Praise for the "Kids Love" Guidebook Travel Series
On-Air Personality Comments (Television Interviews)

"The great thing about these books is that your whole family actually lives these adventures" – (**WKRC-TV**, Cincinnati)

"Very helpful to lots of families when the kids say, I'm bored...and I don't want to go to same places again!" – (**WISH-TV**, Indianapolis)

"Dividing the state into many sections, the book has something for everyone...everywhere." – (**WLVT-TV**, Pennsylvania)

"These authors know first-hand that it's important to find hands-on activities that engage your children..." (**WBNS-TV**, Columbus)

"You spent more than 1000 hours doing this research for us, that's really great – we just have to pick up the book and it's done..." (**WTVR-TV**, Richmond)

"A family that's a great source for travel ideas..." (**WBRA-TV**, Roanoke)

"What a great idea...this book needed to be done a long time ago!" (**WKYT-TV**, Lexington)

"A fabulous idea...places to travel that your kids will enjoy" (**WOOD-TV**, Grand Rapids)

"The Zavatskys call it a dream come true, running their own business while keeping the family together. Their goal, encourage other parents to create special family travel memories." - (**WLVT-TV,** Pennsylvania)

"It's a wonderful book, and as someone who has been to a lot of these places...you hit it right on the money!" – (**WKRC-TV**, Cincinnati)

Praise for the "Kids Love" Guidebook Travel Series
Customer Comments (actual letters on file)

"I wanted to tell you how helpful all your books have been to my family of 6. I rarely find books that cater to families with kids. I have your Indiana, Ohio, Kentucky, Michigan, and Pennsylvania books. I don't want to miss any of the new books that come out. Keep up the great ideas. The books are fantastic. I have shown them to tons of my friends. They love them, too." – H.M.

"I bought the Ohio and Indiana books yesterday and what a blessing these are for us!!! We love taking our grandsons on Grammie & Papaw trips thru the year and these books are making it soooo much easier to plan. The info is complete and full of ideas. Even the layout of the book is easy to follow...I just wanted to thank you for all your work in developing these books for us..." – G.K

"I have purchased your book. My grandchildren and I have gone to many of the places listed in your book. They mark them off as we visit them. We are looking forward to seeing many more. It is their favorite thing to look at book when they come over and find new places to explore. Thank you for publishing this book!" - B.A.

"At a retail price of under $17.00, any of the books would be well worth buying even for a one-time only vacation trip. Until now, when the opportunity arose for a day or weekend trip with the kids I was often at a loss to pick a destination that I could be sure was convenient, educational, child-friendly, and above all, fun. Now I have a new problem: How in the world will we ever be able to see and do all the great ideas listed in this book? I'd better get started planning our next trip right away. At least I won't have to worry about where we're going or what to do when we get there!" – VA Homeschool Newsletter

"My family and I used this book this summer to explore our state! We lived here nearly our entire life and yet over half the book we never knew existed. These people really know what kids love! Highly recommended for all parents, grandparents, etc.." – Barnes and Noble website reviewer

KIDS

LOVE

Pennsylvania

Your Family Travel Guide to Exploring "Kid-Friendly" Pennsylvania

600 Fun Stops & Unique Spots

George & Michele Zavatsky

Dedicated to the Families of Pennsylvania

In a Hundred Years...It will not matter, The size of my bank account...The kind of house that I lived in, the kind of car that I drove...But what will matter is...That the world may be different Because I was important in the life of a child.

- author unknown

For the latest major updates corresponding to the pages in this book visit our website:

www.KidsLoveTravel.com

Although the authors have exhaustively researched all sources to ensure accuracy and completeness of the information contained in this book, we assume no responsibility for errors, inaccuracies, omissions or any other inconsistency herein. Any slights against any entries or organizations are unintentional.

- **REMEMBER:** *Museum exhibits change frequently. Check the site's website before you visit to note any changes. Also, HOURS and ADMISSIONS are subject to change at the owner's discretion. If you are tight on time or money, check the attraction's website or call before you visit.*

- **INTERNET PRECAUTION:** *All websites mentioned in KIDS LOVE PENNSYLVANIA have been checked for appropriate content. However, due to the fast-changing nature of the Internet, we strongly urge parents to preview any recommended sites and to always supervise their children when on-line.*

- **EDUCATORS:** *There are suggestions for finding FREE lessons plans embedded in many listings as helpful notes for educators.*

ISBN-13: 978-0-9822880-2-3

KIDS ♥ PENNSYLVANIA ™   Kids Love Publications, LLC

TABLE OF CONTENTS

(Amusements, Animals & Farms, Museums, Outdoors, State History, Tours, etc.)

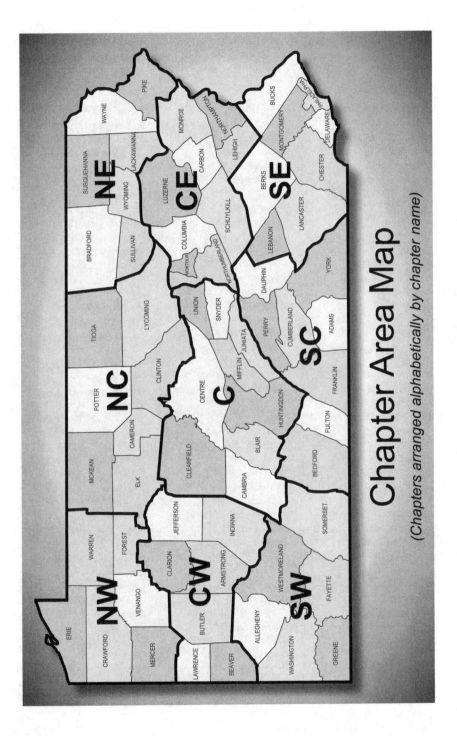

Chapter Area Map

(Chapters arranged alphabetically by chapter name)

CITY INDEX *(Listed by City, Area, Page Numbers)*

CITY INDEX *(Listed by City, Area, Page Numbers)*

HOW TO USE THIS BOOK

(a few hints to make your adventures run smoothly:)

BEFORE YOU LEAVE:

- Each chapter represents a two hour radius area of the state or a Day Trip. The chapter begins with an introduction and Quick Tour of favorites within the chapter. The listings are by City and then alphabetical by name, numeric by zip code. Each listing has tons of important details (pricing, hours, website, etc.) and a review noting the most engaging aspects of the place. Our popular Activity Index in back is helpful if you want to focus on a particular type of attraction (i.e. History, Tours, Outdoor Exploring, Animals & Farms, etc.).
- Begin by assigning each family member a different colored highlighter (for example: Daniel gets blue, Jenny gets pink, Mommy gets yellow and Daddy gets green). At your leisure, begin to read each review and put a highlighter "check" mark next to the sites that most interest each family member or highlight the features you most want to see. Now, when you go to plan a quick trip - or a long van ride - you can easily choose different stops in one day to please everyone.
- Know directions and parking. Use a GPS system or print off directions from websites.
- Most attractions are closed major holidays unless noted.
- When children are in tow, it is better to make your lodging reservations ahead of time. Every time we've tried to "wing it", we've always ended up at a place that was overpriced, in a unsafe area, or not super clean. We've never been satisfied when we didn't make a reservation ahead of time.
- If you have a large family, or are traveling with extended family or friends, most places offer group discounts. Check out the company's website for details.
- For the latest critical updates corresponding to the pages in this book, visit our website: www.kidslovetravel.com. Click on *Updates*.

ON THE ROAD:

- Consider the child's age before you stop at an exit. Some attractions and restaurants, even hotels, are too formal for young ones or not enough adventure for teens. Read our trusted reviews first.
- Estimate the duration of the trip and how many stops you can afford to make. From our experience, it is best to stop every two hours to stretch your legs or eat/snack or maybe visit an inexpensive attraction.
- Bring along travel books and games for "quiet time" in the van. (see tested travel products on www.kidslovetravel.com) As an added bonus, these "enriching" games also stimulate conversation - you may get to know your family better and create memorable life lessons.

ON THE ROAD: (cont.)

- In between meals, we offer the family snacks like: pretzels, whole grain chips, nuts, water bottles, bite-size (dark) chocolates, grapes and apples. None of these are messy and all are healthy.
- Plan picnics along the way. Many Historical sites and State Parks are scattered along the highway. Allow time for a rest stop or a scenic byway to take advantage of these free picnic facilities.

WHEN YOU GET HOME:

- Make a family "treasure chest". Decorate a big box or use an old popcorn tin. Store memorabilia from a fun outing, journals, pictures, brochures and souvenirs. Once a year, look through the "treasure chest" and reminisce. "Kids Love Travel Memories!" is an excellent travel journal and scrapbook template that your family can create (available on www.kidslovetravel.com).

WAYS TO SAVE MONEY:

- Memberships - many children's museums, science centers, zoos and aquariums are members of associations that provide FREE or Discounted reciprocity to other such museums across the country. AAA Auto Club cards offer discounts to many of the activities and hotels in this book. If grandparents are along for the ride, they can use their AARP card and get discounts. Be sure to carry your member cards with you as proof to receive the discounts.
- Supermarket Customer Cards - national and local supermarkets often offer good discounted tickets to major attractions in the area.
- Internet Hotel Reservations - if you're traveling with kids, don't take the risk of being spontaneous with lodging. Make reservations ahead of time. We don't use non-refundable, deep discount hotel "scouting" websites (ex. Hotwire) unless we're traveling on business - just adults. You can't cancel your reservation, or change them, and you can't be guaranteed the type of room you want (ex. non-smoking, two beds). Instead, stick with a national hotel chain you trust and join their rewards program (ex. Choice Privileges) to accumulate points towards FREE night stays.
- State Travel Centers - as you enter a new state, their welcome centers offer many current promotions.
- Hotel Lobbies - often have a display of discount coupons to area shops and restaurants. When you check in, ask the clerk for discount pizza coupons they may have at the front desk.
- Attraction Online Coupons - check the websites listed with each review for possible printable coupons or discounted online tickets good towards the attraction.

MISSION STATEMENT

At first glance, you may think that this is a book that just lists hundreds of places to travel. While it is true that we've invested thousands of hours of exhaustive research (*and drove over 3000 miles in Pennsylvania*) to prepare this travel resource…just listing places to travel is <u>not</u> the mission statement of these projects.

As children, Michele and I were able to travel extensively throughout the United States. We consider these family times some of the greatest memories we cherish today. We, quite frankly, felt that most children had this opportunity to travel with their family as we did. However, as we became adults and started our own family, we found that this wasn't necessarily the case. We continually heard friends express several concerns when deciding how to spend "quality" and "quantity" family time. 1) What to do? 2) Where to do it? 3) How much will it cost? 4) How do I know that my kids will enjoy it?

Interestingly enough, as we compare our experiences with our families when we were kids, many of our fondest memories were not made at an expensive attraction, but rather when it was least expected.

It is our belief and mission statement that if you as a family will study and <u>use</u> the contained information <u>to create family memories</u>, these memories will grow a stronger, tighter family. Our ultimate mission statement is, that your children will develop a love and a passion for quality family experiences that they can pass to another generation of family travelers.

We thank you for purchasing this book, and we hope to see you on the road (*and hear your travel stories!*) God bless your journeys and Happy Exploring!

EXTRA SPECIAL THANKS TO:

We are most thankful to be blessed with our parents, Barbara (Darrall) Callahan and George & Catherine Zavatsky who help us every way they can – researching, proofing and baby-sitting. More importantly, they are great sounding boards and offer unconditional support. So many places around Pennsylvania remind us of family vacations years ago…

We also want to express our thanks to the many Convention & Visitor Bureaus' staff for providing the attention to detail that helps to complete a project. We felt very welcome during our travels in Pennsylvania and would be proud to call it home!

Our own kids, Jenny and Daniel, were delightful and fun children during our trips across the state. What a joy it is to be their parents…we couldn't do it without them as our "kid-testers"!

We both sincerely thank each other – our partnership has created an even greater business/personal "marriage" with lots of exciting moments, laughs, and new adventures in life woven throughout. Above all, we praise the Lord for His so many blessings through the last few years.

We think Pennsylvania is a wonderful, friendly area of the country with more activities than you could imagine. Our sincere wish is that this book will help everyone "fall in love" with all of Pennsylvania.

General State Agency & Recreational Information

Call *(or visit websites)* for the services of interest. Request to be added to their mailing lists.

CHARTER DAY

Statewide - Free admission to the Pennsylvania Military Museum, Boalsburg; Railroad Museum of PA, Strasburg; Hope Lodge & Mather Mill, Fort Washington and other select Pennsylvania Historical and Museum Commission sites on this date to commemorate the granting of the Charter from Charles II to William Penn which founded "Penn's Woods" in 1681. Go on your favorite PA Historical attraction website to see if they are participating. FREE. (usually second Sunday in March)

- Biking Directory of PA. (717) 787-6746. Free through PENN DOT.
- ExplorePAHistory.com
- PA State Association of County Fairs. (717) 365-3922 or www.pafairs.org/FairsAlpha.htm
- PA Tourism. (800) VISIT-PA or www.visitpa.com
- PCOA. PA Campground Owners Assoc. Directory. (888) 660-7262. www.pacamping.com
- PA Fish and Boat Commission. (717) 657-4518 or www.fish.state.pa.us. Information on FISH FARMS/HATCHERIES is here. Fun place to tour.
- PA State Forests. (717) 783-7941 or www.dcnr.state.pa.us/forestry/stateforests/
- PA State Parks. (888) PA-PARKS or www.dcnr.state.pa.us/stateparks/index.htm. Junior Naturalist Program and Cabin/Camping Rentals.
- Statewide Fall Foliage Hotline. (800) FALL-IN PA or www.fallinpa.com

---

C Penn State Athletics, State College. Nittany Lions. (800) 833-5533 or (800) 863-1000 tickets or www.gopsusports.com. Baseball, basketball, fencing, field hockey, football, golf, gymnastics, soccer, softball, swimming, tennis, track, volleyball and wrestling.

CE Dam Releases. LeHigh River Area. (717) 424-6050. Releases create whitewater and rapids. Call for rafting outfitters. Late Spring and Early Fall.

NE POCONOS Tourist Information. (800)-POCONOS or www.800poconos.com. Ask about selection of whitewater rafting, canoeing and riding stables.

NW Erie Area CVB. www.visiteriepa.com or (800) 524-3743.

SE Philadelphia. www.gophila.com or Visitors Center at Independence Historical Park Center. Check out their FAMILY PHILADELPHIA packages that are truly an economical way to explore some of Philly's best sites while staying at "kid-friendly" hotels in town.

SW Laurel Highlands River Tours. www.laurelhighlands.org

SW Pittsburgh CVB. (888) 849-4753 or www.visitpittsburgh.com.

SW University of Pittsburgh Athletics. (412) 648-PITT or (800) 643-PITT or www.pittsburghpanthers.com.

AIRPORTS - All children love to visit the airport! Why not take a tour and understand all the jobs it takes to run an airport? Tour the terminal, baggage claim, gates and security / currency exchange. Maybe you'll even get to board a plane.

ANIMAL SHELTERS - Great for the would-be pet owner. Not only will you see many cats and dogs available for adoption, but a guide will show you the clinic and explain the needs of a pet. Be prepared to have the children "fall in love" with one of the animals while they are there!

BANKS - Take a "behind the scenes" look at automated teller machines, bank vaults and drive-thru window chutes. You may want to take this tour and then open a savings account for your child.

CITY HALLS - Halls of Fame, City Council Chambers & Meeting Room, Mayor's Office and famous statues.

ELECTRIC COMPANY / POWER PLANTS - Modern science has created many ways to generate electricity today, but what really goes on with the "flip of a switch". Because coal can be dirty, wear old, comfortable clothes. Coal furnaces heat water, which produces steam, that propels turbines, that drives generators, that make electricity.

FIRE STATIONS - Many Open Houses in October, Fire Prevention Month. Take a look into the life of the firefighters servicing your area and try on their gear. See where they hang out, sleep and eat. Hop aboard a real-life fire engine truck and learn fire safety too.

HOSPITALS - Some Children's Hospitals offer pre-surgery and general tours.

NEWSPAPERS - You'll be amazed at all the new technology. See monster printers and robotics. See samples in the layout department and maybe try to put together your own page. After seeing a newspaper made, most companies give you a free copy (dated that day) as your souvenir. National Newspaper Week is in October.

PETCO - Various stores. Contact each store manager to see if they participate. The Fur, Feathers & Fins™ program allows children to learn about the characteristics and habitats of fish, reptiles, birds, and small animals. At your local Petco, lessons in science, math and geography come to life through this hands-on field trip. As students develop a respect for animals, they will also develop a greater sense of responsibility.

PIZZA HUT & PAPA JOHN'S - Participating locations. Telephone the store manager. Best days are Monday, Tuesday and Wednesday mid-afternoon. Minimum of 10 people. Small charge per person. All children love pizza – especially when they can create their own! As the children tour the kitchen, they learn how to make a pizza, bake it, and then eat it. The admission charge generally includes lots of creatively made pizzas, beverage and coloring book.

KRISPY KREME DONUTS - Participating locations. Get an "inside look" and learn the techniques that make these donuts some of our favorites! Watch the dough being made in "giant" mixers, being formed into donuts and taking a "trip" through the fryer. Seeing them being iced and topped with colorful sprinkles is always a favorite with the kids. Contact your local store manager. They prefer Monday or Tuesday. Free.

SUPERMARKETS - Kids are fascinated to go behind the scenes of the same store where Mom and Dad shop. Usually you will see them grind meat, walk into large freezer rooms, watch cakes and bread bake and receive free samples along the way. Maybe you'll even get to pet a live lobster!

TV / RADIO STATIONS - Studios, newsrooms, Fox kids clubs. Why do weathermen never wear blue/green clothes on TV? What makes a "DJ's" voice sound so deep and smooth?

WATER TREATMENT PLANTS - A giant science experiment! You can watch seven stages of water treatment. The favorite is usually the wall of bright buttons flashing as workers monitor the different processes.

U.S. MAIN POST OFFICES - Did you know Ben Franklin was the first Postmaster General (over 200 years ago)? Most interesting is the high-speed automated mail processing equipment. Learn how to address envelopes so they will be sent quicker (there are secrets). To make your tour more interesting, have your children write a letter to themselves and address it with colorful markers. Mail it earlier that day and they will stay interested trying to locate their letter in all the high-speed machinery.

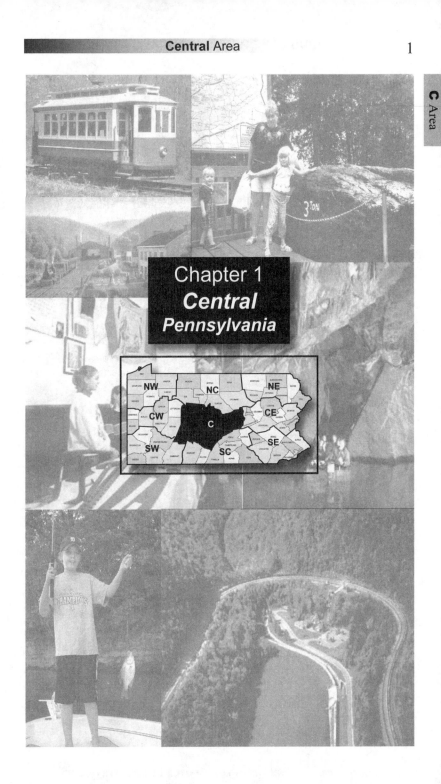

Chapter 1
Central
Pennsylvania

Altoona
- Fort Roberdeau Historic Site
- Quaint Corner Children's Museum
- Horseshoe Curve Landmark
- Lakemont Park
- Railroader's Memorial Museum

Altoona (Lakemont)
- Altoona Curve Baseball Club

Altoona (Tyrone)
- Gardner's Candy Museum

Boalsburg
- Boal Mansion/Columbus Chapel

Boalsburg
- Pennsylvania Military Museum
- Tussey Mountain Ski Area

Centre Hall
- Penn's Cave

Claysburg
- Blue Knob All Seasons Resort

Gallitzin
- Allegheny Portage Railroad
- Gallitzin Tunnels Park, Caboose And Museum

Hollidaysburg
- Canoe Creek State Park

Howard
- Bald Eagle State Park

Johnstown
- Johnstown Inclined Plane
- Johnstown Children's Museum
- Johnstown Flood Museum
- Johnstown Heritage Center

Johnstown (South Fork)
- Johnstown Flood Nat'l Memorial

Mifflinburg
- R.B. Winter State Park
- Mifflinburg Buggy Days

Milroy
- Reeds Gap State Park

Patton
- Prince Gallitzin State Park
- Seldom Seen Coal Mine

Penfield
- Parker Dam State Park

Philipsburg
- Black Moshannon State Park

Raystown Lake (Entriken)
- Lake Raystown Resort

Raystown Lake (Hesston)
- Seven Points Cruises

Raystown Lake (Huntingdon)
- Greenwood Furnace State Park
- Lincoln Caverns/Whisper Rocks
- Swigart Antique Auto Museum
- Rothrock State Forest

Raystown Lake (James Creek)
- Trough Creek State Park

Rock Springs
- Ag Progress Days

Rockhill Furnace
- East Broad Top Railroad
- Rockhill Trolley Museum

Spruce Creek
- Indian Caverns

State College
- Penn State University Campus
- Stone Valley Recreation Area
- Central Pennsylvania Festival Of The Arts

Sunbury
- Shikellamy State Park

Tipton
- Delgrosso's Amusement Park

Windber
- Windber Coal Heritage Center

Woodward
- Woodward Cave

C Area

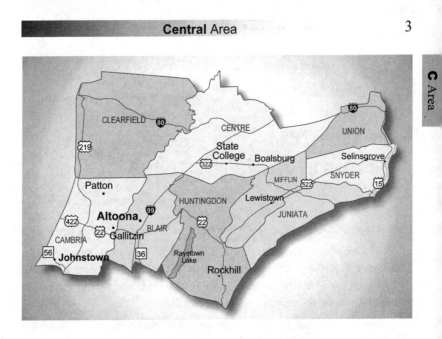

Travel Journal & Notes:

A Quick Tour of our Hand-Picked Favorites Around...

Central Pennsylvania

Central Pennsylvania is all about Caves, Curves, a Chapel, a horrible Flood, and a wonderful Campus.

That wonderful campus is found in Happy Valley, at **Penn State University**. Walking around and peeking in the little museums scattered around campus is fun but topping the trip off with a homemade ice cream sundae from the Creamery is always the highlight.

Nearby, in Boalsburg, is an extremely interesting mansion. While the **Boal Mansion** tour is full of hidden corners and stories, what is tucked away in an outbuilding is really magical. A real Spanish Chapel – the **Columbus Chapel** houses one of the best displays of real Christopher Columbus family articles. Kids think his sea chest is cool!

As transportation progressed west, carving out railroads through the mountains proved very difficult. Ingenious engineers decided to climb up or go around the mountainous terrain. **Horseshoe Curve** was developed because, even if a bridge could be built, no locomotive could climb the steep grade – so, they built track around the inside curves. No trains or canals could get through the Allegheny Mountains before the idea of the "incline" was introduced. **Allegheny Portage Railroad National Historic Site** demonstrates solving the problem by using a combo of 10 inclines. It's difficult to imagine until you see the working scale models in both of these railroad museums. Or, go outside and see it for yourself. It's like a giant physics lesson. Plus, the kids love the demonstration model trains – many with interactive features.

The Central PA area is riddled with **Caves**. Some are crystal caverns with Kids' Cave Crawls. Two others are massive – one has the nickname of "the Big One." One cave even features America's only all-water cavern and is a boat tour.

The power of nature was also severely demonstrated in Johnstown. The flood of 1889 left the town a wasteland for a while. The whole town of

Johnstown is one big experiment in survival and culture. Families probably find the best place to start is downtown. While the Flood Museum is more historical and vivid, young families may gravitate to the **Johnstown Heritage Discovery Center**. It now includes a museum on the first floor where you choose a character to follow through various daily life tasks and decisions OR play pretend coal miner or incline operator in the **Children's Museum** on the third floor. They were so clever to disguise history as play or acting, most kids don't even know you've been sneaking in some history lessons.

So that the townspeople never felt trapped by the fear of floods again, they built an incline tram up to the top of the highest point in town. The **Johnstown Inclined Plane** still exists and you can ride it! It's the steepest, yet slowest "roller coaster" ride you can go on in Pennsylvania...

Sites and attractions are listed in order by City, Zip Code, and Name. Symbols indicated represent:

 Festivals   Restaurants   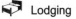 Lodging

Altoona

FORT ROBERDEAU HISTORIC SITE

Altoona - RD #3 Box 391 (I-99, Bellwood Exit) 16601. Phone: (814) 946-0048. www.fortroberdeau.org. Hours: Tuesday-Saturday 11:00am-5:00pm, Sunday 1:00-5:00pm (May-October). Admission: $4.00-$5.00.

A reconstructed 1778 fort with exhibits. Original site of a Revolutionary War fort established to mine lead for the army. The rural 230-acre tract features a reconstructed Revolutionary War stockade surrounding six log cabins. It also includes an 1858 barn containing exhibits and a museum shop, and an education center in an 1860 farmhouse; miners quarters, officers quarters, barracks and blacksmith. A costumed guide will show you around and tell you the story of the Lead Mine Fort. Enjoy the sights and sounds of the past. Hear musket fire, wood chopping, and the daily work of a rangers and craftsmen. Take part in the fort's everyday life. Shoulder a musket, mend clothes, smell the stew, and meet the soldiers. If your kids are antsy, there are 47 acres on the property with 3 nature trails and various habitats. Environmental education programs are available to groups from schools, community organizations, etc. Topics include "Discovery Trail Walk", birds, trees, wild edible plants, reading the landscape, and stream study. Living history re-reenactments. (Summer)

REVOLUTIONARY WAR DAYS

Altoona - *Fort Roberdeau Historic Site* - *Experience danger on the 1778 frontier when British Rangers and Iroquois attack patriots and ruin bullet-making at General Roberdeau's lead mine fort. Admission. (second weekend in July)*

QUAINT CORNER CHILDREN'S MUSEUM

Altoona - *2000 Union Avenue (Downtown SR36) 16601. Phone: (814) 944-6830. www.quaintcorner.org. Hours: Friday-Saturday 10:00am-5:00pm. Admission: $3.00 general. Miscellaneous: This museum is a quick walk from the Altoona Railroaders Museum.*

This is a real Victorian home that kids are allowed to explore - in fact, they're encouraged to snoop around. Probably the cutest and most popular areas are the closets and climbing the ladder into Grandma's Attic at the very top of the house. "Gus Guts" is the highlight of the Medical Room - pick him up, pull out his "guts" and look at a chart to see what the organs are and what they do for the body. Draw on the wall in the Craft Kitchen or dig in the sand and pretend you're an archeologist in the Dinosaur Dig. Visit the International Closet to see displays from other countries, examine the Pirates Treasure or the Amish Closet, explore nature in the Audubon Room, and see doll houses and antiques. There's even a sandbox in the basement. Cool.

HORSESHOE CURVE NATIONAL HISTORIC LANDMARK

Altoona - *Horseshoe Curve Road (6 miles West of Altoona) 16602. Phone: (888) 4-ALTOONA. www.railroadcity.com. Hours: Monday-Saturday 10:00am-6:00pm, Sunday 11:00am-6:00pm (May-October). Other times of year, weekends only 11:00am-4:00pm. Admission: $10.00 adult, $8.00 senior (62+), $7.00 child (4-12). Includes Memorial Museum and Horseshoe Curve admission. Miscellaneous: Large Gift shop. Picnic areas.*

Developed in 1854, the Penn Railroad needed to expand west, but through the mountainous terrain. This curve was developed because, even if a bridge could be built, no locomotive could climb the steep grade. To solve this crossing problem, they built a track around the inside curves of the large mountain range. Inside the Interpretive Center, you can view a video of the curve's history and see a model of what the land looked like before the railroad changed the landscape. Kids like the push button display of train sounds as they make the turn (gaining speed, upgrade and downgrade). The highlight is the funicular ride up to the elevation area (or you can walk up - 200 steps) where you can look out onto the horseshoe track. There's a good chance a train (the railroad still uses this curve) will pass through while you are visiting.

Built with just hand tools and dynamite - wow!

LAKEMONT PARK

Altoona - *700 Park Avenue (I-99 to Frankstown Road) 16602. Phone: (814) 949-PARK or (800) 434- 8006. www.lakemontparkfun.com. Hours: Daily 11:00am-dark (Summers). Weekends only in May and September, Noon-8:00pm. Admission: Buy individual ($1.00) or package ($9.95) tickets. Some rides are a separate fee of $2.50-$3.00 - even if you have the all day ride & slide pass.*

Lakemont Park, the eighth oldest amusement park in the United States, opened its gates for the first time in 1894 as a trolley park in Altoona. One of Lakemont's most prized possessions is the world's oldest roller coaster, Leap-the-Dips. Over 30 rides and attractions. In addition, the park holds an 18-hole miniature golf course, the Island Waterpark and several other rides to thrill visitors of all ages. Go-Kart tracks, picnic areas and arcade. Kids Mini-Indy and Kiddie Lane.

DECEMBER - Glistening lights. Visit with Santa. Hot chocolate. Freshly baked cookies. Toy/gift shops. Model train display. Weekend entertainment. Admission. (Evenings - late November through New Year's Day)

RAILROADER'S MEMORIAL MUSEUM

Altoona - *1300 Ninth Avenue (off 17th Street on I-99) 16602. Phone: (814) 946-0834. www.railroadcity.com. Hours: Monday-Saturday 10:00am-5:00pm, Sunday 11:00am-5:00pm (early May-October). Weekends only (November-December). Admission: $10.00 adult, $8.00 senior (62+), $7.00 child (4-12). Includes Memorial Museum and Horseshoe Curve admission. Miscellaneous: Museum store.*

"Here in Altoona an army of railroaders designed, built, maintained, and moved the Pennsylvania Railroad, the largest railroad in the world...in so doing, they changed the face of America...this is their story!" Why was Altoona chosen to be the heart of construction? (watch a 27 minute film to find out). Listen to the folks talk about their life at local scenes depicting a home, church, newsstand, and clubs. The "News Boy" is funny to listen to. Learn how railroad workers laid the tracks, worked in shops (the test lab is pretty eye opening) and designed and built locomotives. This museum has less focus on displays of trains and more on the lives and work habits of people involved. Nice change.

ALTOONA CURVE BASEBALL CLUB

Altoona (Lakemont) - *1000 Park Avenue (games played at Blair County Ballpark) 16602. Phone: (814) 943-5400 or (877) 99-CURVE. www.altoonacurve.com.*

The Altoona Curve is the AA affiliate of the Pittsburgh Pirates and has been thrilling local fans with hometown baseball since 1999. Housed at the Blair County Ballpark in Lakemont, the Curve games end with fantastic fireworks displays and popular giveaway events. The team also hosts concerts and other community events. Single game tickets run $5.00-$12.00.

GARDNER'S CANDY MUSEUM

Altoona (Tyrone) - *30 West 10th Street (I-99 to SR453 or SR220) 16686. Phone: (814) 684-0857. www.gardnerscandies.com. Hours: Monday-Saturday 9:30am-9:00pm, Sunday 1:00-9:00pm. Admission: FREE*

Gardners is famous for the Original Peanut Butter Melt-away, a creamy, smooth peanut butter dipped in rich chocolate. Many have tried, but none can duplicate the Gardner's family recipe. Take a Nostalgic walk through a penny candy store. Big candy counters with large jars of candy. Also stop in the Candy Kitchen where old-time (mostly brass) equipment is displayed. Take a look at their giant Taffy Hook. Mr. Gardner started "the sweetest place in town" in 1897 and still has licorice whips and candy buttons for sale.

Boalsburg

BOAL MANSION MUSEUM / COLUMBUS CHAPEL

Boalsburg - *300 Old Boalsburg Road (US322 - Business Route) 16827. Phone: (814) 466-6210. www.boalmuseum.com. Hours: Tuesday-Saturday 10:00am-*

5:00pm, Sunday Noon-5:00pm (Summer). Tuesday-Sunday 1:30-5:00pm (May, September, October). Admission: $10.00 adult, $8.00 senior (59+), $6.00 child (7-16). Miscellaneous: Still privately owned. Educators: an eighth grade unit study is found here: http://boalmuseum.com/unitplan.htm.

COLUMBUS CHAPEL: Want to see a real part of Christopher Columbus? On the grounds of the originally furnished mansion is the Columbus Chapel that was brought here from Spain in 1909. They actually have a sea desk once owned by Columbus and many Columbus family heirlooms dating back to the 1400s. The highlight of this place begins with your first step inside the chapel. If you're like us...your mouth will drop wide open in disbelief as

Columbus' actual sea desk...

The view from the loft

you begin to notice the centuries-old heirloom pieces. Many of the artifacts look like movie props (the natural way they have aged makes it hard to believe they are real!) Actual parchment family documents, the family cross, a copy of the family tree and 2 actual pieces of the "true" cross are awesome to see up close. The Columbus Chapel is something else. When your family steps into the Columbus Chapel, they step into Spain in the time of Christopher Columbus. Nowhere else in America can they experience this connection both with the Old World and with Columbus himself. Through it all, Columbus remains the man who opened the door from the Old World to the New World, one of the most important events of the last one thousand years. It's just incredible that all of this history is in a small town museum!

Two pieces from Jesus' cross...amazing!

BOAL MANSION: Also on the grounds are the mansion and several exhibit rooms. The Boal Mansion Museum contains the original furnishings, papers, portraits, tools and weapons of nine generations of this American family. The first exhibit room contains medieval armor, a scale model of the Santa Maria and other family memorabilia. The "Country Life" room contains a beautifully restored 1850s stage coach, a buckboard buggy, farm tools, the 1816 accounts book from David Boal's tavern and many more farm and kitchen implements. The Weapons Room contains a large collection of swords, rifles and pistols from the Revolutionary War through World War I, including David Boal's Pennsylvania long rifle from the 1790's and Captain John Boal's officer's sword from the Civil War. Hearing stories about the Boal family and their home can be interesting, too.

PENNSYLVANIA MILITARY MUSEUM

Boalsburg - *South Atherton Street (Business Route 322) (US322) 16827. Phone: (814) 466-6263. www.pamilmuseum.org. Hours: Wednesday-Saturday 10:00am-4:00pm, Sunday Noon-4:00pm (April-October). Weekends only (November/ December). Admission: $6.00 adult, $5.50 senior, $4.00 child (3-11) and FREE to uniformed military personnel.*

Honoring Pennsylvania's soldiers from Benjamin Franklin's first volunteer unit to Operation Desert Storm. Start your visit viewing the short movie: "Answering the Call: Pennsylvanians in Service to the Nation." Discover why a tank is called a "tank" and how evacuating a patient off the battlefield changed so drastically in less than 50 years. Size yourself up against a World War II era tank and compare that to other armored vehicles from the 1950s and 60s. Younger children enjoy climbing on tanks and cannons outside in the park, but it takes older kids to enjoy the museum. As they study American History, this place brings it to life, especially the World War I trench scene, complete with sound and light effects. The museum only focuses on citizen soldiers – "the men and women of Pennsylvania who served their country in time of war."

> **DID YOU KNOW?**
>
> Did you know that this is the birthplace of Memorial Day?

WAR ENCAMPMENT

Boalsburg - *Pennsylvania Military Museum. Museum Parade Grounds. Military units encamped throughout the area. Daily living history demonstrations. Live fire artillery demonstrations. Day-long festivities in nearby Boalsburg. Parking fee only. (Memorial Day Weekend)*

TUSSEY MOUNTAIN SKI AREA

Boalsburg - *301 Bear Meadow Road - Route 322 16827. Phone: (814) 466-6266 or (800) 733-2754. www.tusseymountain.com.*

Longest Run: 2700 ft.; 8 Slopes & Trails plus snowboarding in winter. Skatepark, driving range, batting cages and par 3 golf in the fall.

Centre Hall

PENN'S CAVE

Centre Hall - *222 Penns Cave Road (SR 192 East, Near I-80, Exit 14) 16828. Phone: (814) 364-1664. www.pennscave.com. Hours: Generally daily 9:00am-5:00pm. Open later summers. Closed January. Weekends Only 11:00am-5:00pm (December & February). Closed Thanksgiving and Christmas Day. Admission: CAVERN: $15.95 adult, $14.95 senior (65+), $8.50 child (2-12). WILDLIFE, FARM AND NATURE TOURS: $19.95 adult, $18.95 senior, $11.50 child (2-12). Combo pricing available. Tours: Cave-1 mile guided tour by motorboat - approximately 1 hour long. Miscellaneous: Gemstone panning (extra fee). There are 48 steps that lead to the main entrance to the cave. Educators: Teachers Guide to Caves here: www.pennscave.com/penns_teachers.pdf.*

America's only all-water cavern and wildlife (1000 acre) sanctuary. Colored lights enhance "The Statue of Liberty", "The Garden of Gods" and "Niagara Falls". The farm and wildlife tour is a guided 90-minute motorized tour over the thousand acres of Penn's Cave forests and fields and a natural habitat for birds, plants, and animals. North American animals, such as deer, elk, wolves, bears, bison, and mustangs are seen, as well as longhorn cattle. Come to Penn's Cave and enjoy both tours.
You will be educated about the geology, biology, and geography of Central Pennsylvania.

NITTANY ANTIQUE STEAM ENGINE DAYS

Centre Hall *- Penn's Cave. Tractor pulls, antique steam engines, parades, food (made with steam), threshing, baling, cider and apple butter making, hayrides, children's activities, petting zoo & fall crafts. Admission. (first week of September)*

C Area

Claysburg

BLUE KNOB ALL SEASONS RESORT/ SKI AREA

Claysburg - *PO Box 247 (between Altoona & Johnstown, in north corner of Bedford County) 16625. Phone: (814) 239-5111. www.blueknob.com.*

Activities include skiing/snowboarding, a tubing park, and cross country skiing. In the warmer months, golfing, hiking and trail biking are big attractions. All condos are furnished with fully equipped kitchens and fireplaces. Longest Run: 2 miles; 34 Slopes & Trails.

Gallitzin

ALLEGHENY PORTAGE RAILROAD NATIONAL HISTORIC SITE

Gallitzin - 110 Federal Park Road (US22, Gallitzin exit - follow signs) 16641. Phone: (814) 886-6150. www.nps.gov/alpo/. Hours: Daily 9:00am-5:00pm. Closed winter holidays. Admission: $4.00 adult (age 16+). FREE for children and park pass holders. Miscellaneous: Visitor Center with 20 minute film. Costumed presentations during the summer. Lemon House - restored tavern and business office on premises along with the Engine House and walking trails to the incline site. Educators: http://www.nps.gov/history/NR/twhp/wwwlps/lessons/23allegheny/23allegheny.htm - link to full array of complete lesson plans & activities for students.

You'll be amazed at the ingenuity of railroad engineers back then! The problem was the Allegheny Mountains. No trains or canals could get through them before the idea of the "incline" was introduced. Called "an engineering marvel" at its opening, travel that took three weeks by wagon took only four days by railroad and canal. It used a combination of 10 inclines and horses or steam locomotives pulling cars on levels in between. A system of inclined planes and a nine hundred foot tunnel carved through solid rock by Welsh coalminers made this feat possible. It's difficult to visualize until you see the working small-scale model in the center of the museum - then it all makes sense

It's just like "The Little Engine that Could"

(still in amazement of course!). With a hands-on demonstration, you can personally try turning a wheel hooked to balanced and unbalanced weights. This clearly demonstrates the need for balanced (one car up - one car down at the same time) inclines. Park rangers give guided tours in costume while demonstrating log hewing, stone cutting, coal mining and musket firing. Be sure to catch the movie about this special railroad.

GALLITZIN TUNNELS PARK, CABOOSE AND MUSEUM

Gallitzin - 702 Jackson Street (off Route 22 - Follow signs) 16641. Phone: (814) 886-8871. www.gallitzin.info/. Hours: Daily, daylight hours. Museum open Tuesday-Sunday 11:00am-5:00pm, weather permitting. Admission: FREE. Miscellaneous: there's a video tour of the west slope of the mtn. Rail online on their front page.

See and feel the awesome power of the trains passing through the Allegheny Tunnel (modified 1854). View the tunnels that were built with picks and shovels using over 300 immigrants to complete it. Twin tunnels, the Allegheny and Gallitzin Tunnels, are the highest and longest on what once was the Pennsylvania Railroad. Because of their integral role in the transportation system, these tunnels were guarded during times of war. Also on site is a PRR walkway and railroad signal and a restored PRR caboose - climb aboard to see the sleeping

> **DID YOU KNOW?**
> Trains run through the tunnels 24 hours a day. Chances are you'll get to see at least one pass by and feel its rubble while you're there.

quarters and pot-bellied stove. This is a cute side trip between visits to the Allegheny Portage Railroad and Horseshoe Curve. The museum shows a video called "Once Upon a Mountain" illustrating the fascinating transportation history of the area - especially trains.

Hollidaysburg

CANOE CREEK STATE PARK

Hollidaysburg - RR 2, Box 560 (US 22) 16648. Phone: (814) 695-6807. www.dcnr.state.pa.us/stateparks/parks/canoecreek.aspx. Admission: to PA State Parks is FREE however swimming, marina and camping/lodging fees apply, with reservation or entrance.

The park boasts one of the largest bat colonies in the Eastern US. The visitor center has natural and historical exhibits and information. Modern Cabins:

C Area

Eight modern cabins overlook the lake. They are within walking distance of the swimming area and are available for year-round rental. Beach, Boat Rentals, Horseback Riding, Sledding, Limestone kilns, Trails, and Cross-Country Skiing. A nine-hole disc golf course begins on the sidewalk near the beach house.

Howard

BALD EAGLE STATE PARK

Howard - 149 Main Park Road (off PA Route 150, midway between Milesburg and Lock Haven, it is accessible by I-80) 16841. Phone: (814) 625-2775. www.dcnr.state.pa.us/stateparks/parks/baldeagle.aspx. Admission: to PA State Parks is FREE however swimming, marina and camping/lodging fees apply, with reservation or entrance.

The 5,900-acre park lies in the broad Bald Eagle Valley of North Central Pennsylvania. Two geologic provinces create Bald Eagle's scenic beauty. The Allegheny Plateau to the north and west holds smooth uplands. The Ridge and Valley Province to the south and east contains numerous long, narrow mountain ridges separated by valleys. Opening soon is the new Nature Inn at Bald Eagle. This 16-room inn will provide full-service accommodations overlooking the lake. The rugged Bald Eagle Mountain and Allegheny Plateau of the 1,730-acre lake features unlimited horsepower boating, hiking and butterfly trails (1.5 miles long, marked & maintained). An interpretive area provides information and examples of butterfly habitats. In September, migrating monarchs are often seen drinking nectar on the abundant goldenrod. This trail is a popular family hike. Swimming is available at the sand beach. The 1,200-foot long sand and turf beach has a children's playground, a snack bar, changing rooms, public restrooms, and parking. The beach is open from late-May to mid-September, 8:00am to sunset, unless otherwise posted. Boat Rentals, Year-round Education & Interpretation Center, Sledding, Campsites, Hiking, and Fishing.

Johnstown

JOHNSTOWN INCLINED PLANE

Johnstown - 711 Edgehill Drive (off SR56, 403 or 271 & Johns St.) 15905. Phone: (814) 536-1816. www.inclinedplane.com. Hours: Daily 9:00am-10:30pm (May-September). Daily 11:00am-9:00pm (October-April). Closed Christmas and New Years. Admission: $4.00 adult, FREE senior (65+), $2.50 child (2-12). Round Trip.

Miscellaneous: Gift shop. Visitor's center. Observation deck on top. Educators: here's a complete lesson plan: http://www.jaha.org/edu/inclined_plane/index. html. FREEBIES: Scavenger Hunt: http://www.jaha.org/edu/inclined_plane/ documents/rise_challenge.pdf.

Brightly lit, it is the world's steepest vehicular inclined plane (71 % grade) with a panoramic view of the city through viewing windows. After the flood, many residents wanted to live up on the hill...but they needed a way to commute.

It was also used as an escape route during subsequent floods. A viewing window looking into the motor room explains the "physics" behind the scenes. Hang on tight to those little ones! Ride on the incline and then grab a snack or ice cream at the top. Spectacular views of the valley and you get to see the largest American flag in the county.

The **JAMES WOLFE SCULPTURE TRAIL** is the first nature trail with sculptures made from steel. It honors the city's steel heritage with ten pieces, eight on the trail. Most photographed and visible is "Steel Floats" (Bottom of the incline).

JOHNSTOWN CHILDREN'S MUSEUM

Johnstown - *201 6th Avenue, Discovery Center, 3rd Floor (Route 56, at the corner of Broad Street and Seventh Ave.) 15906. Phone: (814) 539-1889. www.jaha.org. Hours: Daily 10:00am-5:00pm. Closed major holidays. Admission: $5.00-$7.00 per person. Includes admission to the Heritage Center and Flood Museum in town.*

The Johnstown Children's Museum is a new project of the Johnstown Area Heritage Association. This museum allows children to learn through play about Johnstown's geography, history, culture, industry and more.

The third floor of the Johnstown Heritage Discovery Center is fully devoted to kids and play. From the beginning, kids are transported along a colorful timewarp wall of recognizable buildings and landmarks including the Stone Bridge. Wooden toys can be played with or quiet reading at Morley's Dog café. The Water Room gets lots of attention as kids love splashing around water. As the kids "play" with water from rain in the mountains and valleys, they learn the concept of dam-building and why solid, reliable dams are essential to a town. The Inclimber Slide mimics Yoder Hill, including mine tunnels that climb high to the ceiling. When you reach the top, take a "coal chute" slide down, where you'll land in a padded coal car full of foam coal. (this slide and incline are probably the favorite area for families). While you're up hill, you can control the incline or dress up like coal miners, including hard hats with lights, orange vests and coal picks. Now you can choose to work in a Steel Mill - trying your hand at making molds or being a boss. Kids can "cook" in The Kitchen or pretend "shop" in the General Store. Other interactives include a Fashion studio and a Music Mix-Master studio. During mild weather, The Overlook Garden is a rooftop delight. Kids can see displays of native Pennsylvania plants. A rain meter keeps track of how much rain we get each month. Enjoy the spectacular view of Cambria City and the Conemaugh Gap -- and use the telescope to take a closer look.

JOHNSTOWN FLOOD MUSEUM

Johnstown - 304 Washington Street (off SR56 West to Walnut Street Exit) 15907. Phone: (814) 539-1889. www.jaha.org. Hours: Daily 10:00am-5:00pm. Admission: $5.00-$7.00 (age 6+). Your ticket includes admission to the Heritage Discovery Center. Miscellaneous: Museum store. Film shown hourly (25 minutes long). Film has some shrill screaming that may frighten young children. Educators: middle school students may benefit from their extensive Teacher's Guides downloadable here: www.jaha.org/edu/index.html.

On May 31, 1889, a neglected dam and a phenomenal storm led to a catastrophe in which 2,209 people died, tens of thousands were left homeless, and a prospering city became a wasteland. Hear and see the story of the infamous disaster of 1889 focusing on both the tragedy and triumph of the human spirit. View the Academy Award Winning "The Johnstown Flood" documentary film (shown hourly) with multi-media exhibits including an animated map with sound and light effects showing water movement. ... "it was a roar and a crash and a smash...". In 2000, an original "Oklahoma" house, one of the first types of temporary houses erected to shelter the people left homeless by the flood, was installed. Originally manufactured for

homesteaders in the Oklahoma Territory, these buildings were a very early example of prefabricated housing. Many Johnstown families combined one large and one small Oklahoma to accommodate their needs. The houses were not attractive -- nor were they suitable for the harsh Southwestern Pennsylvania winters. The Oklahoma House was moved from the Moxham neighborhood and placed on an existing patio adjacent to the museum. It is a telling display of how survivors deal with disaster. Other exhibits include: A Quilt - used as a rescue rope, A Wall of Wreckage in 3-D (17 feet tall - flood wall was actually 40 feet tall). It really captures the horror of the moment, yet is subtle enough to not scare school-aged children.

JOHNSTOWN HERITAGE DISCOVERY CENTER

Johnstown - *(Route 56, at the corner of Broad Street and Seventh Ave.) 15907. Phone: (814) 539-1889. www.jaha.org. Hours: Daily 10:00am-5:00pm. Closed Thanksgiving, Christmas, Easter and New Years. Admission: $5.00-$7.00 (age 6+). ticket includes admission to the Johnstown Flood Museum. Miscellaneous: Galliker's Café eatery. Educators: downloadable elementary aged Teachers Guide is online here: www.jaha.org/edu/discovery_center/index.html.*

All Johnstown's immigrants were history-makers - ordinary men, women, and children who made a contribution to the rise of industrial America. And, as they kept traditions and values alive for their families and communities, they enriched the life and culture of a changing city and nation. When you visit the museum, you will be able to assume the persona of such immigrants as Josef and Maria (as well as Prokop, Katerina, Andrej, and Stefan) as you journey through the exhibit that examines the world the immigrants made in Johnstown, Pennsylvania. The visitor will be able to see and touch the environments - you will feel the sharpness of the coal mine walls and smell the scent of incense in the church. One coal-mining exhibit depicts a mining accident, while another gives you the chance to try working at the picking tables, separating rock from coal. You'll see the flames and sparks in the open-hearth steel furnace exhibit and become bystanders to an argument between management and an immigrant worker expressing his mounting frustration with immigrant working conditions. You will hear the thoughts of a young immigrant girl as she sells eggs and butter on the street to help the family's finances. Play "History Jukeboxes" -You sit down in front of the computer and tell your story. The "jukebox" records your voice and image. Rather than simply looking at artifacts, you'll actually experience the sights, sounds and even the smells of immigrants' daily lives, and come away with a more complete understanding of the sacrifices and achievements of these Americans in the making.

C Area

JOHNSTOWN FLOOD NATIONAL MEMORIAL

Johnstown (South Fork) - *733 Lake Road (US219 to St. Michael Exit - SR869east) 15956. Phone: (814) 495-4643. www.nps.gov/jofl. Hours: Daily 9:00am-5:00pm. Closed winter holidays. Admission: $4.00 adult (age 16+). Educators: a complete lesson plan about the Flood is found here: www.nps.gov/ history/nr/twhp/wwwlps/lessons/5johnstown/5johnstown.htm.*

The flood began here - see what little is left of South Fork Dam. It is operated by the National Park Service and features exhibits an actual size "debris wall" which dramatically illustrates the wall of water that devastated Johnstown. The film Black Friday chillingly recreates that day in 1889 - a little frightening for youngsters. Remember over 2200 people died in about 10 minutes. In addition, visitors can enjoy a picnic area, hike nearby trails around the dam's remains, take part in the park's interpretive program journey hikes or view exhibits created by the South Fork Fishing and Hunting Club. Other recreational activities available: bird watching and cross country skiing.

Mifflinburg

R.B. WINTER STATE PARK

Mifflinburg - *RR 2, Box 314 (on PA Route 192, 18 miles west of Lewisburg) 17844. Phone: (717) 966-1455. www.dcnr.state.pa.us/stateparks/parks/rbwinter.aspx. Admission: to PA State Parks is FREE however swimming, marina and camping/ lodging fees apply, with reservation or entrance.*

This park is situated in a narrow valley surrounded by oak forests on steep mountain ridges. A spring-fed mountain stream flows through the valley. Beach, Visitor Center, Year-round Education & Interpretation Center, Campsites, Camping Cabins, Trails, and Winter Sports. The swimming beach features 300 feet of white sand. The beach is open from late-May to mid-September, 8:00am to sunset. Halfway Run Environmental Learning Center is equipped with many educational tools, the center is a classroom and base for educational programs, and features a hands-on science area, a computer center with environmental software, a library of field guides, classic environmental works and children's books, and displays of native wildlife. Visitors can test their knowledge of lumber on the Wall of Woods display. Others enjoy sitting at the center's observation window listening to birds gathered at the microphone-

C Area

equipped feeding station. Large porches provide opportunities to relax and enjoy the surrounding forest scenery.

RAVENSBURG STATE PARK: This pretty valley is especially beautiful when the mountain laurel blooms in late June and during the fall foliage of early October.

MIFFLINBURG BUGGY DAYS

Mifflinburg - SR 45, Downtown www.buggymuseum.org/festival_events.htm.Explore the actual home, carriage house, and workshop of the Heiss Coach Works, the only operation rescued from almost 50 different buggy works in the area (early 1900's). It looks as it did before the Heiss family left. Working demonstrations and buggy rides. FREE. (first weekend in June)

Milroy

REEDS GAP STATE PARK

Milroy - 1405 New Lancaster Valley Road (U.S. Route 322 from Milroy by following park signs for seven miles) 17063. www.dcnr.state.pa.us/stateparks/parks/reeds. htm. Phone: (717) 667-3622. Admission: to PA State Parks is FREE however swimming, marina and camping/lodging fees apply, with reservation or entrance.

The Self-guiding Interpretive Trail is a 1.1-mile trail following the scenic banks of Honey Creek. Interpretive waysides focus on the various ecological communities. This green-blazed trail starts at the kiosk beside the snack bar and follows parts of Blue Jay and Honey Creek trails between the swimming pool complex and Picnic Pavilion #3. Two, free, guarded swimming pools offer about 4,000 square feet of water for swimming. Also offered: Sledding, Campsites, Fishing, Winter Sports. POE PADDY STATE PARK is located at the confluence of Big Poe Creek and Penns Creek, a trout angler's paradise featuring the nationally recognized green drake mayfly hatch in June. You can hike through the 250-foot long Paddy Mountain Railroad Tunnel on the Mid State Trail by following the trail upstream along Penns Creek, crossing a pedestrian bridge and then going to the tunnel. POE VALLEY STATE PARK's hiking trail system connects to the extensive trail network of Bald Eagle State Forest. The hiking trails vary from easy hiking to very rugged, steep trails. Boating, Fishing, Swimming with beach, Hiking, and Winter Sports.

Patton

PRINCE GALLITZIN STATE PARK

Patton - *966 Marina Road (SR 1021) (reached by PA Routes 36 and 53 and U.S. Route 219) 16668. Phone: (814) 674-1000. www.dcnr.state.pa.us/stateparks/parks/ princegallitzin.aspx. Admission: to PA State Parks is FREE however swimming, marina and camping/lodging fees apply, with reservation or entrance.*

The major attractions to the park are the 1,600-acre Lake Glendale and the large campground. Beach, Visitor Center, Boat Rentals, Horseback Riding, Sledding, Campsites, Modern Cabins, Fishing, Trails, and Cross-Country Skiing.

SELDOM SEEN TOURIST COAL MINE

Patton - *PO Box 83 (I-76 to US219 to US22 East to Patton - Route 36) 16668. Phone: (814) 247-6305. www.seldomseenmine.com. Hours: Open 11:00am-5:00pm, Memorial Day weekend, July 4th, and Labor Day weekend. Open Saturday & Sunday in June, Thursday through Sunday in July and August, and for scheduled tours only in April, May, and September. Admission: $9.00 adult, $6.00 child (4-12). Tours: The visitor Center opens at 11am with the first tour entering the Mine at Noon. The last tour enters the Mine at 5:00pm.*

This once working historic coal mine now operates solely as a tourist mine, with underground tours run by miners who once worked in the mine. After you pay admission, you'll be given hardhats. Next, go underground using a mini-

a 3-ton hunk of coal...

train that took real miners down to their worksites. Most stops along the guided tour are while still on-board. You will have one opportunity to deboard and walk around one large mine "room." Learn first hand the lives and working conditions of coal miners from the past to the present. Family run operations, so tours are given by miners or descendants. You'll learn that coal was dug by hand, loaded on cars and hauled from the mine by mules - for as little as 25 cents per ton! Patton is close to Altoona so if in that area, stop on in.

Penfield

PARKER DAM STATE PARK

Penfield - *RD 1, Box 165 (I- 80, take Exit 18 onto Route 153 North, Turn right onto Mud Run Road) 15849. Phone: (814) 765-0630. www.dcnr.state.pa.us/stateparks/ parks/parkerdam.aspx. Admission: to PA State Parks is FREE however swimming, marina and camping/lodging fees apply, with reservation or entrance.*

This rustic, remote park in the heart of **MOSHANNAN STATE FOREST** is almost entirely wooded and offers picturesque areas of forest and swamp meadows, pine plantations and mixed hardwoods. The CCC Interpretive Center interprets the Civilian Conservation Corps. Parker Dam is a good base to explore the surrounding state forest. The swimming area in Parker Lake features a beautiful sand beach and is open from late-May to mid-September, 8:00am to sunset. Beach, Visitor Center, Boat Rentals, Sledding, Campsites, Rustic Cabins, Hiking Trails, and Cross-Country Skiing. Of all the hiking trails, we think the Logside Trail (0.5 mile) is easy and takes you by an authentic repro of a logslide, used at the turn of the century to haul logs out of the forest. Other shorter trails are labeled Stumpfield or Tornado Alley - can you guess why? Wayside exhibits interpreting the tornado are located outside of the Cabin Classroom.

A small-scale, interpretive maple sugaring operation runs throughout March. Apple-cidering is demonstrated each October. A visitor center attached to the park office offers interpretive displays, games and resource and children's' books. It is open during park office hours.

S.B. ELLIOTT STATE PARK is a quiet, rustic, mountaintop recreational area just off of I-80 near the mid-point of the state. This 318-acre park, in the heart of the Moshannon State Forest, is entirely wooded and offers picturesque areas of forest and swamp meadows and typical second growth mixed hardwood and oak timber. Camping, Rustic Cabins and Winter Sports.

WOODHICK WEEKEND

Penfield - Parker Dam State Park. A hands-on competition in old logging events to see who is the best woodhick of the year. X-cut sawing, log rolling, shoe pitching, seed spitting, and more. FREE. (Sunday of Labor Day Weekend)

C Area

Philipsburg

BLACK MOSHANNON STATE PARK

Philipsburg - *RR 1, Box 185 (PA Route 504) 16866. Phone: (814) 342-5960. www.dcnr.state.pa.us/stateparks/parks/blackmoshannon.aspx. Admission: to PA State Parks is FREE however swimming, marina and camping/lodging fees apply, with reservation or entrance.*

Black Moshannon State Park features the Black Moshannon Bog Natural Area. Trails and a boardwalk help people explore the birds and plants of the bog and surrounding forests. According to local tradition, American Indians called this watershed "Moss-Hanne," meaning "moose stream," thus the origin of the park's name. Appropriately, the "black" in the park name describes the tea-colored waters. Beach, Mountain Biking, Boat Rentals, Campsites, Modern Cabins, Trails, and Cross-Country Skiing. One of their trails is accessible and takes you on a boardwalk to explore wetlands (Bog Trail, .3 mile).

Raystown Lake

LAKE RAYSTOWN RESORT

Raystown Lake (Entriken) - *100 Chipmunk Crossing (Route 994) 16638. Phone: (814) 658-3500. www.raystownresort.com.*

The Resort is located between Harrisburg and Pittsburgh in Entriken on Pennsylvania's largest inland lake with 118 miles of scenic shoreline and thousands of acres of pristine woodlands and streams. Lodge rooms, boating and boat rentals, Hiking, Biking and Fitness Trails, Camping and Cottages, Swimming and Beach Areas. Other attractions:

- **PROUD MARY TOURBOAT**: Sightseeing cruises. Food available. Scheduled departures by season (April - October). Admission: Adults $9.50+, Children (under 6) 50% off Adult pricing, (for most cruises). Breakfast with Captain Chipmunk is $13.95 for everyone.

- **WILDRIVER WATER PARK**: Speed slides, twisting slides, whitewater tubing slides, Children's splash pool and mini-golf. $5.00-$14.00 depending on activity.

SEVEN POINTS CRUISES

Raystown Lake (Hesston) - *RD #1, Route 26 (Seven Points Marina) 16647. Phone: (814) 658-3074. www.7pointsmarina.com. Hours: May - mid-October. Summers usually have 3 cruises. Admission: $10.50 adult, $9.50 senior, $5.00 child (4-12). (15 passenger minimum on all cruises so they may have to cancel some cruises if attendance is poor). Tours: 90 minutes, 23 miles. Heated and air-conditioned.*

Public sightseeing boat cruises where you can view wooded shoreline (esp. cedar trees), wild turkey, deer, beaver, bald eagles, and ravens. Close to Lake Raystown Resort (waterpark and activities). Ask for the "Kids Kruz" that includes tour, box lunch, fish feeding, and demonstration of "rack storage" of 200+ boats in a warehouse (real neat if you're not a boater and already familiar with this).

RAYSTOWN REGATTA

Raystown Lake (Entriken) - *(888) RAYS-TOWN. www.raystown.org. Boat racing, concerts, kids' activities, area Pow Wows, & fireworks. (June weekend)*

GREENWOOD FURNACE STATE PARK

Raystown Lake (Huntingdon) - *RR 2, Box 118 (SR 305 North) 16652. Phone: (814) 667-1800. www.dcnr.state.pa.us/stateparks/parks/greenwoodfurnace.aspx. Admission: to PA State Parks is FREE however swimming, marina and camping/ lodging fees apply, with reservation or entrance.*

Relive the 1800s by visiting this 423-acre park, site of an active iron furnace community. Greenwood Furnace was the site of an active iron furnace community from 1834 to 1904. The visitor center is a restored blacksmith shop and provides historical programming. Along the Mid-State Trail to the Greenwood Forest Fire Lookout Tower, you can view charcoal hearths where wood was made into charcoal.

- GREENWOOD HISTORIC WALKING TOUR: Greenwood Furnace was once a thriving ironmaking village. Today, only a handful of its 127 buildings remain. This walking tour explores a portion of the historic district and includes parts of the town, tramway, historic roads and charcoal hearths. A free guide to the historic district is available at the park office and visitor center.

GREENWOOD FURNACE STATE PARK (cont.)

- **BLACKSMITH SHOP**: This historic building has displays on the history of the park and offers blacksmithing demonstrations in the summer. It is open Wednesday, Friday, Saturday and Sunday through the summer months and weekends in May, September and October.

- **VISITOR CENTER / PARK OFFICE**: The Visitor Center/Park Office is open 8:00am-4:00pm, Monday through Friday and seven days a week from Memorial Day to Labor Day. There are temporary exhibits on display. Campsites. A 300-foot sand beach is open from May to mid-September, 8:00am to sunset.

LINCOLN CAVERNS & WHISPER ROCKS

Raystown Lake (Huntingdon) - RR#1 Box 280 (I-76 to US 522 north to US 22 west) 16652. Phone: (814) 643-0268. www.lincolncaverns.com. Hours: Daily open at 9:00am until dark. Daily 9:00 am-4:00pm (March and November, December - Weekends only). Admission: $12.00 adult, $11.00 senior (65+), $7.00 child (4-12). Child Combo Ticket: $11.00 Includes Cave tour and regular bag of mineral rough to pan for gems - available mid-March thru mid-November. Miscellaneous: Gift shop, nature trails, gem panning. They also have Fall festivals and winter batfests. Educators: They provide lesson plan packets with each group reservation.

Nature's handiwork has been protected and preserved for your visit since they were first discovered in 1930 and 1941. Two crystal caverns - Lincoln and Whisper Rock have winding passages, large "rooms" with massive and delicate flowstones, pure white calcite and crystals. The interpretive tours of two spectacular crystal caverns features history, geology, bat facts, and trivia, while offering guests plenty of time for questions and picture taking. The caverns are a comfortable 50 year round, making them the ideal place to spend a hot summer afternoon. Ask about seasonal "Kids' Cave Crawls". Kids can suit up like a real spelunker and move through the simulated Kids Cave Crawl.

SWIGART ANTIQUE AUTO MUSEUM

Raystown Lake (Huntingdon) - 12031 William Penn Highway (US22 East) 16652. Phone: (814) 643-0885. www.swigartmuseum.com. Hours: Daily 9:00am-5:00pm (Memorial Day weekend- October). Admission: $3.00-$7.00 (age 6+).

See over 40 cars on display and the world's largest collection of cars, toys, license plates, bicycles and clothing. The 1908 Studebaker Electric sits in mint condition. It is one of two that belonged to the United States government and were used to transport people in the tunnel between the House and the Senate in Washington, D. C. The 12-passenger vehicle was designed with two front ends so it could reverse direction without turning around. Fun for nostalgic boys and grandparents.

ROTHROCK STATE FOREST

Raystown Lake (Huntington) - *Rothrock Lane - Box 403 16652. Phone: (814) 643-2340. www.dcnr.state.pa.us/forestry/stateforests/rothrock.aspx.*

Vistas or scenic overlooks are a major attraction for many forest visitors. The best known and most easily accessible is the well-known overlook atop Tussey Mountain along PA Route 26 at the Centre/Huntingdon County line. 93,349 acres of Fishing, Camping, Hiking, Cross-Country Skiing, Snowmobile and Bike Trails, and Picnic Areas.

TROUGH CREEK STATE PARK

Raystown Lake (James Creek) - *16362 Little Valley Road (PA Route 994) 16657. Phone: (814) 658-3847. www.dcnr.state.pa.us/stateparks/parks/troughcreek.aspx. Admission: to PA State Parks is FREE however swimming, marina and camping/ lodging fees apply, with reservation or entrance.*

Located along a scenic gorge where Great Trough Creek cuts through Terrace Mountain and empties into Raystown Lake. Rugged hiking trails lead to wonders like Balanced Rock and Rainbow Falls. Rothrock State Forest and Raystown Lake Recreation Area border the park, making a large, contiguous area of public land for recreation Campsites, Modern Cabins, Fishing and Hiking. IN the winter, the park serves as a trailhead for snowmobiling in nearby Rothrock State Forest lands.

WARRIORS PATH STATE PARK About 12 miles southwest of Trough Creek State Park in Saxton, Bedford County, the park is just off of PA 26. Natural cliffs, boating, and part of Raystown Lake area.

Rock Springs

AG PROGRESS DAYS

Rock Springs - Larson AG Research Center. http://apd.psu.edu. AG museum (open mid-April to Mid-October). One of the largest agricultural shows in the country features a petting zoo, live animal expos, games and food, and farming technology demos. Kids Climb a 25 foot tree, fishing center, corn maze and ImAGination Station with other fun things for kids. FREE (Tuesday – Thursday, mid-August)

Rockhill Furnace

EAST BROAD TOP RAILROAD

Rockhill Furnace - PO Box 158 (I-76, exit 13 to US522 North, Orbsonia Station) 17249. Phone: (814) 447-3011. www.ebtrr.com. Hours: Weekends at 11:00 am, 1:00 & 3:00pm. (June-October). Admission: $13.00 adult, $8.00 child (2-11). Tours: Your relaxing ride through fields and forests will last about 1 hour and 15 minutes. 10 mile trip Miscellaneous: Handcar and speeder rides are available between 11:00am and 4:30pm. These unique maintenance cars depart across the street from the railroad station and travel south on recently cleared track that the train does not run on. $2.00 extra. Special themed trains run at least one weekend during each month of operation. Station gift shop.

Take a trip back to the early 1900's when steam ruled the rails. Hear the whistles blow as the train makes its way down the track where coal was once king. With its truly unique shop complex, over-100-year-old station, and early 1900's equipment, the East Broad Top Railroad is a must-see for any family railroad enthusiast. Excursions are usually pulled by one of four mikado steam locomotives, built for the EBT by Baldwin between 1911 and 1918. Vintage diesel locomotives operate as backup power. The train passes through wooded areas and farmland and passes through cuts and over hills and bridges. As you ride an authentic steam powered train through a valley, you'll learn railroad history.

ROCKHILL TROLLEY MUSEUM

Rockhill Furnace - PO Box 203 (PA Turnpike, exit 13 to US522 North to Route 994 - Meadow Street) 17249. Phone: (814) 447-9576 (weekends only) (610) 437-0448. www.rockhilltrolley.org. Hours: Weekends and Holidays 11:00am-4:00pm (Memorial Day-October). Special events only in November and December. Admission: $7.00 adult, $4.00 child (2-12). Tours: Every 1/2 hour service. Miscellaneous: Pennsylvania Transportation Museum and restoration shop where volunteers are always working on new projects.

Take the 2 1/2 mile trolley rides along with a motorman on an antique streetcar - unlimited rides on many different varieties of streetcars. Even though they run on a standard railroad track, streetcars or "interurbans" (city to city) are powered by electricity. Wires running along the

a fun way to travel...wish more cities still used them!

length of main streets were connected to rods moving along a set track. The grandparents will remember this form of transport and have fun memories to share of the friendships that freely developed on the way to work or to the movies.

PUMPKIN PATCH TROLLEY

Rockhill Furnace - *Rockhill Trolley Museum. Visit the Pumpkin Patch while riding aboard a historic trolley. All children 12 years and under receive a free pumpkin with their paid fare. All riders are welcome to ride as often as they like all day long. Admission. (weekends in October)*

POLAR BEAR EXPRESS & SANTA'S TROLLEY

Rockhill Furnace - *Rockhill Trolley Museum. Polar Bear Express - Ride to Blacklog Narrows aboard a closed or open trolley during the evening and see lighted decorations along the trolley line. Rides operate from 6:30-9:00pm. (last weekend in November, first weekend in December). Santa's Trolley - Ride aboard a real trolley car, where each child will personally visit with Santa and receive a gift. Rides from 10:00am-4:00pm. (first Saturday in December)*

Spruce Creek

INDIAN CAVERNS

Spruce Creek - *(Turnpike exit 180: follow Rt. 522 north, take Rt. 22 west to Waterstreet then Rt. 45) 16683. Phone: (814) 632-7578. www.indiancaverns.com. Hours: Daily 10:00am-6:00pm (Summers). Extended weekends 10:00am-4:00pm (May, September, October). Admission: $12.00 adult, $10.50 senior and military, $6.50 child (4-12). Online coupon. Miscellaneous: Catch and release trout fishing in spruce creek on cave property. Hourly Rod rental fees apply.*

Pennsylvania's largest limestone cavern is known for its massive formations. The tour is conducted by a knowledgeable guide who explains the complete history of the caverns and points out various rock formations. Learn a bit of geology as the guide takes you through nearly a mile of lighted walkways - including a one-of-a-kind "Star Room" grotto and the "Frozen Niagara". Concrete and gravel walkways enable even elderly visitors to tour the cave with ease. Authentic Indian history - 150 relics and a tablet of picture writing were found in the cave. Be sure to look for the pre-Columbian "lacrosse" ball. A photogenic Indian totem pole and teepee grace the grounds and there is a free picnic area.

C Area

State College

PENN STATE UNIVERSITY PARK CAMPUS

State College - *(Hetzel Union Building) (off US322) 16801. Phone: (800) PSU-TODAY.*   *www.alumni.psu.edu/VRPennState/VirtualAmbassador/links.html.* *Hours: Mostly weekdays. Some museums also open Saturday & Sundays - Call first. Tours: Call for reservations.*

Things you can see:

- NITTANY LION SHRINE - The 13 ton block of Indiana limestone shaped like the mascot, Nittany Lion.

- FOOTBALL HALL OF FAME - Greensburg Sports Complex, (814) 865-0411. Nittany Lion football greats. Greenberg Sports Complex, along with containing the ice rink, houses the PSU Football Hall of Fame and the Football offices. Greenberg's ice pavilion is open to students and the public and is very popular year round.

- FROST ENTOMOLOGICAL MUSEUM - (814) 865-2865. 250,000 insects!

- EARTH & MINERAL SCIENCES MUSEUM - (814) 865-6427. Steidle Building. Minerals and paintings depicting Pennsylvania's mineral industries.

- PALSNER MUSEUM OF ART - (814) 865-7672.

- PENN STATE BOOKSTORE - (814) 863-0205.

- COLLEGE OF AGRICULTURAL SCIENCES - Dairy, beef and sheep research center, deer pens. Look for Coaly the mule.

- THE CREAMERY - www.creamery.psu.edu. west on Bigler Road (814-865-7535). Approximately 500,000 cones of ice cream are sold here each year. Most visitors to the Creamery at Penn State know only of its famous ice cream, sherbet, and cheeses sold at the store or over the Internet, but what they don't know is that it is the largest university creamery in the nation. Each year, approximately 4.5 million pounds of milk pass through the Creamery's stainless steel holding tanks. These dairy products are produced in the Food Science Lab, located directly behind the

Always something yummy here...

Creamery. These products are used throughout the campus. Ben and Jerry actually took a correspondence course through Penn State to learn about ice cream production.

STONE VALLEY RECREATION AREA

State College - *(CR1029 - off SR26 South) 16801. Phone: (814) 863-1164. Center - (814) 863-2000. www.psu.edu/dept/Stone_Valley/. Hours: Dawn - Dusk (AREA). Daily 10:00am-5:00pm (CENTER). Closed mid-December through January. Admission: FREE Note: be sure to check status of dam repairs before planning water activities. They may close Lake Perez to the public if work is being done.*

Boating, fishing, hayrides, ice skating, sledding, cross-country skiing, hiking, equipment rental for most sports, and cabins. Hikers enjoy many trails around Lake Perez, including the boardwalk over the wetlands at the head of the lake. The trails are also used for mountain biking and, in the winter, snow shoeing and cross-country skiing.

SHAVER'S CREEK ENVIRONMENTAL CENTER - www.outreach.psu.edu/ shaverscreek/. Raptor Center (rehabilitate injured large birds) and Day Camps. FREE Admission. Fees for rentals. Shaver's Creek Environmental Center is nestled in the ridge-and-valley area of central Pennsylvania, between State College and Huntingdon, in the Stone Valley Recreation Area of the Penn State Experimental Forest. Explore discovery rooms, tour the raptor center, walk the network of trails, and visit the gardens and the Pennsylvania nature book and gift shop. Explore animal tracks, constellations, and other cultural and natural history games. Under the Children's Loft, you will find live Pennsylvania frogs, toads, turtles, and snakes, just waiting for your visit.

MAPLE SUGARING

State College - *Stone Valley Recreation Area. Actual tapping of trees. Syrup making. Demonstrations of coopering and sugaring off in a realistic sugar camp. Pancakes and syrup served.*

CENTRAL PENNSYLVANIA FESTIVAL OF THE ARTS

State College - *Downtown & PSU Campus. www.arts-festival.com. The first day is usually Children and Youth Day featuring art creations of local kids ages 8-18. Art and mask parade with costumed characters, storytelling, marionettes, and concerts. (second Full Week of July, Monday - Friday)*

Sunbury

SHIKELLAMY STATE PARK

Sunbury - *Bridge Avenue (Blue Hill is reached from the town of Shamokin Dam on US 11north. Marina off of PA 147) 17801. Phone: (717) 988-5557. www.dcnr.state. pa.us/stateparks/parks/shikellamy.aspx. Admission: to PA State Parks is FREE however swimming, marina and camping/lodging fees apply, with reservation or entrance.*

The marina provides access to unlimited horsepower boating on Lake Augusta that is formed by an inflatable dam on the Susquehanna River. The Blue Hill area is across the river from the Marina and provides panoramic views of the confluence of two branches of the Susquehanna River. Paved paths encircle Shikellamy Marina. A walk around the one-mile nature trail on Shikellamy Overlook can reveal the wildlife that abounds in the park, like deer, songbirds and wildflowers. Unique geologic formations can be studied in the park and on the eastern boundary cliff trail extension. Bicycling: A one-mile, paved hiking and biking path encircles Shikellamy Marina. Bicycle rentals are available at the boat rental during the summer.

Tipton

DELGROSSO'S AMUSEMENT PARK

Tipton - *Old Route 220 (I-99 North, Exit Grazierville or Bellwood) 16684. Phone: (814) 684-3538. www.delgrossos.com. Hours: Daily (Summer). Weekends in May and September. Open at 11:00am. Admission: FREE. (All-day passes, ~$13.00-$16.00 and individual ride prices, ~50c each available). Mini golf and go karts extra fee per ride. All water park guests must have a Fun Pass Wristband to enter.*

North of Altoona sits DelGrosso's Amusement Park, originally established in 1919 as Bland's Park, it is a perfect example of a vintage amusement park. Offering "America's best amusement park food," the park is home to the famous, award-winning DelGrosso's spaghetti sauce, Murf's famous potato salad and their fresh-made pizza. Visitors can also take a ride on the antique Carouselle. Today, more than six decades after they started a spaghetti sauce company, Mafalda's and Fred's seven sons and daughters, 22 grandchildren and 20 great-grandchildren make millions of jars of spaghetti sauce and host hundreds of thousands of guests at their amusement park. 30 rides and attractions. Most of the rides are old-fashioned spinning rides and roller coasters. Mini-golf - (18 holes with lakes and waterfalls), Go-Karts, mini-train rides and an Interactive water park. Free concert series during the summer. This pay-by-ride park offers free admission, free parking and free live entertainment.

Windber

WINDBER COAL HERITAGE CENTER

Windber - *501 15th Street (off SR56) 15963. http://echf.windberpa.org. Phone: (877) 826-3933. Hours: Tuesday-Saturday 10:00am-5:00pm (May-October). Admission: $6.00 adult, $1.50 child (7-16), $3.00 student, $4.50 senior.*

Travel back to a turn-of-the-century coal town and experience the everyday life of a coal miner and his family. State-of-the-art exhibits, media presentations and archives also chronicle the evolution of coal mining technology, the struggle for unionization and the impact of the Berwind-White Co. and the coal industry has on small, rural areas. Mine #40 Scenic Overlook has 3 floors of exhibits, videos, and interactive maps. A working mine seam exhibit is interesting and other

exhibits help you to experience the life of a miner and his family. See working and living conditions - "The Underground Farmer" as they were called. Cities were created overnight by mining companies - Windber being a model town. Unique coal gift shop.

QUECREEK MINE EXHIBIT: The nightshift of Black Wolf Coal Company in the Quecreek Mine started out at 3:00pm on July 24th 2002. The day began like any other day, but at 8:50pm "All hell broke loose." A nine man mining crew breached a wall at entry No. 6, 245 feet underground. The abandoned Saxman Mine No. 2 instantly flooded their workplace with 150 million gallons of water. The rescue efforts took place over a 78 hour period, with hundreds of individuals, agencies, and organizations contributing to the rescue itself and the support efforts. Photos and artifacts displayed try to personally tell the rescue story.

C Area

Woodward

WOODWARD CAVE

Woodward - *SR 45 (US 22 east to Water Street, then SR 45 east) 16882. Phone: (814) 349-9800. www.woodwardcave.com. Hours: Generally Daily 9:00am-4:30pm (Summer). Friday-Sunday 10:00am-4:00pm (Spring, Fall). Admission: $5.25-$10.50 (age 2+). Tours: 50 - 60 minutes, guided*

Experience spectacular Woodward Cave, nicknamed "The Big One". One of the largest caverns in Pennsylvania, its nickname reflects its five spacious rooms, one of which, "The Hall of Statues" is 200 feet long. Experienced guides conduct a well explained, easily walked tour. Five big, well-lit rooms include the "Ball Room", "Square Room". "Hanging Forest", "Tower of Babel" (largest stalagmites in U.S.) and "Upper Room" (cathedral ceiling). Indian burial room and the passageways are wide and flat. On tour, did you notice any cave pearls? Your guide might even sneak in some cave chemistry - you'll feel smarter afterwards.

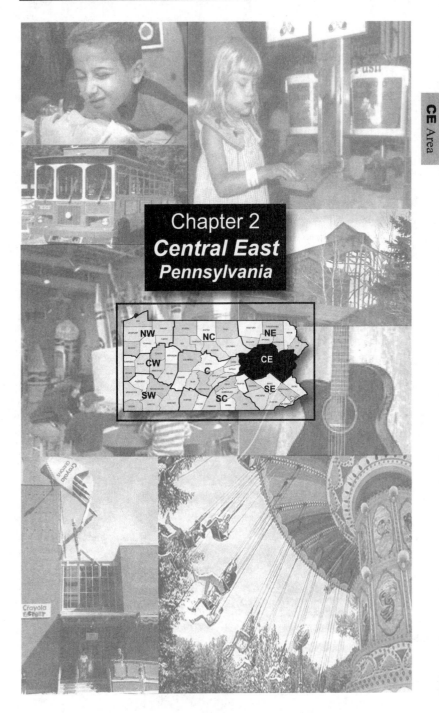

Chapter 2
Central East
Pennsylvania

CE Area

Allentown
- Allentown Art Museum
- Lehigh Valley Heritage Center
- America On Wheels
- Da Vinci Science Center
- Museum Of Indian Culture
- Dorney Park & Wildwater King
- Lehigh Valley Ironpigs
- Lights In The Parkway

Allentown (Schnecksville)
- Lehigh Valley Zoo

Analomink
- Alpine Mountain Ski Area

Ashland
- Pioneer Tunnel Coal Mine

Barnesville
- Tuscarora State Park

Benton
- Ricketts Glen State Park

Bethlehem
- Pennsylvania Youth Theatre
- Bethlehem Historic Area
- Blueberry Festival
- Celtic Classic Highland Games

Bloomsburg
- Children's Museum, The

Breinigsville
- Grim's Corny Maze

Catawissa
- Pumpkin Fall Festival

Danville
- Iron Heritage Festival

Delaware Water Gap
- Water Gap Trolley

Easton
- Crayola Factory
- Hugh Moore Canal Ride Park
- National Canal Museum

Elysburg
- Knoebel's Amusement Resort

Hellertown
- Lost River Caverns

Jim Thorpe (Summit Hill)
- Mauch Chunk Lake Park & Environmental Education Center

Lake Harmony
- Split Rock Resort

Lehighton
- Beltzville State Park

Minersville
- Big Diamond Raceway

Nazareth
- Martin Guitar Company

Palmerton
- Blue Mountain Ski Area

Poconos (Blakeslee)
- Jack Frost Mountain & Big Boulder Ski Areas

Poconos (Marshalls Creek)
- Pocono Snake & Animal Farm

Poconos (Scotrun)
- Great Wolf Lodge Resort & Indoor Waterpark

Poconos (Shawnee-On-Delaware)
- Shawnee Mountain Ski Area

Stroudsburg
- Quiet Valley Living Historical Farm

Swiftwater
- Delaware State Forest

Tannersville
- Camelback Beach Water Park (Camelback Ski Area)

Weatherly
- Eckley Miners' Village

White Haven
- Hickory Run State Park

Wind Gap
- Jacobsburg Park
- Lenape Nation Pow Wow

Wyoming
- Frances Slocum State Park

Travel Journal & Notes:

A Quick Tour of our Hand-Picked Favorites Around...

Central East Pennsylvania

See how some of the region's most famous products are made, including **Martin Guitars** and **Crayola** crayons. Be sure you're in the creative mode because both of these "factory tours" engage the hidden spirit of creativity in all of us. What a great way to introduce your kids to the Arts – music, artistry and crafts. Who knows, someone in your family may have talent?

No matter what time of year, the **Pocono Mountains** are full of activity. Beat the winter blues by skiing fresh powder or splashing indoors at a waterpark. Dive into summer by rafting, kayaking or canoeing in the Delaware and Lehigh rivers or take a bike ride through one of the area's state parks. Next, cool off at an outdoor waterpark or resort pool; visit the petting zoo or go-carting at one of their numerous family fun parks.

Many hard-working immigrants landed jobs in this part of the country. Early transport of goods was done using canals. Try your hand at packing for a trip at the **National Canal Museum**. Your admission to the Crayola Factory includes this museum (parents note: a nice, quiet diversion from the chaos upstairs). Now, head down the road and actually have a chance to ride a real canal boat – kids may even get a turn at steering. Other immigrants performed super-human feats coal mining. With poor conditions, these miners chiseled through rock all day to find veins of precious coal. A "ghost town" workers village is found at **Eckley Miners' Village** in Weatherly and an actual "train" tour of an underground mine is offered at **Pioneer Tunnel Coal Mine** in Ashland. All these transportation options are grand adventures for kids!

Sites and attractions are listed in order by City, Zip Code, and Name. Symbols indicated represent:

 Festivals   Restaurants   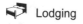 Lodging

Allentown

ALLENTOWN ART MUSEUM

Allentown - 31 North Fifth Street (5th & Court Streets) 18101. Phone: (610) 432-4333. www.allentownartmuseum.org. Hours: Wednesday-Saturday 11:00am-5:00pm, Sunday Noon-5:00pm. Admission: $3.00-$6.00 (over age 6). Admission includes audio tour. Children under 6 are admitted at no charge. Free Museum admission every Sunday. Art Ways is always open during regular Museum hours, free with Museum admission.

European to architecture of Frank Lloyd Wright to American art. Gem Collection, photography, textiles, museum shop. Art Ways with hands-on and touchable art & Family Time or ArtVentures. In Art Ways, a unique interactive learning center, throw caution to the wind and invite your family to look, learn, play, read, create, and yes, even touch together! Through a variety of hands-on, activity-based stations, your family members can make themselves at home in this fun-filled space while learning all about the world of art.

LEHIGH VALLEY HERITAGE CENTER MUSEUM

Allentown - 432 West Walnut Street (US-22 take PA 145 south 1.8 mi. to Walnut St. Turn left on Walnut .2 miles to 5 th St.) 18101. www.lchs.museum. Phone: (610) 435-1074. Hours: Tuesday-Saturday 10:00am-4:00pm, Sunday Noon-4:00pm. Admission: $3.00-$6.00 per person. Miscellaneous: Geology Garden adjacent. Educators: online exhibit and lesson plans here: http://www.lchs.museum/ww2/teachers.htm.

Here you can trace the main lines of the county's story: from the region's indigenous peoples, through the rural life of early Pennsylvania German immigrants, to the developments that made Lehigh County a birthplace of the American Industrial Revolution. From the Lenni Lenape, through the settlement of the Pennsylvania Germans, to the development of nationally important industries such as iron, cement and silk, and into the present. Take a trip into the world of the Pennsylvania Dutch rural community and tour the:TROXELL-STECKEL HOUSE (PA-German farmhouse), Claussville One-Room School, and Haines Mill. Or learn how Lehigh County served as a birthplace of the American Industrial Revolution as you view the soaring remains of the Lock Ridge Iron Furnace and Saylor Cement Kilns. Other properties worth a look in this county are: (small adult fee required to tour) CLAUSSVILLE ONE-ROOM SCHOOLHOUSE- 2917 Rte. 100; SAYLOR CEMENT INDUSTRY MUSEUM

- 245 N. 2nd. On site, 9 cement kilns from beginnings of cement industry; HAINES MILL MUSEUM - 3600 Dornay Park Road. Operating gristmill built in 1760 shows milling techniques; LOCH RIDGE FURNACE MUSEUM (Alburtis) - 525 Franklin. Iron furnaces, industry park. Most of these are only open weekends (May-September). Ask the Heritage Center front desk staff for details before you traverse out.

AMERICA ON WHEELS

Allentown - 5 North Front Street 18102. www.americaonwheels.org. Phone: (610) 432-4200. Hours: Tuesday-Saturday 10:00am-5:00pm, Sunday Noon-5:00pm. Admission: $7.00 adult, $5.00 senior (62+), $3.50 students (6-16).

Start a rainy morning trip to Allentown with a visit to the America On Wheels museum to see the Mack Trucks archives and learn how these world-famous trucks were made in the region for decades. Much more than just cars, the museum features everything on wheels, from racing lawn mowers and bicycles, to carriages and trucks. It has over 23,000 sq. ft. of exhibit space in three exhibit areas including subjects such as the American trucking industry, and also has a long-term education exhibit on alternative fuels. Nice place to get some ideas for kids' science reports about future fuels.

DA VINCI SCIENCE CENTER

Allentown - 3145 Hamilton Blvd. Bypass, Cedar Crest College (corner of the Hamilton Blvd. Bypass and Cedar Crest Blvd.) 18103. Phone: (484) 664-1002. www.davinci-center.org. Hours: Monday-Saturday 9:30am-5:00pm, Sunday Noon-5:00pm. Closed only Christmas Day and New Years Day. Admission: $11.95 adult; $8.95 children, seniors, military members and veterans; children under 3 are free.

This new center is based on the understanding that each young person, like Leonardo da Vinci, is insatiably curious about the world around them, uses multiple modes of investigation, embraces creativity, and seeks to make connections among all the things they are learning. The Center contains more than 200 fun, interactive, hands-on exhibits that stimulate curiosity and intellectual exploration. Its mission is to promote learning about science, math, and technology through hands-on problem solving. Learn what makes the Earth work and become a real weather forecaster. Investigate forces and discover how machines make work easier. Can you lift 1,000 pounds? Ever pet hermit crabs? Other Family favorites include:

WHAT HURTS? You are the doctor, and Justin needs your help! When your body is hurt or sick, it provides clues to what is wrong. You can use these clues to figure out the problem and how to fix it.

WATTS UP? Experiment with energy as you explore light, electricity, and magnetism. Enjoy images from deep space and dance in the Shadow Room.

WHAT'S THE MATTER? Atoms can join together in many unique, but predictable, ways to form new materials with new properties. Have you ever rearranged some atoms?

...watch water freeze

Some of their lab experiments actually encourage you to get "shocked" or messy.

MUSEUM OF INDIAN CULTURE

Allentown - *2825 Fish Hatchery Road (I-78 exit Cedar Crest Blvd. Take Rte. 29 south and then left on Fish Hatchery) 18103. www.lenape.org. Phone: (610) 797-2121. Hours: Friday-Sunday Noon-4:00pm. Admission: $3.00-$4.00 (over age 12).*

Hands-on exhibits enhance the learning of the Native American culture. Pretend you're walking in an Indian's moccasins and head dress as you look at exhibits of their crafts and tools. Special events include corn planting in May and Time of Thanksgiving in October.

TIME OF THANKSGIVING FESTIVAL

Allentown - *Museum Of Indian Culture. Drums, dancers, singing, music, native lifeways demos (flint knapping, basketry, cookery), and kids crafts. Admission. (third weekend in October)*

DORNEY PARK AND WILDWATER KINGDOM

Allentown - *3830 Dorney Park Road (I-78 West to Exit 16 B) 18104. Phone: (610) 395-3724. www.dorneypark.com. Hours: Daily (Memorial Day-Labor Day), Weekends (May and September). Admission: $21.00 (starlight/junior) to $42.00 general (includes wet and dry park rides). Parking $10.00.*

By comparison, this old-fashioned amusement park may be smaller, but it's full of good rides. Dorney Park & Wildwater Kingdom is home to more than 100 rides and attractions, including eight roller coasters and dozens of state-of-the-art thrill machines. Steel Force is the longest, tallest, fastest coaster in the East. Hang Time - "hang out" thrill ride and Water Works interactive aquatic play ride. Also, high energy live shows.

- CAMP SNOOPY — Dorney Park & Wildwater Kingdom is the only place on the East Coast where families can visit Snoopy, Charlie Brown and the PEANUTS™ gang.

- WILDWATER KINGDOM — Dorney Park & Wildwater Kingdom offers two great parks for the price of one. Splash around and beat the heat in one of the country's best-ranked water parks. . . Includes 18 water slides, a giant wavepool and Lollipop Lagoon for little kids. Aquablast is the longest elevated water slide (701ft.) in the world.

The park can get really crowded on hot summer days with long lines to enter and lines to ride so be prepared with a backpack of frozen water bottles and lite snacks to subdue your brood.

LEHIGH VALLEY IRONPIGS

Allentown - *Coca-cola Park, 1050 IronPigs Way 18109. Phone: (610) 841-PIGS. www.ironpigsbaseball.com.*

The Lehigh Valley region of eastern Pennsylvania celebrated the arrival of the Lehigh Valley IronPigs, its new AAA Minor League baseball team, in 2008. Affiliated with the Philadelphia Phillies, the team plays ballgames at Coca-Cola Park in Allentown. The name is a reference to pig iron, used in the manufacturing of steel, for which the Lehigh Valley region of Pennsylvania is world-renowned. The icon of Coca-Cola Park comes to life following every IronPigs home run. The giant Coca-Cola bottle on top of the videoboard, towering 90-feet above ground level, shoots fireworks and illuminates the sky. Kids Zone features a free playground area - a number of games, including speed pitch, slides and more.

LIGHTS IN THE PARKWAY

Allentown - LeHigh Parkway. www.lightsintheparkway.com. This drive-through light display covers more than a mile of one of Allentown's most beautiful parks (Lehigh Parkway) and features lighted trees, light tunnels and animated displays. Horse-drawn wagon rides. The Gift Barn features fine crafts and unique gift ideas for everyone on your holiday shopping list as well as refreshments and Lights In The Parkway souvenirs. Visit with Santa. Admission. (evenings mid-December thru New Years weekend)

This drive-through light display covers more than a mile of one of Allentown's most beautiful parks (Lehigh Parkway) and features lighted trees, light tunnels and animated displays. Horse-drawn wagon rides. The Gift Barn features fine crafts and unique gift ideas for everyone on your holiday shopping list as well as refreshments and Lights In The Parkway souvenirs. Visit with Santa. Admission. (evenings mid-December thru New Years weekend)

LEHIGH VALLEY ZOO

Allentown (Schnecksville) - *5150 Game Preserve Road (I-78 follow SR309 north) 18078. Phone: (610) 799-4171. www.lvzoo.org. Hours: Daily 9:30am-5:00pm (Late April - October). Admission: $6.50-$9.00 (age 2+).*

For more than 90 years, the Game Preserve - located north of Allentown/Lehigh Valley, PA - has entertained and educated more than five million people inside and outside Pennsylvania. Founded by General Harry C. Trexler, a local industrialist, the Game Preserve played a significant role in saving the North American Bison from extinction.

Native, exotic birds, and petting zoo inhabit a 25 acre zoo. The zoo's newest attraction is the addition of penguins moving around an open space with rock border. The zoo skips the large animals like tigers, elephants or giraffes and instead focuses on onyx, zebra, bobcats, prairie dogs, river otter, kangaroo, owl, etc. Investigation Station: Become an Investigative Agent and solve eco-crimes or solve the earth's dilemmas. Catch live animal presentations daily (look on the announcement board). Conserving species of endangered animals is a specialty. Look for their mascot bison, Wooly Bully. Because the zoo is small, you can get very close to the animals and the zoo is rarely crowded.

Analomink

ALPINE MOUNTAIN SKI AREA

Analomink - *Route 447 18320. Phone: (717) 595-2150. (800) 233-8240 (Lodging). Snow Report: (800) 233-8100. www.alpinemountain.com.*

One of the oldest ski areas in the state, Alpine Mountain Ski & Ride Center offers great facilities for skiing, snowboarding and snowtubing, as well as group facilities, a full-service cafeteria, private party room and a lounge that overlooks the Mountain, with live entertainment and events every weekend. Alpine's Snowtubing Park has been expanded and now includes a new "Kiddie Park" area. Longest Run: 2640 ft.; 20 Slopes & Trails.

Ashland

PIONEER TUNNEL COAL MINE

Ashland - 19 th & Oak Streets (SR61 North to Downtown Area - Follow signs off Center Street SR61) 17921. Phone: (570) 875-3850. www.pioneertunnel.com. Hours: Daily 10:00am-6:00pm (Summer). Weekdays 11:00am, 12:30pm, 2:00pm and Weekends 10:00am-6:00pm (May, September, October). Weekdays only in April. Some reserved group tours in November. Admission: $7.50-$9.50 adult, $5.50-$6.50 child (each activity). Save money purchasing the combo of both tours. Tours: Approximately 35 minutes long, given by real coal miner guides. Miscellaneous: Snack bar, Gift shop where most novelties are made from coal. Wooden "train" playground.

Two tour options are available and we highly recommend both. (Pre-schoolers may find the mine tour frightening due to darkness, dampness, and confined areas...but will love the lokie train tour).

- COAL MINE TOUR - Watch you children's eyes light up with fascination as you enter and travel 400' deep into a real working coal mine! Though closed in 1931 (because of the Great Depression), you will see and have explained all the features of a real mine. Learn how and why tunnels were built to access the coal. See the Mammoth Vein (the largest in Pennsylvania) and learn why all miners carried a safety lamp (not for light, but for safety from dangerous gases). Our guide was a real miner who carefully explained what we were seeing. He even turned out all of the lights to show how dark a real mine is! If you're concerned, the mine is inspected regularly by the state to insure its safety. If your parents or grandparents were miners, this will surely bring their stories to life. A top 10 Pennsylvania tour and we definitely agree!

- TRAIN RIDE - OPEN COAL FIELD TOUR - A "lokie" (steam locomotive) called the "Henry Clay" takes real mine cars to show you strip mining - where a "vein" of coal is discovered and dug out of the side of a mountain. Also stop by a relic "bootleg" coal mine where men risked life and the law during the Great Depression. They used these small illegal mines to get bags of coal to sell and heat their homes.

Barnesville

TUSCARORA STATE PARK

Barnesville - *687 Tuscarora Park Road (Off I-81, exit 131A, Hometown) 18214. Phone: (717) 467-2404.   www.dcnr.state.pa.us/stateparks/parks/tuscarora.aspx. Admission: to PA State Parks is FREE however swimming, marina and camping/ lodging fees apply, with reservation or entrance.*

This popular camping spot is heavily forested and the only cleared area is the 52-acre lake. Nestled against Locust Mountain, visitors will find many year-round recreational opportunities like boating and fishing, and opportunities to see wildlife. The hiking trails are short enough (most well under one mile) for younger ones to follow. A seasonal beach, swimming and boat rentals are available, too.

<u>LOCUST LAKE STATE PARK</u> is six miles upstream from Tuscarora. The park was developed as a family tent and trailer campground and has 282 campsites. Additional camper facilities include modern restrooms, swimming beach, boat rental, campstore, bicycle trail, hiking trails, fishing, playgrounds, and nature programs.

Benton

RICKETTS GLEN STATE PARK

Benton - *RR 2, Box 130 (PA Route 487) 17814. www.dcnr.state.pa.us/stateparks/ parks/rickettsglen.aspx. Phone: (717) 477-5675. Admission: to PA State Parks is FREE however swimming, marina and camping/lodging fees apply, with reservation or entrance.*

A series of trails, covering a total of five miles, parallel the streams as they course down the Glens. A shorter hike of 1/2 mile, the Evergreen Trail, offers an excellent view of the final series of falls as it meanders through a majestic stand of giant hemlocks and white pine. Twenty-one waterfalls are along the Falls Trail within the Glens Natural Area, while one (Adams) is only a few hundred feet from the Evergreen Parking Lot off of PA 118. Take the Falls Trail and explore the Glens which boasts a series of wild, free-flowing waterfalls, each cascading through rock-strewn clefts in this ancient hillside. The 94-foot Ganoga Falls is the highest of 22 named waterfalls. Beach Trail: 0.8-mile, easiest hiking. Campers in both camping areas can access the Lake Jean day-use and swimming areas without having to travel on a road. Beach/ Swimming, Boat Rentals, Horseback Riding, Campsites, Modern Cabins.

Bethlehem

PENNSYLVANIA YOUTH THEATRE

Bethlehem - *211 Plymouth Street 18015. Phone: (610) 332-1400. www.123pyt.org.*

Pennsylvania Youth Theatre (PYT) is a nonprofit performing arts organization with the mission of educating, entertaining, and enriching the lives of young people and their families through the art of theatre. Productions for/by youth like Cinderella, Babes in Toyland and Charlie and the Chocolate Factory.

BETHLEHEM HISTORIC AREA

Bethlehem - *459 Old York Road (off SR378 - Historic area) 18018. Phone: (800) 360-8687. www.historicbethlehem.org. Hours: Daily, except Christmas Admission: FREE (Walking self-guided tours). Guided, scheduled tours are $4.00-7.00/person. Miscellaneous: Best to visit during re-enacted history festivals around Christmas, Bach Festival in May, Celtic Festival in September or Musicfest in August.*

Points of interest include:

- VISITORS CENTER - Learn about Moravian Missionaries who first developed this town using pre-Revolutionary German architecture. Watch a video before you take a self-guided walking tour. Open daily until 5:00pm.

- MORAVIAN MUSEUM - 66 West Church Street. Can you imagine a 5 story log cabin, built without nails? Once used as a church, dorm and workshop, now it's a Moravian historical museum. (open Thursday-Sunday)

- INDUSTRIAL QUARTER - Start at the Luchenbach Mill (HistoryWorks! Children's interactive gallery located on the first floor), stop at a 1761 tannery or 1762 waterworks - the first pumped municipal water system in the colonies.

CHRISTMAS OPEN HOUSE

Bethlehem - *Bethlehem Historic Area. Tours of decorated, historical buildings. Refreshments and musical entertainment. Admission. (Thanksgiving weekend thru weekend after New Years)*

BLUEBERRY FESTIVAL

Bethlehem - *Burnside Plantation, Schoenersville Road. www.historicbethlehem.org. Enjoy blueberry delights galore on a 250 year old restored Moravian farm. Crafts, demonstrations, children's activities, and special tours are featured. Petting Zoo, Pony Rides, Horse Drawn Carousel, RCN Pie eating contests, Colonial Games. Admission. (third weekend of July)*

CELTIC CLASSIC HIGHLAND GAMES & FESTIVAL

Bethlehem - *Historic Downtown Area. www.celticfest.org. Exciting & educational weekend celebrating the cultures of Ireland, Scotland, and Wales. Music, dance, bag piping, athletic competition, children's activities, and authentic vendors. FREE. (last full weekend of September)*

Bloomsburg

CHILDREN'S MUSEUM, THE

Bloomsburg - *2 West Seventh Street   17815. www.the-childrens-museum.org. Phone: (570) 389-9206.   Hours: Tuesday-Saturday 10:00am-5:00pm. Admission: $5.00 ages 3+. No admission fee for children two years old and younger.*

Explore, discover and have fun while learning with over 50 different interactive exhibits. Walk into an Egyptian Tomb, set jet balls in motion, track rain, snow, sleet and hail by radar (then give your own live TV broadcast), crawl underground, build a body, try on a spacesuit, brush some giant teeth, or go outside to the Butterfly Garden (seasonal). Although it's a children's museum, some areas focus on interactive history: explore a full-sized longhouse, sit in a classroom with a wood stove, pretend you're a pioneer at the general store and then take a tour of a mini-coal mine. Special programs are offered each month.

Breinigsville

GRIM'S CORNY MAZE

Breinigsville - *9941 Schantz Road. www.grimsgreenhouse.com. 4 acre maze. FREE Straw maze and corn box. Admission for maze. (Weekends, last week of September - last week of October)*

CE Area

Catawissa

PUMPKIN FALL FESTIVAL

Catawissa - *Rohrbach's Farm Market. www.rohrbachsfarm.net. Petting zoo, refreshments, pumpkin patch, corn maze, pony or wagon rides. Flashlight nights too. (Corn Maze begins Labor Day weekend. Pumpkin Patch weekends in October)*

Danville

IRON HERITAGE FESTIVAL

Danville - *www.ironheritagefestival.net. The Iron Age, 1829 thru 1950 and Danville, PA are truly synonymous. In 1829, the first Iron foundry was established in Danville to manufacture wagon boxes, plowshares, andirons sadiron and griddles. In 1839-1840 Iron Ore started to be mined locally and in 1840 the first Anthracite furnace to efficiently produce iron was opened in Danville. On October 8, 1845, the first T-rail in America was rolled out at the Montour Iron Works, the largest iron manufacturing plant in the United States. The T-rail made it possible for Pennsylvania and America to become the leader in the industrial revolution. This festival is a celebration of America's ingenuity and foresight and is of interest for all of our Nation's citizens. Charcoal pit and iron ore tours and demonstrations, parade, costumed crafters and demos. Admission. (mid-July weekend)*

Delaware Water Gap

WATER GAP TROLLEY

Delaware Water Gap - *Main Street, Rte. 611 (I-80, exit 310) 18327. Phone: (570) 476-9766. www.watergaptrolley.com.*

Hours: Daily 10:00am-4:00pm (April-November). Admission: $9.50 adult, $4.00 child (2-11). Tours: All weather trolleys, narrated scenic, historical tour of area. 1 hour long. Trolley leaves every 1 1/2 hours (generally) Miscellaneous: Picnic areas and miniature golf on premises. Only $2.00 per person to play as much as you want. Hole in 1 on 10 is a FREE Ice Cream.

Replica streetcars take a relaxed tour of the Water Gap - Shawnee area where you can learn about Indians, early settlers, and some history. The first half of tour may be boring to kids but the second half stops at Chief Taminy's face formed from rough edges in the mountain rocks (like a natural profile - Mt. Rushmore). Also stop at the Cold Air Cave (regardless of the outside temperature; the air rushing out of the entrance to the small cave is always 38 degrees F. – your kids will say – really cool!). Now that you have a feel for the area, go wander back to some attractions you'd like to visit further or just have a picnic and play mini-golf.

Easton

CRAYOLA FACTORY

Easton - *30 Centre Square, Two Rivers Landing (Look for giant box of crayons on top at Two Rivers Landing) 18042. Web: www.crayola.com/factory. Phone:*

...it's fun just walking through the front door...

(610) 515-8000. Hours: Tuesday-Saturday 9:30am-5:00pm (earlier winter/ spring weekday closing - usually 3:00pm), Sunday Noon- 5:00pm. Also open holiday and summer break Mondays. Closed Christmastime, New Years, Easter and Thanksgiving & first two weeks of January. Admission: $9.75 general (3+), $9.25 senior(65+), $8.75 military. Includes admission to the National Canal Museum. Miscellaneous: The Crayola Store - Colorful collection of anything using color to create is sold. Also area to try new products. McDonald's Express eatery on premises. To get the most benefit from the full admission price, be prepared to do most of all of the activities (that includes you Mom & Dad - you get to be kids...again!)

No, The Crayola Factory is not the real manufacturing plant. Instead, it is a family hands-on discovery center that not only provides live demonstrations on how Crayola Crayons and Markers are made but also has more than a dozen hands-on art activities for guests to create mementos of their visit. Each person is asked to learn and think "Outside the Lines" here. Do you know what

Creative fun at every station

celebrity molded the 100 billionth crayon? "Color on the Wall" - Go ahead, it's glass and is wiped clean easily. You can color, draw and create with the latest Crayola® product without the worry of cleanup afterwards. Hurry kids, this

may be your only chance to break the rules! Everyone creates "their own souvenirs to take home". Especially great is the Factory Floor exhibit where a worker mixes melted wax and colors to help you make your own souvenir crayons to take home. The most favorite color is red and our kids got to help put the wrappers on real (just manufactured)

Jenny gets her freshly made souvenir box to take home!

crayons. The Meltdown area allows you to actually paint with melted crayons or re-create Prints, Stamps and Sculptures in another exhibit. The Color Park has a section for preschoolers that includes a ball play area with a series of tubes and bins that collect, sort and move colored balls from one location to another; and a soft play area for children ages two and under that includes a crawl space, oversized puzzle pieces and interactive panels. Older kids will like the Light Zone area where you experiment with color and light combinations. The Crayola Factory went through a $1.5 million redesign, adding two Animation Stations, a manufacturing theatre and new exhibits to give visitors an improved experience. Parents, it does get crazy in here, but if you go with the flow and start creating yourself…you CAN survive and have FUN!

HUGH MOORE CANAL RIDE PARK

Easton - 2750 Hugh Moore Park Road (off I-78 or off US22 to Lehigh Drive) 18042. Phone: (610) 559-6613. http://canals.org/visitors/Josiah_White_II_Canal_Boat_ Ride. Hours: Wednesday-Saturday 1:00-4:00pm (mid-June - Labor Day). Weekends only in September. Admission:$9.25 adult, $8.75 senior (65+), $6.50 child (3-15). Admission includes the Emrick Technology Center. Tours: Costumed interpreter guides you on a 30- minute ride. Miscellaneous: Canoes and pedalboats can be rented at the canal boat boarding area for use on the canal. Trails, picnic, boat rentals, gift shop.

The mule-drawn canal boat Josiah White II rides is on a restored section of the LeHigh Canal. The large boat and costumed drivers are carried by a mule or two (Dixie and Daisy). Why are mules better to use than horses or donkeys? Visit the Loctender's House Museum - lifestyle of his family and also a great view of the dam, lock, and bridge. You can also view the piers and cables of the Change Bridge, including the oldest machine-made wire rope in America.

Admission includes entrance to the <u>EMRICK TECHNOLOGY CENTER</u>. Through dynamic exhibits and education programs, the Emrick Technology Center explores the Lehigh Valley's rich industrial heritage. Visitors will see the 26-ton stationary steam engine once used to power the Buehler Furniture Factory; learn the history of the paper drinking cup, the Dixie Cup Company and its founder, Hugh Moore; and view a World War I cannon produced by Bethlehem Steel.

<u>LOCKTENDER'S HOUSE</u> - Where the life and work of a locktender's family is shown by period room exhibits and costumed interpreters. You can also view the piers and cables of the Change Bridge, including the oldest machine-made wire rope in America.

CANAL FESTIVAL

Easton *- Hugh Moore Canal Ride Park. Annual canal festival featuring canal boat rides, 19th century living history encampments and reenactments, Locktender's House tours, continuous music and entertainment, food. Parking $5.00. (last Sunday of June)*

NATIONAL CANAL MUSEUM

Easton *- 30 Centre Square (I-78, Easton exit & US22 - 3rd floor - Two Rivers Landing) 18042. Phone: (610) 559-6613. www.canals.org. Hours: Tuesday-Friday 9:30am-3:00pm, Saturday 9:30am-5:00pm, Sunday Noon-5:00pm (Closed Mondays except school holidays). Admission: Included in the purchase price of Crayola Factory tickets. (not available separately) Miscellaneous: Admissions are limited based on building capacity. Call ahead if you're traveling from out of town. Educators: a whole slew of pdfs from the National Science Foundation on canals is online here: http://canals.org/ educators/My_Curriculum. Strong, curriculum - based Scavenger Hunts for grades 3-8 links are found on that same page.*

The National Canal Museum is the only museum in the country dedicated to telling the story of America's historic towpath canals. Visit a short time in history before railroads, highways, and airplanes. Follow the story lines of immigrants and locals who built and ran the canals. Hear the boatman tell stories and sing canal songs. Walk through the middle of a full size replica

boat. Hands-on exhibits help kids understand this mode of transport. Load up your cargo and take a journey down a 90-foot long model canal featuring locks and incline planes! Actually operate a lock model and pilot your play boat through it. Don't miss the miniature train display and the interactive water table. Find out how

Waterworks lock experiments

boats float and how mules were able to pull boats weighing over 100 tons. Then dress up as socialites traveling the canal in luxury with Mr. Tiffany (of Tiffany glass in 1886). The Molly Polly Chunker was a luxury liner canal boat decorated in Victorian fashion. This is the best interactive way to truly understand canals and this brief era of time.

Elysburg

KNOEBEL'S AMUSEMENT RESORT

Elysburg - PO Box 317 (I-80 West to Bloomsburg exits 232, 236, 241. Rte. 232, PA 42 South to Catawissa & SR 487) 17824. www.knoebels.com. Phone: (800) ITS-4-FUN. Hours: Daily 11:00am-10:00pm (Summer). Weekends only (May & September). Admission: FREE. Pay-One-Price Plans are available for $0.75-$5.00 per ride. Ticket books save 10-15%. Would rather Pay-One-Price? For $20.00-$38.00, you can get a pass to nearly all the rides. Miscellaneous: Pool and water slides. Games, entertainment. Restaurants. Gift shops. Mini-golf. Swimming and Camping. Overnight Cabin rentals.

This is America's largest FREE admission park! Designed to allow every style of family to enjoy (and pay for) the rides they like best with 41 rides including the "Phoenix" - rated one of America's 10 best roller coasters. Knoebels recently

built their own version of a "Classic" wooden ride called Flying Turns. This is a roller coaster like ride where you sit in a train and roll down a wood track much like a bobsled run. Just as many family rides as thrill or kiddie rides. Ride in the Antique Cars or get a birds-eye view from the Giant Wheel. Want a little more action? Try the Whipper or shriek in the Haunted Mansion. Compose yourself with a nice quiet ride on the Pioneer Train before you return home from a fun filled day at Knoebels. An extremely family-friendly, old-fashioned attraction!

Museums have been added to the park (free admission):

- KNOEBELS COAL MINING MUSEUM. Free admission to Knoebels' tribute to the anthracite coal mining industry.

- KNOEBELS HISTORY MUSEUM - View a time line and photo exhibit detailing the history of Knoebels. Located in the rear of the Mining Museum.

- KNOEBELS CAROUSEL MUSEUM - Learn about the history of the carousel in America and see examples of the work of all of the major carousel carvers.

COVERED BRIDGE AND ARTS FESTIVAL

Elysburg - Knoebel's Amusement Resort. Crafters, demonstrations, entertainment, and food. For the children, face painting, clowns, and a selection of rides will be open in the park. End your day with a bus tour of several covered bridges including the nation's only twin covered bridges. FREE. (second weekend in October)

Hellertown

LOST RIVER CAVERNS

Hellertown - 726 Durham Street (I-78, Exit 21, Rt. 412 South) 18055. Phone: (610) 838-8767. Web: www.lostcave.com. Hours: Year-round. 9:00am-6:00pm (Memorial Day-Labor Day), Rest of year closes at 5:00pm. Closed Thanksgiving, Christmas, and New Year's Day. Admission: $10.50 adult, $6.50 child (3-12).

Lost River Caverns is a natural limestone cavern. It was discovered in 1883 by a limestone quarry operation which was digging where the parking lot now stands. At that time, the operation accidentally created the entrance to the cave. Since that is the only entrance to the caverns, they don't have any bats, rats or snakes or any Native Americans, dinosaurs or cavemen in the cave. Experience the wonder of abundant crystal formations, an underground river and five unique chambers. Moving through the cavern is the Lost River, whose clear waters mysteriously originate from an unknown source, then disappear once more beneath the earth's surface. One of the cavern rooms is a dedicated chapel, so visitors can even book Lost River for underground weddings or events. Guided walking tours take guests through beautiful crystal formations. Indoor tropical garden, rock museum and gift shop are on the premises.

Jim Thorpe (Summit Hill)

MAUCH CHUNK LAKE PARK & ENVIRONMENTAL EDUCATION CENTER

Jim Thorpe (Summit Hill) - *151 E. White Bear Dr. 18250. Phone: (570) 645-8597. www.carboneec.org. Hours: Monday-Friday 8:00am-4:30pm. Park trails and raptor cages are open daily from dawn to dusk.*

Located on the outskirts of historical Jim Thorpe, this County Park is perfect for that family getaway. While lodging at the park you can enjoy the art of Mother Nature on the 2.8 mile Mauch Chunk Lake, walk or bike the renovated Switchback Gravity Railroad and many other trails throughout the park, rent a boat, hike or stroll through the woods to the Environmental Center to see the birds of prey. Then unwind on the parks sandy beach.

Every visit brings you to the <u>CARBON COUNTY ENVIRONMENTAL EDUCATION CENTER</u>, where you'll see a spectacular collection of live birds of prey. This attraction is also a Pennsylvania-licensed wildlife rehabilitation center, so you may have an opportunity to see some of the state's wild residents up close while they recuperate. The center is housed in an old converted dairy barn; it occupies about 70 acres of woodland, wetland, and meadow habitat within Mauch Chunk Lake Park, so you're sure to see a good cross-section of Pennsylvania wildlife.

Lake Harmony

SPLIT ROCK RESORT

Lake Harmony - *1 Lake Drive (I-80 East to Exit 277 or I-476 to exit 95, follow Rte.940 East 18624. Phone: (717) 722-9111. (800) 255-ROCK (Lodge). Snow Report: (717) 722-9111. www.splitrockresort.com.*

Lodge with 2 indoor pools, whirlpools or sauna, 18 hole championship golf course, sail on beautiful Lake Harmony, mountain bike or hike to Hickory-Run State Park, or do some skiing. Three restaurants, a pizza parlor and water park snack bar provide multiple dining options. Longest Run: 1700 ft.; 7 Slopes & Trails.

H2O.O.O.O.H.H Indoor Family Waterpark is located adjacent to the Galleria at Split Rock Resort in Lake Harmony, PA. This complete indoor water park features attractions for all ages, including the Komodo Dragon - Pennsylvania's 1st indoor flow rider. Daredevils will want to try the Viper, Piranha And Amazon Blast slides, which drop 4 stories. Those looking for refreshing relaxation will enjoy the lava springs hot tubs. The little ones will have a great time at the jungle falls & leapin' lizards play areas. The water park is open to the general public. Overnight accommodations are not required for use of the waterpark. Please bring your own towels...they do not supply them. Separate admission: ~$40.00 Adult, ~$35.00 Kids under 42 inches tall. $15.00 Passes for observers and seniors.

Lehighton

BELTZVILLE STATE PARK

Lehighton - 2950 Pohopoco Drive (US 209) 18235. Phone: (215) 377-0045. www.dcnr.state.pa.us/stateparks/parks/beltzville.aspx. Admission: to PA State Parks is FREE however swimming, marina and camping/lodging fees apply, with reservation or entrance.

Beltzville Lake is seven miles long and features fishing, swimming, water sports and unlimited horsepower boating. Along the shore, you can sometimes find fossils. A 525-foot sand beach is open from late-May to Labor Day, 8:00am to sunset. A hike along Wild Creek Trail leads to waterfalls and Sawmill Trail wanders through forests and by a creek. Beach, Boat Rentals, & Cross-Country Skiing.

Minersville

BIG DIAMOND RACEWAY

Minersville - (Near Forestville, off Rt. 901) 17901. www.bigdiamondraceway.com. Phone: (570) 544-6434. Hours: Fridays at 8:00pm (April-Labor Day). Nationals end of September weekend.

Wide, banked, 3/8-mile clay oval located In Forestville, hosts NASCAR Series for Modifieds, Sportsman and Roadrunners. NASCAR - Winston Series Stock Car Racing.

Nazareth

MARTIN GUITAR COMPANY

Nazareth - 510 Sycamore Street (I-80 to SR33 South to SR191 South to North Broad to Beil St - Follow Signs) 18064. www.martinguitar.com. Phone: (610) 759-2837. Hours: Monday-Friday 8:30am-5:00pm (shop and museum). Closed Holidays and week of Christmas. Public Tours: Conducted at regular intervals between 11:00am and 2:30pm, Monday through Friday. First-come, first-served basis. No charge. Lasts one hour. Recommended for school-aged children and above because of length of tour. Miscellaneous: 1833 shop memorabilia, strings, books and accessories.

Founded in 1833, Martin guitars are known as "America's guitar". Used by many legendary performers, you'll start your tour in the museum shop of vintage guitars. Children are encouraged to "gently play" several guitars in the waiting area. If any of your children play the guitar, they will be especially interested in all the posters of famous performers who use Martins. Follow a guitar from rough lumber to a finished product which requires more than 300 steps to complete. The tour shows step-by-step production and is very educational. See the types of wood (cured for 4 months prior to production) used - from the usual to the exotic. Watch how each piece is computer-routed or bent in special jigs. Martin even makes their own strings to insure that "one of a kind" Martin sound. They've even produced a $50,000 custom order guitar with diamonds in the guitar neck! Sometimes famous performers (or their band members) stop by the Martin plant…maybe even on your tour!

DID YOU KNOW?

The company is the oldest surviving maker of guitars in the world.

Palmerton

BLUE MOUNTAIN SKI AREA

Palmerton - *1600 Blue Mountain Drive 18071. Phone: (610) 826-7700. Snow report: (800) 235- 2226. www.skibluemt.com.*

Since its opening in 1977, Blue Mountain has grown into one of the premiere skiing and snowboarding destinations in the Pocono area, attracting snow sports enthusiasts from the Philadelphia, Wilmington, New York, New Jersey and beyond. The ski and snowboard area boasts the highest vertical in Pennsylvania, a half pipe, two terrain parks and night skiing. 1,082-foot vertical, plenty of trails for ALL abilities plus a half-pipe and two terrain parks. Longest Run: 6400 ft.; 29 Slopes & Trails plus snowboarding.

Poconos Area

JACK FROST MOUNTAIN & BIG BOULDER SKI AREAS

Poconos (Blakeslee) - *PO Box 707 (I-476 exit 95 or I-80 exit 284, head north to Jack Frost, head south to Big Boulder) 18610. www.jfbb.com. Phone: (800) 468-2442. Admission: per activity Miscellaneous: Baby sitting provided. Choose from Poconos resorts' townhouses, condominiums, cabins, or campsites. SnowMonsters skiing and snowboarding programs are geared towards kids to teach them basic techniques and important safety tips in a fun environment! Chairlifts and SkiCarpets (make it easier for younger skiers to move up the mountains).*

Big Boulder was built on the site of the first commercial ski resort in Pennsylvania, and it was here that snowmaking was first used successfully in a commercial application. Five parks make Jack Frost/Big Boulder the premier destination for skiers and riders to come and test their skills. Visitors can ski two mountains for the price of one when they purchase a lift ticket.

- BIG BOULDER SKI AREA - Longest Run: 2900 ft.; 14 Slopes & Trails. Five family and seven single tubing chutes.

- JACK FROST SKI AREA - Longest Run: 2700 ft.; 21 Slopes & Trails.

- RIDE ATV PARK - 4 wheeler vehicle park with curves, hill, whoop-de-doos, mud pits. Smaller course and ATV's for youngsters. Fee includes rentals.

- SPLATTER - 2500 acres of paintball fields (with special themes). Year round.

- WHEELS SKATE PARK - In-line skate and board park with half pipes, quarter pipes, rail slides and pyramids. Kids area. Rentals. Daily (April - October).

POCONO SNAKE AND ANIMAL FARM

Poconos (Marshalls Creek) - *Route 209 (I-80 exit 309, US209 Northeast) 18335. Phone: (570) 223-8653. http://poconosnakeandanimalfarm.com/. Hours: Daily Noon-5:00pm, weather permitting. Admission: $5.50 to $7.50 (age 2+).*

Visit the "Great Little Zoo". They have over 100 animals including a giant Anaconda, Alligators, Emus, and Mountain Lions. Some of the most popular attractions include a 100 year old, 150 pound Alligator snapping turtle (ugly!), a giant python, Grey Wolves, and the beloved wolf Max whose best friend for over 13 years is a bear - watching them play is an unforgettable experience. Many of the animals are extra large for their species. The antics of the monkeys, or more engaging pot belly pigs, may make your kids "squeal". Petting and bottle-feeding areas, too. It's worth it to get the $2.00 cup of peanuts and fruit to feed the monkeys. Each visit is different as you never know what new animal may appear on the scene (or be left on their doorstep). They are designed to be visited in about an hour's time, a perfect interval for children.

GREAT WOLF LODGE RESORT & INDOOR WATERPARK

Poconos (Scotrun) - *1 Great Wolf Drive (just off I-80, Scotrun exit, Route 611 north) 18355. Phone: (800) 905-WOLF. www.greatwolflodge.com. Admission: Rates (include admission to waterpark) for lodging run $169-$300 per night depending on package. Note: want to save money? Check for off peak season specials and use the micro/frig in your room to prepare at least one economical meal per day.*

The Poconos first new family destination resort in nearly three decades. The 401-suite Great Wolf Lodge has an array of amenities including: a huge indoor Waterpark, an Arcade, Cub Club activity/crafts room, Spa, Fitness Room, the Camp Critter Bar & Grille, The Loose Moose Cottage gourmet buffet and food court, Claw Café confectionery and an animated Great Clock Tower to greet you. The Pocono Great Wolf indoor waterpark is the largest of any in the chain. They have a new, state-of-the-art water roller coaster ride that defies the law of gravity, winding up and down hill, and the cannon bowl tube ride, which offers a whirling water ride.

SNOWLAND

Poconos (Scotrun) - *Great Wolf Lodge Resort. The lodge is decorated in a winter scene. It snows 3x daily, hot cocoa and live music, clock tower sing along, Rowdy the Reindeer Storytime. Attend the North Pole University for Elves. Admission (includes lodging and indoor waterpark passes). (month-long in December)*

SHAWNEE MOUNTAIN SKI AREA

Poconos (Shawnee-on-Delaware) - *PO Box 339 (Exit 309, Off I-80) 18356. Phone: (570) 421-7231. (800) VILLA-4-U. (Lodge). Snow Report: (800) 233-4218. www.shawneemt.com.*

SKIwee Bowl Teaching Area: This exclusive contoured teaching terrain, located between lower Bushkill Trail and Little Chief Slope, features new extended carpet lifts, colorful teaching aides, permanent fencing and automated snow-making.

- INCUBATOR TERRAIN PARK: Complementing Shawnee's huge 3000' Bushkill Super Park, this new terrain park will be located on the Country Club Slope and will offer beginner/novice skill level rails, boxes and snow features. The Incubator Park will serve as a learning area for those Riders and Skiers not yet at a comfortable skill level to challenge the Bushkill Park.

- TANDEM SNOW TUBES: Shawnee's Pocono Plunge Snow Tubing Park will be adding a limited number of two person snow tubes able to accommodate one adult and one small child in the same snow tube.

22 Trails, Terrain Park, Snowboarding, "Pocono Plunge" Snow Tubing Park & Half-Pipe. Open Day & Night. Longest Run: 5100 ft. Comfortable rooms, dining, indoor pool/jacuzzi, & the only full-size indoor ice rink in the region.

Stroudsburg

QUIET VALLEY LIVING HISTORICAL FARM

Stroudsburg - *1000 Turkey Hill Road (I-80 to exit 304, US209 SW (Bus Rte), right at Shafer's School House Road, left on Business Route 209. 18360. Phone: (570) 992-6161. www.quietvalley.org. Hours: Tuesday-Saturday 10:00am-5:00pm, Sunday 1:00-5:00pm (June 20-Labor Day). Admission: $10.00 adult, $5.00 child (3-12). Online coupon. Tours: 90 minute, costumed guided. Last tour leaves at 4:00pm. Educators: you'll find so many pre-and-post visit activities here: http://www.quietvalley.org/programs/schoolprograms/resources.htm. Even lesson plans, crosswords, quizzes, a story to tell and a field trip workbook.*

Meet a Pennsylvania Dutch family as they go about their numerous daily chores – pretend the time is the early 1800s. "Family" guides in period clothing share the daily routine of a typical Pennsylvania German family and its descendants who lived at this location from 1765 to 1913. There are fourteen buildings, including original and reconstructed, on the farm. Daily activities include spinning, weaving, smoking and drying meats, vegetables and fruits; cooking, gardening, and tending to animals. Kids can touch barnyard animals and jump in a giant haystack! Usually one craft is highlighted weekly - ex. quilting, butter churning, candle dips, basket making, natural wool dying (how do they get color naturally?) and blacksmithing. Actual aunts, uncles, cousins, and siblings escort you around the farm & treat you like visiting relatives.

POCONO STATE CRAFT FESTIVAL

Stroudsburg - *Quiet Valley Living Historical Farm . www.poconocrafts.com. Craft demonstrations, musical entertainment and an interactive children's play area are among the activities held under tents at this lakeside center. Admission (12+). (late August)*

HARVEST FESTIVAL

Stroudsburg - *Quiet Valley Living Historical Farm. Tractor pulls, antique steam engines, parades, food (made with steam), threshing, baling, cider and apple butter making, hayrides, children's activities, petting zoo & fall crafts. Admission. (second weekend in October*

OLD TIME CHRISTMAS FARM

Stroudsburg - *Quiet Valley Living Historical Farm. Tours of decorated, historical buildings. Refreshments and musical entertainment. Tours led by lantern lights. Admission. (first two weekends in December)*

Swiftwater

DELAWARE STATE FOREST

Swiftwater - HC 1, Box 95A 18370. Phone: (570) 895-4000. www.dcnr.state. pa.us/forestry/stateforests/delaware.aspx.

Messing Nature Center leads to Trails, Horse Trails, ATV Trails (35 miles), Fishing, Cross-Country Skiing.

MAPLE SUGARING

Swiftwater - *Delaware State Forest. Actual tapping of trees. Syrup making. Demonstrations of coopering and sugaring off in a realistic sugar camp. Pancakes and syrup served. Messing Nature Center area.*

Tannersville

CAMELBACK BEACH WATER PARK (CAMELBACK SKI AREA)

Tannersville - *PO Box 168 (I-80, Exit 299) 18372. Phone: (570) 629-1661. www. camelbeach.com or http://skicamelback.com/. Hours: Waterpark open Daily at 10:00am (Summers). Weekends only (early Fall and late Spring). Skiing (December-March). Admission: Avg. $24.00 (twilight) to $30.00 (adult day rate). See website for skiing.*

WATERPARK: The Flow Rider, the ultimate surfing ride! 22 Water-slides- The most in the region featuring Checkered Flag Challenge with Kahuna Lagoon wave pool, two kids play zone, the Blue Nile Adventure River, bumper boats, mini golf, swimming pool, scenic chairlift & more. The Pharoah's Phortress expansion has eight waterslides, a four-story-high tipping bucket, fountains, spray guns and much more! 3200 foot long Alpine Slide, bumper boats, go-carts, mini-golf, chairlift rides, Cameltop Restaurant (lunch only).

SKI AREA: The largest ski resort in the Pocono Mountains is Camelback, which offers 33 trails and 13 lifts, including two high-speed quads, snowboard halfpipe, two terrain parks, and a wide selection of trails for all ability levels. In 2008, Camelback installed 110 new low-energy snow guns in a move that should save 50,000 gallons of diesel fuel annually. PA Ski & Winter Sports Museum is located here.

MOUNTAIN ADVENTURES: Treetop Adventure Course, Mountain Segways, Zip lines, Euro bungee & Climbing Wall. Call for package rates as they are not typically shown online.

OCTOBERFEST

Tannersville - *Camelback. German music, dance, foods & cultural exhibits. "Um-pah-pah" bands & cloggers. Pumpkin painting and hayrides. FREE. (late October)*

Weatherly

ECKLEY MINERS' VILLAGE

Weatherly - *2 Eckley Main Street (I-80 West to Exit 40 - SR940 West - then follow signs) 18255. Phone: (570) 636-2070. www.eckleyminers.org. Hours: Monday-Saturday 9:00am-5:00pm, Sunday Noon-5:00pm. Closed State Holidays except summer holidays. Admission: $6.00 adult, $5.50 senior (65+), $4.00 child (3-*

CE Area

11). Tours: Guided tours available for small extra charge (recommended) in the summertime only. Miscellaneous: Great supplement to a nearby tour of a coal mine.

What is a Patch Town? A patch was a cluster of a few dozen company houses along a crooked, unpaved street built within the shadow of black silt ponds

and strip mining pits. See an actual town (only slightly restored) just as it appeared in a movie (in the 1970s). Retired miners, miner's widows, and children still live here. Watch a 15 minute video at the Visitor's Center first, then walk by audio displays of a typical miner's day or week (including church on Sunday). School-aged kids will want to take the tour which includes going inside a house (1870s -

A large "breaker" tower, built as a movie prop, but it looks so real...

1890s - notice all of the updates!), a company store, and a doctor's office. Just imagine having to be a young boy then, helping to support the family by being a "breaker boy" in the smoky, dangerous mill. Boy, can you feel the coal miner ancestry here!

PATCH TOWN DAYS

Weatherly - *Eckley Miners' Village. Family-oriented living history festival featuring street fair, coal mining and dance troupes, wagon rides, huge craft show with period demos, children's activities, and ethnic food. Admission. (third weekend of June)*

CIVIL WAR ENCAMPMENT

Weatherly - *Eckley Miners' Village. Living history event. Civil War re-enactors display authentic camp life, cavalry drill demonstrations, and cannon firings. Period music, wagon rides, house tours, town ballgame, and period church service. Admission. (second or third weekend in August)*

CHRISTMAS OPEN HOUSE

Weatherly - *Eckley Miners' Village. Tours of decorated, historical buildings. Refreshments and musical entertainment. Wagon rides, arts & crafts, and storytelling. Admission. (Thanksgiving weekend)*

White Haven

HICKORY RUN STATE PARK

White Haven - *RD 1, Box 81 (PA Route 534, I-80 exit 274) 18661. Phone: (717) 443-0400. www.dcnr.state.pa.us/stateparks/parks/hickoryrun.aspx. Admission: to PA State Parks is FREE however swimming, marina and camping/lodging fees apply, with reservation or entrance.*

The Boulder Field, a striking boulder-strewn area, is a National Natural Landmark. This large park has over 40 miles of hiking trails, three natural areas and miles of trout streams. Every trail in the park can be hiked. Hiking-only trails have yellow blazes. Blue-blazed trails allow cross-country skiing and orange-blazed trails allow snowmobiling. While at the park, learn about lumbering history at the Visitors Center, observe wildlife or see Hawk Falls. A sand beach is open from late May to mid- September, 8:00am to sunset. Beach & Swimming, Sledding, and numerous Campsites.

Wind Gap

JACOBSBURG ENVIRONMENTAL EDUCATION PARK

Wind Gap - *835 Jacobsburg Road (PA 33) 18091. Phone: (610) 746-2801. www.dcnr.state.pa.us/stateparks/parks/jacobsburg.aspx. Hours: The center office is open 8:00am-4:00pm, Monday through Friday. The center's main parking area on Belfast Road is open from sunrise to sunset, seven days a week for your enjoyment. Miscellaneous: Heritage programming includes displays and demonstrations of early gunmaking at the Pennsylvania Longrifle Heritage Museum currently in the Henry Homestead. Living history programs include mid-1840s rendezvous and period military encampments. Gunmaking and blacksmithing classes are offered and historic buildings are open for tours. Please contact the center office for a schedule and reservation information.*

Environmental Education Center offers many programs. Once the site where the famous Henry Rifle was made, the Jacobsburg National Historic District lies almost entirely within the park. Heritage programming includes displays and demonstrations of early gunmaking at the Pennsylvania Longrifle Heritage Museum, currently in the Henry Homestead. Henrys Woods offers scenic hikes and the rest of the center grounds have multi-use trails. Horseback Riding and Mountain Biking are most popular here.

CE Area

AMERICAN FUR TRADE RENDEZVOUS

Wind Gap - *Jacobsburg Environmental Education Park. Annual pre-1840s era living history encampment at Boulton, one Jacobsburg Environmental Education Center`s three historical gun and iron making communities. See what living on America`s eastern frontier was really like! Complete with knife and tomahawk throwing competitions, blackpowder shooting, primitive fishing and archery, hearth cooking, and all the sights, sounds and smells of real history! Crafts and trade goods will be available for sale. The Pennsylvania Longrifle Museum at the 1812 Henry Homestead will be open all day each day, and scheduled tours will be offered of the 1834 John Joseph Henry House Museum both days. Admission fee for adults. (last weekend in October)*

LENAPE NATION POW WOW

Wind Gap - *Mountain View Park. www.lenapenation.org/events.html. Native American singing and dancing. Arts and crafts. Native food storytelling and much more! Admission. (last weekend in September)*

Wyoming

FRANCES SLOCUM STATE PARK

Wyoming - 565 Mt. Olivet Road (exit 170B of I- 81, take Rte. 309 North) 18644. Phone: (717) 696-3525. www.dcnr.state.pa.us/stateparks/parks/francesslocum.aspx. Admission: to PA State Parks is FREE however swimming, marina and camping/ lodging fees apply, with reservation or entrance.

The horseshoe-shaped lake provides 165 acres for boating and fishing. An environmental interpretive center located in the day use area features exhibits on American Indians and ecological topics. The park is named for a young girl who was kidnapped by a Lenni Lenape raiding party in 1778. Frances Slocum spent her first night of captivity in a rock shelter in the park. Deer Trail: yellow blazes, 1.3-mile, 2.5 miles, 3.8 miles This interpretive trail has three loops of varying lengths which allow you take a short walk or an adventure of almost four miles. Pool, Campsites, Boat Rentals, Ice Skating and Sledding.

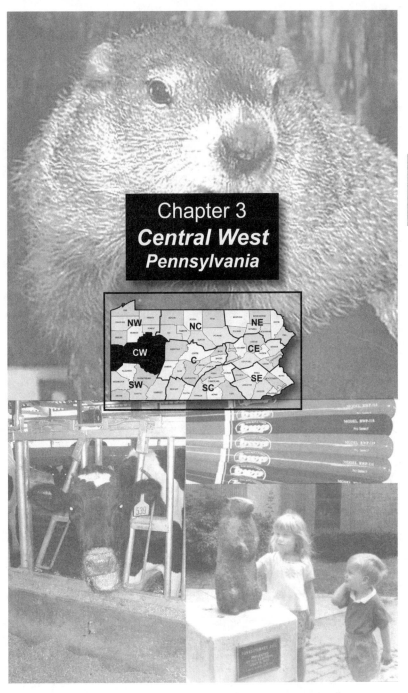

Chapter 3
Central West
Pennsylvania

CW Area

Brookville
- BWP Bats Factory Tour

Butler
- Playthings, Etc. Toy Store
- Butler County Museums
- Schramm's Fall Fest

Cooksburg
- Cook Forest State Park

Cooksburg (Clarington)
- Double Diamond Deer Ranch

Evans City
- Marburger Dairy Farm

Harmony
- Log Cabin Inn

Hookstown
- Raccoon Creek State Park

Indiana
- Jimmy Stewart Museum

Moraine
- Living Treasures Animal Park

New Castle
- Harlansburg Station's Museum Of Transportation
- Fireworks Capital Of America Fireworks Festival
- Cascade Of Lights

Penn Run
- Yellow Creek State Park

Portersville
- McConnell's Mill State Park
- Moraine State Park

Punxsutawney
- Punxsutawney Groundhog Zoo
- Weather Discovery Center
- Groundhog Day

Saxonburg
- Armstrong Farms Bed & Breakfast

Sigel
- Clear Creek State Park

Slippery Rock
- Jennings Environmental Education Center
- North Country Brewing Company

Valencia
- Harvest Valley Farms Fall Festival

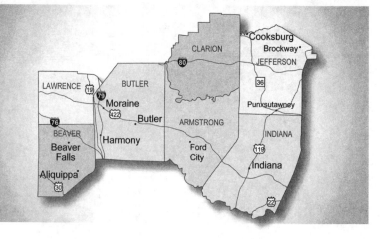

A Quick Tour of our Hand-Picked Favorites Around...

Central West Pennsylvania

This chapter contains many unpretentious towns – one famous little town and others that you may not have heard of. But that's what makes this area so special for families – no frills, just small town folks who allow you to explore their wares and nature in peace.

If the idea of exploring unique shops where you are allowed to touch EVERYTHING is appealing – **Playthings, Etc**. is the place. Don't worry about asking for directions, if you're along Rte. 8, north of Butler, you can't miss the giant silver spaceship building!

Another outdoor adventure can be scheduled at **Marburger Farms** where guests (best to schedule ahead) can come and learn about the giant barn full of Holstein cows and the milking parlor next door. Free milking observation is at 3:00pm each day. In neighboring towns, fresh local products can be found at a handful of Farmers Markets.

On Groundhog Day (February 2), the world looks for "Punxsutawney Phil" each year to peek out of his burrow on Gobbler's Knob and see if his shadow appears. His prediction indicates how much of the winter season is left. Phil and his descendants have been popping out every year since February 2, 1887. He and his family reside at a free **Punxsutawney Groundhog Zoo** in town. But that wasn't enough. These townsfolk realized kids enjoyed Phil so much; why not partner that interest with a **Weather Discovery Center**? Kids and adults alike pass through the door of a 12-foot tall tree stump and into Phil's famous burrow, completely immersing themselves in groundhog culture and science. Did you know this town is the Weather Capital of the World?

Play Ball? Ever seen how a baseball bat is made? **BWP Bats**, located in the heart of the Pennsylvania Wilds, constructs completely hand-made baseball bats from red oak and maple trees taken from the hills of northwestern Pennsylvania. They now offer tours.

State Parks offer recreation and exploration. One park has a 400 ft. deep gorge with giant boulders. Others offer boating and beaches on property near Deer or Animal Parks. Hiking alongside ancient pines, prairies and creek beds is another option.

Sites and attractions are listed in order by City, Zip Code, and Name. Symbols indicated represent:

 Festivals | O | Restaurants   Lodging

Brookville

BWP BATS FACTORY TOUR

Brookville - *80 Womeldorf Lane (Exit 86 on I-80 Pennsylvania) 15825. Phone: (814) 849-0089. www.bwpbats.com.   Tours: They have free factory tours 8:00am thru 4:00pm, Monday-Saturday at the Factory Outlet. Before 2:00pm is best.*

Welcome to the Home of the handmade professional Bats. BWP Bats, located in the heart of the Pennsylvania Wilds, constructs completely hand-made baseball bats from red oak and maple trees taken from the hills of northwestern Pennsylvania.   BWP Bats are known as the hardest and most durable wooden bats in the Major Leagues. Harder wood equates to better performance. All bats are precision kiln dried and double dipped for maximum hardness. This factory is also a full service lumber company so they have control over wood quality. On the free factory tour, visitors can see how the highest quality bats are produced - from a rough forest log to finely crafted baseball bat.

Butler

PLAYTHINGS, ETC. TOY STORE

Butler - *2483 William Flynn Hwy (7 miles north of Butler on SR 8) 16001. Phone: (724) 285-PLAY. www.playthings-etc.com.   Hours: Monday-Saturday 10:00am-8:00pm (closed Sundays).*

If the idea of exploring unique shops where you are allowed to touch EVERYTHING is appealing – Playthings, Etc. is the place. Don't worry about asking for directions, if you're along Rte. 8, north of Butler, you can't miss the giant silver spaceship building! This is the World's Coolest Toy Store inside and out...mostly because, even in a short visit, we played with a plasma car, rubber band guns, an electric train table, pogo sticks (even one that's turbo), a water and sand table, and the largest slot car set we've ever seen. Kids like to play pretend? Let them go wild pushing brightly colored flashing buttons and gears at the space station. Families are encouraged to enjoy a long visit and to try out the many interactive toys inside. Their motto is so cool – "families that pray together and play together will stay together."

BUTLER COUNTY MUSEUMS

Butler - *119 West New Castle Street, downtown 16003. Phone: (724) 283-8116. www.butlerhistory.com. Hours: open to the public Sundays, 1:00pm-3:00pm and Wednesdays 11:00am-1:30pm, May through August and for special events. Admission: $5.00 adult, $2.00 youth ages 5-17.*

Country life at 4 different sites: **COOPER CABIN** - (off Rte. 356, Cooper Rd.). The 1810 cabin is still furnished with family heirlooms and memorabilia as well as other period pieces. Out buildings include a spinning house, spring house and tool shed. A self-guided nature trail winds through the more than four acres of land surrounding the cabin. There is also a model oil well and an extensive herb garden. Cooper Cabin is open to the public for tours and a program on the 2nd and 4th Sundays of June, July, and August, 1:00pm-4:00pm. Admission fees: $3.00 per adult, $1.00 for youth ages 5-17.**SHAW HOUSE** - a summer residence for Butler's only U.S. Senator, Walter Lowrie (1828). **LITTLE RED SCHOOLHOUSE** - (1838) living history museum on 200 Jefferson St. which recreates the one-room school experience for visitors and school classes.

HERITAGE CENTER - 119 West New Castle Street. Industry in the area including tin shop, Bantam Jeep, and Franklin glassworks. A mini-circus is on display and includes an elephant that squirts innocent bystanders, girls walking a tightrope and a train that circles the perimeter.

CIDER AND SAUERKRAUT FESTIVAL

Butler - Butler Heritage Center. Cooper Cabin Pioneer Homestead. Applebutter making, cider pressing, sauerkraut making, lap hoop quilting demonstrations, and tours of the cabin. Hot dogs with chili or sauerkraut, chips, beverages, and baked goods will be available for purchase. www.butlercountyhistoricalsociety-pa.org. Admission. (mid- September)

CHRISTMAS OPEN HOUSE

Butler - *Butler Heritage Center. Tours of decorated, historical buildings. Refreshments and musical entertainment. Admission.*

SCHRAMM'S FALL FEST

Butler - *291 Crisswell Road. www.schrammfarms.com. Petting zoo, refreshments, pumpkin patch, corn maze, pony or wagon rides. Scarecrows display. Admission. (weekends in October)*

Cooksburg

COOK FOREST STATE PARK

Cooksburg *- River Road - PO Box 120 (I-80 exit 78, PA 36 north) 16217. Phone: (814) 744-8407. www.dcnr.state.pa.us/stateparks/parks/cookforest.aspx. Admission: to PA State Parks is FREE however swimming, marina and camping/lodging fees apply, with reservation or entrance.*

Virgin white pine and hemlock timber stands nick-named the "Black Forest". Highlights are the Forest Cathedral, Log Cabin Inn Visitor Center, Sawmill Craft Center and Theater, the Fire Tower and Seneca Point Overlook. Log Cabin Inn: Cook Forest's environmental learning center is a large log building built in 1934 by the CCC. It is at one end of Longfellow Trail and contains a variety of displays, taxidermy animals and logging tools from early lumbering days. Near the entrance on Route 36 is Double Diamond Deer Ranch, where deer are raised from birth. Children can bottle-feed fawns June -August. Pool, Horseback Riding, Campsites, Rustic Cabins, Boating, Fishing, Cross-Country Skiing, Sledding and Snowmobiling. Several private canoe rentals are in the Cooksburg area.

DOUBLE DIAMOND DEER RANCH

Cooksburg (Clarington) *- 12211 Route 36 (I-80, Brookville exit north on SR36, South of Cook Forest) 15828. www.doublediamonddeerranch.com. Phone: (814) 752-6334. Hours: Daily 10:00am-Dusk (May-November). Admission: $6.00+ (age 5+). Miscellaneous: A Buck Barn with stuffed animals is also on the property. Glow-in-the-Dark Mini Golf is located inside a former flea market building (so your family can have fun playing golf in any kind of weather), it features many unusual creatures. They were created by Roland Metal art, and were painted with glow in the dark paint.*

Photograph or watch white tail deer in natural habitats. Covered walkways, scenic trails, and a Museum & gift shop. In the summer months you can see the newborn fawns, plus the regular cast of characters including Tweety, an all white deer with blue eyes. Come see how tiny they are. Kids can help bottle feed the fawns at 2 and 6 p.m. That's also treat time for the adult deer who get apples and carrots." Bottle times" and "Treat Times" are scheduled in June, July and August. The deer do not drop their antlers until February, March and April. The last buck always sheds his antlers around April 15th.

Evans City

MARBURGER DAIRY FARM

Evans City - *1506 Mars-Evans City Road (I-79 exit 83 east on Rte. 528. South on Rte 68 to Rte 309) 16033. Phone: (724) 538-4800.   www.marburgerdairy.com. Tours: Group tours are scheduled ahead of time - usually near afternoon milking*

time. FREEBIES: click on their Fun and Games link for coloring and puzzles related to dairy farms.

Another outdoor adventure can be scheduled at Marburger Farms where guests (best to schedule ahead) can come and learn about the giant barn full of Holstein cows and the milking parlor next door. Free milking observation is at 3:00pm each day. The Marburger farm uses a 12 cow milking parlor; which means that they can milk 12 cows at a time. This farm milks over 150 cows which are fed by the surrounding fields of corn and hay. Be sure to wear your old clothes as you are on a real working farm! Off all the varieties of beverages they package, which is the most popular? Buttermilk. Want some recipes, go to the Recipes icon. We highly recommend their Buttermilk Waffles.

Did You Know?

A cow that eats only grass can make about 50 glasses of milk a day, but a cow that eats grass, corn, and hay can make about 100 glasses.

Harmony

LOG CABIN INN

Harmony - *430 Perry Highway (just 5 minutes north of Zelienople on Rt. 19) 16037. Phone: (724) 452-4155. www.springfields.com/lci_files/logcabininn.html. The Log Cabin Inn is just north of the hustle and bustle of Cranberry. Rural and rustic, it is built around a 160 year old cabin. The original dining room area floor is tilted and the logs are huge. Casual Dress. Relaxing atmosphere. Showing all Steeler football games and a great outdoor (heated) deck overlooking the 'Backwoods'.... you'll love it. All American fare with children's menu complete with coloring and crayons. The best appetizer to share: Loaded Cabin Fries - Generous portion of crispy potato cubes smothered in ranch dressing, mozzarella and cheddar cheeses, bacon and red onions-$5.99. Daily, Lunch & Dinner.*

🍽️

Hookstown

RACCOON CREEK STATE PARK

Hookstown - RD 1, Box 900 (3000 SR 18, or enter from US 22 or US 30) 15050. www. dcnr.state.pa.us/stateparks/parks/raccooncreek.aspx. Phone: (724) 899-2200. Hours: 8:00am-Sunset Admission: to PA State Parks is FREE however swimming, marina and camping/lodging fees apply, with reservation or entrance.

A centrally located 100-acre lake provides opportunities for outdoor recreation like fishing, boating, and photographing and viewing waterfowl and other wildlife. Wild Flower Reserve (899-3611, Rte 30.) A 315 acre tract of land with over 500 species of wildflowers and wildlife. Frankfurt Mineral Springs - explore the reported "medicinal" properties of the water. There are many hiking trails scattered throughout the park, some only about one mile in length with moderate hills. The 800-foot, accessible sand/turf beach is open from late-May to mid-September, 8:00am-sunset. Visitor Center, Boat Rentals, Horseback Riding, Sledding, Winter Sports, Campsites, and Modern Cabins.

Indiana

JIMMY STEWART MUSEUM

Indiana - 835 Philadelphia St (Indiana Public Library - 3rd Floor, corner of 9th) 15701. Phone: (724) 349-6112 or (800) 83-JIMMY. www.jimmy.org. Hours: Monday-Saturday 10:00am-5:00pm, Sunday & Holidays Noon-5:00pm. Closed Christmastime and New Years time. Admission: $7.00 adult, $6.00 senior (62+), military and students, $5.00 child (7-17).

A legendary actor (every Christmas we still all watch "It's a Wonderful Life") who had accomplishments in film, radio and television plus civic and family roles. Displays of his great grandfather's uniform, baby photographs, furniture from the family hardware store, original movie posters, props and costumes. Watch films that are shown in a small 1930s vintage movie theatre most weekends.

CW Area

FESTIVAL OF LIGHTS

Indiana - "It's A Wonderful Life". Blue Spruce Park. Jimmy Stewart's home town. See "Blue the Spruce Ness Monster". Sleigh and pony rides. Drive-thru. Admission. (Evenings-late November through New Year's Day)

Moraine

LIVING TREASURES ANIMAL PARK

Moraine - US422   16101. Phone: (724) 924-9571.   www.ltanimalpark.com. Hours: Daily 10:00am-8:00pm (Summer). Daily 10:00am-6:00pm (April and May, September, October). Admission: $8.50 adult, $7.00 senior, $5.50 child (3-11).

Perfect for the whole family, this large petty zoo features animals from around the world, including timber wolves, lambs, kangaroos, sheep, camels, llamas, pot belly pigs, yaks, zebras, monkeys, bears, turkeys, alligators, snakes and deer.

Watch kangaroos, tigers and wolves and ride the miniature horses. Kids love the petting area (babies, reindeer, and camels) and feeding areas (bears, otters, monkeys, goats, sheep, and llamas). Cups of animal feed are available in the gift shop or at coin-operated food dispensers throughout the park. Spring means babies at Living Treasures - even mini donkeys. Leave your binoculars at home but don't forget your camera for those once in a lifetime photo opportunities.

New Castle

HARLANSBURG STATION'S MUSEUM OF TRANSPORTATION

New Castle - *West Pittsburgh Road, 424 Old Rt. 19 (US19 & SR108) 16101. Phone: (724) 652-9002. www.harlansburgstation.com/. Hours: Tuesday-Saturday 10:00am-5:00pm, Sunday Noon-5:00pm. Weekends Only (March, April, May, November, December) Admission: $2.00-$3.00.*

This is a story on the creation of one man's dream, his own personal museum that he now shares with the public. Olde time railroad station with display of real Pennsylvania railroad cars outside and memorabilia displayed inside the cars. Meet the mascot conductor and see lots of railroad uniforms. In the station are trains, cars, planes, trucks, and trolleys. The scale train layout depicts four scenes of Western Pennsylvania. Tours of silver-sided passenger cars are available.

FIREWORKS CAPITAL OF AMERICA FIREWORKS FESTIVAL

New Castle - *Downtown area. www.fireworkscapitalofamerica.com. Children's activities, street dancing, musical entertainment, "Ducky Derby", Ice Cream Social, plus a Fireworks Spectacular. No Admission. (second Saturday of July)*

CASCADE OF LIGHTS

New Castle - *Cascade Park. www.newcastlepa.org/Events/events.html. Glistening lights. Visit with Santa. Hot chocolate. Freshly baked cookies. Toy/gift shops. Weekend entertainment. Admission. (Evenings - late November through New Year's Day)*

Penn Run

YELLOW CREEK STATE PARK

Penn Run - *170 Route 259 Highway (PA 422 or PA 259) 15765. Phone: (724) 357-7913. www.dcnr.state.pa.us/stateparks/parks/yellowcreek.aspx. Admission: to PA State Parks is FREE however swimming, marina and camping/lodging fees apply, with reservation or entrance.*

Yellow Creek State Park is in Indiana County along one of the first "highways" in the state, the Kittanning Path. This trail was used by the Delaware and

Shawnee nations and by early settlers. Today, US 422 roughly follows the old Kittanning Path, and provides the main access to the park from Indiana and Ebensburg. The park is named for Yellow and Little Yellow creeks, which create the lake. The creeks have lots of yellow clay in the banks and bottoms. Laurel Run Trail is a 0.5-mile loop which starts at the park office. This easy hike is especially beautiful in the spring when wildflowers abound. Ridgetop Trail is a challenging 2-mile trail. It begins in the beach/day-use area and winds through a variety of habitats. Damsite Trail is a 2.5-mile trail that offers a view of the Yellow Creek dam. Yurts: These four Mongolian-style tents are round, on a wooden deck and sleep five people in single bunks and double/single bunks. Yurts have a cooking stove, refrigerator, countertop, table, chairs, electric heat and outlets, fire ring and picnic table. Restrooms are nearby. The 800-foot beach is open from late-May to mid-September, 8:00am to sunset. Visitor Center, Boat Rentals, Sledding, Fishing, and Trails.

Portersville

MCCONNELL'S MILL STATE PARK

Portersville *- RD 2, Box 16 (near the intersection of PA 19 and U.S. 422) 16051. www.dcnr.state.pa.us/stateparks/parks/mcconnellsmill.aspx. Phone: (724) 368-8091. Admission: to PA State Parks is FREE however swimming, marina and camping/lodging fees apply, with reservation or entrance.*

A 400 ft. deep gorge with giant boulders and unique eco-system. Slippery Rock Creek flows through the gorge. The steep-sided gorge contains numerous rocky outcrops, boulders, old growth forest, waterfalls and rare plants. Cleland Rock Vista is a great place to view the gorge. You can tour the restored rolling gristmill or the covered bridge. There is also scenic hiking, whitewater boating and two rock climbing and rappelling areas. Historical Center, sledding, boating, fishing, swimming, biking, camping, skiing, and snowmobiling. The park is open sunrise to sunset, daily.

HERITAGE FESTIVAL

Portersville - McConnell's Mill State Park. The festival celebrates the operational era of the Old Mill (1852-1928). Visitors can witness artisans and craftspeople making art and try old time games and crafts. Other activities include mill tours, corn grinding demonstrations, musical entertainment, a Civil War encampment and food vendors. (last full weekend in September)

MORAINE STATE PARK

Portersville - *225 Pleasant Valley Road (bisected by PA Route 422 running east/west and PA 528 running north/south) 16051. Phone: (724) 368-8811. www. dcnr.state.pa.us/stateparks/parks/moraine.aspx. Admission: to PA State Parks is FREE however swimming, marina and camping/lodging fees apply, with reservation or entrance.*

Moraine State Park is the third largest park in Pennsylvania so you know they'll have plenty to do for the outdoorsy type. There are 10 boat launches around Lake Arthur and sailing is very popular. Races and regattas for sailboats are held throughout the summer. At the Crescent Bay Area, sailboats, rowboats, paddleboats, canoes, kayaks, motorboats and pontoon boats may be rented in the summer. Guests who want to be passengers vs. participants can take a pleasant ride around Lake Arthur by sightseeing pontoon boat during warm weather season (www.morainepreservationfund.com, $5.00-$7.00 sightseeing cruises). On tour, you'll learn about the osprey and other wildlife that linger around the water's edge. The park has a nice beach open each summer and many hiking and biking trails that would meet the needs of a family just wanting a short ride or walk. Look for the nesting Bald Eagles. And, Moraine State park has about two dozen geocach sites within its borders. Of special interest is the Frank Preston Conservation Area and a 7-mile paved bike trail that winds around the north shore of the lake. Also on premises: Visitor Center, Horseback Riding, Mountain Biking, Modern Cabins, and Winter Sports.

Punxsutawney

PUNXSUTAWNEY GROUNDHOG ZOO

Punxsutawney - *East Mahoning Street, off Barclay Sq.@ Library (I-80 to exit 97, US119) 15767. Phone: (800) 752-PHIL. www.groundhog.org. Hours: Museum: Tuesday-Saturday 1:00-4:00pm, Sunday 2:00-4:00pm. Zoo: (Dawn to Dusk. Call first to confirm hours of museum. Admission: FREE Miscellaneous: At 401 West*

Mahoning Street, (814) 938-2555 is the Punxsutawney Museum devoted to groundhog history and legend. All around the town, colorful, whimsical, 6-foot tall fiberglass Phantastic Phils! adorn the public spaces of the Weather Capital of the World. Each of the large fiberglass groundhogs is an individual work of art created by artists from across the state and the country. FREEBIES: Printable Puzzles, games and activities are found here: www.groundhog.org/index.php?id=66.

...gotta love me!

For updates & travel games visit: **www.KidsLoveTravel.com**

On Groundhog Day (February 2), the world looks for "Punxsutawney Phil" each year to peek out of his burrow on Gobbler's Knob and see if his shadow appears. His prediction indicates how much of the winter season is left. The legend was brought to this country by German immigrants. Phil and his descendants have been popping out every year since February 2, 1887. He and his family reside at this zoo. We might suggest you watch the movie "Groundhog Day" starring Bill Murray prior to your visit to get into the spirit of things! By the way, Phil gets almost as much mail as Santa Claus and on Groundhog Day up to 35,000 people come to see him each

"Now Phil, you gotta help me out", says Jenny. "Daniel likes summer, but I like winter...shadow please!"

year! (they have pictures to prove it). It's worth a trip anytime of the year to meet a live groundhog up close … your family may be surprised how they can change their shape to fit around the landscape.

WEATHER DISCOVERY CENTER

Punxsutawney - 201 North Findley Street (one block off the main street in Punxsutawney) 15767. Phone: (814) 938-1000. www.weatherdiscovery.org. Hours: Daily 10:00am-4:00pm, closed Wednesday and Sunday. Admission: $4.00 per person.

DID YOU KNOW? Punxsutawney is the "Weather Capital of the World".

The Weather Discovery Center excites and educates visitors about the old and new ways of predicting and studying weather. Kids and adults alike pass through the door of a 12-foot tall tree stump and into Phil's famous burrow, completely immersing themselves in groundhog culture and science. Have you ever seen a tornado from the safety of inside? Tried your hand at being a TV meteorologist? Make a "Perfect Storm" with your friends--it's electrifying! "Twist & Shout" your way right into a tornado! Through interactive, hands-on exhibits, visitors learn about tornadoes, thunderstorms, meteorology, winds, weather folklore and more. A theater shows age-appropriate weather videos for the extreme weather fans in all of us, and a weather-themed gift shop is also part of the building.

GROUNDHOG DAY

Punxsutawney - *Downtown. (800) 752-PHIL. www.groundhog.org. Join thousands of Phil's faithful followers for his annual prediction. Fun for everyone. What many people don't know is Groundhog Day is just the culmination of an entire weekend of family-friendly activities - most of which are completely free of charge. For instance, kids can explore the science behind meteorology and even try their hand at forecasting (just like Phil) at the Weather Discovery Center. There's the Groundhog Zoo, where kids can meet Phil before his big day. All weekend, there's storytellers, facepainting, ice carving, and more. Hours vary. (morning of February 2)*

Saxonburg

ARMSTRONG FARMS BED & BREAKFAST

Saxonburg - *1020 Ekastown Road   16056. www.armstrongfarms.com. Phone: (724) 352-2858. Come on down to the farm. Start your first morning with a steamy fresh ground cup of Kiva Han coffee (roasted locally) and some Buckwheat pancakes (milled locally each fall/winter at Zanella Mill in West Sunbury) made with best-selling Marburger Buttermilk . Ah! Now, step outside your Farm Bed n Breakfast doorstep to a view of grazing Black Angus cattle. Armstrong Farms invites guests to breakfast (Kathy makes a mean infused French toast) with an overview of cattle farm ranching and a meet n greet with a mini-donkey, cute baby calves and Stella the Goose. If you're brave, ask to help with the chores today. We'd recommend The Bonnie House at Westminster Preserve for families. The common areas include a large equipped kitchen, dining room with table that seats 12 and living room. Sliding glass doors in the dining & living room areas open to a large wrap-around deck that overlooks the Love Pond, pastures and woodlands. Guests are served breakfast on the deck or in the dining room. You can rent by the room ($105/night) or by the house ($500/night).*

Sigel

CLEAR CREEK STATE PARK

Sigel - *RR 1, Box 82 (1-80 to exit 73) 15860. Phone: (814) 752-2368. www.dcnr. state.pa.us/stateparks/parks/clearcreek.aspx.   Admission: to PA State Parks is FREE however swimming, marina and camping/lodging fees apply, with reservation or entrance.*

Set along the Clarion River, Clear Creek is a cozy getaway and a canoeist's paradise. Whether you bring your own canoe or rent one, a popular activity is the 11-mile trip from Clear Creek to Cook Forest State Park. Rustic log and stone cabins are nestled among ancient pines and hemlocks, making this park the perfect place to spend a secluded, rustic vacation. For a unique experience, try yurts. Yurts: The two round, Mongolian-style tents at Clear Creek State Park are on wooden decks and sleep four people in bunk beds. Yurts have a cooking stove, refrigerator, countertop, table, chairs, electric heat and outlets, fire ring, picnic table and are adjacent to a water pump. The park also has a Beach, Visitor Center, Historical Center, Boat Rentals, Sledding, Campsites, Fishing, Winter Sports, and Trails.

Slippery Rock

JENNINGS ENVIRONMENTAL EDUCATION CENTER

Slippery Rock - *2951 Prospect Road 16057. www.dcnr.state.pa.us/stateparks/ parks/jennings.aspx. Phone: (724) 794-6011. Hours: Daily, Dawn - Dusk. Educational Center Monday-Friday 8:00am-4:00pm. Admission: FREE. Miscellaneous: Hiking trails. Picnic areas.*

This park's main attraction are the surviving remnants of a Midwest Prairie. A unique attraction at the center is its relict prairie, which includes the spectacular and well-known prairie flower, the blazing star. The relict prairie ecosystem is rare in Pennsylvania. In late July, blooms of blazing star (wild prairie flowers) along with other assorted wildflowers of all varieties are full peak color. Due to the glacial activity, the ground is mostly clay and only supports growth of thin grasses and plants. Community programs present various environmental topics in an informative and entertaining way through slide presentations, trail walks and public workshops.

MAPLE SUGARING

Slippery Rock *- Jennings Environmental Education Center. Actual tapping of trees. Syrup making. Demonstrations of coopering and sugaring off in a realistic sugar camp. Pancakes and syrup served. (mid-March)*

NORTH COUNTRY BREWING COMPANY

Slippery Rock - 141 S Main St (I-79 exit 105 - three miles east) 16057. Phone: (724) 794-2337. http://northcountrybrewing.com. Like root beer or cream soda? Homemade sodas (and in-house brews) all honor the area with local names everyone recognizes as it flows 10 feet and into your mug. Try some fresh-brewed at North Country Brewing Company restaurant in the quaint little college town of Slippery Rock. Sunday's are great for a rewarding family get together. Lunch Specials run under $10.00 and include sides. Hardly anything on the menu is prepared the way you're used to so come here hungry (big portions) and adventuresome. We'd recommend a root beer with a Hummus Plate or Pub Pretzels to start. They have many vegetarian offerings that actually made for a nicer lunch than the heavy sandwich options. But, if you like meat - boy do they have it - especially burgers - and with some homemade sauces or sides. Any frequent visitor to Pittsburgh knows 'Burghers love french fries on everything - even salad! Seafood and pasta available, too. Best time to come with the kiddos? Lunch or Sundays. Note: after dark, the place is very crowded with more of a social scene. Open daily for lunch and/or dinner. The owner is so "go green" he told us he composts all his scrap produce (leftovers from plates), has a grass roof, uses biodegradable straws, recycled wood for tables, and just recently moved to a farm where he'll raise beef cattle and chickens to serve as entrees!

Valencia

HARVEST VALLEY FARMS FALL FESTIVAL

Valencia - 125 Ida Lane (off Rte 8). www.harvestvalleyfarms.com. Petting zoo, refreshments, pumpkin patch, corn maze, pony or wagon rides. Entertainment on weekends. FREE. (weekends, end of September thru October)

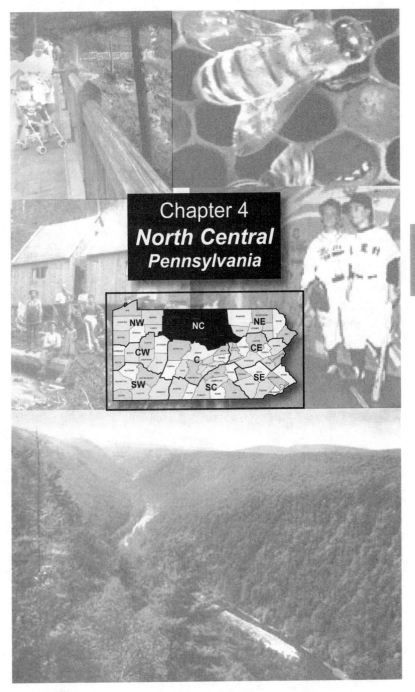

Chapter 4
North Central
Pennsylvania

NC Area

Austin
- Sinnemahoning State Park

Coudersport
- Ski Denton

Cross Fork
- Ole Bull State Park

Emporium
- Bucktail State Park
- Sizerville State Park

Galeton
- Cherry Springs State Park
- Lyman Run State Park

Galeton (Coudersport)
- Pennsylvania Lumber Museum

Hughesville
- Crystal Lake Ski Center

Hyner
- Hyner Run State Park

Johnsonburg
- Bendigo State Park

Millerton
- Draper's Super Bee Apiaries

Morris
- Ski Sawmill Mountain Resort

Renovo
- Kettle Creek State Park

Wellsboro
- Animaland Zoological Park
- Hills Creek State Park
- Leonard Harrison State Park

Williamsport
- Hiawatha Riverboat Tours
- Lycoming County Museum - Taber Museum
- Williamsport Trolleys

Williamsport (Allenwood)
- Reptiland, Clyde Peeling's

Williamsport (Waterville)
- Little Pine State Park

Williamsport, South
- Little League Museum

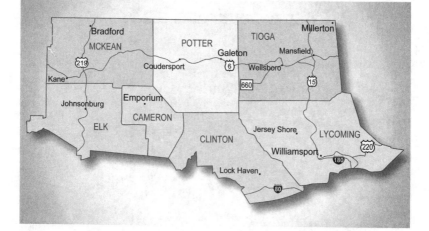

A Quick Tour of our Hand-Picked Favorites Around...

North Central Pennsylvania

Here, you can wish upon a star in Cherry Springs State Park, Pennsylvania's first dark sky preserve, and hike or bike the Pine Creek Gorge, Pennsylvania's Grand Canyon. Camping is also popular here; many state and national parks offer wilderness buffs the opportunity to get back to nature and even do some whitewater rafting. Imagine more than two million acres of public lands set aside for your enjoyment offering unlimited recreational opportunities.

The "Grand Canyon" of Pennsylvania begins just south of Ansonia, along U.S. Route 6 and continues south for about 47 miles. At **Leonard Harrison** and **Colton Point State Parks**, the depth of the canyon is about 800 feet and these park locations have the most spectacular scenic overlooks. Well worth the drive off the beaten path for the scenic views! If your children are able, we suggest hiking one of the trails up or down the gorge. If not, the Overlook Trail is a short .6-mile loop taking you to Otter View, a vista looking south with good photo ops.

This area is all natural and several family-run nature and animal parks have sprung up. **Draper's Super Bee Apiaries** is one "sweet spot." Every visit warrants a view of the observation hive (don't worry, it's enclosed in safety glass). On tour, you'll learn about different products produced from beehives. Hopefully, you'll be able to get to a bee site, help extract some honey, and then take a taste test.

In Williamsport your family can visit with reptiles or take a Hiawatha Trolley or Paddleboat tour past lumber baron mansions. Of course, the main attraction in town is the **Little League Museum**. The birthplace of Little League is host to the world championship (nationally televised-last weekend in August). From its humble beginnings in 1939 through today and its 3 million participants in over 90 countries, the museum is a tribute to Little League Baseball. Learn about the legends, swing the bat or test your arms pitching.

NC Area

Did you know Pennsylvania once had a prosperous lumber heritage? The **Pennsylvania Lumber Museum** displays 3000+ objects including old-fashioned logging tools and a logging locomotive. The best part of the visit is the short walk to the preserved remains of, a once very busy, logging camp.

Sites and attractions are listed in order by City, Zip Code, and Name. Symbols indicated represent:

 Festivals   Restaurants   Lodging

Austin

NC Area

SINNEMAHONING STATE PARK

Austin - *8288 First Fork Road (junction of PA 872 and US 6 or PA 120) 16720. www.dcnr.state.pa.us/stateparks/parks/sinnemahoning.aspx. Phone: (814) 647-8401.   Admission: to PA State Parks is FREE however swimming, marina and camping/lodging fees apply, with reservation or entrance.*

The diverse habitat supports the American eagle, black bear and white-tailed deer. Interpretive pontoon boat rides on George B. Stevenson Reservoir are available during the summer to allow a closer look at lake wildlife. Boating, Fishing, some Trails, Modern Campsites, and one Modern Cabin.

ELK STATE FOREST: Principally in Elk and Cameron Counties, the 200,000 acres of forest land are open to hunting, fishing and general recreation. Within Elk State Forest is a portion of the Quehanna Wild Area, which is south of Sinnemahoning. The Quehanna Trail System provides access for primitive-type forest recreation limited to day use activities and backpack hiking. 814-486-3353

Coudersport

SKI DENTON

Coudersport - *PO Box 367 (on US 6) 16915. www.skidenton.com. Phone: (814) 435-2115.*

With slopes ranging from the steepest in the Eastern states to long, gentle beginner trails, Ski Denton draws skiers of all levels. Addition of a lighted Snowboard Park and new tube slide. Longest Run: 1 mile; 20 Slopes & Trails. Located in Denton Hill State Park. There are five cabin chalets and hostel-style group lodging located on the Ski Denton grounds. They now have mountain-biking, too.

Cross Fork

OLE BULL STATE PARK

Cross Fork - *Box 9 (PA Route 144) 17729. Phone: (814) 435-5000. www.dcnr. state.pa.us/stateparks/parks/olebull.aspx. Admission: to PA State Parks is FREE however swimming, marina and camping/lodging fees apply, with reservation or entrance.*

The park area is referred to as the Black Forest of Pennsylvania. Its dense tree cover and mountainous terrain attracts thousands of campers along Kettle Creek. The park is named after Ole Bornemann Bull, the famous Norwegian violinist who toured this country in the 1850s. Ole Bull Trail leads to the historic foundation remains of Ole Bull's "home site" and a panoramic view of the park area. The Beaver Dam Nature Trail provides an introduction to the habitats along Kettle Creek. This 0.75-mile trail starts at the concrete fordway and has a flat trail surface. The 85-mile Susquehannock Trail System passes through Ole Bull State Park. The beach is in Camping Area 1 across from the picnic area. The 150-foot sandy beach along Kettle Creek is open from late-May to mid-September, 8:00am to sunset. Modern Cabin rental, Fishing, Trails, and Cross-Country Skiing.

Emporium

BUCKTAIL STATE PARK

Emporium - *RD 1, Box 1-A (Route 120) 15834. Phone: (814) 486-3365. www. dcnr.state.pa.us/stateparks/parks/bucktail.aspx. Admission: to PA State Parks is FREE however swimming, marina and camping/lodging fees apply, with reservation or entrance.*

Hemmed in by mountains, this state park scenic drive follows PA Route 120 as it winds from Lock Haven to Emporium along the West Branch of the Susquehanna River and the Sinnemahoning Creek. It stretches through a narrow valley which has for years been called the Bucktail Trail, named after the famous American Civil War regiment of Woodsmen, the Bucktails or Bucktail Rangers. This is the old Sinnemahoning Trail used by American Indians on their way to and from the eastern continental divide between the Susquehanna and Allegheny rivers. Aside from the three towns named above, the valley is mostly forested land with an occasional small village or isolated farm. The scenic drive has no recreational facilities. In June, the mountain laurel is in bloom and in early October the fall colors are breathtaking. Boating permitted, Fishing, and some Trails.

SIZERVILLE STATE PARK

Emporium - *RD 1, Box 238-A (PA Route 155) 15834. Phone: (814) 486-5605. www.dcnr.state.pa.us/stateparks/parks/sizerville.aspx. Admission: to PA State Parks is FREE however swimming, marina and camping/lodging fees apply, with reservation or entrance.*

The Bottomlands, Campground and North Slope trails take the visitor through a variety of lowland habitats and are relatively easy to walk making them ideal for hikers of any age. The Sizerville Nature Trail is a three-mile loop that nearly everyone can enjoy. It has educational stopping points. Maps are available in the park office. Nady Hollow Trail is a 1.5-mile loop that ascends a 1,900-foot mountain. The "Cutback" section takes the hiker halfway up the mountain and then, gradually runs down along the mountainside. Due to the slope of this trail, it is more challenging. Sizerville State Park is also a trailhead for the Bucktail Path Trail, which is part of an extensive trail system throughout the northern tier region of central Pennsylvania. Within the park, you will find beautiful white pines, hemlocks, spring wild flowers, a butterfly garden and flaming fall foliage in early October. Pool, Visitor Center, and Campsites.

Galeton

CHERRY SPRINGS STATE PARK

Galeton - *RD 1, Box 136 (PA Route 44 - Potter County) 16922. Phone: (814) 435-5010. www.dcnr.state.pa.us/stateparks/parks/cherrysprings.aspx. Admission: to PA State Parks is FREE however swimming, marina and camping/lodging fees apply, with reservation or entrance.*

Cherry Springs State Park is nearly as remote and wild today as it was two centuries ago, a haven for campers who like to rough it and who can appreciate one of the finest scenic drives in Pennsylvania. Its dark skies make it a haven for astronomers. Named for the large stands of black cherry trees in the park, the 48-acre state park is surrounded by the 262,000-acre Susquehannock State Forest. The Susquehanna Trail passes nearby and offers 85 miles of backpacking and hiking. Public Stargazing Saturdays.

CHERRY SPRINGS WOODSMAN SHOW

Galeton - *Cherry Springs State Park. www.woodsmenshow.com. Lumberjack competition and horse pulling contest. Entertainment, displays, food. No Admission. (first weekend of August)*

LYMAN RUN STATE PARK

Galeton - *545 Lyman Run Road 16922. Phone: (814) 435-5010. www.dcnr.state. pa.us/stateparks/parks/lymanrun.aspx.* Admission: *to PA State Parks is FREE however swimming, marina and camping/lodging fees apply, with reservation or entrance.*

Lyman Run State Park has been carved from the Susquehannock State Forest. The shaded picnic area is popular for picnicking and hiking, and the lake is a fishing hot spot. Beach, Campsites, Fishing, Trails.

Hiking is available on many trails in the **SUSQUEHANNOCK STATE FOREST**, though the main trail is the Susquehannock Trail System, an 85-mile loop through the forested hills and valleys of the region. During the summer months, a 43-mile-ATV trail is available within Susquehannock State Forest. The trail passes through Lyman Run State Park, where parking and sanitary facilities are located. 261,784 acres of Fishing, Trails, Winter Sports, and ATV Trails.

PENNSYLVANIA LUMBER MUSEUM

Galeton (Coudersport) - *5660 US 6 West (just west of PA 449) 16922. Phone: (814) 435-2652. www.lumbermuseum.org. Hours: Wednesday-Sunday 9:00am-5:00pm (April-November). Closed state holidays. Admission: $2.00-$4.00 (age 5+).* Miscellaneous: *The museum is set in the heart of the Susquehannock State Forest, where an abundance of State Parks, campgrounds, rental cabins and motels are available for an overnight stay.*

Pennsylvania once had a prosperous lumber heritage with its wealth of white pine and hemlock trees. Now on display, are 3000+ objects including old-fashioned logging tools and a logging locomotive. The best part of the visit is the short walk to the preserved remains of, a once very busy, logging camp. See the huge sawmill (buzzing logs that have floated down river),

Courtesy of Pennsylvania Historical & Museum Commission

mess hall, dormitories, rails, and engines used for transport. The well kept operational facility is extremely interesting and educational. By 1920, why did they blow the final whistle and leave?

NC Area

BARK PEELER'S CONVENTION

Galeton (Coudersport) - Pennsylvania Lumber Museum. Annual woods festival. Events include crafts, music, saw milling, woodhick demonstrations. Contests: birling, fiddling, tobacco spitting, frog jumping. Admission (weekend before or after July 4th)

Hughesville

CRYSTAL LAKE SKI CENTER

Hughesville - 1716 Crystal Lake Rd (off US 220) 17737. Phone: (570) 584-2698. Snow Report: (570) 584-4209. www.crystallakeskicenter.com.

The facilities include an unusual natural setting of 960 acres of mountain woodlands at elevations from 1550 to 2100 feet, several lakes and ponds, dining facilities for up to 200 in a modern, fully winterized dining hall, lodging for up to 180 in the winter months and recreational facilities. Cross-country skiing, ice skating and snowshoeing.

Hyner

HYNER RUN STATE PARK

Hyner - Box 46 (Hyner Run Road, PA 1014) 17738. Phone: (717) 923-6000. www. dcnr.state.pa.us/stateparks/parks/hynerrun.aspx. Admission: to PA State Parks is FREE however swimming, marina and camping/lodging fees apply, with reservation or entrance.

The terrain of the park is generally level and occupies the small valley created by Hyner Run, with steep mountains on both sides. The park is entirely surrounded by **SPROUL STATE FOREST**. Hyner Run State Park and Hyner View State Park are in the heart of the 276,764-acre Sproul State Forest. There are many miles of scenic state forest roads, foot trails, snowmobile trails and scenic overlooks. The very first purchase of public lands by the Commonwealth is not far from the park on the Young Womans Creek at Bull Run, where a monument commemorates this event. Pool, Campsites, one Modern Cabin, Fishing, Winter Sports, and Trails. Horse Trails, ATV Trails (32 miles). Hang gliding is a very popular activity at the park. Hang gliders take off from the scenic vista and sail out over the West Branch of the Susquehanna River.

Johnsonburg

BENDIGO STATE PARK

Johnsonburg - *533 State Park Road (four miles northeast of Johnsonburg on SR 1004) 15845. www.dcnr.state.pa.us/stateparks/parks/bendigo.aspx. Phone: (814) 965-2646. Admission: to PA State Parks is FREE however swimming, marina and camping/lodging fees apply, with reservation or entrance.*

Located in a valley on a bank of the East Branch of the Clarion River, a charming streamside picnic area sits amidst a mixture of hardwood trees. A trout stream provides ample opportunities for anglers and the swimming pool is a big hit in summer. Sledding. Kinzua Bridge (very high railroad bridge).

Millerton

DRAPER'S SUPER BEE APIARIES

Millerton - *RR #1, Box 96 (SR15 & SR238. Follow signs. Close to NY border) 16936. Phone: (570) 537-2381 or (800) 233-4273. www.draperbee.com. Hours: Monday-Friday 8:00am-5:00pm, Saturday 8:00am-1:00pm. Admission: FREE. Tours: Vary per day. Can accommodate any size group but they prefer a call in advance for larger groups. Miscellaneous: Gift shop with honey products galore and bee keeping equipment for sale. They even sell "bee" theme "knick knacks" which the owner said is also found in her house.*

Every visit warrants a view of the observation hive (don't worry, it's enclosed in safety glass). On tour, you'll learn about different products produced from bee hives. Hopefully, you'll be able to get to a bee site, help extract some honey, and then take a taste test. If you call ahead, Mrs. Draper might make some baked goods and beverages (Kool-Aid with honey) for you to sample. TIDBITS YOU MIGHT LEARN - Wildflower honey has the most nutrients (why? - Find out!); the Queen Bee lays 2000 eggs per day (the larva are what bears really love!). Speaking of bears, can you guess how they keep the "locals" away from their outdoor hives?

a bee...hard at work
making honey...

Learn why honey is liquefied in a "hot room" and not boiled. Learn how to identify the difference between worker bees, male drones, and the Queen. This is an extremely family-oriented, educational, and helpful (health-wise) tour given by people who care deeply about what they do. Well worth the trip into the "Endless Mountains".

Morris

SKI SAWMILL MOUNTAIN RESORT

Morris - *PO Box 5 (Rte. 220 to Rte. 287) 19963. Phone: (570) 353-7521. Snow Report: (800) 532-SNOW. www.skisawmill.com.*

They have 12 slopes and 3 lifts. Peak elevation is 2,215 feet and base elevation is 1,770 feet - giving a vertical drop of 515 feet. There is also a terrain park adjacent to the double chairlift. Beginner area and tubing area. New in summer/ fall season for groups will be: Paintball Rentals, Mountain Bike Rentals, and Canoe Trips down the pine creek. Also ask about hay rides, bonfires, archery classes and more off-peak season.

Renovo

KETTLE CREEK STATE PARK

Renovo - *Box 96 (SR 4001) 17764. Phone: (717) 923-6004. www.dcnr.state. pa.us/stateparks/parks/kettlecreek.aspx. Admission: to PA State Parks is FREE however swimming, marina and camping/lodging fees apply, with reservation or entrance.*

A 250-foot sandy beach area is open from late-May to mid-September, 8 a.m. to sunset. Horseback Riding, Sledding, Campsites, Fishing, Trails, Winter Sports.

Wellsboro

ANIMALAND ZOOLOGICAL PARK

Wellsboro - *4181 Route 660 (1.2 miles east of Leonard Harrison St. Park) 16901. Phone: (570) 724-4546. www.animalandzoo.com. Hours: Daily 10:00am-5:00pm (May-November 1). Extended summer hours. Weather permitting, open at random (November-April). Admission: $8.00 adult, $7.00 senior (65+) and students (13+), $5.00 child (3-12). Miscellaneous: Snack Barn and Gift Shop.*

Located near Leonard Harrison State Park and overlooking the picturesque Pennsylvania Grand Canyon, Animaland Zoolological Park is home to more than 200 exotic, wild, and domestic animals. Stroll through 12 acres of exhibits ranging from monkeys and kangaroos to pygmy goats and even a Siberian tiger. Animaland is a 2 mile walk-thru zoo which is all handicapped accessible. The asphalt paved pathway winds though the outdoor zoo exhibits with park benches along the way for resting. Stroller rental and animal food are available for purchase.

HILLS CREEK STATE PARK

Wellsboro - *RD 2, Box 328 (US Route 6 or PA Route 287) 16901. Phone: (717) 724-4246. www.dcnr.state.pa.us/stateparks/parks/hillscreek.aspx. Admission: to PA State Parks is FREE however swimming, marina and camping/lodging fees apply, with reservation or entrance.*

Osprey, loon and waterfowl visit the lake that boasts a variety of warm water fish species. A sand beach is open from late-May to mid-September, 8:00am-to sunset. Lake Side Trail - 1.5-mile - This trail begins at the entrance to the camping area and follows the lake shore in a westerly direction for about one mile, finally arriving at the Beaver Hut Boating Area. A beaver house plus many signs of beaver activity may be seen in this area. Camping, camping cottages, modern cabins, yurts, and picnicking. Visitor Center and Boat Rentals.

LEONARD HARRISON STATE PARK

Wellsboro - *RR 6, Box 199 (take PA Route 660 west from Wellsboro for 10 miles) 16901. Phone: (717) 724-3061. www.dcnr.state.pa.us/stateparks/ parks/leonardharrison.aspx. Admission: to PA State Parks is FREE however swimming, marina and camping/lodging fees apply, with reservation or entrance. Miscellaneous: The environmental interpretive center, at the Leonard Harrison main overlook entrance, is open during the summer season through the fall foliage season. A video and educational displays interpret the area and its wildlife. Water, soda and juice vending machines are available from late April to late October.*

The "Grand Canyon" of Pennsylvania begins just south of Ansonia, along U.S. Route 6 and continues south for about 47 miles. At Leonard Harrison and Colton Point State Parks, the depth of the canyon is about 800 feet and these park locations have the most spectacular scenic overlooks. Well worth the drive off the beaten path for the scenic views! If your children are able, we suggest hiking one of the trails up or down the gorge. If not, the Overlook Trail is a short .6 mile loop taking you to Otter View, a vista

...a walk with a view!

looking south with good photo ops. There is no bridge across Pine Creek at the bottom. A beautiful vista, one-half mile down the Turkey Path Trail, was constructed by the Youth Conservation Corps in 1978. Shortly after the vista, there is a scenic waterfall along the path on Little Four-Mile Run. Major improvements on the Turkey Path Trail, including steps, observation decks and hand rails were completed in the 1990s. The Pine Creek Trail runs through the bottom of the gorge and provides great bicycling. Bring along quarters (for viewers) or binoculars to get detailed views. Rustic camping and Canoe/Raft liveries threaded throughout the park system.

Williamsport

HIAWATHA RIVERBOAT TOURS

Williamsport - *Susquehanna State Park (Docked at Arch Street - US220 to Reach Road Exit - Follow signs) 17701. www.ridehiawatha.com. Phone: (570) 326-2500 or (800) 248-9287. Hours: Tuesday-Sunday, 1:00, 2:30, and 4:00pm. (Summer). Weekends Only in May, September & October Admission: $7.50 adult, $7.00 senior (60+), $3.50 child (3-12). Online coupon. Tours: 1 hour*

An old-fashioned paddlewheel boat cruises along the river as your narrator tells tales of the river when "lumber was king". Snacks and gifts are available on board. Tuesday night is "Family Night" during the summer (reduced family rates) and feature a "make your own ice cream sundae."

LYCOMING COUNTY MUSEUM
TABER MUSEUM

Williamsport - *858 West 4th Street 17701. www.tabermuseum.org. Phone: (570) 326-3326. Hours: Tuesday-Friday 9:30am-4:00pm, Saturday 11:00am-4:00pm, Sunday 1:00-4:00pm. Closed Sundays (November-April). Admission: $7.50 adult, $6.00 senior, $5.00 child (2-12).*

Over 12,000 square feet of exhibits include the history of lumbering, The LaRue Shempp model train exhibit, an American Indian gallery, and period rooms. This unique model train exhibition, one of the finest in the U.S., also features two working layouts for visitors to operate and enjoy. Peek through the windows of a re-created general store to see some of the things people needed, wanted, or thought were extravagant. Visit a one-room school to view a collection of inkwells, slates, and books that illustrate children's education at the turn of the 19th & 20th centuries. Get a glimpse into the homes of 19th century residents through the Greek Revival and Victorian Parlor period rooms. See a blacksmith shop and a working gristmill. A changing art gallery is on the premises, also.

WILLIAMSPORT TROLLEYS

Williamsport - *1500 West Third Street (Trolley Gazebo Downtown) 17701. Phone: (800) CITY-BUS or (570) 326-2500. www.ridehiawatha.com/trolley.asp. Hours: Tuesday-Friday 10:45am & 12:15pm or 1:45pm (Summer) . Call ahead to confirm times -Only 10:45am & 12:15pm departures on Saturdays. Admission: $3.00-$5.00 general. Tickets for the Williamsport Trolley Tour may be purchased from the Trolley Driver or at the Hiawatha House, Susquehanna State Park. Tours: Taped narration in replica streetcars - lasts about 70 minutes. Miscellaneous: During the Hiawatha's operating season, You can combine your Trolley Tour with a ride on the Hiawatha Riverboat when the Trolley stops at the Susquehanna State Park where the boat docks.*

Millionaires Row (impressive mansions built by lumber barons) is the focus of this tour. Kids enjoy Memorial Park (the site of the first Little League Baseball game). For fidgety children, there are several on and off stops throughout the trip.

The Peter Herdic Transportation Museum/Williamsport Trolley Hub Project consists of renovations to the existing railroad freight station, development of a trolley turnaround area (including a gazebo), construction of two Victorian bus shelters, purchase of a railway passenger "parlor" car, historic bus stop signs.

REPTILAND, CLYDE PEELING'S

Williamsport (Allenwood) - *18628 US 15 (I-80 exit 210B head north 6 miles) 17810. Phone: (570) 538-1869 or (800) REPTILAND. www.reptiland.com. Hours: Daily 9:00am-7:00pm (Summer). Daily 10:00am-5:00 or 6:00pm (September-May). Admission: $12.00 adult, $10.00 child (3-11) Shows: Every 90 minutes beginning at 10:30. Miscellaneous: Enjoy a healthy selection of hot and cold sandwiches and salads at Crocodile Creek Café*

Since opening in 1964, Reptiland has provided the public a link to the less-loved members of the animal kingdom. A visit to Reptiland explodes common myths and inspires scientific curiosity. The newly renovated indoor exhibit complex allows comfortable viewing of more than 40 species in recreated natural habitats. During summer months, Cobras, alligators, pythons, vipers, are all slithering around in a tropical garden setting. Visitors experience daily feedings and touch a variety of reptile skins to feel the difference between turtles, snakes and crocodiles. You even get to touch a real snake! Meet "Big Boy" the alligator or poison dart frogs. A multi-media show reveals the close-up world of reptiles and there's often live lecture demonstrations.

LITTLE PINE STATE PARK

Williamsport (Waterville) - *Box 100 (four miles north of PA 44 at Waterville and eight miles south of PA 287) 17776. www.dcnr.state.pa.us/stateparks/parks/ littlepine.aspx. Phone: (570) 753-6000. Admission: to PA State Parks is FREE however swimming, marina and camping/lodging fees apply, with reservation or entrance.*

Little Pine State Park is located in one of the most beautiful sections of the **TIADAGNTON STATE FOREST** in the Appalachian Mountains. A sand beach with grass turf is open from late-May to mid-September, 8:00am to sunset. Boat Rentals, Sledding, Campsites, Camping Cottages, Yurts, Fishing, 14 miles of Trails, and Winter Sports.

LITTLE LEAGUE MUSEUM

Williamsport, South - *US 15 17701. www.littleleague.org/learn/museum.htm. Phone: (570) 326-1921. Hours: Monday-Saturday 10:00am-5:00pm, Sunday Noon-*

5:00pm (Memorial Day-September). Closed Tuesdays and Wednesdays in June. Friday and Saturday 10:00am-5:00pm (Labor Day-Memorial Day). Admission: $5.00 adult, $3.00 senior (62+), $1.50 child (5-13). Miscellaneous: The museum is next to the Little League International Headquarters and overlooking the Howard J. Lamade Little League World Series Stadium.

The birthplace of Little League is host to the world championship (nationally televised-last weekend in August). From its humble beginnings in 1939 through today and its 3 million participants in over 90 countries, the museum is a tribute to Little League Baseball. Learn about the legends, swing the bat or test your arms. Actually "Play Ball" in the batting and pitching areas, and then watch your form on instant replay. Experience the running track, push-button quiz panels, and the opportunity to do your own play-by-play commentary on a World Series game. Learn about nutrition that will help you play your best. Watch videotaped highlights of the most exciting moments of the Little League World Series. Uniforms, balls, gloves, bats, etc from different baseball eras shows how much the sport has grown. And, if you've never seen how a ball, bat and glove are made - they have a display on the process of making them.

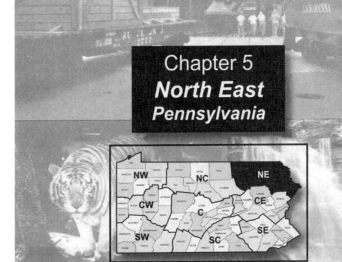

Chapter 5
North East
Pennsylvania

Beach Lake
- Carousel Water And Fun Park

Bushkill
- Bushkill Falls

Dalton
- Lackawanna State Park

Estella
- Endless Mountains Winterfest/ Sled Dog Races

Forksville
- World's End State Park

Hamlin (Lake Ariel)
- Claws And Paws Animal Park

Hawley
- Lake Wallenpaupack

Honesdale
- Stourbridge Rail Excursion

Le Raysville
- LeRaysville Cheese Factory

Milford
- Grey Towers Historic Site
- Waterwheel Café

Poconos (Bushkill)
- Delaware Water Gap Area
- Pocono Indian Museum

Poconos (Greentown)
- Promised Land State Park

Poconos (Long Pond)
- Pocono Raceway

Scranton
- Electric City Trolley Museum
- Lackawanna Coal Mine
- Steamtown Nat'l Historical Site
- Pennsylvania Anthracite Heritage Museum
- Sno Mountain Ski Area
- Houdini Tour & Magic Show
- Everhart Museum
- La Festa Italiana

Scranton (Moosic)
- Scranton/Wilkes-Barre Yankees

Tobyhanna
- Tobyhanna State Park

Towanda
- French Azilum Historic Site

Troy
- Mt. Pisgah State Park

Union Dale
- Elk Mountain Ski Area

Wilkes-Barre
- Wilkes-Barre/Scranton Penguins Hockey

NE Area

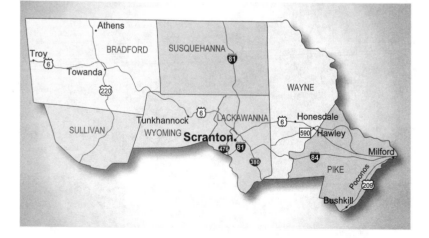

A Quick Tour of our Hand-Picked Favorites Around...

North East Pennsylvania

A Northeastern Pocono Mountains family vacation is a wonderful location for families to reconnect in an escape environment not like home. Among the family attractions include a NASCAR raceway or go-carting at one of the family fun parks.

For a more laid back family experience, sightseeing on horseback or taking a ride on America's first locomotive on the Stourbridge line may be fun. **Steamtown** is a land of wonderment for young conductors at heart. It looks like the site popped out of a Thomas Train movie – especially the roundhouse. This fully restored roundhouse and turntable are incredible to watch. As the Baldwin #26 enters the yard, it stops on the turntable, advances to the correct "house" where it sleeps for the night.

The Northeast Pennsylvania Mountains Region is chock-full of wildlife, so if you love communing with cuddly critters, this is the place for you! For 40 miles the Middle Delaware River passes between forested mountains with barely a house in sight. Then the river cuts through the mountain ridge to form the famed **"Delaware Water Gap."** Also in the Bushkill area is the "Niagara of Pennsylvania" – **Bushkill Falls** with its eight waterfalls and Native American village home. Trails and bridges lace the area and the trails are manageable for young families on a scavenger hunt for scenic "bests."

Stretching over miles along the Delaware River, you'll find extremely scenic roads and trails to wander along. This area takes you up around Hamlin and beyond to the forests and nature centers that some of Pennsylvania's wildest residents call home – in nature or in a delightful interactive animal park called **Claws and Paws**.

NE Area

Sites and attractions are listed in order by City, Zip Code, and Name. Symbols indicated represent:

 Festivals   Restaurants   Lodging

Beach Lake

CAROUSEL WATER AND FUN PARK

Beach Lake - *Box 134 (Rte 6 East to Honesdale, then Rte 652 East) 18405. Phone: (570) 729-7532. www.carousel-park.com. Hours: Daily 11:00am-10:00pm (Summers) Weekends 11:00am-6:00pm (late spring/late summer). Waterslides close at 6:00pm. Admission: Free Parking, Free Admission. Pay one price ticket ($12.00-$19.50) or pay per activity ($2.00-$4.00).*

Water slides (regular and juvenile), Go-karts, bumper boats, water slides, kiddie-kars and mini-golf all included in our pay-one price ticket. Also available: hardball and softball batting range, arcade and snack bar.

Bushkill

BUSHKILL FALLS

Bushkill - *Bushkill Falls Road (I-80 to Exit 309 - SR209 North) 18324. Phone: (888) 628-7454 or (570) 588-6682. www.visitbushkillfalls.com. Hours: 9:00am - 5:00-7:00pm (April-November). Basically closes before dusk sets in. Due to weather conditions, some trails may be restricted partly or in full. Admission: $10.00 adult, $9.00 senior, $6.00 child (4-12). Mini golf, gemstone mining, trail guide and adventure maps, fishing and paddleboats are additional small fee. Miscellaneous:*

Check out the Pennsylvania Wildlife Exhibit, fish Twin Lakes, visit a variety of gift shops, stop at the Fudge Kitchen for delectable sweets in the Wagon Wheel Pavilion, take a paddle-boat ride, or enjoy a round of miniature golf. Additional activities run $3.00-$5.00.

"The Niagara of Pennsylvania," has eight waterfalls. The main falls include Upper Canyon (craggy glen), Bridle Veil Falls (long, misty), Laurel Glen (mountain laurel wildflowers), Pennell Falls and Main Falls (over 100 foot cliff). Trails and bridges lace the area. Visitors may take part in a new Map Adventure while they hike. An official

NE Area

trail map that is especially detailed and accurate has been developed. The map includes 20 "control points" that can be found on the trails. When five, ten, or twenty locations have been found and verified with a unique punch, the hiker becomes eligible for a monthly prize drawing. Waterfalls are just the beginning of your visit to Bushkill Falls. Step into a Native America long-house and experience the Lenni Lanape Native Americans longhouse exhibit where kids can walk into an Indian home with "beds" - pretty neat! Plan to spend at least one-half day here.

Dalton

LACKAWANNA STATE PARK

Dalton - RD 1, Box 230 (I-81 exit 60, travel 3 miles west on PA Route 524) 18414. Phone: (570) 945-3239. www.dcnr.state.pa.us/stateparks/parks/lackawanna.aspx. Admission: to PA State Parks is FREE however swimming, marina and camping/ lodging fees apply, with reservation or entrance.

Includes Salt Spring - a 36 acre natural area with old-growth hemlocks, streams and 3 waterfalls. Also Archbold Pothole - world's largest geological pothole - 38 ft. deep, 42 ft. wide. There is a campground, organized group tenting sites and a pool. Boaters and anglers enjoy the 198-acre Lackawanna Lake, and Kennedy Creek. This park is a favorite of canoeists, hikers, nature enthusiasts and campers. A series of looping trails wander through the campground and day use areas of the park, and additional loops explore forests, fields, lakeshore areas and woodland streams. Biking, skiing, and snowmobiling.

NE Area

Estella

ENDLESS MOUNTAINS WINTERFEST
SLED DOG RACES

Estella - *Camp Brule. Phone: (570) 836-5431. Sled dog teams compete for cash prizes. Mid-distance and sprint races. Food, displays. Admission. (Last weekend in January or first weekend in February)*

Forksville

WORLD'S END STATE PARK

Forksville - *PO Box 62 (PA Route 42 from 1-80, then to Rte. 184) 18616. Phone: (570) 924-3287. www.dcnr.state.pa.us/stateparks/parks/worldsend.aspx. Admission: to PA State Parks is FREE however swimming, marina and camping/ lodging fees apply, with reservation or entrance.*

Virtually in a class by itself, this wild, rugged and rustic area seems almost untamed. Camping, rustic cabins and hiking on the Loyalsock Trail attracts many visitors. Be prepared for rocky pathways. Use proper hiking footwear. The scenery is spectacular, especially the June mountain laurel and Fall foliage. Canyon Vista, reached via Mineral Spring and Cold Run Roads, has outstanding views. Beach, Horseback Riding, Visitor's Center, Fishing, Boating, Horse Trails, and Winter Sports.

World's End State Park is adjacent to the **LOYALSOCK STATE FOREST** and offers hiking, hunting fishing and other outdoor recreation. 570-387-4255.

Hamlin (Lake Ariel)

CLAWS AND PAWS ANIMAL PARK

Hamlin (Lake Ariel) - *1475 Ledgedale Road (SR590 East - then follow signs) 18436. Phone: (570) 698-6154. www.clawsnpaws.com. Hours: Daily 10:00am-6:00pm (May- mid- October). Admission: $14.95 adult, $13.95 senior, $10.95 child (2-11). Miscellaneous: Snack bar. Gift shop. Picnic Area. Large walk-in petting zoo. Dino dig and Turtle Town interactive areas.*

When was the last time you saw a parrot ride a bike or you got to pet an alligator? This "zoo in the woods" in the Pocono Mountains region offers unique hands on activities for the entire family. "Get Close to the Animals" is their theme…and you will! Many cages have glass front enclosures - so animals can walk right up to your face and you're still protected. During posted times, you can feed giraffes using a long stick or hand-feed fruits and vegetables to Lory Parrots (colorful, small, tame parrots). The animals are comfortable with visitors and they're not bashful about getting close to get a good nibble from your snack-filled hands. During the summer months they have unique Performing Parrot shows and Wildlife Encounter shows. Claws n' Paws features more than 120 unique species of animals, including a white tiger, black panther, and African lion, as well as educational programs and demonstrations throughout the day.

Hawley

LAKE WALLENPAUPACK

Hawley - US 6 18428. www.hawleywallenpaupackcc.com. Phone: (570) 226-3191 Area Chamber.

Located in the Poconos, it's the third largest lake in the state, offering a diversity of water recreation activities.

- RITZ COMPANY PLAYHOUSE - (570) 226-9752. www.ritzplayhouse. com. 512 Keystone Street.

- BOAT TOURS - US6, Gresham Landing. www.eastshorelodging.com (570) 226-3293. (June - October). Sit back and relax on our 28-foot patio boat. Enjoy a breath taking hour-long cruise on picturesque Lake Wallenpaupack as your tour guide describes the area and the history behind this charming lake region. Daily scenic tours for one half hour. Tour boats run daily from 11:00am to 7:00pm on weekends from May 1 through October and daily from June 15 through Labor Day. Admission: $10.00-$14.00.

- TRIPLE "W" RIDING STABLE RANCH - Beechmont Drive - off Owego Turnpike. (570) 226-2670 or www.triplewstable.com. Horse ranch and western riding trips from one hour to overnight camping ($25 - 100+). Overnight accommodations at Double "W" Bed and Breakfast. Year round except hunting season.

Honesdale

STOURBRIDGE RAIL EXCURSION

Honesdale - (I-84, exit 5 - SR191 north - to Main Street) 18431. Phone: (570) 253-1960. www.waynecountycc.com. Hours: Sundays @ 1:00pm (Sunday before July 4th - Sunday before Labor Day), plus seasonal tours listed on their website. Admission: Start at $17.00 and up depending on excursion.

Honesdale is the birthplace of the American railroad and the small brick building which now houses the Wayne County Historical Society was once the D&H Canal's company office. On August 8, 1829, the Delaware & Hudson operated the first commercial locomotive on rails in the western hemisphere. That locomotive left from this spot, ran three miles to Seelyville and returned. On the Great Train Robbery Run, see masked men from the "Triple W Ranch" ambush the train on a 3 hour round trip (includes a one-hour stop for sightseeing). Or, take a Fall Foliage Tour or one of the many holiday tours.

EASTER BUNNY TRAIN RIDES

Honesdale - *Stourbridge Rail Excursion. Candy treats with the Easter Bunny riding along. Mr. Mouse, too. Entertainment. Admission. (Easter Weekend)*

SANTA TRAINS

Honesdale - *Stourbridge Rail Excursion. Sing songs and eat treats as you ride the train with Santa aboard. Admission. www.hawleywinterfest.com. Mrs. Claus and Rudolph, too! Stop at Winterfest in Hawley. (first two weekends in December)*

Le Raysville

LERAYSVILLE CHEESE FACTORY

Le Raysville - *RR 2 Box 71A, Cheese House Road (Off SR467 - turn on dirt road 1/2 mile from town) 18829. www.leraysvillecheese.com. Phone: (800) 859-5196 or (570) 744-2554. Hours: Daily 9:00am-5:00pm (March - December) Admission: FREE Tours: Twice per week they make cheese in 6000 pound vats. Call for viewing times.*

The majority of the region's Amish community resides in the Le Raysville area. Their horse-drawn carriages are a common sight along the local roadways. This factory uses local milk from several local farms in the town. This Old Order Amish farm based factory hand-makes several different types of pasteurized whole milk Cheddars, as well as a Havarti-style called Udder Delight a Pennsylvania jack and a Cherry Smoked Havarti called Smokey Delight. Want to try Cheddar Curds? This unique country snack is best straight from the factory store - eaten fresh.

NE Area

Milford

GREY TOWERS NATIONAL HISTORIC SITE

Milford - 151 Grey Towers Drive (84 East to Exit 46, Milford. Bear right off ramp onto Highway 6 East) 18337. Phone: (570) 296-9630. www.fs.fed.us/na/gt/. Tours: Tours of the mansion and surrounding gardens are conducted daily on the hour from 10:00am until 4:00pm from May 27 - October 3. Fees are: $5.00 adult, $4.00 senior, $2.00 youth (12-17). Under 12 are FREE.

Grey Towers is the ancestral home of Gifford Pinchot, first chief of the US Forest Service and twice Governor of Pennsylvania. House and garden tours are offered every day from Memorial Day weekend through October 31. A guided tour of the mansion and grounds is an interesting and unique way to learn about how one family shaped and influenced our conservation ideals and values, while experiencing what life might have been like at Grey Towers in the early 20th century. The guided tour takes the visitor through three first-floor rooms of the mansion and several garden areas and takes about one hour. Other Grey Towers activities include short hiking trails, on-site programs, and conservation education programs for all ages.

CHRISTMAS OPEN HOUSE

Milford - Grey Towers National Historic Site. Tours of decorated, historical buildings. Refreshments and musical entertainment. Admission.

WATERWHEEL CAFÉ

Milford - (off US6 - follow signs) 18337. www.waterwheelcafe.com. Phone: (570) 296-2383. Hours: Daily 8:00am-5:00pm (May-October). Other times of year, by season. Weekend (Thursday-Sunday) evening dinner served by reservation. An early 1800s water-powered 3 story gristmill still operates and you can watch the giant water wheel turn which drives a series of shafts, gears, and pulleys. Through the glass walls of the café, you can see the stones and grain milling equipment at work. Water rushes over the three-story high waterwheel, driving a series of shafts, gears, pulleys and belts that power the stones and grain milling equipment. A self-guided tour enables you to understand this whole fascinating process. Sit down and enjoy whole grain pancakes, muffins, and scones or multi-grain bread sandwiches.

Poconos Area

DELAWARE WATER GAP NATIONAL RECREATION AREA

Poconos (Bushkill) - *(I-80 to US209 north along the Delaware River) 18324.*
Phone: (570) 588-2451. www.nps.gov/dewa. Admission: *Only for guarded beaches (per vehicle) and boat ramp access. Generally $7.00-$10.00 per vehicle.*
Educators: The Many Faces of Delaware Water Gap program curriculum outline is found here: www.nps.gov/dewa/forteachers/curriculummaterials.htm.

For 40 miles the Middle Delaware River passes between low forested mountains with barely a house in sight. Then the river cuts through the mountain ridge to form the famed "Water Gap." Stretching over miles along the Delaware River, you'll find extremely scenic roads and trails to wander along. Great canoeing & rafting (some short - kid friendly), fishing, skiing, and snowmobiling. (For updated brochures or information call 1-800-POCONOS or www.800poconos.com).

- **DINGMAN'S FALLS** - A flat boardwalk trail, accessible to wheelchair-users, leads through a hemlock ravine to the base of Dingmans Falls (1/2 mile round-trip, no climb.) From the base of the falls, a steep climb of 240 steps reaches the top of the falls. Rangers give guided walks to the falls on summer weekends at 2:00 p.m. The visitor center at Dingmans Falls is closed indefinitely for construction. Dingmans Falls is on Johnny Bee Road, which is just south of the traffic light on Route 209 in Dingmans Ferry PA (milepost 13). www.nps.gov/dewa/planyourvisit/dingmans-falls.htm.

- **BUSHKILL VISITOR'S CENTER** - Daily 9:00am-5:00pm (summer). Weekends only in late spring and early autumn.

- **RAYMONDSKILL FALLS** - A 1/4-mile round-trip hike leads through a hemlock ravine to the Upper Falls. (70 ft. climb) The Middle Falls are a 1/2-mile round-trip, using steep, uneven stairs (150 ft. climb.) Raymondskill Creek at the bottom of the ravine is a 1 mile round-trip with a steep ascent on the return (200 ft. climb.) Directions: Raymondskill Road is a sharp left turn, if northbound on Route 209, just north of milepost 18.

Both Visitor's Centers offer "ranger picked must sees" during each season. They also have a Junior Ranger program which includes a kid's self-guided exploring booklet. During the summer, rangers present programs just for kids, as well as family campfire programs and guided walks suitable for children as well as adults.

NE Area

POCONO INDIAN MUSEUM

Poconos (Bushkill) - *PO Box 261 (SR209 North off I-80 exit 309) 18324. Phone: (570) 588-9338. www.poconoindianmuseum.com. Hours: Daily 10:00am-5:30pm. Extended summer hours. Admission: $2.50-$5.00 (age 6+).*

The museum recreates the life of the Delaware Indians from B.C. to the contact period with Europeans to post American Revolution. You will be given a cassette player which will guide you step by step through the museum in great detail. See their lifestyle through homes (some made of bark - and you thought they only lived in tee-pees!), weapons, and kitchen pottery. Most of these items were unearthed in the Delaware Water Gap. Boys like the "150 year old scalp" and buying an authentic "peace pipe".

PROMISED LAND STATE PARK

Poconos (Greentown) - *RD 1, Box 96 (PA Route 390) 18426. Phone: (717) 676-3428. www.dcnr.state.pa.us/stateparks/parks/promisedland.aspx. Admission: to PA State Parks is FREE however swimming, marina and camping/lodging fees apply, with reservation or entrance.*

Promised Land lies in the heart of the Poconos. Two lakes, campgrounds, many hiking trails and beautiful scenery make the park popular in all seasons. There are about 50 miles of hiking trails in Promised Land State Park and the surrounding state forest, providing access to many natural scenic places. Hike Bruce Lake Road to a natural glacial lake, or see the little waterfalls along Little Falls Trail, or walk a loop around Conservation Island. A seasonal museum explores CCC contributions and area wildlife. There are two sand beaches that are open from late-May to mid-September, 8:00am to sunset. Boat Rentals, Rustic Cabins, Fishing, Boating, Hiking, and Winter Sports.

POCONO RACEWAY

Poconos (Long Pond) - *184 Sterling Road 18344. Phone: (800) RACEWAY. www.poconoraceway.com.*

Pocono Raceway has long been recognized as one of NASCAR's most competitive raceways. Pocono's unique 2.5 mile track features three turns, each with its own degree of banking. NASCAR 2.5 Mile super speedway - NASCAR racing, mid-June and early August.

Scranton

ELECTRIC CITY TROLLEY MUSEUM

Scranton - *(at Cliff Street, on the grounds of the Steamtown National Historic Site, I-81 exit 185) 18503. Phone: (570) 963-6590. www.ectma.org/museum.html. Hours: The trolley museum is open seven days a week (Wednesday through Sunday only - during the Winter) from 9:00am-5:00pm, except Christmas, New Years and Thanksgiving Day. Special excursions for holidays. Admission: Average $5.00 museum fee. Additional avg. $7.50 fee for trolley ride. Combo rates are $8.00-$10.00. Tours: During the operating season, trips are scheduled four days a week at 10:30am, 12:00 Noon, 1:30pm and 3:00pm, Wednesday thru Sunday.*

A late 19th century mill building serves as the museum. Trolleys are exposed for viewing and rides. Interactive displays, where visitors will actually generate electricity and learn how this energy form is harnessed to serve transportation needs. The Electric City, a hands-on interactive kids exhibit, puts children in the operator's seat of a recreated open-style trolley car as they view a model trolley in operation on a suspended track.

- TROLLEY EXCURSIONS: The scenic route follows a portion of the former Lackawanna & Wyoming Valley Railroad right-of-way as it parallels Roaring Brook and makes stops at the Historic Iron Furnaces and continues through the Crown Avenue Tunnel. At 4747 feet long, the tunnel is one of the longest interurban tunnels ever built.

LACKAWANNA COAL MINE

Scranton - *McDade Park (I-81, Exit 57B or 51 – follow signs) 18503. Phone: (570) 963-MINE or (800) 238-7245. www.lackawannacounty.org/attractions_coal.asp. Hours: Daily 10:00am–4:30pm (April–November). Closed Easter and Thanksgiving. Admission: $10.00 adult, $9.50 senior (65+), $7.50 child (3-12). Company Store – souvenir coal jewelry and such. Food service. Constant 55 degrees F. below so bring along a jacket. McDade Park has excellent areas for picnics and play.*

"Go down in history" where you descend (by railcar) 300 feet below the ground to see how men "hand harvested" coal. Actual miners are your guides as they share personal stories about the hard life, the work, and the dangers of digging for "black diamonds". A walking tour of three veins of mine floor is started by watching a movie on mining history. After descending (on a steep grade) in a mine car, the rest of the tour is on foot. Can you imagine working 10 hours a day in near pitch darkness? The tour guides and staff are super friendly here.

STEAMTOWN NATIONAL HISTORICAL SITE

Scranton - *150 South Washington Avenue (I-81, exit 185 - toward downtown) 18503. Phone: (888) 693-9391 or (570) 340-5200. www.nps.gov/stea. Hours: Daily 9:00am-5:00pm. Reduced winter hours. Closed New Years Day, Thanksgiving Day, and Christmas Day. Admission: $6.00 adult. The Park Entrance Fee (all visitors age 17 and over) includes admission to the railroad yard, History Museum, Theater, Technology Museum, Roundhouse and all walking tours and theater programs. Tours: Scranton Limited Train Rides ($3.00 per person). Longer excursions are planned often with reservations. The normal fee is $15.00-$21.00 per person. Educators: Their excellent online downloadable Student Activity Guides are age appropriate and include Teaching info plus games and short stories: www.nps.gov/stea/forteachers/index.htm.*

The roundhouse...watch it come to life!

The National Steamtown Historic Site preserves the steam railroading era so visitors can relive that time period as the fire-breathing behemoths lumber back to life. "This is just like Thomas the Train" squealed our kids as we all saw the roundhouse come to life! This fully restored roundhouse and turntable are incredible to watch. As the Baldwin #26 enters the yard, it stops on the turntable and advances to the correct numbered house where it will "sleep" or receive maintenance. While you are out walking around the roundhouse, talk with the crew as they share stories about their jobs and the engines. The conductors love to wave and are good photograph opportunities.

The Visitor's Center (mostly oriented for older kids) has both a Technology Center and History Museum of American Steam Railroading. The theater at Steamtown shows an 18-minute film called Steel and Steam. This short film follows one man's career on the railroad, and illustrates the massive changes railroads underwent in a fairly short time during the early 20th century. Join a Park Ranger or a Volunteer

The Union Pacific #4012 "Big Boy" - over a million pounds of hardworking iron!

for a walking tour through a portion of the former locomotive shops to see and learn what it takes to keep steam-era railroad equipment operational. On select weekends, the Chilidren's Discovery Center is open to storytelling

NE Area

activities. The express train ride is a short excursion best for younger children who can't endure the longer 2 hour train rides.

RAILFEST

Scranton - *Steamtown National Historical Site. FREE w/ park admission. (Labor Day Weekend)*

🏃 _____

HOLIDAY EXPRESS SANTA TRAINS

Scranton - *Steamtown National Historical Site. Sing songs and eat treats as you ride the train with Santa aboard. Admission. Face painting, live music. Polar Express. (last weekend of November & first weekend in December)*

🏃 _____

PENNSYLVANIA ANTHRACITE HERITAGE MUSEUM

Scranton - **RD #1 - Bald Mountain Road (I-81 - Exit 57B or Exit 51 - Follow signs to McDade Park) 18504. www.anthracitemuseum.org. Phone: (570) 963-4804 or (570) 963-4845. Hours: Monday - Saturday 9:00am-5:00pm, Sunday Noon-5:00pm (Closed holidays - except summer holidays). Admission: $4.00 to $6.00 (ages 3+).. Educators: Lesson plans are found here: http://explorepahistory.com/story.php?storyId=11**

Explore the culture created by life and work in the coal towns. Their collections include highlights of the mines, canals, railroads, mills, and factories. Scenes also peak into family's homes and neighborhoods with a scene in the kitchen and a seat at the local Church. This was really hard work! To see a close-up of the mills producing iron "T" rails for America's railroads, stop over to the park setting of Scranton Iron Furnaces.

SNO MOUNTAIN SKI AREA

Scranton - *1000 Montage Mountain Road 18505. Phone: (570) 969-7669. Snow Report: (800) GOT-SNOW. www.snomtn.com.*

Sno Mountain offers day and night skiing and a professionally staffed ski school. Last season, Sno Mountain became one of only five Zip Rider attractions currently operating in the U.S. The mile-long Zip Rider zip line cable ride offers a completely hands-off adventure down the terrain of the resort at speeds reaching 50 mph. Longest Run: 1+ miles; 21 Slopes & Trails. Ice skating and snow tubing, too.

HOUDINI TOUR & MAGIC SHOW

Scranton - *1433 North Main Avenue (I-81 to exit 190, left two miles) 18508. Phone: (570) 342-5555. http://houdini.org/. Hours: Weekends 1:00-4:00pm (Memorial Day – June), Daily (July, August – Labor Day Weekend). Open Holiday Weekends throughout the year. Reservations best for weekends. Admission: $14.95 per person. Tours: Guided tours plus the show offered several times each afternoon. Miscellaneous: Gift/Magic Shop. Admission includes video presentation and live magic shows (check website or call for exact times of shows). Very enthusiastic magicians answer questions and perform illusions before your eyes.*

The world's only exhibit devoted entirely to Houdini. It helps to know the magic word if you want to get into the Famous Houdini Museum (Houdini Lives!). Houdini and his brother Hardeen toured through this area often. The show is perfect for all ages featuring noted professional magicians and live animals, as well as a fun guided tour of the collection in the 100-year-old historic building and see rare film footage of Houdini doing escapes. Nationally known magicians re-create these shows daily using Houdini-style equipment and live doves, a rabbit and two poodles. They float an audience member up in the air, pass a hoop around them and float them back down. Wander around and see Houdini's favorite trick props and photographs.

EVERHART MUSEUM

Scranton - *1901 Mulberry Street (Mulberry and Arthur Avenue) 18510. Phone: (570) 346-7186. www.everhart-museum.org. Hours: Generally, Daily Noon-4:00 pm. Closed Wednesday and Tuesday. PLEASE CALL FOR HOURS as they change each season. Admission: $5.00 adult, $3.00 senior, $2.00 child (6+). Educators: This website has quizzes just for kids: www.everhart-museum.org/Education/Kids/Kids.htm*

Housing exhibits of American Folk, Native American, Oriental and primitive art. They also have fun exhibits for kids in dinosaur hall and the bees and bird collections. Children's store.

LA FESTA ITALIANA

Scranton - Courthouse Square. www.lafestaitaliana.org. Italian style festival features delicious ethnic food, crafts and live entertainment to suit young and old. Great fun for the whole family. FREE. (Labor Day weekend)

SCRANTON/WILKES-BARRE YANKEES

Scranton (Moosic) - *PNC Field, 235 Montage Mountain Rd. 18507. Phone: (570) 969-2255. www.swbyankees.com. Admission: Single game tickets run $10.00-$14.00.*

Wear your best pinstripes to catch a game by the 2008 Governor's Cup Champions and AAA affiliate of the New York Yankees, the Scranton/Wilkes-Barre Yankees. With stunning batting performances from Cody Ransom and strikeouts from Kei Igawa, there's no wonder why this team gathers an annual average attendance of 400,000 fans. Local families love to come by on Domino's Family Dinner nights - great value or on a promo night for t-shirt giveaways, live entertainment and fireworks.

Tobyhanna

TOBYHANNA STATE PARK

Tobyhanna - *PO Box 387 (accessible from I- 84 via PA Routes 507, 191 and 423) 18466. Phone: (570) 894-8336. www.dcnr.state.pa.us/stateparks/parks/tobyhanna. aspx.   Admission: to PA State Parks is FREE however swimming, marina and camping/lodging fees apply, with reservation or entrance.*

The 5,440-acre park includes the 170-acre Tobyhanna Lake. Tobyhanna is derived from an American Indian word meaning "a stream whose banks are fringed with alder." Beach, Boat Rentals, Campsites. Also in this location are Big Pocono and Gouldsboro State Parks. Trails and Winter Sports are on rugged terrain.

Towanda

FRENCH AZILUM HISTORIC SITE

Towanda - *RD #2, Box 266 (Rte. 6 take SR 187 south. off SR187 - follow signs) 18848. Phone: (570) 265-3376.   www.frenchazilum.com.   Hours: Wednesday-Sunday 11:00am-4:00 pm. (late May thru late October). Weekends 11:00am-4:30pm (May) Admission: $4.00-$6.00 (age 12+).   Miscellaneous: Picnic pavilion. Nature trails.*

Few sites in Pennsylvania address another country's historic events like this one does. Founded in 1793, 50 log cabins were created as a refuge for French nobility fleeing the Revolution. After Napoleon's pardon, most left the area. Although no structures from the original town survive, an original foundation has been left exposed for public viewing. A reconstructed and relocated log cabin, circa 1790, serves as a small museum with artifacts pertaining to the settlement. Nearby is the 1836 LaPorte House containing period furnishings. Warm weather archeological digs occur frequently. Stand around and ask what they're finding.

Troy

MT. PISGAH STATE PARK

Troy - *RD 3, Box 362 (2 miles north of US Route 6) 16947. Phone: (570) 297-2734. www.dcnr.state.pa.us/stateparks/parks/mtpisgah.aspx. Admission: to PA State Parks is FREE however swimming, marina and camping/lodging fees apply, with reservation or entrance.*

At the base of Mt. Pisgah and set along Mill Creek. A dam on Mill Creek forms Stephen Foster Lake, named after the famous composer and onetime local resident. The 75-acre lake provides fishing, boating and skating. Adjacent to the park are Mt. Pisgah County Park. Also Pool, Visitor Center, Trails, and Winter Sports.

MAPLE SUGARING

Troy - *Mt. Pisgah State Park. Actual tapping of trees. Syrup making. Demonstrations of coopering and sugaring off in a realistic sugar camp. Pancakes and syrup served. (last weekend in April)*

NE Area

Union Dale

ELK MOUNTAIN SKI AREA

Union Dale - *RR 2, Box 3328 (I-81 exit 206) 18470. Phone: (570) 679-4400. Snow Report: (800) 233-4131. www.elkskier.com.*

Elk Mountain was one of the first commercial ski areas to open in Pennsylvania in 1959. Today, Elk has seven lifts and 27 slopes, including some of the most challenging terrain in the region. The resort also has its own distinctive character; the resort regularly plants Norway Spruce and red and white pines. Since the mid-1980s, more than 13,000 trees have been planted. Skiing and Snowboarding. Longest Run: 1.75 miles; 27 Slopes & Trails.

FALL FESTIVAL

Union Dale - *Elk Mountain. Petting zoo, refreshments, pumpkin patch, corn maze, pony or wagon rides. Scenic chair lift rides, entertainment. (second weekend in October)*

Wilkes-Barre

WILKES-BARRE/SCRANTON PENGUINS HOCKEY

Wilkes-Barre - *Ice Rink at Coal Street 18702. www.wbspenguins.com. Phone: (570) 208-PENS.*

Kids Club activities, section and skate. AHL Hockey (October-early April). Join their Kids Club or come on promo nights for bobbleheads and such.

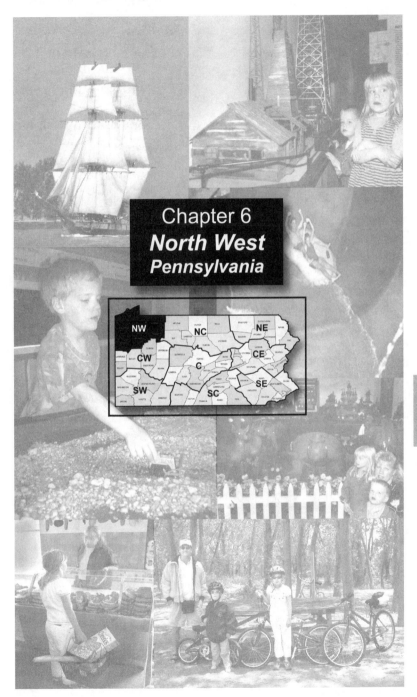

Chapter 6
North West
Pennsylvania

General
- Maple Sugaring Taste Weekend

Clarendon
- Chapman State Park

Clarion
- Clear Creek State Forest

Conneaut Lake
- Conneaut Lake Park

Edinboro
- Wooden Nickel Buffalo Farm
- Edinboro Highland Games

Erie
- Bicentennial Observation Tower
- Erie County Historical Museum
- Erie Otters Hockey
- Erie Sea Wolves Baseball
- Presque Isle Scenic Boat Tours
- Presque Isle State Park
- Waldameer Park & Water World
- Erie Maritime Museum / U.S. Brig Niagara
- Experience Children's Museum
- Firefighter's Historical Museum
- Erie Zoo
- Splash Lagoon

Franklin
- DeBence Antique Music Museum

Greenville
- Greenville Canal Museum
- Greenville Railroad Park

Grove City
- Wendell August Forge

Hermitage
- Philadelphia Candies

Jamestown
- Pymatuning Deer Park
- Pymatuning State Park

North Warren
- Cornplanter State Forest

Oil City
- Oil Creek State Park

Sandy Lake
- Goddard State Park, Maurice K.

Sharon
- Daffin's Candies

Titusville
- Drake Well Museum
- Oil Creek & Titusville Railroad

Warren
- Kinzua Dam/ Big Bend Visitor's Center

NW Area

A Quick Tour of our Hand-Picked Favorites Around...

North West Pennsylvania

Northwest Pennsylvania is the center of ingenuity. Here you'll find some old-fashioned amusement parks, a newer indoor waterpark (**Splash Lagoon**) where we love the tall, tall slides, industrial Erie, family-friendly state parks, the discovery of oil, and some fun factory tours.

Presque Isle State Park is a wonder with seven miles of sandy beaches (one of the top 100 swimming holes) and it has the only surf beach in the Commonwealth. On a nice day, many locals and visitors head to Presque Isle for boating, fishing, nature walks or biking. The park is so clean, the beaches multi-purpose paths allow easy transport around most of the 14 miles of the isle. It's really one of the best state parks for families we've found.

The **United States Brig Niagara**, restored and moored on Erie's bayfront, is the only ship of her type, which is still in existence from the War of 1812. The Niagara is the tallest "tall ship" on the Great Lakes and you can board it! Once aboard, see over 200 oars, steered with a tiller instead of a wheel, sleeping quarters, and rows of cannons. Inside the **Erie Maritime Museum** is another ship to tour and pretend you're a sailor on the treacherous Lake Erie.

Erie Zoo has monkey and otter habitats that are especially fun to watch and they even have one area with gorilla that get so close to the clear wall you feel they're trying to communicate with you. There are some deer parks and loads of ducks near Pymatuning State Park.

If you like factory tours, this area has got one that hammers metal (**Wendell August Forge**) and others that produce some yummy and funny chocolates. **Philadelphia Candies** has covered most every sweet thing in chocolate and **Daffins** has a display of some chocolate animals that are hundreds of pounds each!

Finally, Titusville is the home of the discovery of oil and the birthplace of the petroleum industry. **Drake Well Museum** and the **Oil Creek & Titusville Railroad** are really interesting to tour. Inside the museum there are many push button exhibits and squeeze and sniff oil samples from all over the world. Outside, they occasionally demonstrate how they fired the hole. See the first oil fields in the world as they tell a story of the oil rush boom days in the valley from a railcar scheduled train ride located near the museum.

Sites and attractions are listed in order by City, Zip Code, and Name. Symbols indicated represent:

    🏃 Festivals   🍽️ Restaurants   🛏️ Lodging

MAPLE SUGARING ANNUAL TASTE & TOUR WEEKEND

General - *www.pamaple.org/tour.html. You're invited to spend the weekend exploring the heart of the Pennsylvania Maple Producer. Each of these sugaring operations are unique in their own way. Demonstrations all day both days, and the little sugarhouse is packed with people. A local Boy Scout troop camps at the site that weekend and demonstrates how Indians and early settlers made sugar and syrup. There's free maple hot chocolate and samples of other maple goodies. Hot dogs boiled in maple water are for sale at a nominal price. (Yummy with maple mustard, too!) The warming tent has hay bales for seating as well as a kids table with crayons and maple scene pictures for coloring. The sugarhouse is off the road about 3/4 of a mile, so you can either walk or take a haywagon drawn by a tractor or teams of draft horses. All quite picturesque. FREE. Note: Hurry Hill site in Edinboro: The owner has produced a video for teachers on /Miracles on Maple Hill, a children's storybook that won a Newberry Award which would be excellent for homeschoolers / educators in connection with the book. That video runs on a loop in a warming tent near the sugarhouse and the stand where a large variety of maple products are sold. (mid-March weekend)*

🏃 _____

Clarendon

CHAPMAN STATE PARK

Clarendon - *RD 2 Box 1610 (off US Route 6) 16829. Phone: (814) 723-0250. www.dcnr.state.pa.us/stateparks/parks/chapman.aspx. Admission: to PA State Parks is FREE however swimming, marina and camping/lodging fees apply, with reservation or entrance.*

Chapman sits on the banks of the West Branch of Tionesta Creek. Among its many recreational offerings, the park boasts a 68-acre lake that provides swimming at a beach and warm and cold water fishing. A sand beach is open from late-May to mid-September, 8 a.m. to sunset. Boat Rentals, Campsites, Fishing, Trails, and Winter Sports.

Clarion

CLEAR CREEK STATE FOREST

Clarion - *158 South Second Avenue 16214. Phone: (814) 226-1901. www.dcnr. state.pa.us/forestry/stateforests/clearcreek.aspx.*

Points of interest within the State Forest are the Clear Creek State Park with overnight camping facilities, swimming, fishing, hiking trails, and day-use areas; Bear Town Rocks, a vista with an excellent view accessible by trail or automobile; and Hays Lot Fire Tower with a panoramic view of great distances. Visitors can tour the laurel fields located on Spring Creek Road during the early June wildflower season.

Conneaut Lake

CONNEAUT LAKE PARK

Conneaut Lake - *12382 Center St (I-79, exit 147B west on Rte. 322, follow signs to PA 618) 16316. Phone: (814) 382-5115. www.conneautlakepark.com. Hours: Saturdays 1:00 to 10:00pm, Sundays 1:00-6:00pm. (Memorial Day weekend-Labor Day weekend). Most summer Thursdays and Fridays open 4:00-10:00pm. Admission: FREE, pay for each ride or combos. Ride-A-Rama does not include the Pony Track, Cascade Express Miniature Golf, or the Kaylee Belle Paddlewheel Boat. Single Tickets are $1.00 and Day Passes are $15.00-$20.00.*

Old-fashioned 100 year old park with rides, water attractions, kiddie land, restaurant, Camperland and beach/boardwalk. Conneaut Lake Park has dozens of old-fashioned rides, including the famous Blue Streak Wooden Roller Coaster (1938) - set to reopen late 2010 season. Splash City Water Park, too.

NW Area

PUMPKIN FESTIVAL

Conneaut Lake - *Conneaut Lake Park. Pumpkin painting and carving, pie-eating contests. Pumpkin patch (wagon rides out there). Refreshments. (second weekend)*

Edinboro

WOODEN NICKEL BUFFALO FARM

Edinboro - *5970 Koman Road (I-79 to exit 166 - go east - follow signs) 16412. Phone: (814) 734-BUFF. www.woodennickelbuffalo.com. Hours: Daily 11:00am-5:00pm (Friday-Sunday only in winter). Admission: $4.00 per person ($20.00 per tour, minimum charge). Reservations required. Before leaving, every person in the group will receive one newsletter and a Wooden Nickel as a souvenier. Miscellaneous: Wooden Nickel Restaurant casual dining serving Bison burgers and other snacks.*

This 150-acre farm is home to more than 50 wild buffalo and offers visitors the opportunity to learn more about these wild animals as well as the health benefits of bison meat. The owners loved the meat when they first tried it and decided to breed and sell buffalo products. The tour includes a talk on Bison as you view them in the pastures. The buffalo herds roam the farm pastures freely, and guests may have the opportunity to watch cows tending to their young or witness the challenges between bulls in the herd. You will learn about their history and relationship with Native Americans, see the handling facilities, and view authentic Native American art and Bison products in the Gift Shop. This is done with visuals and videos to keep the kids attention. Ribs and fur from the animals (not live animals!) can be touched. American Indian folklore and festival in July. Feel a real buffalo hide or admire cute baby bison (late July).

CORN MAZE

Edinboro - *Wooden Nickel Buffalo Farm. Have fun wandering around the miles of the 6-acre maze to find game sheet stations. Admission. (weekends in September, daily in October).*

EDINBORO HIGHLAND GAMES & SCOTTISH FESTIVAL

Edinboro - *Edinboro University. http://cslab103.cs.edinboro.edu/~HIGHGAMES/ home.php. Highland dance, pipe band competition, music, sheep-herding, medieval camp, kids games & crafts. FREE. (late July weekend)*

Erie

BICENTENNIAL OBSERVATION TOWER

Erie - *Dobbins Landing 16501. www.visiteriepa.com/bicentennial_tower.shtml. Phone: (814) 455-6055. Hours: Open at 10:00am - closing varies seasonally between 6:00-10:00pm (April-October). November - March (open Saturday & Sunday only) 12PM - 4PM. Admission: $1.00-$2.00 (age 7+). Free admission on Sundays (excluding holidays).*

Enjoy an aerial view of the city and Presque Isle Bay. The 187-ft tower features two observation decks, and markers of Erie's harbor history and geography. 210 stairs to the observation deck (or, yes, there is an elevator!). If you climb the stairs, follow the 16 stations that highlight various landmarks. Souvenirs and food available in tower lobby.

ERIE COUNTY HISTORICAL MUSEUM

Erie - *419 State Street (I-79 to Bayfront Parkway) 16501. Phone: (814) 454-1813. www.eriecountyhistory.org. Hours: Wednesday-Saturday 11:00am-4:00pm. Extended to Tuesday in the summer. Admission: $3.00-$5.00 (age 5+). Educators: go to this website link: www.eriecountyhistory.org/education/teacher-resources/ for some really interesting historical links to U.S. History - even one on toys.*

Local history, architecture and industry. "Voices from Erie County History" offers glimpses into Erie County's rich heritage from the days of pre-settlement to the turn of the twenty-first century. The two-building complex contains the Museum of Erie County History, which features Voices, an interactive exhibit offering selective views of Erie County's rich heritage from pre-settlement to present day, the Admiral Curtze Maritime Hall, an exhibit presenting the region's ongoing maritime legacy, the Kovacs Kids Korner children's area filled with captivating educational, fun activities. The Cashier's House, adjacent to the History Center, is a beautifully restored 1839 Greek Revival style townhouse which features life in Erie during the Antebellum period.

ERIE OTTERS HOCKEY

Erie - 809 French Street (office) (Louis J. Tullio Civic Center) 16501. Phone: (814) 452-4857 (Box Office) or 455-7779 (office). www.ottershockey.com. Admission: $6.00-$10.00

Ontario Hockey League (players between the age of 16-20). The Otters play a 68-game regular season schedule (34 home, 34 away), plus playoffs, in the Ontario Hockey League. Since the franchise relocated to Erie prior to the 1996-1997 season, a total of 23 players have been selected at the National Hockey League Entry Draft.

ERIE SEA WOLVES BASEBALL

Erie - 110 East 10th Street (office) (Jerry Uht Ballpark) 16501. Phone: (814) 456-1300. www.seawolves.com. Admission: $6.00-$10.00

The Erie Seawolves are the Class AA Affiliate of the Detroit Tigers and 2007 Southern Division Champions. You can visit Jerry Uht Park and see future MLB stars as alumni include Curtis Granderson, Justin Verlander, Aramis Ramirez, and more than 100 others. Fireworks, giveaways, on-field stunts, kids' zones and more make the game on the field just one aspect of the excitement. Check out the deals on Friends & Family Nights.

PRESQUE ISLE SCENIC BOAT TOURS

Erie - (Departing from Perry Monument on Presque Isle State Park) 16505. Phone: 814-836-0201 or toll free 800-988-5780. www.piboattours.com. Admission: Rates are adults: $14.00 child: $9.00 and under 5 free. Cruise schedules and prices are subject to change. Any trip may be cancelled due to sever weather, mechanical difficulties, or fewer reservations than required. Tours: Tour departures vary seasonally: Mid-May through Mid-June and after Labor day through September 30; are Saturdays and Sundays. The summer season of mid-June through Labor day; are 7 days per week and sunset cruises which depart 1 hour prior to sunset.

Experience the scenic beauty of the Peninsula and Erie waterfront while viewing three historic lighthouses on the 65-foot great lakes vessel, "Lady Kate." The 14-mile, 90-minute tour ventures out onto the open waters of Lake Erie. You will view Presque Isle's shores, Erie's skyline, lighthouses, ships, the beaches, Gull Point Nature Preserve, wildlife and numerous other sights. Live narration takes place on each tour by knowledgeable guides that identify and describe points of interest while they supply enlightening information about the area's ecology, history, development, nature and more.

NW Area

PRESQUE ISLE STATE PARK

Erie - PO Box 8510 (Lake Erie, reached by PA Route 832 or by boat) 16505.
Phone: (814) 833-7424. www.dcnr.state.pa.us/stateparks/parks/presqueisle.aspx.
Admission: to PA State Parks is FREE however swimming, marina and camping/
lodging fees apply, with reservation or entrance.

Seven miles of sandy beaches (Top 100 swimming holes) and it has the only surf beach in the Commonwealth. Because of the many unique habitats, Presque Isle contains a greater number of the state's endangered, threatened and rare species than any other area of comparable size in Pennsylvania. On a nice day, many locals and visitors head to Presque Isle for boating, fishing, nature walks or biking. The park is so clean, the beaches well-maintained, and the paved multi-purpose paths allow easy transport around most of the 14 miles of the isle. We

A break from our 5 mile trip...

especially recommend biking 5 miles of the trails, stopping every now and then to enjoy a beverage or dip in the water along the beaches. The Karl Boyes Multi-purpose National Recreation Trail makes a 13.5-mile circuit of the park. This paved trail is designated as a National Recreation Trail. This ADA accessible trail is popular with bicyclists, in-line skaters and joggers.

The beaches were beautiful...but we were dressed for biking!

A boat rental concession is located in the Grave Yard Pond area and provides a variety of powered and non-powered craft. Beaching of boats along Presque Isle shoreline is permitted except at the Gull Point Natural Area between April 1 and November 30, and within 100 feet of designated swimming areas.

Stop in their nature center first to discuss your plans with a ranger...they were most helpful!

The gateway to Presque Isle is the new <u>TOM RIDGE ENVIRONMENTAL CENTER</u> (TREC). An educational center at heart, TREC is dedicated to teaching visitors about Presque Isle and the many different forms of life that inhabit this unique peninsula. TREC also serves as a center for research, contributing to conservation efforts and promoting environmental awareness, helping to preserve the unparalleled beauty of Presque Isle. There is free admission to the interactive exhibits and the 75-foot observation tower. Also offered: Canoe and Boat Livery. Lighthouses. Camping, Skiing, & Snowmobiling.

In addition to the 'Big Green Screen' movies and the changeable exhibit area, there are special activities like scavenger hunts, family night at the movies, and music concerts planned throughout the year. Check out the web-site at www.trecpi.org or call 814-833-7424 to find out what's new.

WALDAMEER PARK AND WATER WORLD

Erie - *220 Peninsula Drive (Close to entrance of Presque Isle State Park) 16505. Phone: (814) 838-3591. www.waldameer.com. Hours: Tuesday-Sunday (Mid-May - Labor Day) Admission: General Admission to entire park ranging from $17.00 - $24.00. There is no admission fee to enter the amusement park. ALL Parking is FREE! Individual ride tickets also available for everyone. (Due to ride restrictions, we recommend the use of individual ride tickets, not wrist band, for children under two years old.) Amusement park only wristbands and waterworld only wristbands available for a few dollars less. Everyone must pay to enter Water World. Miscellaneous: Restaurants. Tubes and life jackets are free. Smoke free environment. Bring your own towel.*

Five incredible body slides, Three fabulous double tube slides, The Wild River single tube slide, A daring free fall slide, a speed slide, A refreshing Endless River innertube ride, A heated relaxing pool, Three tad pool areas with five great kiddie slides, and Beautiful parks. Thunder River log flume ride plus many more classic amusement rides in Waldameer Park. They have a coaster called Ravine Flyer II, also. Puppet shows and concerts, too! Although the park has grown, this park has kept its low key approach to fun and family. Because they offer free admission into the park, parents or grandparents that are not interested in riding can go along (and hold loose items!) at no charge. If you're a rider, the lines aren't usually that long.

ERIE MARITIME MUSEUM / U.S. BRIG NIAGARA

Erie - *150 East Front Street (I-79 North to Bayfront Parkway) 16507. Phone: (814) 452-BRIG. www.brigniagara.org/museum.htm. Hours: Monday-Saturday 9:00am-5:00pm, Sunday Noon-5:00pm. Closed Sunday-Wednesday (January, February, March) Admission: $8.00 adult, $7.00 senior, $5.00 youth (3-11). Active duty military and their immediate families are admitted to the Erie Maritime Museum* *and all other Pennsylvania free of charge. Miscellaneous: Shipwright gift shop. First-person costumed interpreters are featured on weekends and for special events.*

The United States Brig Niagara, restored and moored on Erie's bayfront, is the only ship of her type which is still in existence from the War of 1812. Now the official Flagship of Pennsylvania, the Niagara, with homeport in Erie, she was re-commissioned August 1990. The Niagara is the tallest "tall ship" on the Great Lakes. She was the relief flagship of Commodore Oliver Hazard Perry from which he won the Battle of Lake Erie.

Berthed within yards of the museum, Niagara is visible from the building's bay side picture window. Tour the flagship "Niagara" (when in port) built to fight in the War of 1812 - the Battle of Lake Erie - Commodore Perry's ship. Once aboard, see over 200 oars, steered with a tiller instead of a wheel, sleeping quarters, and rows

Courtesy of Pennsylvania Historical & Museum Commission

of cannons. Do you know the difference between a Brig (2 sails) and a ship (3 sails)? How do you preserve a ship? - Sink it in freshwater! (it's the air & salt that causes deterioration)

New, artistic exhibits about the ship "Niagara" (including video) include: Lake Erie ecology, the bow of the Wolverine, bilge pumps in action, cannon fire, knots and sails. Students can experience aspects of the life of a sailor in Perry's fleet. Maybe drill on the carronade, set the sail, and learn to tie basic knots as part of the museum experience. Inside, the centerpiece exhibits of the museum are a former steam-powered electricity generating station and a reconstruction of the mid-ship section of the Lawrence. The replicated Lawrence, Commodore Oliver Hazard Perry's first flagship during the Battle of Lake Erie, comes complete with mast, spars and rigging to foster hands-on learning in the ways of sail handling. Probably the most powerful display is the adjoining section of the Lawrence replica that has been blasted with live ammunition from the current Niagara's own carronades. This "live fire" exhibit of the Lawrence recreates the horrific carnage inflicted upon both ships and men during the Battle of Lake Erie and throughout the Age of Fighting Sail. Why can't cannons fire all at once on one side of the ship?

NW Area

EXPERIENCE CHILDREN'S MUSEUM

Erie - 420 French Street (Discovery Square) (I-79 North to Bay Front Highway) 16507. Phone: (814) 453-3743. www.eriechildrensmuseum.org. Hours: Tuesday-Saturday 10:00am-4:00pm, Sunday 1:00-4:00pm. Closed Tuesday during school

year. Admission: $5.00 general (ages 2+) Miscellaneous: Aimed at 2-12 year old children. The Much More Store gift shop.

Raining or snowing in Erie? Just head downtown to the Experience Children's Museum. For a smaller museum, we were impressed how they use their space in this old building. A few of our favorites: People At Work where kids move vehicles and stones to change the way a stream flows; Owl Pellet Dissecting Table – yes, that's right, you use picks to discover what the owl ate last!; and their Market was the most colorful,

Daniel's diverting a creek

realistic and well-stocked we've ever seen... check out the meat and seafood market items! The first floor is full of science - from giant bubble creations to energy, light, and motion. Check out Radar Rooster weather, a Bedrock Cave, or the Circles and Cycles (pollution - unregulated and innumerable, and its effects on the Lake Erie watershed). Children are challenged to create a safe community. The second floor is the "The Healer Within" and has career dress up areas, Rookie Reporter newsroom, the Corner Store, Senses, Safety, Construction, and your heartbeat. Aerodynamics is a new colorful assortment of plastic balls that actual pop, chute and slide around the space. Before you know it, kids learn about characteristics of air and how it affects objects - yes, aerodynamics.

...searching for the best steak & seafood

FIREFIGHTER'S HISTORICAL MUSEUM

Erie - 428 Chestnut Street (I-79 to Route 5) 16507. Phone: (814) 456-5969. www. firefightershistoricalmuseum.com. Hours: Saturday 11:00am-4:00pm, Sunday 1:00-4:00pm (June-August). Saturday - Sunday 1:00-4:00pm (September, October). Admission: $1.00-$4.00 (students+)

The #4 Erie Firehouse has 1300+ items on display. Items include antique equipment, uniforms, badges, helmets, masks, fire extinguishers, hand pumps and horse drawn carts. They have the only display of an 1889 horse drawn fire engine and an understandable demonstration of the relay system in fire call boxes.

ERIE ZOO

Erie - 423 West 38th Street (I-90 to exit 27) 16508. www.eriezoo.org. Phone: (814) 864-4091. Hours: Daily 10:00am-5:00pm except Christmas Day and New Year's Day. Children's Zoo is open March through November. Admission: $8.00 adult, $6.00 senior (62+), $5.00 child (2-12). Slightly reduced admission in the winter. Miscellaneous: Train & Carousel rides ($1.50 -$2.00 extra)

The Erie Zoo is home to over 500 animals, representing more than 100 species, from around the world. Winding walkways take visitors through the beautifully landscaped grounds. The Zoo features everything from lowland gorillas to African waterbirds with special events and activities for the entire family. Go on an African safari of sorts to see cheetahs and rhinos at the Zoo's Kiboka Outpost, meet red pandas and orangutans in the Wild Asia exhibit, or meet the Zoo's newest

...the amazing entrance to "Wild Asia"...

resident, Norton the polar bear. The Children's Zoo features special educational

programs, feed & petting area and even an indoor wildlife carousel. Monkey and otter's habitats are especially fun to watch and they even have one area with traditional lions, and tigers and bears. Various gardens include the Butterfly gardens, the Greenhouse, and the great gardens at Kiboka Outpost where the rhinos roam. The animals are so-o-o close and the settings (indoor/outdoor) were well done and easy to manage. Our favorites were the gorillas and orangutans that are so endearing to watch and communicate with!

...this gorilla seemed to be in deep "thought"?

ZOOLUMINATION

Erie - Erie Zoo. Glistening lights. Visit with Santa. Hot chocolate. Freshly baked cookies. Toy/gift shops. Weekend entertainment. Admission. Walk-thru. (mid - to - late December only)

SPLASH LAGOON

Erie - 8091 Peach Street (I-90 exit 24, Rte. 19 south) 16509. Phone: (866) 3-SPLASH. www.splashlagoon.com.   Hours: Generally 9:00am-10:00pm. Closed some weekdays during school year. Admission: Waterpark passes are $25.00-$35.00 each. Spectator Pass is around $13.00. After 4pm, save $3-8.00 off admission. Online coupons. Miscellaneous: 4 hotels are part of the indoor waterpark resort and are directly connected to Splash Lagoon (range $140-$300, include 4-6 waterpark passes and complimentary breakfast). Splash passes are valid from Noon on the day of arrival until Close of the day of departure.

...it looks like a giant "MouseTrap" game...what fun!

A new indoor waterpark resort with a: Tree House packed with interactive water fun, 48-Ft Tall Tipping Bucket regularly dumps 1,000 gallons of water, 4 twisting & turning 4-story high Body Slides, A Swirling Body Coaster with speeds of over 40 MPH, Swirling Tube Coaster for 1 or 2 riders, Two 25 Person whirlpools, Laaaazy River, Activity Pool featuring 8 water basketball hoops, Dancing Water Play Area, Little People Activity Pool with zero depth entry, 6,000 Sq. Ft. Arcade, Lazer Tag Arena, and Food Court. We recommend going online and reserving one of the Splash Lagoon overnight stay packages because you get two day waterpark passes and hotel accommodations in large rooms with complimentary continental breakfast (real value for the money). You'll want to break up your day(s) at the waterpark every two hours or so with a rest - all that play makes you tired and hungry...naps and several light meals at local eateries (our favorite, Quaker Steak & Lube) are recommended. And Splash Lagoon is outstanding! Clean, fresh (check out all the filters they use...both air and water) and full of something for every child and adult to ride and lounge in. Compared to other indoor waterparks, we especially liked that every ride had a different "twist" and they even have some of the new rides

we affectionately call "toilet bowls"...chute down a tube, then swirl around a bowl and drop out the middle. None of the rides are strenuous and plenty of staff are on hand to gently escort you to another area or help you out of your

NW Area

raft. On busy days (esp. rainy day Saturdays), be prepared for long lines up the dozens of steps to the big rides (watch out for your neighbors raft bumping). Everyone in our party, from 6 to 66, enjoyed the park!

Franklin

DEBENCE ANTIQUE MUSIC MUSEUM

Franklin - 1261 Liberty Street, Route 8 (Downtown, off I-80 to exit 29) 16323. Phone: (814) 432-5668 or (888) 547-2377. www.debencemusicworld.com. Hours: Tuesday-Saturday 11:00am-4:00pm, Sunday 12:30-4:00pm (April - October). Admission: $8.00 adult, $7.00 senior (60+), $3.00 child (3-14).

"To See and Hear Museum". 100+ antique, automated music machines from the gay 90's - roaring 20's. See and hear demonstrations of nickelodeons, Swiss & German music boxes, waltzes and polkas, merry-go-round band organs, calliopes, player pianos, and a variety of antique organs. We were most fascinated by the nickelodeons that had glass panel inserts showing the musical instrument "guts". This was the first time we have ever seen a violin or accordion playing as an accompaniment. Bring the grandparents along for this visit.

Greenville

GREENVILLE CANAL MUSEUM

Greenville - 60 Alan Avenue (Lock 22 - Alan Avenue, near Riverside Park) 16125. Phone: (724) 588-7540. www.greenvillecanalmuseum.org. Hours: Saturday-Sunday 1:00-5:00pm (summer). Admission: Small admission for students+.

History of Erie Extension Canal - artifacts like tools and photographs. The Erie Extension Canal played a vital role as the first efficient transportation into northwestern Pennsylvania for settlers and commerce. Great Lakes iron ore was shipped on the canal, which was combined with coal at iron and steel mills. Small settlements along the canal grew, forming new towns. See a full size replica of an 1840s canal boat - Rufus Reed, and view a working model of a canal lock.

GREENVILLE RAILROAD PARK AND MUSEUM

Greenville - *314 Main Street - Rte. 358 16125. Phone: (724) 588-4009. http:// members.tripod.com/~greenville/rrpark.html. Hours: Generally, Weekends 1:00-5:00pm (Summer). Call ahead if driving distance to museum.*

Climb aboard the largest switch engine - #604 - used in the steel industry. Plenty of railroad cars - hopper cars, cabooses, and a 1914 Empire auto touring car. World's first parachute invented by local Stefan Banie in 1914. Stationmasters quarters, dispatch office and displays of railroad uniforms.

Grove City

WENDELL AUGUST FORGE

Grove City - *1605 South Center Street (I-79, exit 31- follow signs-(Route 208, one mile east of outlet mall) 16127. Phone: (800) WAF-GIFT. www.wendellaugust.com. Hours: Monday-Saturday 9:00am-5:00pm, Sunday Noon-5:00pm (except several days surrounding holidays). Admission: FREE Miscellaneous: Country's oldest and largest forge producing aluminum, pewter, sterling silver, and bronze items by hand. Old time Nickelodeon, W.A. Parrot (who talks and does impressions), LGB train on a surrounding track up above and a 225 gallon ocean reef tank. These keep the kids amused while adults gift shop.*

Because of fire early 2010, the original Forge building burned but they have relocated near the Outlet Mall and are still hand-crafting pieces. Real workshop

...*"edging" the metalwork*

tours are unavailable at this time but instead they have set up a neat simulated workshop area for guests, including a history center. A self-guided tour of the simulated production workshop is fascinating to watch as metal is taken through an eleven step process. The gift metal is hammered over a pre-designed template with random hand, or machine-operated hammer motions. At one point, you'll get a chance to pick up a hammer that is used - they weigh up to 3 pounds. You'll understand why a craftsman thought to automate the hammering process - tired, tired hands! Once the impression is set, the item is forged (put in a log fire) to produce smoke marks that bring out the detail of the design. The item is cooled and cleaned and finished by thinning the edges. Each piece is marked with a sign particular to the craftsman. This is a wonderful place to show children the balance between old world craft and new, automated craftsmanship.

NW Area

Hermitage

PHILADELPHIA CANDIES

Hermitage - *1546 East State Street (off SR18 North) 16148. Phone: (724) 981-6341. www.philadelphia-candies.com. Hours: Daily 9:00am-4:00pm (lunch between 12:00-1:00pm). Admission: FREE. Tours: Pre-arranged, 15-20 minutes around floor. Miscellaneous: annual "Chocolate Factory Tour" from 9:00am - 4:00pm, Saturday, two weeks before Easter, showing the public where and how all the delicious candy is made for shipment to its own stores as well as other fine stores throughout the country. You will be able to see skilled candy makers creating milk chocolate bunnies, specialty baskets, and delicious chocolates. The 7,000-pound chocolate tank, chocolate enrobers, a chocolate bunny depositor, and a lollipop machine will be labeled and operating for the self-guided tour.*

Have you ever tried chocolate covered cookies, cherry cheesecake, marshmallows or orange peels? We have - and this is where you can see them being made! Free samples are abundant at the factory store and you can get a peek at whatever chocolate concoction they're sweetening that day. Here are some "fun" numbers for you: 30,000 square foot facility, 80 year old family business, 7000 pounds of chocolate are melted at one time, sugar comes in 50 pounds bags, and corn syrup is delivered in 55 gallon drums!

Jamestown

PYMATUNING DEER PARK

Jamestown - *Route 58, East Jamestown Road (off US 322, 3 Miles South of Pymatuning Dam) 16134. Phone: (724) 932-3200. www.pymatuningdeerpark.com. Hours: Monday - Friday 10:00am-5:00pm, Saturday, Sunday, Holidays 10:00am-6:00pm (Summer). Weekends only in May, September & October (weather permitting). Admission: Average $5.50-$6.50 per person. Animal Food $1.00 per package. Miscellaneous: Train and pony rides.*

While strolling through the wooded setting under a canopy of trees, visitors encounter both domestic and exotic animals including Siberian Tigers, African Lions, Camels, Black Bears, assorted Primates and of course, several species of deer. Some animals you pet and some you don't! The "Kiddie Zoo" welcomes young and old alike to get up-close and personal with featured baby animals and a variety of domestic farm animals. Petting and feeding in the Kiddie Zoo is a highlight for most park visitors. Cracker-crunching deer, bucket-pulling monkeys, and biscuit-begging black bears make for endless feeding adventures throughout the entire park.

PYMATUNING STATE PARK

Jamestown - *Box 425 (accessible by U.S. Route 6, U.S. Route 322, PA Route 18, PA Route 285, and PA Route 58) 16134. Phone: (724) 932-3141. www.dcnr.state. pa.us/stateparks/parks/pymatuning.aspx. Admission: to PA State Parks is FREE however swimming, marina and camping/lodging fees apply, with reservation or entrance.*

Flood control reservoir along the Ohio border. The spillway is perhaps one of the best known locations because the fish being fed are so plentiful that the "ducks walk on the fishes' backs" to compete for the food fed by the visitors. The largest body of water in the state. More people visit Pymatuning than almost any other PA state park. But the biggest thing about Pymatuning is the fun you can have boating, fishing, swimming, camping and enjoying other recreational opportunities. There are trails near Tuttle and Jamestown campgrounds, and the abandoned railroad grade on the Spillway is a flat, wide trail.

In addition to the state park facilities, the PA Fish and Boat Commission operates a fish hatchery and the PA Game Commission has wildlife viewing areas. Wildlife Museum - state's largest colony of nesting eagles. Beach, Boat Rentals, Sledding, Campsites, Modern Cabins, Fishing, and Trails.

PIONEER AND ARTS FESTIVAL

Jamestown - *Pymatuning State Park. Displays, demonstrations, arts and crafts, Indian dancers, frontier activities, encampment, historical program, tour of the Gatehouse, food and live entertainment. No Admission. (last weekend in July)*

North Warren

CORNPLANTER STATE FOREST

North Warren - *323 N. State Street 16365. Phone: (814) 723-0262. www.dcnr. state.pa.us/forestry/stateforests/cornplanteractivities.aspx.*

1,256 acres named for Chief Cornplanter, a famous Indian Chief of the Seneca tribe. Highlights include Hunter Run Demonstration Area and Lasure Trail. This is a combined interpretive area with about 1-1/2 miles of self guided foot trails. It is heavily used by the surrounding schools for environmental education. There are seven miles of cross-country ski trails for the winter sports enthusiast. The trail is located 4 miles N. of Tionesta off SR 36. ATV Trails.

NW Area

Oil City

OIL CREEK STATE PARK

Oil City - *RD 1, Box 207 (the main entrance to the park is off of PA Route 8) 16301. Phone: (814) 676-5915. www.dcnr.state.pa.us/stateparks/parks/oilcreek.aspx. Admission: to PA State Parks is FREE however swimming, marina and camping/ lodging fees apply, with reservation or entrance.*

The site of the world's first commercial oil well, this park tells the story of the early petroleum industry by interpreting oil boom towns, oil wells and early transportation. Many sites can be seen while traveling the 9.5-mile paved bicycle trail through the scenic Oil Creek Gorge, or on an excursion train.

Displays and programs are at Petroleum Centre, the focal point of the early oil boom. "A Contrast in Time" slideshow takes you on a six-minute journey through time. The noise of pumping wells and shouting men in the 1860s contrasts with the rustling leaves in a gentle breeze in present day Oil Creek. The train station is open 11:00am-5:00pm Saturdays and Sundays. Visit the Train Station Visitor Center for historical displays, an exciting diorama and an interactive computer information center. A train still chugs through the valley and stops at the Train Station in Petroleum Centre, just as it did over 100 years ago! Wildcat Hollow - outdoor classroom and 4 theme trails. Hike the "wickedest hollow east of the Mississippi." Choose from one to four trails including: Wetlands Trail (one mile); Geology Trail (one mile); Oil History Trail (0.25 mile); Forestry Trail (0.25 mile). Also: Boat Rentals, Sledding, Fishing, and Cross-Country Skiing.

Sandy Lake

GODDARD STATE PARK, MAURICE K.

Sandy Lake - *684 Lake Wilhelm Road (I-79 exit 34, west on Rte. 358) 16145. Phone: (724) 253-4833. www.dcnr.state.pa.us/stateparks/parks/mauricekgoddard. aspx. Admission: to PA State Parks is FREE however swimming, marina and camping/lodging fees apply, with reservation or entrance.*

The 1,860-acre Lake Wilhelm is an angler's paradise. The large lake, abundant wetlands, old fields and mature forests provide a diversity of habitats which attract wildlife in all seasons. Boat Rentals, Sledding, Trails, & Winter Sports.

PIONEER FROLIC

Sandy Lake - *Goddard State Park. Every June the Friends of Goddard (FROG) co-sponsor the Pioneer Frolic which is two days of festivities that examine what historical rural Pennsylvania life was like along the Sandy Creek during the 1750s to 1840s. Crafters, artisans, and demonstrators display there wares and skills which can include a blacksmith, pioneer toys, spinner, food, entertainment and an encampment. www.orgsites.com/pa/friendsofgoddard/*

Sharon

DAFFIN'S CANDIES

Sharon - *496 East State Street (Factory - 7 Spearman Avenue, SR60 in nearby Farrell) 16146. Phone: (724) 342-2892. www.daffins.com. Hours: Monday-Saturday 9:00am-9:00pm, Sunday 11:00am-5:00pm. Admission: FREE. Tours: Monday - Friday 9:00am-3:00pm (lunch 12:00 - 1:00pm). Tuesday only (summer). By reservations. 15+ people (add-ons to other groups accepted). 45 minutes long. Miscellaneous: Tours in the fall and winter are best - more activity preparing for Christmas and Easter Holidays. The Chocolate Kingdom is available to view whenever the store is open.*

Daffin's Candies has earned a national reputation for its delectable sweet and semi-sweet milk chocolate candy with nearly 100 years of experience and three generations of chocolate makers.

A display made from hundreds of pounds of chocolate...sweet!

Start in the Chocolate Kingdom inside the World's Largest Candy Store. The Kingdom is inhabited by a 400-pound chocolate turtle, a 125-pound chocolate reindeer and 75-pound chocolate frog. Chocolate castles, a train, a village, and a Ferris Wheel bring this whimsical land to life. Snap a picture or pick up free postcard pictures of these unique creatures. Each giant figurine can require up to 700 lbs. of chocolate! As the tour continues, you'll learn how cocoa beans are removed from pods, mashed into paste, and finally processed into the chocolate forms we all know and love.

Daffin's still hosts its annual event known as Swizzle Stick Day on the Sunday before Palm Sunday. The facility holds plant tours that day, drawing nearly 8,000 people during the four-hour session. Patrons also get a free sample of a swizzle stick dipped in fresh candy filling with fresh chocolate dipped on top.

For updates & travel games visit: **www.KidsLoveTravel.com**

Regular factory tours are also available year-round. At the Factory, the group will see a short video tape of Daffin's and the History of chocolates. The seven foot Rabbit and other artistic chocolate items are also on display at the factory. Then, the group will take a tour thru the factory and see how some chocolates are made. At the end of the tour, each person will receive a candy sample.

Titusville

DRAKE WELL MUSEUM

Titusville - *East Bloss Street, 205 Museum Lane (I-80 to exit 3, off SR8 North) 16354. Phone: (814) 827-2797. www.drakewell.org. Hours: Tuesday-Saturday 9:00am-5:00pm, Sunday Noon-5:00pm (May-October). Admission: $6.00 adult, $5.00 senior (65+), $3.00 child (3-11). Miscellaneous: Head over to Pithole City (off SR227 between Pleasantville and Plummer) Visitor's Center (June-Labor Day). Within the park is a bike trail and tourist train ride depot. Magic Lantern Shows (old-fashioned movies using glass slides to illustrate stories, songs and comedy) and Blacksmith demos occasional Saturdays each month. Look at Calendar of Events. Educators: before you visit, ask when they are offering a Nitro Show to student groups and ask to tag along. Their education dept. has lesson plan materials they can send you.*

The birthplace of the petroleum industry. Edward Drake drilled the first oil well in 1859 through layers of sandstone. Start your visit with a video about the challenges Drake and his driller, "Uncle" Billy Smith faced to succeed. The museum's indoor and outdoor exhibits explain the progress of the oil industry. Operating oil field machinery, historic buildings, and scale models demonstrate primitive

Lots of fun pushin' the buttons and learning...

and modern drilling processes. Many exhibits have "push buttons" and "cutaways" of the machinery in action (the kids will really like pushing the small button to make all the working parts move). And, they can "squeeze and sniff" oil samples from all over the world, make plastic, send telegraph messages, and find unusual items made from oil in the museum lobby. Some will surprise you (ex. Tape, aspirin). Be sure to purchase a souvenir vial of real crude Pennsylvania oil in the Museum Store and eat your ice cream on the patio.

NW Area

OIL FESTIVAL

Titusville - Drake Well Museum. Heritage festival celebrating the history of oil. Festival includes sporting events, concerts, parades, children's events, historic tours, and a stagecoach robbery. FREE. (early August)

OIL CREEK & TITUSVILLE RAILROAD

Titusville - 409 South Perry Street (I-80 exit Route 8 north to Perry Street Station) 16354. Phone: (814) 676-1733. http://octrr.org/. Hours: Weekend departures at 1:00pm (June-October). Selected weekday runs in July, August and October. Admission: $17.00 adult, $15.00 senior (60+), $11.00 child (3-12). Tours: 2 1/2 hour narrated trip by guide and audio recording. Miscellaneous: Railroad memorabilia displays, souvenir area, and snack shop. Caboose Motel right across the street. The Motel features 21 caboose units.

A railcar post office?

See the first oil fields in the world tell a story of the oil rush boom days in the valley (similar to the gold rush). Stop by Rynd Farm and Drake Well Park. Ride in restored 1930s passenger cars. One car is the only working railway Post Office car - have your postcard to grandma hand-stamp cancelled while on board.

EASTER BUNNY TRAIN RIDES

Titusville - Oil Creek & Titusville Railroad. Candy treats with the Easter Bunny riding along. Admission. (Weekend before Easter)

SANTA TRAINS

Titusville - Oil Creek & Titusville Railroad. Sing songs and eat treats as you ride the train with Santa aboard. Admission. (second weekend in December)

NW Area

Warren

KINZUA DAM/ BIG BEND VISITOR'S CENTER

Warren - *1205 Kinzua Road* - *Route 59 (I-79 to Route 6 east to Route 59 east)*
16365.   Phone: (814)   726-0661.   www.lrp.usace.army.mil/rec/lakes/kinzuala.
htm. Hours: Daily 10:00am-4:00pm (Summer). Weekends (September, October).
Admission: FREE.

A flood control dam has created a vast waterway known as the Allegheny
Reservoir (within the Allegheny National Forest). Center features exhibits,

displays, and slide programs which
explain the purpose of the dam
and power plant. In the summer,
there are numerous activities
ranging from swimming, boating
and water-skiing, to camping,
fishing and sightseeing. During the
autumn, the Kinzua countryside
produces colorful displays of fall
foliage with miles of hiking trails
and country roads from which to
enjoy the brilliant fall scenery. Winter doesn't signal an end to the enjoyment
of the outdoors. Hikers turn to cross-country skiing, fishermen continue their
sport on the ice and snowmobiles speed along the many trails and forest
roads. The blossoming of the woodland wildflowers signals the arrival of spring
in Kinzua Country; and with it, the arrival of trout fishermen, canoeists and
nature enthusiasts.

BIG BEND OVERLOOK VISITOR CENTER - The U.S. Army Corps of
Engineers maintains a nice visitor center and picnic area just downstream
of the Kinzua Dam. The visitor's center, which is open daily from Memorial
Day weekend through Labor Day, and weekends in September and October,
contains exhibits, displays and brochures which illustrate the purpose of the
Kinzu Dam, and highlight recreational and sightseeing opportunities in the
area. Several overlooks provide great views of the Kinzua Dam and Allegheny
Reservoir.

NW Area

Travel Journal & Notes:

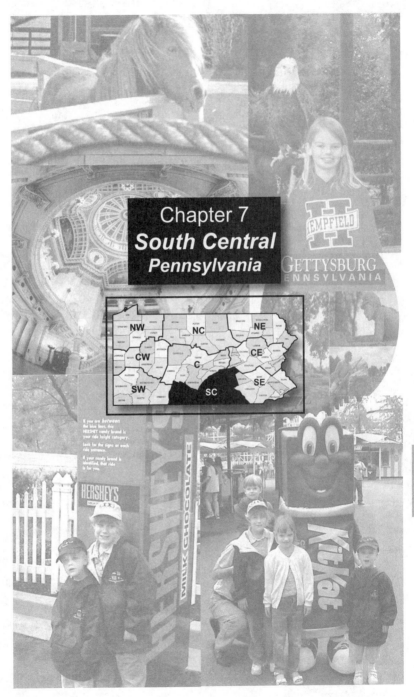

Chapter 7
South Central
Pennsylvania

Bedford
- Fort Bedford Museum
- Old Bedford Village

Bedford (Manns Choice)
- Coral Caverns

Bedford (Schellsburg)
- Gravity Hill

Carlisle
- Kings Gap State Park

Carroll Valley
- Liberty Mountain Ski Area

Fayetteville
- Caledonia State Park

Fort Loudon
- Cowan's Gap State Park

Gardners
- Pine Grove Furnace State Park

Gettysburg
- American Civil War Museum
- Battlefield Bus Tours
- Boyd's Bear Country
- Eisenhower Nat'l Historic Site
- Explore & More Children's Museum
- Gettysburg History Center
- Gettysburg Nat'l Military Park
- Hall Of Presidents
- Jennie Wade House & Olde Town
- Land Of Little Horses
- Lincoln Train Museum
- Soldier's National Museum
- Lincoln's Lost Treasure - Downtown Adventure
- Battle Of Gettysburg

Gettysburg (Biglerville)
- National Apple Museum

Halifax
- Lake Tobias Wildlife Park

Hanover
- Codorus State Park
- Utz Potato Chips
- Snyders Of Hanover

Harrisburg
- Fort Hunter Mansion & Park
- Pennsylvania State Capitol Building
- Whitaker Center For Science And The Arts
- Pennsylvania National Fire Museum
- National Civil War Museum
- City Island
- Pride Of The Susquehanna Riverboat Tour
- Harrisburg Senators Baseball
- State Museum Of Pennsylvania
- Wildwood Lake Sanctuary
- Pennsylvania Farm Show

Hershey
- Antique Automobile Club Of America Museum
- Hershey Bears Hockey
- Hershey Gardens
- Hershey Lodge
- Hershey Story - The Museum On Chocolate Avenue
- Hershey Trolley Works
- Hersheypark
- Hershey's Chocolate World Visitors Center
- Zoo America North American Wildlife Park

Hummelstown
- Indian Echo Caverns

Imler
- Blue Knob State Park

Lewisberry
- Gifford Pinchot State Park
- Ski Roundtop

Mercersburg
- Whitetail Ski Resort And Mountain Biking Center

Middletown
- Middletown And Hummelstown Railroad

New Park
- Maize Quest Fun Park

SC Area

Newport
- Little Buffalo State Park

Newville
- Colonel Denning State Park

Orrtanna
- Mr. Ed's Elephant Museum

Schellsburg
- Shawnee State Park

Thomasville
- Martin's Potato Chips

York
- Harley-Davidson Motorcycle Museum Tour

York *(cont.)*
- Agricultural & Industrial Museums
- York County Heritage Museums
- York Little Theatre
- York County Fire Museum
- Wolfgang Candy Company
- Christmas Magic - A Festival Of Lights

York (Hellam)
- Shoe House

Zionsville
- Stahl's Pottery Festival

Travel Journal & Notes:

A Quick Tour of our Hand-Picked Favorites Around...

South Central Pennsylvania

Take a roadtrip honoring our Civil War past in the beautiful South Central PA region. The Road to Gettysburg tells the story of the cost and sacrifice of the Commonwealth, for the common good. This memorable journey will take you beyond the battlefields. Your family can also experience firsthand the people, places, and events that shaped our Civil War heritage. The area is also well-known for its yummy farm and factory tours.

Your road to Gettysburg begins in the capital city, Harrisburg. The painful and proud history of the American Civil War is recounted here at the **National Civil War Museum**. Who wants to see Dinosaur bones? Who wouldn't! Then come to **The State Museum of Pennsylvania** next on your itinerary and plunge through the pages of Pennsylvania history. Lots of hands-on activities for the little explorers are in the Curiosity Connection. Take a late lunch or give the family a mid-day snack at the one of the yummy pizza joints downtown. Round two can begin with a production at the Popcorn Hat Players inside Strawberry Square or head over to Harrisburg's City Island for a host of activities. **Whitaker Center for Science and the Arts** sparks the imagination and encourages thought provoking conversations with your family as you try all of the hands-on exhibits in the Harsco Science Center.

Hershey Harrisburg is great for stimulating little ones senses when it comes to experiencing the outdoors or darting indoors on rainy days. No matter what season, this region is a wonderland to behold and traverse through. Play along the Susquehanna River, relax at a state park or be really brave and try a new thrill ride at **Hershey Park**! Many of the attractions surrounding the amusement park enrich the trip – whether it's a trolley tour of town or experimenting in the Chocolate Lab or being treated to chocolates on your pillow each night at Hershey Lodge.

Once in York, there's a historic site nearly everywhere. One of its museums, the **Agriculture and Industry Museum**, houses a collection of York County-built automobiles, an authentic Conestoga Wagon, and a 1937 Aeronca K airplane. Part of the fun is trying to figure out what each piece of machinery did. It's like a quirky game to meander through the museum maze of "junk." Nearby is a factory favorite – **Wolfgang Chocolates** and many snack food tours in the Hanover area.

Enjoy a living history re-enactment of the war at the American Civil War Museum. At the **Gettysburg National Military Park Museum and Visitors Center**, experience one of the largest Civil War collections brought to life with interactive exhibits. They've added more flare and engagement to the site allowing kids to enjoy history from simple, colorful displays. Later, take a simulated ride to Gettysburg on the **Lincoln Train**.

Many who visit the Gettysburg area may miss the chance to escape the historical district and venture out into the countryside. The **National Apple Museum** is nearby and offers a cute, homespun museum plus periodic tours of the apple orchards. Why are the trees so small? Kids get involved right from the beginning (they eat an apple snack with juice). As you sip on your juice, watch a film about apple varieties, picking, and production. They show footage of actual apple product factory production lines located in town.

Another enchanting part of the Gettysburg countryside is off US 30 west to the **Land of Little Horses**. As you enter you'll be greeted by adorable small horses (most only a few feet tall) that seem to be just the right size for kids to enjoy. Take in a horse show or costume parade.

Sites and attractions are listed in order by City, Zip Code, and Name. Symbols indicated represent:

 Festivals   Restaurants   Lodging

SC Area

Bedford

FORT BEDFORD MUSEUM

Bedford - *Fort Bedford Drive (I-76, exit 11, SR320 - Pitt Street - Downtown) 15522. Phone: (814) 623-8891 or (800) 259-4284. www.fortbedfordmuseum.org. Hours: Daily 11:00am-5:00pm (mid-May thru mid-October). Admission: Generally $3.00-$5.00*

The French and Indian War fort site - "The Fort in the Forest". A blockhouse structure that houses the large scale model of the original fort along with Native American household artifacts. From flint rock rifles to hand tools to clothing – each help you explore pioneer and frontier days in western Pennsylvania. In order to secure the water and secure the banks of the stream, a gallery with loopholes extended from the central bastion on its north front down to the water's edge. A ladder-like arrangement of steps led down the river's bluff-like south bank. This enclosed gallery was a real military curiosity. The fort controlled the river gap and served a British stockade against the French for years.

OLD BEDFORD VILLAGE

Bedford - *220 Sawblade Road (1/2 mile south of PA Turnpike (I-70/76), exit 11-Route 220) 15522. www.oldbedfordvillage.org. Phone: (814) 623-1156 or (800) 238-4347. Hours: Daily (except Wednesday) 9:00am-5:00pm (Memorial Day-Labor Day). Thursday-Sunday 10:00am-4:00pm (September/October). Admission: $8.00 adult, $5.00 student (age 6+). Ask about senior discount. Tours: Self-guided. Guided tours are available with advance notice. Miscellaneous: Dress for walking on the natural roadways. Pendergrass Tavern. Many warm weather re-enactment weekends.*

Craftsmen are in action as you relive the past walking through 40 log homes and shops (see them making brooms, baskets, bread, pottery). There are seasonal productions such as "Welcome to Early America" - a recreated world of the 1790s Pioneer America or summer theatre musical, comedies or mysteries (814-623-7555 for reservations). In 1794, President George Washington led federal troops with his battle headquarters here in Bedford. After the troops left, the colonial industry flourished with blacksmiths, attorneys, a doctor, distillers, innkeepers, soldiers, millers, and farmers setting up shop in the village. In all, over 14 period skills are represented at the Village, and many of the products made on site can be found at the Village Craft Shop. And don't miss the opportunity to learn one of the many crafts available through Old Bedford Village's educational programs.

SC Area

PUMPKIN FESTIVAL

Bedford - *Old Bedford Village. Pumpkin painting and carving, pie-eating contests. Pumpkin patch (wagon rides out there). Refreshments. (third weekend in October)*

CHRISTMAS OPEN HOUSE

Bedford - *Old Bedford Village. Tours of decorated, historical buildings. Refreshments and musical entertainment. Re-enactors. Admission. (first and second weekend in December)*

CORAL CAVERNS

Bedford (Manns Choice) - *(6 miles west of town on Route 31. Turnpike exit 11) 15550. Phone: (814) 623-6882. www.coralcaverns.com. Hours: Weekends only 10:00am-5:00pm (mid-May through Mid-October). Admission: $11.00 adult, $5.00 child (10 and under).*

At Coral Caverns' underground wonderland, explore the only known coral reef cavern in existence and discover an abundance of fossils, stalactites and stalagmites. The most noted feature is the coral reef, a towering fossil wall containing the fossil remains of coral and other sea creatures buried years ago when Pennsylvania was partially covered by "The Great Inland Sea." Try to find "cave bacon" or a sighting of cave bats.

GRAVITY HILL

Bedford (Schellsburg) - *Bethel Hollow Road 15522. . www.gravityhill.com.*

Tucked away in the "less traveled" area of Bedford County is a marvel. Often talked about, but seldom found, Gravity Hill is a phenomenon. Cars roll uphill, water flows the wrong way ... it's a place where gravity has gone haywire.

Some people like to take water or various other non-flammable, bio-degradeable liquids and pour them onto the road. The liquids will flow uphill. There are directions on the website about finding Gravity Hill with a minimum of wrong turns. Daylight hours suggested.

Carlisle

KINGS GAP STATE PARK

Carlisle - 500 Kings Gap Road   17013. www.dcnr.state.pa.us/stateparks/parks/kingsgap.aspx. Phone: (717) 486-5031. Admission: to PA State Parks is FREE however swimming, marina and camping/lodging fees apply, with reservation or entrance.

Kings Gap offers a panoramic view of the Cumberland Valley. Sixteen miles of hiking trails interconnect three main areas and are open year-round. Kings Gap offers environmental education programs from the pre-school environmental awareness program to environmental problem solving programs.

Carroll Valley

LIBERTY MOUNTAIN SKI AREA

Carroll Valley - 78 Country Club Trail (Rte. 30 to Rte. 116, Liberty Mountain Resort is 8 miles on the left) 17320. Phone: (717) 642-8282.. www.skiliberty.com.

Liberty Mountain Resort is nestled near the scenic Catoctin Mountains on 275 beautiful acres, with more than 100 acres of skiing, snowboarding and snow tubing trails. Just eight miles southwest of historic Gettysburg, the resort is convenient from both the Baltimore, Md., and Washington, D.C., metro areas. Skiing, Snowboarding and Snow Tubing. Longest Run: 5300 ft.; 16 Slopes & Trails. Snow Monsters Kids club.

Fayetteville

CALEDONIA STATE PARK

Fayetteville - 40 Rocky Mountain Rd (US Route 30) 17222. Phone: (717) 352-2161. www.dcnr.state.pa.us/stateparks/parks/caledonia.aspx. Admission: to PA State Parks is FREE however swimming, marina and camping/lodging fees apply, with reservation or entrance.

Known locally as South Mountain, Caledonia located on the northern-most section of the Blue Ridge Mountains fifteen miles west of Gettysburg via Route 30. The Appalachian Trail passes through the central portion of the park. It is a great place for family outings: The park features a large, ADA accessible swimming pool with a small snack bar. The pool is open 11:00am-7:00pm from Memorial Day weekend to Labor Day, unless posted otherwise. Visitor Center, Campsites, Fishing, Trails, and Cross-Country Skiing. Mr. Ed's

Elephant Museum (a collection of 6000 elephants) is open daily just 2 miles east of the park on Rte. 30.

Fort Loudon

COWAN'S GAP STATE PARK

Fort Loudon - (PA 75 North to Richmond Furnace, follow signs) 17224. Phone: (717) 485-3948. www.dcnr.state.pa.us/stateparks/parks/cowansgap.aspx. Admission: to PA State Parks is FREE however swimming, marina and camping/ lodging fees apply, with reservation or entrance.

Logging Road Trail: 1.7-mile, easy hiking. This old logging road can be walked from one end of the park to the other and is a good trail to use to make loop hikes with other trails on the side of Cove Mountain. Lakeside Trail: 1.5-mile, easy hiking. This very pleasant, nearly level, scenic trail encompasses Cowans Gap Lake. This is the most popular trail in the park. Beach, Visitor Center, Boat Rentals, Campsites, Rustic Cabins, and Winter Activities. Buchanan's Birthplace State Historical Park nearby. Environmental Education and Interpretation (April-November). Check out the landslide exhibit on Knobsville Road Trail.

Gardners

PINE GROVE FURNACE STATE PARK

Gardners - 1100 Pine Grove Road (PA Route 233 & 34) 17324. Phone: (717) 486-7174. www.dcnr.state.pa.us/stateparks/parks/pinegrovefurnace.aspx. Admission: to PA State Parks is FREE however swimming, marina and camping/lodging fees apply, with reservation or entrance.

This park was once the site of the Pine Grove Furnace Iron Works that dates from 1764. Historical buildings include the ironmaster's mansion, a gristmill, an inn and several residences. The self-guiding historical trail leads you through the remains of the iron works. The Appalachian Trail passes through the park. Two beaches are open from May 1 to September 30, 8:00am to sunset. Visitor Center, Boat Rentals, Campsites, Kite-flying Area. Fishing, short Hiking Trails, and Cross-Country Skiing.

Gettysburg

AMERICAN CIVIL WAR MUSEUM

Gettysburg - *297 Steinwehr Avenue (US15 - Business Route) 17325. Phone: (717) 334-6245. www.gettysburgmuseum.com. Hours: Daily 9:00am-5:00pm (March-December). Extended spring and summer closing hours. Admission: $5.50 adult, $3.00 child (6-17). Miscellaneous: The program, "Enlist Now!," will give 'new recruits' a first-hand look at what life was like for the common Union soldier. Recruits will be able to taste the food, learn how to march, learn drills and be able to experience what it was like to enlist in the Union army. Summer*

weekends $15.00. Educators: study guide and quiz: http://www.gettysburgmuseum.com/files/ study_guide.pdf

More than 200 life-size wax figures in 30 different scenes re-create crucial moments but also describe the cause and effects of the conflict called the Battle at Gettysburg. Besides strategic planning and battle scenes, voices from history blend with scenes and words to recreate the past. Jennie Wade bakes bread before being fatally shot in her sister's kitchen. John Brown, bound in ropes, walks to the gallows. Slaves using the Underground Railroad try to escape to freedom. And Abraham Lincoln sits in the theatre on that fateful day. The last scene is of an animated wax figure of Lincoln making his speech the night before his famous address. At the end of the tour, you'll enter the Battleroom Auditorium where the battle is re-enacted (with wax figures and lighting). It's an easy explanation of the three days of battle (not too technical for kids). Lincoln arrives and gives his address at the end.

BATTLEFIELD BUS TOURS

Gettysburg - *778 Baltimore Street 17325. www.gettysburgbattlefieldtours.com. Phone: (717) 334-6296.   Hours: Daily 9:00am-9:00pm (Summer), 9:00am-7:00pm (Spring & Fall), 9:00am- 5:00pm (rest of year). Weather permitting. Admission: $24.95 adult, $14.00 child (4-11). Tickets can be ordered or purchased at area hotels.   Tours: 23 mile tour of "The Battle of Gettysburg". 2 hour narration audiotape tours leave several times daily, depending on season. Call to reserve tickets for specific tour times.*

A Hollywood cast of actors, technicians, and special effects recreate the Battle of Gettysburg as you tour the Battlefield from the famous Double Decker buses (seasonal, warm months) that have become a landmark in Gettysburg.

Licensed Battlefield Guide bus tours offer the visitor a truly unique perspective into the struggles of the three days' battle. And you re-live it all under the skies of Gettysburg most famous landmarks: Little Round Top, Devil's Den, Wheatfield, Peach Orchard, Pickett's Charge, and High Water Mark. Enclosed bus for other cold, rainy season tours. Note: a family's only concern may be the length of the tour - too long for squirmy toddlers and hyper young kids. Better to buy the audio drive tour and go on your own.

BOYD'S BEAR COUNTRY

Gettysburg - 75 Cunningham Road (off Bus. Rte. 15, near Emmitsburg Rd.) 17325. Phone: (717) 630-2600. www.boydsbearcountry.com. Hours: Daily 10:00am-6:00pm except New Years, Easter, Thanksgiving and Christmas. Admission: FREE. Miscellaneous: Restaurants on premises. Dress-your-own bears and seasonal crafts area.

The World's Most Humongous Teddy Bear Store and museum-all in one. Get a history of the Boyd's Collection…its product and the life story of the founder. Your tour is led by Bennie B., an overstuffed (and overfed!) Boyd's Bear who serves as the resident historian. The displays include a replica of Gary's father's butcher shop in New York City (where Gary learned business tricks and tips!); neat photos and memorabilia of Gary's growin' up years and experiences as a Peace Corps volunteer; displays of early Boyd's duck decoys, Gnomes Homes, early plush and resin, and other stuff that made Boyd's famous; and sections dedicated to QVC shows, collectors' club, and charitable activities. They've built a display of virtually every Boyd's plush critter ever made.

The Nursery is open…where baby bears are born every day. Nurse Carin welcomes perspective parents of all ages to adopt their beary own cuddly bear. Look at the bears in their cradles, pick one, fill out the adoption papers and get your photo taken. The Super Duper Bear Factory is the place to make your own bear. Also, they have occasional Breakfasts with Molly & Sebastian, a Mother's Day Tea or Father's Day Breakfast, hayrides in October, or Breakfast with Santa in December. Entertainment on the porch most summer weekends, too.

EISENHOWER NATIONAL HISTORIC SITE

Gettysburg - (adjacent to the Gettysburg Battlefield) 17325. www.nps.gov/eise. Admission: $5.00-$7.50 per person (age 6+). Tours: Shuttle buses leave the Gettysburg Battlefield Visitors Center several times each day. More often in the summer and during special events. Less often in dead of winter. FREEBIES: The

Strictly For Kids Eisenhower Home Virtual Tour - Take a tour of the President's home. It's surprising how much you can learn about a President by checking out his house and snooping through his stuff! Online at www.nps.gov/archive/eise/tour1axxA.htm.

During his Presidency, President and Mrs. Eisenhower used the farm as a weekend retreat, a refuge in time of illness, and a comfortable meeting place for world leaders. From 1961 to 1969, it was the Eisenhower's home during a vigorous and active retirement. Today the farm is maintained as it was during the Eisenhower years and the President's home retains nearly all its original furnishings. You are invited to tour the home and grounds, and take a walk to the cattle barns and skeet range.

EXPLORE & MORE CHILDREN'S MUSEUM

Gettysburg - 20 East High Street (near the circle) 17325. Phone: (717) 337-9151. www.exploreandmore.com. Hours: Monday-Saturday 10:00am-5:00pm (April-September). Closed Wednesdays but open Sunday afternoons (rest of year). Admission: $4.00 adult (age 15+), $6.00 child (2-14). Miscellaneous: Toy store.

Located in an historic home, they have seven rooms where children can create a work of art, play house the way people lived around the time of the Civil War, make a bubble large enough to stand inside of, or experiment with mixing colors (make color explosions in milk!) and waterworks. Children can make puppets and then perform a show with them. More pretend play in the Construction Zone area (receiving, conveyor, shipping, recycling – clean up) or the Black Light Dress Up Room (wild!). We especially liked the 1860s Room and all the dress up clothes and play items to play Civil War era "house". At this place, you can even play with an overhead projector, just like a teacher. Best for kids ages 3 to 8. Give your children a break from the battlefield nearby!

GETTYSBURG HISTORY CENTER

Gettysburg - 241 Steinwehr Ave 17325. www.gettysburgdiorama.com. Phone: (717) 334-6408. Hours: Daily 9:00am-8:00pm. Extended weekend and summer evening hours. Admission: $3.00-$5.50 (age 6+).

The famous Gettysburg Diorama is now front and center along one of Historic Gettysburg's most-visited neighborhoods as part of the new Gettysburg

History Center. The Gettysburg Diorama is the largest military scale model in the United States. The fully narrated diorama features more than 20,000 hand-painted soldiers, horses, cannons as well as Gettysburg buildings that became famous during the battle. Learn what role your home state played in the Battle. See the armies' arrival, battle lines forming, and the advances and retreats of the struggling armies. The hills, roads and fields are accurate to scale and provide an overview of all three days of battle with an exciting sound and light show.

GETTYSBURG NATIONAL MILITARY PARK

Gettysburg - *1195 Baltimore Pike (follow signs off US 15) 17325. Phone: (717) 334-1124 Park or (717) 338-9114 Eisenhower Site. www.nps.gov/gett. Hours: Daily 8:00am-5:00pm. Open until 6:00pm (April-October). The park is open at 6:00am each day and closes after dark. Closed Thanksgiving, Christmas and New Years. Admission: VISITOR CENTER/BATTLEFIELD - FREE. MUSEUM: $10.50 adult, $9.50 senior & Active Military, $6.50 youth (ages 6-18). WILLS HOUSE: $4.00-$6.50. Tickets can be purchased on site or online at www.gettysburgfoundation.org.   Tours: Park grounds and roads - Self guided tours 6:00am - 10:00pm. Eisenhower Site - All visits to the Ranger conducted programs, walks, tours, campfire programs, living history programs, children's program and Battle Walks through the summer months. Educators: Find curriculum titled: War for Freedom online under For Teachers/Curriculum.*

The Battle of Gettysburg was a turning point in the Civil War, the Union victory in the summer of 1863 that ended General Robert E. Lee's second and most ambitious invasion of the North. It was the war's bloodiest battle with 51,000 casualties. It also provided President Abraham Lincoln with the setting for his most famous address.

Visitors to Gettysburg National Military Park should begin at the Museum and Visitor Center where the park offers information, a vast museum about Gettysburg and the Civil War, the fully restored Gettysburg Cyclorama and the film "A New Birth of Freedom", narrated by Morgan Freeman, a central feature in the new center that orients visitors to the significance of Gettysburg. The center also provides information on the numerous ways to tour the battlefield park. The center also has an expansive bookstore and a refreshment saloon, which offers snacks, sandwiches and drinks.

SC Area

When visitors tour Gettysburg, they don't have to picture the battle in their minds. The recent restoration of this National Park and the new Cyclorama bring the Civil War to life in dramatic ways. If you haven't visited the park in a while, it is a must see for families. Here is the site of the major Civil War battle and Abraham Lincoln's Gettysburg Address:

- BATTLEFIELD - The most important major blow to the Confederate Army and the most casualties (51,000) on the first few days of early July 1863. See key places: Cemetery Hill and Ridge, Culp's Hill, Little Round Top, and Observation Tower. (We suggest the audio tape tour for kids).

- NOVEMBER 19, 1863, CEMETERY - President Lincoln dedicated the National Cemetery on the battlefield and delivered his famous speech "The Gettysburg Address".

- DAVID WILLS HOUSE: 8 Lincoln Square (downtown). The 1863 house includes the restored office where prominent attorney David Wills coordinated post-battle recovery efforts and invited a war-worn President Lincoln to deliver "a few appropriate remarks" when he dedicated the cemetery. Visitors will be able to see the restored second-floor bedroom where the President finished revising the Gettysburg Address on Nov. 18, 1864. www.mainstreetgettysburg.org/willshouse.html. (Hours: Wednesday-Sunday 10:00am-5:00pm, extended spring and summer hours)

- CYCLORAMA - A 30 minute description while standing in the middle of a 360 degree circular wall painting of the battlefield and Pickett's Charge, the climactic moment of the battle (a sight & sound experience). Climb the stairs into the Cyclorama tower (in the new Museum & Visitors Center) and be taken back to July 3, 1863. As the audio narration begins, you hear the story of the charge and lights highlight certain portions of the canvas. Rocks, weapons and bushes in front of the painting bring a sense of depth...putting you in the middle of the battle. 9:00 am - 4:30pm (every 1/2 hour).

- MUSEUM OF THE CIVIL WAR - A large collection of Civil War artifacts, especially weapons and uniforms. The Camp Life exhibits are the most interesting relating visuals to the life of a soldier.

ANNIVERSARY OF LINCOLN'S GETTYSBURG ADDRESS

Gettysburg - *Gettysburg National Military Park. Daytime, Gettysburg National Cemetery. The annual observance of President Abraham Lincoln's famous address with brief memorial services and noted speakers. (one day in the third week, as announced, in November)*

HALL OF PRESIDENTS

Gettysburg - *789 Baltimore Street 17325. Phone: (717) 334-5717.   Hours: Daily 9:00am-5:00pm (later hours in summer season). (March-Thanksgiving Weekend). Admission: $3.50-$7.25 (age 6+).*

Watch life-sized reproductions tell the "Story of America" through taped messages. First ladies appear in the type of gown they wore at the inauguration of their husbands. They've also added a heartwarming "Eisenhower at Gettysburg" exhibit. If your children are studying Presidential history, this is an easy way to learn important facts about each man. Featuring the area's only complete wax collection of American Presidents and their first ladies, the Hall of Presidents is located across the street from the Gettysburg Tour Center and next to the main entrance of the National Cemetery.

JENNIE WADE HOUSE & OLDE TOWN

Gettysburg - *547 Baltimore Street (Adjacent to Olde Town) 17325. Phone: (717) 334-4100. www.gettysburgbattlefieldtours.com/jennie-wade-house.php. Hours: Daily 9:00am-9:00pm (Summer), Daily 9:00am-5:00pm (March-Thanksgiving Weekend). Admission: $3.50-$7.25 (age 6+). Miscellaneous: Caution: Due to the dramatic nature and story of this tour - parents with children younger than 1st or 2nd grade should probably arrange to be part of a school tour. They only give brief descriptions of the events and not explicit details.*

With minor changes and repairs, the Museum remains much as Jennie must have known it over 140 years ago. Authentically furnished from cellar to attic, the museum is a shrine to Jennie and to life and living during the American Civil War. Jennie Wade was the only civilian killed during the battle of Gettysburg and the situations that led to her death were quite dramatic. While baking bread for the soldiers in her kitchen, a stray bullet hit and killed young 20 year old Jennie. (a realistic hologram of Jennie is seen in the kitchen - and you see the actual bullet hole). A soldier tells you all the details including the fact that her fiancé was killed just days later in battle, but never knew of Jennie's fate!

SC Area

LAND OF LITTLE HORSES

Gettysburg - *125 Glenwood Drive (3 miles West on US30, then follow signs) 17325. Phone: (717) 334-7259. www.landoflittlehorses.com. Hours: Monday-Saturday 10:00am-5:00pm, Sunday Noon-5:00pm (June-Labor Day). Weekends only (May, September, October). Admission: $13.95 adult, $11.95 child (age 2+). Miscellaneous: Air-conditioned arena. The Gift Horse Shop. Carousel, train tram, petting farm. Put on a "feed bag" at the Hobby Horse Café. Wagon and pony rides available for extra.*

As you enter you'll be greeted by adorable small horses (most only a few feet tall) that seem to be just the right size for kids to enjoy. Many are in separate pens throughout the park, some are in the barn, others are getting ready for the show in the arena. We took in the Barn Show first and loved the chance

...just the right size for kids!

to see the horses prance around and be gently petted. Especially cute are the mothers with their young. The highlight of this farm is the Performing Animals Show. They get the kids involved by "kissing a pig" (there's a trick involved - 2 kids volunteered and did it!), or helping with the animal tricks. "Something Special" is a daily event at the Land of Little Horses. The event changes every day, and can be anything from Miniature Horse costume parades (where you dress up horses and show them off to the entire park), fun games with prizes for the winners, goat milking & sheep sheering, photo opportunities with the stars of our daily Arena Performances, and much more! They also have cart races, saddle kids, and host weekend chicken races - so cute, pick your favorite animal and cheer it on! A great attraction for children of all ages.

LINCOLN TRAIN MUSEUM

Gettysburg - *425 Steinwehr Avenue 17325. www.gettysburgbattlefieldtours. com/lincoln-train-museum.php. Phone: (717) 334-5678. Hours: Daily 9:00am-9:00pm (Summer), Daily 9:00am-5:00pm (March-Thanksgiving). Admission: $3.50-$7.25 (age 6+). Miscellaneous: Events (in the diorama display) that led up to this historic train ride. Large train collection layout that reproduces the Civil War Era.*

A simulated 1836 train ride with Lincoln and statesmen on a 12 minute trip. See Civil War grounds and overhear conversations that might have occurred on that trip. They project actual footage of a steam train ride as your seat and floorboards move to the straights, curves, and rumbles of the track. Statesmen speak of this time, in the still present war, Mr. President's ill son, and thoughts of re-election. We suggest this stop for young kids (all ages for that matter) because it easily and uniquely illustrates the emotion/history behind the Gettysburg Address. The Lincoln Toy Train collection in the museum features over 1000 trains and dioramas illustrating the railroad's role during the Civil War.

SOLDIER'S NATIONAL MUSEUM

Gettysburg - *777 Baltimore Street 17325. www.gettysburgbattlefieldtours.com/ soldiers-national-museum.php. Phone: (717) 334-4890. Hours: Daily 9:00am-9:00pm (Summer) 9:00am-5:00pm (March-Thanksgiving Weekend). Admission: $4.00-$6.00 (age 6+).*

10 dioramas depict battles of the Civil War. There's also a life- sized, narrated confederate encampment. The building was once General Howard's headquarters and later the Soldier's National Orphanage. The drama begins with the red glow at Fort Sumter, goes on to Alabama and Chattanooga, seeing the marvel of the Monitor and the Merrimac at Hampton Roads, the fiery battle of Atlanta and Lee's Surrender at Appomattox. Walk through an encampment, hear soldier's fears spoken and the drum roll starting, even see the conditions of orphaned kids housed here for a time.

LINCOLN'S LOST TREASURE - DOWNTOWN ADVENTURE

Gettysburg - *17326. Phone: (800) 838-3006. www.lincolnsLostTreasure.com. Admission: $38.95 per person on scavenger hunt. Often, through website, they offer buy-one-get-one half off tickets. Suggested for kids ages 10 and up (with adult companion) but kids as young as 6 (and curious) get it. Tours: purchase show tickets weekends starting every 30 minutes from 11:00am-3:00pm. Note: A few tastes of food and a few drinks are included (appetizers & light drinks).*

Part Theatre, Part Adventure, Part Mystery. The streets of Gettysburg serve as a backdrop for a story told with elements of improv theatre and scavenger hunt. Hired by a wealthy eccentric entrepreneur, you are thrust into a mission that puts you in the center of a quest to uncover the secret treasure Lincoln left behind.

Lincoln's Lost Treasure is a LIVE two and a half hour adventure through the streets of historic Downtown Gettysburg. Almost like stepping into your own action movie, individuals or groups of up to 6 or 8 people are sent on a thrilling

SC Area

and entertaining quest to uncover a lost secret sparked by President Lincoln's final breath. Aided by a few historical artifacts and LIVE cast members, you are sent off to piece together hidden clues that can unravel the location to treasury gold that has been lost for over a century. Encountering eccentric and engaging cast members, decoding cryptic clues, and dodging FBI agents out to foil your mission, you and friends traverse the city's famous streets, hidden shops and historical landmarks discovering that Lincoln's Gettysburg Address holds the key to a national treasure.

BATTLE OF GETTYSBURG

Gettysburg - Yingling Farm (3 miles outside of town). www.gettysburgreenactment.com. (717) 338-1525. Reenactments, events at Yingling Farm (site of film) include camps, gallant stands and charges. Interpreters give a really nice narrative of what's happening with each battle. Although it's a three day event, if you only had one day to select, pick the day when they re-enact Pickett's Charge. It's the most well known and elaborately staged of the battles. Food concession are plentiful. If sunny day, wear sunscreen, hats, etc. Admission: $15.00-$30.00 per person. (long week of July 4th)

NATIONAL APPLE MUSEUM

Gettysburg (Biglerville) - 154 West Hanover Street (From Gettysburg, take Rt. 34 north 6 miles to Rt. 394, turn left, go three blocks. Museum on left. Look for big red barn) 17307. Phone: (717) 677-4556. www.nationalapplemuseum.com. Hours: Saturday 10:00am-4:00pm, Sunday 1:00-4:00pm (May-October). Call for special group arrangement during other days and times. Admission: $2.00 adult, $1.00 child (6-12). Tours: Guided every 2 hours (last one at 3:00pm). Self-guided audio tape tours. Miscellaneous: Picnic area. Gift shop - guess what...everything in there has apples on it!

Miles and miles of sweet, juicy apples...

What a treat this place is! America's favorite fruit (red delicious, the most popular) is highlighted here. Kids can get involved right from the beginning (they eat a snack of apple juice and cookies). As you sip on your juice, they show a film about apple varieties, picking, and production (bet you didn't know the apple is part of the rose family!). This film is very entertaining (not boring at all) and the kids are thrilled seeing thousands of apples in every scene. Because many apple production facilities don't give tours, you'll get a great video look at how they "produce" apples for applesauce. How do they keep apples unbruised and ripe all year long? Antique equipment displays and old town dioramas are upstairs. The bug displays really appeal to the kids. See the "apple biz" come to life when you drive just up the road through apple orchards. Do you know why orchards love bees, ladybug beetles, and dwarf trees?

APPLE BLOSSOM FESTIVAL

Gettysburg (Biglerville) - *South Mountain Fairgrounds. Live entertainment, orchard tours, scenic wagon rides, delicious apple foods, plus! (first full weekend of May)*

NATIONAL APPLE HARVEST FESTIVAL

Gettysburg (Biglerville) -*South Mountain Fairgrounds. www.appleharvest.com. An Old time festival of apple products, live country music, hundreds of arts and crafters, antique autos and tractors, steam engines, orchard tours and food. Gettysburg Scenic Railway train ride thru apple countryside. Admission. (first and second weekend in October)*

Halifax

LAKE TOBIAS WILDLIFE PARK

Halifax - 760 Tobias Drive (Rt. 322/22 West to Dauphin. Rt. 225 North to Halifax. Four miles on Rt. 225 North to Fisherville) 17032. www.laketobias.com. Phone: (717) 362-9126. Hours: Monday-Friday 10:00am-6:00pm, Saturday & Sunday 10:00am-7:00pm (Summer), Weekends only (May, September, October). Admission: Park admission: $4.00. $1.00-5.00 per additional activity (ages 3+). Tours: Last Safari Tour One Hour Before Closing. Note, the Park closes at 6:00pm in October.

Hundreds of wild and exotic animals - alligators, buffalo, llamas, monkeys and reptile animal shows. Specially designed cruisers take you across 150 acres of rolling land where you see herds of wild and exotic animals from around the world. Tour guides travel with you giving expert information on the various species and their habitats. You will be surprised at how close you come to these animals. Also a petting zoo and fishing ponds for "tamer" activity.

Hanover

CODORUS STATE PARK

Hanover - 1066 Blooming Grove Road (PA Route 216) 17331. Phone: (717) 637-2816. www.dcnr.state.pa.us/stateparks/parks/codorus.aspx. Admission: to PA State Parks is FREE however swimming, marina and camping/lodging fees apply, with reservation or entrance.

The 1,275-acre Lake Marburg is popular with fishermen, boaters and swimmers. Codorus is also an excellent place to observe spring and fall migrations of waterfowl and warblers. The park offers interpretive programs and hikes. Boat rentals are available and a restaurant is convenient to the park. Pool, Visitor Center, Horseback Riding, Sledding, Campsites, Fishing, Trails, Winter Sports. Like Disc Golf? The site of the 2005 and 2010 state championships, Codorus Disc Golf Course is rated one of the most challenging courses in Pennsylvania.

UTZ POTATO CHIPS

Hanover - 900 High Street (SR94 North and Clearview Streets) 17331. Phone: (717) 637-6644. www.utzsnacks.com. Hours: Monday-Thursday 8:00am-4:00pm.

Occasional Fridays, by appt. Admission: FREE Tours: Self-guided. (20 minutes) Miscellaneous: Outlet store just down the road. Lots of sampling and buying goes on there. Try a new flavor - something regional like Crab or Carolina BBQ.

Walk along an elevated, glass enclosed observation gallery to observe potato chips in production. View close up TV monitors and listen to the descriptions of each step of the process. This is a modern and very clean facility. We probably got the closest to large conveyors of fried chips here (behind glass of course!). A new experience was watching home-cooked kettle chips being made. As you study family history photographs, enjoy a free bag of chips! We especially liked the "platform bridges" that they had throughout the tour so the "little ones" could see too!

SNYDERS OF HANOVER

Hanover - *1350 York Street   17731. www.snydersofhanover.com/History/ TourSnydersofHanover/. Phone: (800) 233-7125 ext. 8592. Admission: FREE. Tours: Tuesday, Wednesday, Thursday at 10:00am, 11:00am & 1:00pm. (24 hour*

notice is needed). Ages 5 and up. The tour lasts approximately 1 hour and everyone participating must be able to climb stairs.

Snyder's has been known as America's Pretzel Bakery for a century, and today, the company still makes a variety of snack foods, led by its famous hard pretzels. Free guided tours are offered with advance reservations. Meet at the

factory storefront (where you'll no doubt be nibbling on samples before touring). Watch a short video covering the company history starting with potato chips made at home in the early 1920s to the 1970s when they established sourdough hard pretzels. After that you'll see the oven room where you can

almost taste the pretzels. The guide then finishes up by showing you how potato chips are made from beginning to end. The differences you'll notice on

this snack food tour are the numerous and extra large baking ovens and highly automated packaging systems. Machines build boxes while another machine fills the bags and yet another machine boxes the bags and then seals the cases shut. Kids love all the automation!

DID YOU KNOW?

Pennsylvania is the "Snack Food" capital of the US.

SC Area

Harrisburg

FORT HUNTER MANSION & PARK

Harrisburg - *North Front Street (from US 81 take exit 66. Take North Front Street 2 miles. 17101. Phone: (717) 599-5751. www.forthunter.org. Hours: Park is open daily from 8:00am to dusk. Admission: $3.00-$5.00. Tours: Mansion tours are Tuesday-Saturday 10:00am-4:30pm, Sundays Noon-4:30pm (May-December). The Mansion is closed Mondays, Holidays and January thru April.*

Fort Hunter was part of a chain of forts along the Susquehanna River built by the British in 1756 at the outset of the French and Indian War. Spectacularly situated on a bluff overlooking the Susquehanna River and the Blue Mountain

Range, this 40 acre park invites visitors to relax and explore Pennsylvania history. Professionally guided tours of the elegantly restored Mansion look back in time to sophisticated country living in the nineteenth century. Fort Hunter is a 19th century plantation complex hosting nine structures listed on the National Register of Historic Places.

MAPLE SUGAR FESTIVAL

Harrisburg - *Fort Hunter Mansion & Park. Actual tapping of trees. Syrup making. Demonstrations of coopering and sugaring off in a realistic sugar camp. Pancakes and syrup served. FREE. (early March)*

HOLIDAY EGG HUNT

Harrisburg - *Fort Hunter Mansion & Park. Thousands of plastic eggs filled with candy and scattered on the east lawn. Hunts are scheduled. Take part in special family activities such as face painting, pony rides and more. Pre-register or drop-in. FREE. (Sunday before Easter)*

FORT HUNTER DAY

Harrisburg - *Fort Hunter Mansion & Park. Autumn festival featuring a visit from Abraham Lincoln, children's crafts and games, exhibits, farm animals, music, craft show, demonstrations, food and more. FREE. (third Sunday in September)*

PENNSYLVANIA INDIANS FESTIVAL

Harrisburg - *Fort Hunter Mansion & Park. Curious about how Pennsylvania Indians once lived? Visit a wigwam, learn about the food Indians grew and gathered, how they hunted and made fire. Watch tool making, dancing, beading and hear music. See the clothing, animals and plants they used. Food stand and a specialized museum shop. Small admission. (first Sunday in October)*

CHRISTMAS AT FORT HUNTER

Harrisburg - *Fort Hunter Mansion & Park. Decorated for the season with natural trimmings; guided tours are offered. Toy Train Exhibit. Festival of Trees. Regular admission. (mostly weekends in December but also Mansion tours regular weekday hours)*

PENNSYLVANIA STATE CAPITOL BUILDING

Harrisburg - *Third & State Streets   17101. www.pacapitol.com/. Phone: (800) TOUR-N-PA. Hours: Monday-Friday 8:30am-4:00pm, Saturday, Sunday, & Holiday 9:00am, 11:00am, 1:00pm, & 3:00pm. Closed major holidays. Admission: FREE Tours: Guided - every 1/2 hour, weekdays (except lunch - 12:00 - 1:00pm). Specific times listed for weekends above. Guided tours are only 30 minutes long and worth the time. Miscellaneous: Stop at the Information Center first for a brochure on the self-guided tour. Welcome Center is open weekdays only. Educators: wait until you see all the fun, colorful or coloring worksheets they have under Teachers Tools: www.pacapitol.com/teachers_tools.html*

The 272-foot dome will stun everyone as you stand underneath it and look up. Your neck could get sore because you'll be staring a good while. As you pass though bronze and ornately carved wooden doors, you can climb the stairs to the second and fourth floors to view the elegant and handsome Senate and House chambers. The favorite (and most educational) area is the Welcome Center. From the Ben Franklin video in miniature, to

...inside the rotunda!

Hello History (take a telephone call from famous Pennsylvania leaders and athletes) to the glass window case full of colored balls (representing the number of bills that a state legislator considers in a year - there's a lot!). Other exhibits that encourage learning about laws (for kids and adults) are interactive displays of a "Day in the Life of a Legislator" (try to get your birthday as a holiday), voting (actually sit in a voting desk) and the making of a law (presented through a colorful display - like the game "Mousetrap" full of tracks, pulleys, and chains that follow a funny course). What a wonderful way to teach government!

WHITAKER CENTER FOR SCIENCE AND THE ARTS

Harrisburg - *222 Market Street (Downtown - Diagonal to the State Capitol) 17101. Phone: (717) 214-ARTS. www.whitakercenter.org. Hours: Tuesday-Saturday 9:30am-5:00pm. Sunday 11:30am-5:00pm. Admission: $11.75-$13.75 (age 3+). IMAX additional charge. Combo discounts offered. Miscellaneous: IMAX Theatre - call (717) 214-IMAX for showtimes. Center closed Thanksgiving and Christmas Day. Food court attached by walkway. In addition to hands-on interactive exhibits, the Harsco Science Center also features Stage Two, a "black box" theater; and Big Science Theatre productions.*

WHITAKER CENTER FOR SCIENCE AND THE ARTS (cont.)

Their motto is "Question Everything". Nine different themed exhibit areas use performing arts to teach science concepts. How is dancing linked to science and physics? What are backstage secrets of how lighting and special effects

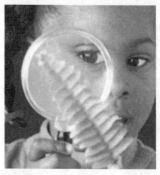

contribute to the theater experience? Have you ever "walked through" a kaleidoscope? (you can here!). The younger kids will spend most of their time in the "kids hall" (ages 8 and below) where they too, get to experiment with light and sound! Other exhibits: Health and Wellness which includes The Gallery of Anatomy, The Five Senses, Medical Technology, and Wellness; The Gallery of Mathematics in Nature and Art; People and Diversity which includes Genetics, and Culture and Communication; Environment and Ecology which includes Global Environment, Watersheds, and Pennsylvania Environments; Physics which includes Forces and Motion, Simple Machines, Bodies In Motion: The Physics of Human Movement (explores the art of the human body as it moves), and Backstage Science. KidsPlace includes a Midtown Market, Storybook Stage, Waterworks, ArtWorks, and a City Building for construction fanatics. What we like best - they are always focused on making each space engaging and change exhibits - for example, Science on a Sphere interactive globe in the Forces of Nature exhibit.

PENNSYLVANIA NATIONAL FIRE MUSEUM

Harrisburg - *1820 N. Fourth St., downtown 17102. www.pnfm.org. Phone: (717) 232-8915. Hours: Tuesday-Friday 10:00am-4:00pm, Saturday 10:00am-4:00pm, Sunday 1:00-4:00pm. Closed Mondays and Holidays. Admission: $6.00 adult, $5.00 senior, $4.00 student. Family: $20.00.*

Housed in the 1899 Victorian firehouse Reily Hose Company No. 10, the Pennsylvania National Fire Museum displays the history of the Fire and Emergency Services. Several displays feature hand and horse-drawn equipment from the 1700 and 1800's and motorized apparatus from 1911 through 1947. There is a wide array of firefighter artifacts throughout the museum including firefighters' tools and fancy parade helmets. The museum is staffed by all volunteers and they gladly answer kids' questions or will show you a video about firefighting history.

NATIONAL CIVIL WAR MUSEUM

Harrisburg - *1 Lincoln Circle at Reservoir Park (Interstate 83, Take Exit 50 West (Progress Exit & US Route 22 / Walnut Street) 17103. Phone: (717) 260-1861 or (866) BLU-GRAY. www.nationalcivilwarmuseum.org. Hours: Monday-Saturday 10:00am-5:00pm, Sunday Noon-5:00pm.Open until 8:00pm on Wednesday evenings. (Closed Thanksgiving, Christmas & New Year's Day). Closed Mondays and Tuesdays in the winter. Admission: $9.00 adult, $8.00 senior, $6.00 student, $35.00 family.*

Their Mission Statement: The only museum in the United States that attempts to portray the story of the Nation's Civil War - Equally balanced presentations are humanistic in nature without bias to Union or Confederate causes. Dioramas, digital videos and simply displayed showcases ease you through the facts. From slavery to camp life, the museum will give your kids a better understanding of our country and its people. A House Divided features comparisons of the Northern and Southern economies, the John Brown raid on Harpers Ferry, the election of Abraham Lincoln, and a map showing the division of the country. The "We the People" video introduces you to ten Americans – Northerners and Southerners, men and women, white and black, military and civilian – who endured typical hardships and heartache in the four-year conflict. Because its emphasis is on the humanness of the conflict, you will see more common artifacts - items found in homes or soldier's pockets. From the beginning at the original Confederate flag that flew over Fort Sumter to the last videotape of the 1938 reunion of Confederate and Union veterans in Vicksburg - you will "see" the war differently. Tours are educational, entertaining, sometimes emotional and look at the issues of slavery, war strategies, motivations and music.

CITY ISLAND

Harrisburg - *Walnut & Market Street Bridges (Susquehanna River) 17104. http://www.harrisburgevents.com/Common/City_Island.html. Hours: Dawn-Dusk Note: accessed by Market Street Bridge and Walnut Street Walking Bridge.*

City Island's 63 acres is hosts a variety of entertainment, food and activity vendors along with Commerce Bank Park that is home to the Harrisburg's Senators baseball club. Once ashore, a miniature train provides a leisurely round-the Island tour of all the sights and attractions. Some of the Island's most popular activities are located on its north end, where the unique Water Golf miniature golf course awaits. Nearby, the distinctive Harbourtown Children's Play area beckons visitors with a scaled-down re-creation of an 1840s canal town. Playhouse-type structures include a pirate ship, lighthouse and stores. Within feet are large sandboxes and volleyball courts, and the city's historic Beachhouse and Beach (one of the cleanest rivers in the nation). Skyline Sports Complex & Riverside Village Park eateries (east shore) include crab cakes, burgers, fries, ice cream and more. This mid-19th Century-themed retail village contains a variety of picnic facilities, gazebos, scenic decks and plenty of places to feed the Island's ever-hungry ducks and geese. Nestled against the Walnut Street Bridge is the City Island Arcade. Visitors can swim in a beautiful setting at City Island Beach, FREE. Signs are posted for lifeguard hours. Beach House is open weekends only Late May through early June from 12:00pm-7:30pm. The beach opens daily starting Mid-June - Labor Day, from 12:00pm-7:30pm. Elegant horse-drawn carriage rides are offered in-season along the waterfront. What a treat for locals and a nice appeal to visitors!

PRIDE OF THE SUSQUEHANNA RIVERBOAT TOUR

Harrisburg - *(Docked at City Island) 17104. www.harrisburgriverboat.com. Phone: (717) 234-6500. Hours: Tuesday-Sunday Noon-3:00pm (June-August) Admission: $9.00 adult, $7.00 senior (59+), $4.00 child (3-12). Wednesday has reduced fares. Tours: Indoor and outdoor seating. 40 minute narrated cruise leaves on the hour. Miscellaneous: Dinner cruises are $35.00 per person from May-October with reservation.*

This short family boat trip passes under 6 bridges and by the grave of the city's founder, John Harris on an authentic paddlewheel boat. Take your children and their special friends back to yesteryear, and experience a unique method of transportation that was used over 150 years ago. The boat is docked on the wonderful city park, City Island, which is situated in the middle of the Susquehanna River. The recorded history talk on the way out tells us that the Susquehannock Indians lived on the islands in the river and fished the waters of the Susquehanna River in the 17th Century.

HARRISBURG SENATORS BASEBALL

Harrisburg - *PO Box 15757 Commerce Bank Park (City Island) 17105. Phone: (717) 231-4444. www.senatorsbaseball.com. Admission: $4.00-$9.00*

The Harrisburg Senators, AA Class farm team of the Washington Nationals, has been a longtime favorite for baseball fans in Pennsylvania's capital city. The first stage of its $45 million renovation project of Commerce Ball Park features a new LED scoreboard, video boards around the stadium, and expanded picnic areas for families. Come see talented players hit it out of the park in the state's capitol. Meet Rascal, the mascot on Sunday afternoons.

STATE MUSEUM OF PENNSYLVANIA

Harrisburg - *300 North Street (3rd & North Street) (Downtown) 17108. Phone: (717) 787-4980. www.statemuseumpa.org. Hours: Thursday-Saturday, 9:00am-5:00pm., Sunday 12:00-5:00pm. (Closed holidays except Memorial Day and Labor Day) Admission: $4.00-$5.00 per person (age 1+). Miscellaneous: Planetarium (additional charge) shows. Gift shop - we bought some neat Dinosaur DNA dust (cherry or grape flavor) to commemorate our Dino Lab experience. FREEBIES: Scavenger Hunt Activity Sheets are here: www.statemuseumpa.org/Assets/pdf-files/scavenger-hunt/Scavenger%20Hunt.pdf. Educators: For Teachers Guides, Student Workbooks: www.statemuseumpa.org/teachers-phmc-resources.html or www.ExplorePAhistory.com.*

The Official Museum of the Commonwealth features 4 floors of historical exhibits: Geology, Archeology (pretend to dig like the professionals - what types of things are found at a typical site?), Military (Gettysburg, etc.), Industry, The Arts and Technology. Do you know what animal has the most highly developed brain? Do you know the difference between a paleontologist and an archaeologist? Do you know what important document served as an instrument of peace during a time of great turmoil? Do you know what camp near Harrisburg had more soldiers trained and organized into regiments than any other camp during the Civil War? Do you know what kind of wagon early Pennsylvania farmers used to haul their products to market? All of ancient and modern Pennsylvania history in one place.

Our favorite was the Dino Lab - a real paleontology lab tech at work carving a skeleton from a fossil rock. It is a fascinating experience - and you can even ask questions while they work! Meet a "Dunkle" fish and a mastodon too. The original charter granted to William Penn by King Charles II in 1861 is also on display. CURIOSITY CONNECTION - Interactive Computer and dress up for kids age 7 and below. The adventure begins in a Child's Magical Bedroom and

Courtesy of Pennsylvania Historical & Museum Commission

...be a bee!

continues through secret portals leading to an entire miniature world of Curiosity. Other areas such as The Living Forest, Industry and Transportation Zone, Farm Land, Construction Zone and Art Wall allow children to discover the world around them and express their creativity through interactive play. Infants and toddlers will find activities, puzzles, puppets and more in their own special place. Kids will want to check out activities that correspond to the displays in the museum.

WILDWOOD LAKE SANCTUARY

Harrisburg - 100 Wildwood Way (Lucknow Industrial Park, north of Harrisburg Area Comm. College) 17110. Phone: (717) 221-0292. www.wildwoodlake.org. Hours: Dawn to dusk. Nature Center Tuesday-Sunday 10:00am-4:00pm. Admission: FREE general admission , small fee for special programs.

It's a 212 acre lake with wonderful walkways through marshes, meadows and woodlands. The nature center has great interactive displays for children...they take a card through the exhibit and get stamps at various stations which teach them about the wetlands while creating a picture. There's also a Discovery Room with quick, easy arts and crafts. Bird enthusiasts can watch the birds from the special glass enclosed bird blind that overlooks the lake and offers numerous bird feeders that attracts an abundant number of species that come to eat. The pathways outside are well marked, paved or mulched, and lend themselves to a lot of discovery...turtles on logs, butterflies, etc. Gift shop with exploration toys. Our relatives from Pennsylvania love this place!

PENNSYLVANIA FARM SHOW

Harrisburg - Farm Show Complex. www.farmshow.state.pa.us/. The largest indoor agricultural event in America. The Farm Show Complex houses 16 acres under roof, spread throughout 7 buildings. Favorite annual events and sights delighted crowds like the 1,000-pound butter sculpture, Sheep to Shawl contest, Farm Show Detectives and Celebrity Cow Milking Contest. Visitors also enjoyed the many new attractions like the Best Burger Showdown, sticky bun contest and Broadway and puppet shows. The famed Food Court lived up to its reputation, offering the best Pennsylvania-produced products. America's Top Rodeo/Livestock Events. FREE. (second week of January)

Hershey

ANTIQUE AUTOMOBILE CLUB OF AMERICA MUSEUM

Hershey - 161 Museum Drive (322 East into Hershey and exit onto HERSHEYPARK Drive) Turn left onto Hershey Road (Rte. 39 West) at GIANT Center) 17033. Phone: (717) 566.7100. www.aacamuseum.org. Hours: Daily 9:00am-5:00pm (except major winter holidays). Admission: $7.00-$10.00 (age 4+). Note: Here's

*an entertaining self-guided childrens tour: http://www.aacamuseum.org/Pdf/
childrens-self-guide.pdf.*

What was your first car? Do you have a Dream Car? You may find them at the Museum. Museum collections currently number over 150 vehicles, at any given time, you can see 85-100 classic cars and trucks on display. The Museum's highly detailed dioramas present carefully restored vintage vehicles in elaborate scenes that bring the history of the automobile to life. From a tiny machine shop in turn-of-the-century New York to the asphalt apron of San Francisco's Golden Gate Bridge. Be sure to see the Lakeland Bus used in the Academy Award winning movie Forrest Gump. For children, the Lower Level is a place to get up close and personal with automotive stuff. In the activity room, younger visitors can ride a pedal car, do a crayon rubbing of an antique license plate and engage in a variety of hands-on projects and activities. At the Photo Stop, kids of ages can dress up in period clothing and have their picture taken sitting in a car from the Museum's sit-in fleet.

HERSHEY BEARS HOCKEY

Hershey - 100 West Hershey Park Drive (Giant Arena) 17033. Phone: (717) 534-3911. www.hersheybears.com. Admission: $16.00-$22.00. Family Four Packs w/ food offered at a discount.

AHL, Washington Capitals affiliate. Join CoCo the Bears Kids Club.

HERSHEY GARDENS

Hershey - 170 Hotel Road (on the grounds of the Hotel Hershey) 17033. Phone: (717) 534-3492. www.hersheygardens.org. Hours: Daily 9:00am-5:00pm (April-October). Extended summer evening hours. Admission: $6.00-$10.00 (age 3+).

This 23-acre botanical gem has over 7,000 roses and seasonal flower displays, 25,000 tulips in the spring, a Japanese garden and an outdoor Butterfly House with 400 butterflies. The Butterfly House Opens first weekend in June and remains open through the third Saturday in September, weather permitting. The Children's Garden provides opportunities for hands-on learning, self-discovery, and fun with water features, hideaways, creatures, surprises, whimsical characters, and more all within nearly 30 themed areas.

HERSHEY LODGE

Hershey - 325 University Drive 17033. Phone: (717) 533-3311. www.hersheylodge.com. A very family-friendly way to stay in the area comfortably. With lodging rates starting in the $159 range, it includes a free shuttle to HersheyPark and other attractions, plus, free admission to Hershey Gardens (seasonal) and Hershey Story. Often, the packages

SC Area

they offer are the best value, especially if you're planning to visit several attractions. You have the opportunity to make reservations for Breakfast in the Park with Hershey Characters, too. On site, at the lodge, are tennis courts, basketball courts, miniature golf, gameroom, bocce ball, bike rentals, and their fabulous pools – indoor and outdoor. Kids will like to eat at Lebbie Lebkichers casual buffet or the Bears' Den hockey-themed sports café. Watch the game on a 9'x12' video wall, check out the game room, and order from the $6.95 Kids Menu (we recommend the Bear Puck Dessert...or anything chocolate!). Great way to enjoy Hershey, PA without a lot of hassle.

🛏 🍽 _____

HERSHEY STORY - THE MUSEUM ON CHOCOLATE AVENUE

Hershey - *63 West Chocolate Avenue (next to arena) 17033. Phone: (717) 534-3439 or (800) HERSHEY. http://hersheystory.org/splash.aspx. Hours: Daily 10:00am-6:00pm (Summer). 10:00am-5:00pm (Winter). Holidays and peak season hours extended. Arrive early to book your Chocolate Lab Class, as they fill quickly. Classes may only be purchased at the admissions desk on the day of the class. Admission: Chocolate Lab or Museum are each: $10.00 adult, $9.00 senior (62+), $7.50 child (3-12). Or, do both and save a little. Miscellaneous: Strollers not allowed. Café Zooka light food and beverage. Apprentice Program: After paying museum admission plus $3.00, visitors can become Milton Hershey's apprentice and receive a special booklet that will help them discover the Chocolate King's secrets to success. By answering questions and solving puzzles throughout the Museum Experience, their efforts will be rewarded along the way, culminating with a commemorative coin and a personalized newspaper page. Educators: go to this link: http://hersheystory.org/education/lesson-plans/ for chocolate related lesson plans. We especially liked Chocolate Graphing.*

KISSTORY - The Story of An American Icon. From their introduction in 1907, HERSHEY'S KISSES chocolates have enjoyed a phenomenal popularity that remains to this day. Explore this fun-filled, interactive exhibit that takes a nostalgic look at one of America's most treasured treats. Learn how Mr. Hershey failed as a candy maker in Philadelphia and New York - but became a millionaire manufacturing caramels in Lancaster, Pennsylvania. He sold that business to start a chocolate factory in his birthplace farmland. See how it developed as Hershey, Pennsylvania. Go behind the scenes of innovations in chocolate (like how do they wrap Hershey Kisses?) as the centerpiece of this area comes to life with a roar and a rumble. Other exhibits explore varied aspects of Hershey, Pennsylvania. They trace its lavish architecture, much of it inspired by Milton and Kitty Hershey's travels abroad, as well as the Hershey mansion and life in the factory. We also fell in love with the Apostolic Clock

Procession which performs at special events each year. A looped video next to the clock shows the procession and explains the clock's history. Elsewhere in the museum, kids can "punch a real time clock" or sit in an original HersheyPark roller coaster car (kind of virtual reality).

CHOCOLATE LAB - Chocolate making is a sweet recipe for learning about art and science! The Chocolate Lab offers participatory classes such as molding, dipping and even making chocolate from scratch. Located on the main floor, it is inspired by Milton Hershey's own candy-making apprenticeship and his flair for experimentation. The Chocolate Lab explores the unique qualities of chocolate through playful, hands-on experiences on a variety of subjects including geography, history, economics and science.

the 13' clock
...built over 11
years

HERSHEY TROLLEY WORKS

Hershey - *(Departs at entrance to Hershey's Chocolate World) 17033. Phone: (717) 533-3000. http://hersheytrolleyworks.com. Hours: Rain or Shine. Same hours as the park. Last tour is 1 hour before closing Admission: $12.95 adult, $11.95 senior (62+), $5.95 child (3-12). Tours: The Trolley Adventure: (only available Memorial Day – Labor Day). The Christmas Adventure: (only available during Christmas Candylane). Due to limited seating, guests are encouraged to purchased tickets upon their arrival to Hershey®'s Chocolate World. Trolley tokens may only be purchased the day of the tour. Each token is valid only for a specific time.*

Family adventure through America's sweetest town. Old time songs and visits throughout from famous "characters" plus lots of little-known facts about the town as you pass historic sites. The conductors are entertaining, informative, and loaded with candy! The tour lasts about 45-60 minutes and usually includes either a stop at Founder's Hall, the focal point the Hersheys' legacy, or a stop in downtown Hershey featuring the grand lobby of the Hershey Theater.

SC Area

HERSHEYPARK

Hershey - *100 W. Hersheypark Drive (Off SR 743 & US 422) 17033. Phone: (800) HERSHEY. www.hersheypa.com. Hours: Daily - opens at 10:00am (summer). Weekends only (May, September). Admission: Range $31.95-$52.95 (Ages 3+). Preview Plan: Purchase a regular full-day admission ticket for tomorrow, 2-1/2* hours prior to Park closing, and be their guest FREE for the remainder of that evening.*

Begin by "measuring up" for size. From "Kisses" on up, the rides are rated by candy type. 110 acre theme park with 60 rides and attractions. You'll also find:

German Area, English Area, Penn Dutch Area (and food to match), a SeaLion & Dolphin Show, Night Lights Musical Laser Spectacular. 21 kiddie rides and live entertainment at Music Box Theater or the Amphitheatres. Rollercoasters you'll find include: GREAT BEAR - inverted looping roller coaster; SUPER DOOPER LOOPER - is a milder form of Great Bear; and ROLLER SOAKER - an awesome interactive water coaster.

As a grand tribute to the boardwalks of the East Coast beaches, The Boardwalk At Hersheypark will captivate you with over 100 fun-in-the-sun experiences - from the flavors, sounds, and activities of an old-fashioned boardwalk, to the exhilarating refreshment of water attractions like Coastline Plunge (with four water slides), the East Coast Waterworks (seven slides), and the largest water-play structure in the world! Just remember not to go swimming on a stomach full of chocolate!

The attractions at Hersheypark are constantly getting upgraded and added to, and new roller coasters appear every few years. The entire park is very clean and the staff, friendly.

CHRISTMAS CANDYLANE

Hershey - *Hersheypark. www.hersheypa.com or (717) 534-3090. More than 1,000,000 lights, unique shops, holiday entertainment, great food and rides. Look for Santa and his live reindeer! Admission for rides, park entrance free. Lodging packages. Breakfast with Santa. (mid-November - New Year's weekend)*

Fun with our cousins & their good friend "KitKat"

HERSHEY'S CHOCOLATE WORLD VISITORS CENTER

Hershey - *800 Park Blvd 17033. www.hersheys.com/chocolateworld/. Phone: (800) HERSHEY. Hours: Daily 10:00am-5:00pm (everyday but Christmas). - Extended hours for special events, weekends and peak season. Admission: FREE. Miscellaneous: Shuttles to other attractions leave from here. 8 unique gift shops. Food court. Chocolate Town Café. HERSHEY'S Really Big 3-D Show, an immersive three-dimensional musical featuring the HERSHEY'S Product Characters as they come to life for the first time on the big screen (movie charges fee).*

A factory tour on an automated tram into the simulated world of chocolate production! Start at the cocoa bean plantation (rainforests and tropic) to dairy farms to making chocolate through the years at Hershey. Actual video footage of a real factory and the wonderful scent of chocolate pervades. It even gets warmer as you pass through the "roaster oven" part of the ride. Souvenir photographs are taken of the passengers in each car. You can purchase them for around $10.00 at the end of the tour. Learn why different chocolate manufacturers have different flavors (the

...a bunch of Hershey bar wrappers - a treat at the end of the tour...

secret is where the cocoa beans came from). The updated Chocolate Making Tour Ride is an exciting and informative immersive experience...and it ends with a free sample!

ZOO AMERICA NORTH AMERICAN WILDLIFE PARK

Hershey - *Park Avenue (opposite Hershey Park) 17033. Phone: (717) 534-3860. www.zooamerica.com. Hours: 10:00am-5:00pm. (Open until 8:00pm in the*

summer). ZOOAMERICA is open year-round except Thanksgiving, Christmas and New Year's Day. Admission: $8.00-$9.50 (age 3+).

An eleven acre North American attraction that hosts wildlife from 5 regions (200+ species) including bears, bobcats and lynx. ZooAmerica began as The Hershey Zoo in 1916, when Milton S. Hershey opened

SC Area

his private animal collection to the public. "Desert of Night" area is unique and wonderful. "Visit" with creatures of the night like owls, snakes and bats. ZooAmerica welcomed another new addition, the black-footed ferret, which can be seen in The Great Southwest. Thought to be extinct at one point, these ferrets are one of the most endangered species on this continent. Feisty ferrets are fun to watch. The American crocodile exhibit and interactive Maze learning stations are fun zoo exhibits. Guests can even take advantage of a special falconry demonstration or naturalist educational sessions.

Hummelstown

INDIAN ECHO CAVERNS

Hummelstown - *368 Middletown Road (Off I-283 and US 322 at Hummelstown / Middletown Exits) 17036. Phone: (717) 566-8131. www.indianechocaverns.com. Hours: Daily 9:00am-6:00pm (Summer). 10:00am-4:00pm (Spring/Fall). Call for times (Winter). Admission:$13.00 adult, $11.00 senior (62+), $7.00 child (3-11). Online coupon. Tours: 45 minutes, guided Miscellaneous: Gift shop - Southwestern, Rocks, quirky items. Pan for gems at Gem Mill Junction (open seasonally). Wagon ride to the Petting Barnyard. Playground with Indian Tepee and Conestoga Wagon. Shaded picnic area.*

You'll walk the same paths that the Susquehannock Indians did hundreds of years ago and be entertained with many stories and legends surrounding Indian Echo. Check out the Wilson Room and the Story of William Wilson who lived in the caverns for 19 years - "the Pennsylvania Hermit". The Indian Ballroom is the largest room. There are 3 lakes and a variety of stalactites, stalagmites, and flowstone. As with any caverns, small, squirmy children may not enjoy the tour and get bored easily.

Imler

BLUE KNOB STATE PARK

Imler - *RR 1, Box 449 16655. Phone: (814) 276-3576. www.dcnr.state.pa.us/ stateparks/parks/blueknob.aspx. Admission: to PA State Parks is FREE however swimming, marina and camping/lodging fees apply, with reservation or entrance.*

Blue Knob State Park is named for the majestic dome-shaped mountain. Bob's Creek is great for trout fishing and Blue Knob boasts the second highest peak in the state, which gives great views of up to 42 miles. Off-peak season, ride the ski resort's chairlift for great views. All park trails are open to mountain biking and many are less than two miles long-easy hiking for families. Weather permitting, the swimming pool is open daily from 11:00am-7:00pm from Memorial Day weekend to Labor Day, unless posted otherwise. Horse-back Riding, Down-hill Skiing, Campsites, Fishing, Winter Sports.

Lewisberry

GIFFORD PINCHOT STATE PARK

Lewisberry - *2200 Rosstown Road (Route 177) 17339. Phone: (717) 432-5011. www.dcnr.state.pa.us/stateparks/parks/giffordpinchot.aspx. Admission: to PA State Parks is FREE however swimming, marina and camping/lodging fees apply, with reservation or entrance.*

Pinchot Lake is a great warm water fishery and is popular for sailing. The trails between the campground and the Conewago Day Use Area are for joint-use by hikers, cross-country skiers and bikers. There are more than 20 miles of marked and maintained trail at Gifford Pinchot State Park. Shorter trails are marked with white, double bar blazes. Most trails interconnect to allow hikers to tailor their outing to meet their individual desires. A large, ADA accessible beach in the Quaker Race Day Use Area is open from late-May to mid-September, 8:00am to sunset. Visitor Center, Boat Rentals, Horseback Riding, Disc Golf course, Sledding, Campsites, Modern Cabins, Yurts, Fishing, and Cross-Country Skiing.

SKI ROUNDTOP

Lewisberry - *925 Roundtop Road 17339. Phone: (717) 432-9631. Snow Report: (717) 432-7000. www.skiroundtop.com.*

Minutes from tourist destinations like Hershey and Gettysburg, Ski Roundtop is a four-season resort with plenty of snow sports to keep visitors busy. Roundtop was one of the first ski resorts in the area to offer tubing, where skiers can shed their skis and slide down a hill in an inner tube. Roundtop and nearby ski resorts – Liberty and Whitetail – are now under the same management, so skier discount cards and season passes are transferable among the three resorts. Magic Mountain area is set aside just for kids. With its own Magic Carpet lift, your children can learn in a secure area physically separated from the other slopes. Longest Run: 4100 ft.; 15 Slopes & Trails - Skiing and Snowtubing.

Mercersburg

WHITETAIL SKI RESORT AND MOUNTAIN BIKING CENTER

Mercersburg - *13805 Blairs Valley Road 17236. www.skiwhitetail.com. Phone: (717) 328-9400.*

Longest Run: 4900 ft.; 17 Slopes & Trails. Terrain Park: 1 rail, 8 snow features, and a fun box for snow tubing and snow boarding. SnowMonsters kids program.

Middletown

MIDDLETOWN AND HUMMELSTOWN RAILROAD

Middletown - *136 Brown Street (SR283 to Middletown exit - Race Street Station) 17057. Phone: (717) 944-4435. www.mhrailroad.com. Hours: Memorial Day Weekends - October. July & August - Tuesday and Thursday also. Admission: Regularly scheduled: $7.00-$12.00 (age 2+). Tours: Generally departures at 10:00am, Noon and 1:30pm. Check schedule for detailed times. You don't want to miss the train. Miscellaneous: Special event trains- Reservations suggested. New: Little Red Caboose Rides.*

The yard has several rail cars on display. During the ride, the train follows the towpath of the historic Union Canal and alongside the peaceful Swatara. The narrator relates the history of the Canal (completed in 1827) and the location of Canal Lock #33, as well as a century old limekiln and Horse Thief Cave. Passengers will want to have their cameras out while crossing a 35-foot bridge above the Swatara Creek. On the return trip from Indian Echo Cave Platform, you will enjoy a "sing-a-long" of tunes from the railroading days, as well as fun songs for young and old alike. Can you still "Chicken Dance"?

EASTER BUNNY TRAIN RIDES

Middletown - *Middletown And Hummelstown Railroad. Candy treats with the Easter Bunny riding along. Live music. Admission. (Easter Weekend and weekend before)*

CIVIL WAR REMEMBERED

Middletown - *Middletown And Hummelstown Railroad. Reenactment with skirmishes along the tracks and during the ride. Trains leave two times each day. Admission. (last weekend in September)*

SANTA EXPRESS OR THE POLAR EXPRESS

Middletown - *Middletown And Hummelstown Railroad. Sing songs and eat treats as you ride the train with Santa aboard. Admission. (Saturdays in December)*

New Park

MAIZE QUEST FUN PARK

New Park - *2885 New Park Road. www.mazefunpark.com. Petting zoo, refreshments, pumpkin patch, corn maze, pony or wagon rides. 10 acres of corn maze with fountains and bridges. Indoor Playground. Admission. (outdoor park open weekends in September and October thru mid-November)*

Newport

LITTLE BUFFALO STATE PARK

Newport - *RD 2, Box 256A (PA Route 34) 17074. Phone: (717) 567-9255. www. dcnr.state.pa.us/stateparks/parks/littlebuffalo.aspx. Admission: to PA State Parks is FREE however swimming, marina and camping/lodging fees apply, with reservation or entrance.*

Explore historical features including a covered bridge, restored grist mill, an old farm house built on the site of a colonial tavern, and a narrow gauge railroad. Programs are offered year-round. Many programs feature Shoaff's Mill. Over 12,000 people visit the mill annually. Today, the Perry County Historical Society operates and maintains a museum and library in the farmhouse. Members volunteer to open the museum every Sunday during the summer months. For more detailed information on programs, contact the park office. Little Buffalo has approximately 8 miles of hiking trails. Sturdy footwear is recommended because of rocky footing on some of the trails. Pool, Visitor Center, Year-round Education & Interpretation Center, Boat Rentals, Sledding, Fishing, and Trails.

SC Area

CHRISTMAS WALK

Newport - *Little Buffalo State Park. This family oriented activity has become a popular holiday event in the county. Thousands of lights and holiday cutouts dot the East Picnic Area and provide the perfect holiday atmosphere. Santa always makes an appearance. Local 4-H Clubs sell cookies and hot chocolate. Local choirs sing carols many of the nights. (evenings one week mid-December)*

Newville

COLONEL DENNING STATE PARK

Newville - **1599 Doubling Gap Road (Doubling Gap, North Cumberland County, along PA Route 233) 17241. Phone: (717) 776-5272. www.dcnr.state.pa.us/ stateparks/parks/coloneldenning.aspx. Admission: to PA State Parks is FREE however swimming, marina and camping/lodging fees apply, with reservation or entrance.**

The wooded park area nestles at the side of a mountain and has a scenic lake and excellent hiking trails. A hike on a 2.5 mile trail rises to Flat Rock for a beautiful vista of the Cumberland Valley. The one-mile, self-guiding Doubling Gap Trail is a moderate hike. The Hiking and Nature Trail Guide is available at the park office and has a map and detailed description of the hiking trails in the park and surrounding forest lands. The sand beach is open from late-May to mid-September, 8:00am to sunset. A visitor center, exhibiting plants, animals and minerals found in the park, is open during the summer season. Campsites, Fishing, and Cross-Country Skiing.

Orrtanna

MR. ED'S ELEPHANT MUSEUM

Orrtanna - **6019 Chambersburg Road (along Rte. 30, 12 miles outside of Gettysburg) 17353. Phone: (717) 352-3792. www.mistereds.com. Hours: Daily 10:00am-5:00pm. Admission: FREE.**

Forty-two years ago Ed Gotwalt began collecting elephants. Now that collection - 6,000 pachyderms in all - is his livelihood. As you approach the place, you're greeted by Miss Ellie, a 9.5 foot tall white elephant with animated eyes and ears who may wink at you as you walk near. Miss Ellie also talks, blathering about the area, telling a few jokes and then goes back to sleep. Inside, although nothing is labeled, Ed is ready to share the story behind any treasure you ask about. You would not believe the different kinds of elephant collectibles you will find.... from an elephant potty chair to a hair dryer.... there is even an elephant pulling a 24-karat gold circus wagon. The reason most kids love this place - Ed sells peanuts and boasts that he has the largest selection of candy in the area - like a room full of Pez candy.

Schellsburg

SHAWNEE STATE PARK

Schellsburg - *Box 67 (Ten miles west of historic Bedford along Route 30) 15559. Phone: (814) 733-4218. www.dcnr.state.pa.us/stateparks/parks/shawnee.htm. Admission: to PA State Parks is FREE however swimming, marina and camping/ lodging fees apply, with reservation or entrance.*

Of particular interest is Shawnee's long sand and turf beach that receives ample use between Memorial Day and Labor Day. The lake is popular for boating and fishing. Boat Rentals, Mountain Biking, Sledding, Campsites, Modern Cabins, Trails, and Winter Sports.

Thomasville

MARTIN'S POTATO CHIPS

Thomasville - *5847 Lincoln Highway (US Route 30) 17364. Phone: (717) 792-3565 or (800) 272-4477. www.martinschips.com. Admission: FREE. Tours: Tuesdays @ 9:00, 10:00 and 11:00am. 45 minutes long. Closed-toe shoes required. Cameras permitted.*

Enjoying the benefit of the rich loamy soil, farmers had to find ways to use their excess crops. From the farm kitchen of Harry and Fairy Martin in 1941, a unique potato chip found its way into homes. All potato chips and popcorn are made in their 40,000 sq. ft. Thomasville facility which produces over one million bags each month. Presidents G.W. Bush, Clinton and Obama may have munched on Martin's Potato Chips at 10,000 feet aboard Air Force One. Take the Martin's tour and you'll get a fresher chip than even the president when you sample them hot off the line.

York

HARLEY-DAVIDSON MOTORCYCLE MUSEUM TOUR

York - *1425 Eden Road (on US30 or Exit 21 East of I-83) 17402. Phone: (877) 883-1450. www.harleydavidson.com. Hours: Tour center and gift shop 8:00am-4:00pm Monday thru Friday and some summer Saturdays. Admission: FREE Tours: Tours begin at regular intervals between 9:00a.m.and 2:00p.m. Monday through Friday. Tickets are distributed on a first-come, first-served basis. It is recommended that you arrive early in the day. Modified tours may be conducted due to manufacturing requirements. Tours are not offered on weekends, major holidays, during the week of July 4th or during production changes and year-end maintenance. Closed toe shoes are required for factory floor tour. (Plant tour is for ages 12+, however there are no age restrictions on the museum tour) Miscellaneous: Tours are wheelchair accessible. Souvenir Shop.*

What little traveler hasn't seen (or better yet - heard) a Harley-Davidson motorcycle pass by? Founded in 1903, Harley-Davidson has become a passion of the American dream. See over 20 vintage and famous Harleys

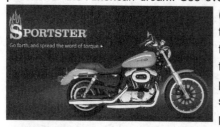

(Malcolm Forbes' custom bike) on the museum tour that is available for all ages (even a Kids Rally area for the little tykes). You will see photographs and videos of the 24 step manufacturing process that produces a completed motorcycle every 6 minutes! They are so confident in their quality and reliability that the first time an engine is started (it contains over 400 parts!) is when the bike is completely finished. An associate takes a few spins around the 1 mile long test track (what a great job!) to be sure that it meets all the standards and expectations of the waiting customer. More than 3,000 employees work around the clock assembling Touring and Softail® models, as well as limited production, factory-custom motorcycles. They perform a variety of manufacturing operations - from machining, polishing and chrome plating, to forming, welding and painting.

DID YOU KNOW?

What does a doctor, a lawyer, machine operator, actor, business owner, and pastor all have in common... a Harley-Davidson motorcycle!

At the Vaughn L. Beals Tour Center, you'll explore exhibits that detail the plant's history, and guide you through the manufacturing and assembly processes. You'll also have the chance to sit on current production motorcycles and visit the gift shop for tour-related souvenirs. The Kids' Rally, a specially designed area for visitors under the age of 12, makes the York facility an ideal family destination.

AGRICULTURAL & INDUSTRIAL MUSEUMS

York - *480 East Market Street / 217 West Princess Street (US30 to George Street exit, Rte. 462 into downtown) 17403. www.yorkheritage.org. Phone: (717) 852-7007. Hours: Tuesday-Saturday 10:00am-4:00pm. Admission: $5.00-$10.00 for One ticket for Ag & Industrial, Fire & Historical Museums-all York Cty heritage trust sites. We recommend the Industrial Museum (Princess Street) most. Educators: Ask for the scavenger hunt before you venture into this maze of artifacts. Pre/ Post Visit Resources on Colonial and Civil War times are found on this link: http:// yorkheritage.org/ep_tp.asp*

Learn about York County's many contributions to agricultural and industrial progress on a visit to the Agricultural and Industrial Museum. Agricultural artifacts produced or used in the county over three centuries include locally made wagons, tractors, steam engines and farm tools. Visit the newest exhibit Marvelous Milk: From the Farm to Your Table, where students learn about the dairy industry in York County and get the opportunity to milk a (reproduction) cow, Annabelle. A lot of products produced here have clothed, sheltered, transported, fed, and entertained the nation. Learn how the modern day farm evolved from the time of Native Americans. Then, go a few streets away to explore the numerous products made in York. Begin in an old gristmill (still working - you'll see), pull a factory whistle (time to go home!) or use an old rotary phone to dial up a friend next door (watch the mechanics of the operation station tapping out the numbers). The Pfaltzgraff pottery exhibit is well done with several stages of pottery being made (sometimes a potter comes in for live demonstrations). Since the Pfaltzgraff tour has age restrictions and is rather long, you may vote this exhibit more family-friendly than an actual tour. Don't forget about CAT trucks (get in the cab) and York Peppermint Patties!

YORK COUNTY HERITAGE MUSEUMS

York - *250 East Market Street (US 30 to George Street exit, follow signs to downtown) 17403. Phone: (717) 848-1587. www.yorkheritage.org. Hours: Tuesday-Saturday 10:00am-4:00pm, Sunday Noon-4:00pm. Winter hours only*

York industry has reached around the world!

weekends. Admission: $5.00-$10.00 for One ticket for Ag & Industrial, Fire & Historical Museums-all York Cty heritage trust sites. Educators: Ask for the scavenger hunt before you venture into this maze of artifacts. Pre/Post Visit Resources on Colonial and Civil War times are found on this link: http:// yorkheritage.org/ep_tp.asp

When you venture downtown, be sure to visit the campus of historical buildings on West Market Street. These buildings include a replica of the courthouse where the Second Continental Congress met, as well as an authentic tavern dating back to 1741. A reproduction of original York village square with Bonham House (beautiful home), General Gates House, and Bobb Log House.

- GOLDEN PLOUGH TAVERN (c. 1741), the city's oldest structure, gives a taste of life during the years when the Tavern housed travelers and served local residents.

- GENERAL HORATIO GATES HOUSE (c. 1751): this English-style house was the General's home while he attended the Continental Congress, and is said to have been the site of LaFayette's famous toast to Washington that sent a signal to conspirators that the French would not support a plot to replace Washington with Gates.

- BOBB LOG HOUSE (c. 1812) is an example of the simple structures popular along the Pennsylvania frontier at the turn of the 19th century.

- HORACE BONHAM HOUSE, with original furnishings of the artist, reveals the social and cultural changes that took place between the Civil War and the turn of the century.

YORK LITTLE THEATRE

York - *27 South Belmont Street 17403. Phone: (717) 854-3894. www.ylt.org.*

Family hits like Sound of Music and Seuss….Many productions include youth performers. Children's Shows - all tickets are $8.00.

YORK COUNTY FIRE MUSEUM

York - *757 West Market Street 17404. www.yorkheritage.org. Phone: (717) 843-0464. Hours: Saturday 10:00am-4:00pm. Closed winter. Admission: $5.00-$10.00 for One ticket for Ag & Industrial, Fire & Historical Museums-all York Cty heritage trust sites.*

The Fire Museum of York County displays more than 200 years of firefighting. All seventy-two fire companies of York County are represented here, with some of them dating back to before the American Revolution. The beautiful turn-of-the-century fire house contains a series of displays of how firefighters progressed from the early Leather Bucket Brigades to Hand Drawn Carts and Pumps, to Horse Drawn Apparatus, and finally to Motorized Equipment. All of the equipment is original and full-size. Pull a Fire Alarm Box or visit an old fashioned Fire Chief's Sleeping Quarters, complete with brass slide pole.

WOLFGANG CANDY COMPANY

York - *50 East 4th Avenue (SR30 to North George Street - south to Fourth Avenue) 17405. Phone: (717) 843-5536 or (800) 248-4273. www.wolfgangcandy.com. Hours: Monday-Friday 8:00am-4:30pm, Saturday 10:00am-3:00pm. Admission: FREE Tours: Walk in Tours are Monday - Thursday 10:00am and 2:00pm. 1/2 hour long. Groups by appointment only. Miscellaneous: Candy shoppe and soda fountain (Das Sweeten Haus Center). Relax on an antique stool (and watch the girls make hand dipped raisin clusters) as you enjoy a dish of Wolfgang's ice cream and sip a coffee or hot chocolate.*

I really was excited about the tour... just didn't like the hair net...

Recently voted one the "Top 5 Tasty Tours" in the Nation by the Food Network, a tour of Wolfgang Candy allows you to see, smell, and taste your favorite candy being created and learn about the unique history behind this fifth generation, family-owned business. When you enter the Bavarian style shop to wait for your tour, you undoubtedly first glance at the antique truck parked in the middle of the main floor. This was the original delivery truck used to sell chocolate candies door to door back in the 1920s. It is also the truck that helps "Candy Dan" in his flying video tour of the factory. If you choose not to go on the tour at all, this video is a great "birdseye view" of a tour but with a children's twist. The actual facility started in the back of the Wolfgang house and grew and grew. You'll pass retired family members' homes as you adorn a white hair net and walk up to the factory. You will be amazed as you watch peanut butter centers covered in creamy milk chocolate and feast your eyes on the process that transforms tiny salty pretzels into chocolate-covered delights. At the conclusion of your Wolfgang tour, watch it all come together on a hand-packing line reminiscent of that signature I LOVE LUCY episode we all know and love. Smell and taste samples as you go. The guide kept the kids' attention by pointing out lessons they learn in school. The girls and guys on the line must pick partners and pay attention (sound like school?). We recommend Fall through Easter as the best time to see candy and fillings actually made on the line (it's easier to understand the tour during full production). Summertime has minimal production.

CHRISTMAS MAGIC - A FESTIVAL OF LIGHTS

York - *Rocky Ridge County Park.   http://www.yorkcountyparks.org/chmagic.html. Christmas Magic is a 0.5 mile long walking trail (accessible to anyone) that meanders through 400,000 Christmas lights, holiday scenes and five enclosed heated pavilions. Walk thru glistening lights in a village with Santa, a mini-train display, Penguin village, food & entertainment. Admission per person. (Thanksgiving weekend thru December)*

SHOE HOUSE

York (Hellam) - *197 Shoe House Road (Just south of Rt. 30, 4 miles east of York, north off Hwy 462) 17315. Phone: (717) 840-8339. www.shoehouse.us. Hours: Wednesday-Sunday 11:00am-5:00pm (summer). Weekends 1:30-5:00pm (September, October). Admission: $3.00-$4.50 (age 4+).*

Haines Shoe House along the Lincoln Highway is a home stuffed into a white, 25-foot stucco boot. The odd shaped building seen from the Lincoln Highway

 was built by a shoe store chain owner as a promotional gimmick. Colonel Haines was a flamboyant millionaire aptly named the "Shoe Wizard." The house measures 48 ft. in length, 17 ft. in width at the widest part and 25 ft. in height. The interior consists of three bedrooms, two baths, a kitchen and living room. Take a personal tour of the Shoe House and view the interesting rooms on the five different levels. See the curved eating booth in the kitchen located in the heel of the shoe house. Count the number of stained-glass windows with pictures of shoes. Relax in the soul of the shoe with a snack and some homemade ice cream, or picnic on the grounds. Look for the shoe dog house and the shoe mailbox.

SC Area

Zionsville

STAHL'S POTTERY FESTIVAL

Zionsville - *Stahl's Pottery, 6826 Corning Road www.stahlspottery.org. Tour historic, early 20th century wood-fired kiln and pottery site. Potting techniques demonstrated. Over 15 contemporary potters display and sell their wares. Light lunch available. FREE. (third Saturday of June)*

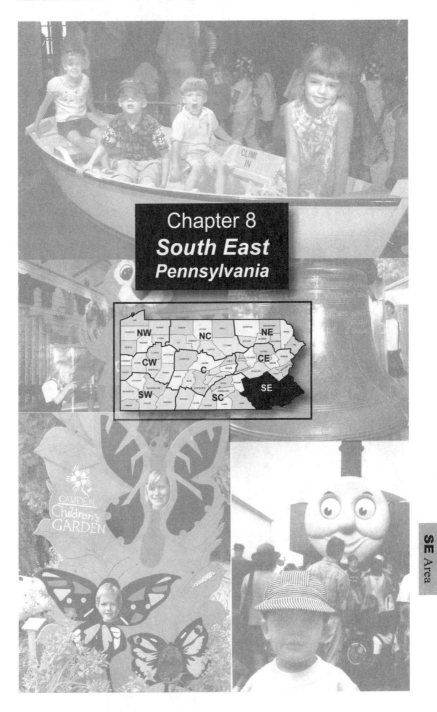

Chapter 8
South East
Pennsylvania

Audubon
- Mill Grove, The Audubon Wildlife Sanctuary

Bensalem
- Neshaminy State Park

Bernville
- Koziar's Christmas Village

Bird-In-Hand
- Americana Museum
- Plain & Fancy Farm

Birdsboro
- Daniel Boone Homestead

Boyertown
- Boyertown Museum Of Historic Vehicles

Chadds Ford
- Brandywine Battlefield Park
- Brandywine River Museum

Collegeville
- Evansburg State Park

Columbia
- National Watch & Clock Museum
- Wright's Ferry Mansion

Cornwall
- Cornwall Iron Furnace

Downingtown
- Marsh Creek State Park

Doylestown
- Mercer Museum
- Moravian Pottery And Tile Works & Fonthill
- Polish American Festival

Doylestown (Chalfont)
- Byers' Choice Ltd

Doylestown (Pipersville)
- Ralph Stover State Park

Elverson
- French Creek State Park
- Hopewell Furnace National Historic Site

Fort Washington
- Fort Washington State Park

Grantville
- Memorial Lake State Park

Intercourse
- Intercourse Pretzel Factory
- Kitchen Kettle Village

Kempton
- Hawk Mountain
- W.K. & S. Steam Railroad

Kennett Square
- Longwood Gardens

King Of Prussia
- Scottish And Irish Music Festival And Fair, Greater Philadelphia

Kutztown
- Crystal Cave
- Rodale Institute Farm
- Kutztown Folk Festival

Lahaska
- Peddler's Village

Lancaster
- Dutch Apple Dinner Theatre
- Hands-On House Children's Museum
- Landis Valley Museum
- Amish Farm And House
- Biblical Tabernacle Reproduction / Mennonite Information Center
- Dutch Wonderland Family Amusement Park
- Fulton Steamboat Inn
- Lancaster Science Factory
- Lancaster Barnstormers Baseball
- North Museum Of Natural History And Science
- Wheatland
- American Music Theatre

Lancaster (Paradise)
- National Christmas Center

Lancaster (Willow Street)
- Hans Herr House

Lancaster / Strasburg
- Sight & Sound Theatres

Langhorne
- Sesame Place

Langhorne (Newtown)
- Tyler State Park

Lititz
- Sturgis Pretzel Bakery
- Wilbur Chocolate Co.
- Wolf Sanctuary Of PA

Manheim
- Celtic Fling & Highland Games

Manheim
- Pennsylvania Renaissance Faire

Media
- Linvilla Orchards

Media (Newtown Square)
- Ridley Creek State Park

Morgantown
- Hay Creek Apple Festival

Morrisville
- Pennsbury Manor

New Hope
- New Hope & Ivyland Railroad
- New Hope Boat Rides

Norristown
- Elmwood Park Zoo

Nottingham
- Herr's Snack Factory Tour

Penns Creek
- T & D 'S Cats Of The World Wild Animal Refuge

Philadelphia
- Philadelphia Sports
- Philly Cheesesteak
- Philly Transportation & Tours

Philadelphia (cont.)
- Philadelphia Orchestra
- Academy Of Natural Sciences
- Franklin Institute Museum
- Philadelphia Zoo
- Univ. Of Pennsylvania Museum Of Archaeology & Anthropology
- World Café Live
- Atwater Kent, Museum Of Philadelphia
- Betsy Ross House
- Carpenter's Hall
- Christ Church
- City Tavern
- Declaration (Graff) House
- Federal Reserve Bank
- Fireman's Hall
- Franklin Court
- Franklin Fountain
- Franklin Square
- Independence Hall
- Independence Seaport Museum
- Independence Visitor Center (For The Nat'l Historical Park)
- Jones Restaurant
- Liberty Bell
- Lights Of Liberty
- National Constitution Center
- National Liberty Museum
- Ride The Ducks Tours
- Shane's Candies
- Thaddeus Kosciuszko Memorial
- Todd House
- U.S. Mint
- Doubletree Hotel Philadelphia
- Philadelphia City Hall Obsv.Deck
- Reading Terminal Market
- Eastern State Penitentiary
- Philadelphia Museum Of Art
- Fairmount Park
- Please Touch Museum
- Insectarium
- Mummers Museum
- Philadelphia Phillies Park Tours
- Wachovia Center Tours
- Fort Mifflin
- Heinz National Wildlife Refuge
- Philadelphia International Children's Festival
- Battle Of Germantown Re-Enactment

SE Area

Philadelphia (Chestnut Hill)
- Morris Arboretum

Philadelphia Area (Camden, Nj)
- Adventure Aquarium
- Battleship New Jersey
- Camden Children's Garden

Quakertown
- Nockamixon State Park

Quarryville
- Fulton (Robert) Birthplace

Reading
- Mid Atlantic Air Museum
- Reading Phillies Baseball
- Nolde Forest Environmental Education Center
- Reading Public Museum

Ronks
- Amazing Maize Maze

Schaefferstown
- Alexander Schaeffer Farm Museum

Shartlesville
- Roadside America

Spring Mount
- Spring Mountain Adventures

Strasburg
- Ed's Buggy Rides
- Amish Village
- Choo Choo Barn, Traintown Usa
- Railroad Museum Of Pennsylvania
- Strasburg Railroad

Strasburg (Paradise)
- National Toy Train Museum

Upper Black Eddy
- Delaware Canal State Park
- Ringing Rocks Park

Valley Forge
- Valley Forge National Historical Park

Warminster
- Bucks County Zoo & Animal Junction

Washington's Crossing
- Washington Crossing Historic Park

West Chester
- American Helicopter Museum
- QVC Studio Tour

Wyomissing
- Berk's County Heritage Center

A Quick Tour of our Hand-Picked Favorites Around...

South East Pennsylvania

Lancaster County is home to America's oldest Amish settlement, where tens of thousands still live an old "Plain" lifestyle. Horse & buggy remain a primary form of transportation and windmills dot the countryside. **Pennsylvania Dutch Country** offers tours of authentic Amish Homes or, stay on a nearby farm where kids can help milk cows or gather eggs, make preserves, help with planting or harvest activities, and learn about what goes into living an agricultural life.

With the Amish come decisions about food – where to eat and what food stores to visit. Pretzel Factories and buffet dining options abound. There is at least one dozen of each to choose from. The oldest factory, **Sturgis Pretzel**, is in Lititz and still offers a pretzel "ticket" and a quick lesson on twisting your own pretzel by hand. Probably one of the best food factory tours in the USA is found south of Lancaster, off Rte 1 in Nottingham – **Herr's Snack Factory Tour**. Following a curious mascot video tour, your guide takes you through the whole process of making potato chips – with free, warm chip samples at the end-of-the-line!

Families visiting the Lancaster area can enjoy all of the fun and entertainment the county has to offer. Take the kids to Dutch Wonderland for a day of rides (a very manageable park for 2 to 10 year olds), games and live show theaters. Our favorite theater is **Sight & Sound** – it's like the stories you heard as kids come to life.

The **Strasburg Rail Road** and neighboring **Train Museums** also have your ticket to fun. Travel past Amish farms aboard authentically restored passenger cars pulled by a steam locomotive. "Meet" giant locomotives or be dazzled by miniature train displays. **Roadside America**, a touristy indoor mini-railroad in Shartlesville, is in the northern part of this region of the state. Even though it looks old-fashioned, the interactive display engages every kid or "kid-at-heart" as you discover small details around every bend.

Early America was full of new businesses. One such business was pottery and tile works – best displayed in quirky ways in Doylestown at the **Mercer Museum**. While the tile works are down the street (next to the mansion), kids really gravitate to the old stone castle full of objects made obsolete by the Industrial Revolution. Grab a scavenger hunt worksheet and try to find your way through the most eccentric, yet curiously fun, museum you'll ever find. And, Sesame Place is not too far away.

Begin your Philadelphia adventure on a **Ride The Ducks** quacking tour through Old Town. On board, you'll learn about all there is to see and do – from a humorous perspective! After grubbing on some delicious Philly Cheesesteaks from a street vendor, head east to the Historic District, where you'll find **The Liberty Bell**, **Independence Hall** and **Franklin Court**. First check in at the **Independence Visitor Center** to get your free timed tickets (or order them online for a small fee before you arrive) before heading off to see the sights. Scattered throughout this area are also several Once Upon a Nation storytelling benches, where you can rest your feet and hear a tale about Colonial Philadelphia. In the evening, be sure to make reservations for the imaginative **Lights of Liberty** tour. You won't believe how magical the night sky brings historic figures back to life.

Once you've gotten your fill of history, other options like the **Insectarium** (north of town) and Art, Children's (younger set) or Science museums (older kids) like Franklin Institute prevail. This city allows you to look under a microscope at bugs, crawl like bugs and even eat bugs!

Sites and attractions are listed in order by City, Zip Code, and Name. Symbols indicated represent:

 Festivals   🍽 Restaurants   🛏 Lodging

SE Area

Audubon

MILL GROVE, THE AUDUBON WILDLIFE SANCTUARY

Audubon - *Audubon & Pawlings Roads 19407. http://pa.audubon.org. Phone: (610) 666-5593. Hours: Tuesday-Saturday 10:00am-4:00pm, Sunday 1:00-4:00pm. Admission: $2.00-$4.00 (age 4+).*

Early 1800s home of noted artist, author and nature lover, John James Audubon. The house displays Audubon's paintings of birds and a complete set of his greatest work, "The Birds of America". Kids seem to admire the stuffed bird collection and birds' eggs. Grounds with nature trails and bird sanctuary are open dawn to dusk.

HOLIDAY OPEN HOUSE

Audubon - *Mill Grove. Celebration of John James Audubon's love of nature. They've brought the outside in and decked the halls of the Audubon art museum with natural decorations and whimsical teasel critters. A critter scavenger hunt for the children and holiday treats await you. Museum gift shop open for holiday shopping. FREE. (first Sunday in December)*

Bensalem

NESHAMINY STATE PARK

Bensalem - *3401 State Road (follow PA 132 signs towards Delaware River @ State Road and Dunks Ferry Road) 19020. Phone: (215) 639-4538. www.dcnr.state.pa.us/ stateparks/parks/neshaminy.aspx. Admission: FREE. Pool and camping require fees. Miscellaneous: The Playmasters Theatre Workshop: The playhouse, on State Road, offers entertainment throughout the year. Visit www.playmasters.org.*

Can you feel the ocean's tides in Pennsylvania? You can at Neshaminy State Park. Waves won't knock you down, but if you watch the river, you'll see it rise or fall an inch a minute. Even though the river flows another 116 miles from here to the ocean, you're at sea level. When the tide comes in at a New Jersey beach, the water rises here also. Because tides affect this part of the river, it's called an estuary.

Neshaminy State Park provides boating access to the Delaware River. The picnic areas and seasonal swimming pool are the most popular park attractions. River Walk Trail: The trailheads for both River Walk trails begin and end on Logan Walk. The River Walk Trail follows the shoreline and gives views of the river with its boating traffic, and also explores the tidal marsh. The River Trail Inner Loop explores the interior of the park and is a great way to discover animals and plants. The River Walk Brochure compares the past to the present, and describes some of the river inhabitants like sturgeon, shad and eel. Puzzles help children explore the estuary, river and tidal marsh. This self-guiding brochure is available at the park office. Fishing, Boating (unlimited hp motors permitted), and Cross-Country Skiing.

Bernville

KOZIAR'S CHRISTMAS VILLAGE

Bernville - *Off SR 183. www.koziarschristmasvillage.com. Glistening lights. Visit with Santa. Hot chocolate. Freshly baked cookies. Toy/gift shops. Weekend entertainment. Top 10 PA Travel Attractions. Walk-thru. Admission. (Evenings - late November through New Year's Day)*

Bird-in-Hand

AMERICANA MUSEUM

Bird-in-Hand - **2709 Old Philadelphia Pike, Rte. 340 17505. Phone: (717) 391-9780. www.bird-in-hand.com/americanamuseum/. Hours: Tuesday thru Saturday 10:00 AM to 5:00 PM (April thru November). Admission: $2.00-$4.00 (age 6+).**

Step back to a time when cigars were two for a nickel, a can of soup cost a dime, and a shave was only fifteen cents. Take a nostalgic walk through small town America at the dawn of the 20th century. Museum exhibits include a barber shop, woodworking shop, tea parlor, print shop, millinery, toy store, blacksmith shop, tobacco shop, apothecary, wheelwright shop, and a country general store, where neighbors often gathered to share news and play a friendly game of checkers beside the potbelly stove. Self-guided tours are offered throughout the day.

PLAIN & FANCY FARM

Bird-In-Hand - **3121 Old Philadelphia Pike (7 miles east on SR340) 17505. Phone: (717) 768-4400 or (800) 441-3505. www.plainandfancyfarm.com. Hours:) Monday-Saturday 8:30am-5:00pm,   Sunday 10:30am-6:00pm (April-October). Extended summer hours. Monday-Sunday 10:00am-5:00pm (November-March). Admission: $5.00-$10.00 per person/ per activity (Depending on Activity). Combo**

pricing packages and coupons online. Miscellaneous: Plain & Fancy Restaurant - all you can eat home style meals served family style (pass around large tables). Go with an appetite to get your money's worth. There are gift shops, one with ice cream and another serving soft pretzels.

Here's what you can do (choose one or a combo):

*   "THE AMISH EXPERIENCE" - Only one of three "experimental" F/X theatres in North America - they use actual props, 5 projectors, 3D imagery, dramatic stage lighting and "surround sound" to tell a story. The story is of an Amish family and their teenage son who is in a "runabout time" - trying to decide which world he wants to embrace. (85% of Amish teens stay within the church even after experiencing the outside world). It tells a great Amish story (past and present) and is very dramatic - probably best for ages 8 and older. www.amishexperience.com.

The Amish Experience Theater ♥ Bird-in-Hand ♥ Pennsylvania

*   AMISH COUNTRY HOMESTEAD - see how Amish live today through a 9-room house. Learn about Amish living, furniture, chores and clothing, and adapting to life without electricity. Includes new Amish schoolroom.

*   AARON & JESSICA'S BUGGY RIDES - 3.5 mile buggy ride tour of Amish farmlands. Sleigh rides too (winter)! www.amishbuggyrides.com (717) 768-8828. Usually runs $10.00-$12.00 per person. Children half price.

Birdsboro

DANIEL BOONE HOMESTEAD

Birdsboro - 400 Daniel Boone Road (off US422 - 1 mile north) 19508. Phone: (610) 582-4900. www.danielboonehomestead.org. Hours: Grounds: Daily 9:00am-5:00pm. Visitor Center and historic area are open Sundays from 12:00 - 4:30pm. Admission: Grounds fee $3.00 (age 6+). Guided tour of Boone House (tours last 30-45 minutes) is $4.00-$6.00 per person and includes the Grounds fee. Tours: Miscellaneous: The Daniel Boone Homestead offers a variety of walking/hiking possibilities throughout the site. The gravel path winds around the historic area and is about ¾ of a mile in distance. A short trail takes you around the Lake and there are hiking/bridle trails. Daniel Boone Lake, created by damming the Owatin

Creek, runs through the Homestead property. Fishing is permitted with a valid fishing license during regular visiting hours.

Historic and legendary, Daniel Boone embodies the cherished American characteristics of rugged individual and adventurer. Born here in 1734, the birthplace interprets the colonial Pennsylvania rural life of Daniel Boone. Daniel spent his first 16 years here before his family migrated to North Carolina. Today, the site tells the story of

Courtesy of Pennsylvania Historical & Museum Commission

Daniel's youth and the saga of the region's 18th century settlers by contrasting their lives and cultures. You'll be able to sort through fact and fiction as you tour the historic site which includes the Boone House, 18th century structures, a lake, picnic areas, and recreational facilities. A restored 10 room Boone homestead (originally a log cabin), a similar cabin, sawmill, smokehouse, spring kitchen, blacksmith, and barn are on site. Be sure to watch the video presentation (re-enacted) to get a sense of the Boone family's life here and out-of-state. The Daniel Boone Homestead offers a variety of walking/hiking possibilities as well. The local Amity Lions Club has provided a ¼ mile sensory trail for the visually impaired.

Boyertown

BOYERTOWN MUSEUM OF HISTORIC VEHICLES

Boyertown - *28 Warwick Street (SR73 and 562 - South to Warwick) 19512. Phone: (610) 367-2090. www.boyertownmuseum.org/. Hours: Tuesday-Sunday 9:30am-4:00pm. Admission: $4.00-$6.00 (age 6+).*

See Pennsylvania's transportation heritage - carriages, wagons, trucks, bicycles, and cars. Also on display are 18th and 19th century vehicles built by Pennsylvania Dutch craftsmen and the tools that were used to assemble them. Discover rare and handsome vehicles you have never seen before and won't find anywhere else. See custom bodied cars by Fleetwood, steam and electric vehicle technology, high wheel bicycles, children's vehicles and tools of the craftsman.

SE Area

Chadds Ford

BRANDYWINE BATTLEFIELD PARK

Chadds Ford - *Box 202 (US1, 1 mile east of SR100) 19317. Phone: (610) 459-3342. www.ushistory.org/brandywine. Hours: Tuesday - Saturday 9:00am-4:30pm, Sunday Noon-4:30pm (March-November). Open Thursday - Sunday (December-February). Closed most federal holidays. Admission: Grounds FREE. General admission $5.00 adult, $3.50 senior (65+), $25.50 youth (6-17). Parking free. Tours: Maps for self-guided tour at Visitor's Center. House Tours daily except in March. Miscellaneous: Museum shop. Plenty of picnic areas. Battle re-enactment every September. Educators: click on History Articles for some great material for research reports on characters of the battle. FREEBIES: click on KIDS CORNER for several fun activities to play.*

The peaceful nature of the Brandywine Valley was shattered in the summer of 1777, when British and Hessian forces fought American Continentals and local militia under George Washington and the young Marquis de Lafayette in the largest land battle of the Revolutionary War.

This giant park and museum are focused on actual Revolutionary War events. Watch the audiovisual introduction to the park first, then drive along a tour that includes 28 historic points taking you back to 1777. Remember, this defeat of American forces (led by George Washington) left the Philadelphia area open to attack and conquest by the British.

BATTLE OF BRANDYWINE

Chadds Ford - *Brandywine Battlefield Park. Annual re-enactment of the Battle of Brandywine, the largest single day battle of the American War for Independence. Admission. (weekend nearest September 11)*

BRANDYWINE RIVER MUSEUM

Chadds Ford - *US 1 & PA Rte. 100 (from Wilmington, DE head northwest on Rte. 52 to Rte. 1. Left on Rte. 1. Follow signs) 19317. Phone: (610) 388-2700. www.brandywinemuseum.org. Hours: Daily 9:30am-4:30pm. Closed Christmas. Admission: $10.00 adult, $6.00 senior (65+), student/child (age 6+). $3.00 for Children's Audio Tours (highly recommended in addition to, or replacing the Game Sheets). Tours: Kuerner Farm Tours (April through November). For more than 70 years, the historic Kuerner Farm has been a major source of inspiration to Andrew Wyeth. Since his earliest painting of the farm in 1932 at the age of 15, Wyeth has found subjects in its people, animals, buildings and landscapes for* *more than 1,000 works of art. Educational tours departing from the museum are offered at timed intervals. Wednesday through Sunday. $5 per person in addition to museum admission. Due to uneven walking surfaces, the Kuerner Farm is not accessible to disabled individuals. Read-Aloud Tours w/Storytimes are offered occasionally. Miscellaneous: Restaurant open daily 10:00am-3:00pm except Mondays & Tuesdays and winters. FREEBIES: go on a gallery hunt and see if you can find items on the Discovery Game Sheets.*

American art in a 19th century gristmill. Known for collections by three generations of Wyeths. The house where N.C. Wyeth raised his extraordinarily creative children and the studio in which he painted many of his memorable works of art have been restored to reflect their character in 1945, the year of the artist's death (House & Studio Tour $5.00 extra, April-November).

CHRISTMAS OPEN HOUSE

Chadds Ford *- Brandywine River Museum. Tours of decorated, historical buildings. Refreshments and musical entertainment. Admission. Model railroad, Victorian dollhouse and whimsical "critter" ornaments. Thanksgiving weekend thru weekend after New Years)*

Collegeville

EVANSBURG STATE PARK

Collegeville *- 851 May Hall Road (off US Route 422) 19426. Phone: (610) 409-1150. www.dcnr.state.pa.us/stateparks/parks/evansburg.aspx. Admission: to PA State Parks is FREE however swimming, marina and camping/lodging fees apply, with reservation or entrance.*

This park is a haven for hikers, equestrians and folks who want to picnic and relax. You can take a walk along Skippack Creek or visit the Friedt Visitor Center that provides insight into German Mennonite living in the 18th and 19th centuries. This farmhouse was built in the early 1700s. This historic building interprets the lifestyles of the German Mennonite families who owned the home for 190 years. Outside, the root cellar, well, and herb and sensory gardens add to the eighteenth century atmosphere. An exhibit room in the house is devoted to the natural history of the area, and the house also provides an area for visitors to watch songbirds and other animals. Fishing, Hiking, Cross-Country Skiing.

SE Area

Columbia

NATIONAL WATCH & CLOCK MUSEUM

Columbia - *514 Popular Street (off US30 west - follow signs) 17512. Phone: (717) 684-8261. www.nawcc.org/index.php/museumlibrary. Hours: Tuesday-Saturday 10:00am-4:00pm (year round). Sunday Noon-4:00pm (April-December). Open Tuesday-Saturday until 5:00pm (April-December). Admission: $4.00-$7.00 (age 6+). Miscellaneous: "Yours, Mine and Hours" Museum Shop. Library. Educators:*

You've got the time, they've got the place! The National Association of Watch and Clock Collectors have a school (of horology), offices, and this fabulously renovated museum. One staff member described it as the "Disneyland of Clocks and Time". Start at the beginning, Stonehenge, then travel through time as you browse past displays of time-keeping history. You'll see thousands of watches (many still working),

> **DID YOU KNOW?**
>
> This museum houses over 12,000 watches and clocks.

unique water and candle clocks, sundials and even an alarm clock that pinches you when it rings! Bells, chimes, music boxes, and organs sound on the hour as each clock chimes.

WRIGHT'S FERRY MANSION

Columbia - *38 South 2nd Street (US30 - Columbia/Marietta Exit SR 441 South) 17512. Phone: (717) 684-4325. . Hours: Tuesday & Wednesday, Friday & Saturday 10:00am-3:00pm, Closed July 4 (May- October). Open hours vary from year to year. PLEASE VERIFY OPEN HOURS BEFORE VISITING. Admission: $5.00 adult, $2.50 child (6-18). Group tours (Call for reservations - 30 days in advance).*

Discover the fascinating and visionary life of Susanna Wright, a bright, creative Quaker woman whose diverse talents have benefited many. She ran a ferry here, was an unofficial doctor and lawyer, launched the silk industry in this region, and shared ideas with people like Ben Franklin with whom she corresponded regularly. The 1738 house reflects Quaker lifestyles prior to 1750 and its collections are one of the most complete and representative in the country. Because this is an "open" museum (no velvet ropes separating you from the displays) you certainly get the feeling that the occupants have just left for a little while…and may be returning shortly! We recommend close supervision for younger children, or better yet only bring them if your children are age 8 or older.

Cornwall

CORNWALL IRON FURNACE

Cornwall - 94 Rexmont Road (4 miles North of US76 off SR 72 on SR419) 17016. Phone: (717) 272-9711. www.cornwallironfurnace.org. Hours: Thursday-Saturday 9:00am-5:00pm, Sunday Noon-5:00pm. Closed most holidays, except Summer holidays. Admission: Visitors Center is FREE. Guided tours are $4.00-$6.00 per person (age 6+). Note: on tour, there is no heat or air conditioning in the furnace building. Educators: an easy to follow pre-visit discussion and vocabulary worksheet is found online: www.cornwallironfurnace.org/Vocabulary-Students.pdf.

A 1742 - 1833 iron making complex. The preserved facility once produced farm tools, kitchenware, stoves, cannons and ammunition. Self-guided tours examine an orientation exhibit that provides a clear understanding of the once active iron plantation. Housed in the third bay of the old charcoal barn, the exhibit tells the story of two families and their iron plantation workers. You can see the original furnace stack, blast machinery, blowing tubs, and a Great Wheel (76 feet around). Remember this site was water-powered. An ironmaster's mansion and the Charcoal House Visitor's Center are on the premises. Start by watching the video showing the making of charcoal and preparing molds for casting in the 19th century. The Visitors Center gallery also provides information on charcoal making, pig iron, and different types of employees, such as indentured servants and slaves. The exhibit is comprised of period artifacts, text panels, and colorful graphics. Text is written at the comprehension level of middle school-aged children. There is no admission fee for the gallery or video, which is accessible to all. The property is a 5-acre historic site that offers a picnic area and beautiful grounds for a nice walk on a warm day.

Downingtown

MARSH CREEK STATE PARK

Downingtown - 675 Park Road (two miles west of the village of Eagle on PA 100) 19335. Phone: (610) 458-5119. www.dcnr.state.pa.us/stateparks/parks/marshcreek.aspx. Admission: to PA State Parks is FREE however swimming, marina and camping/lodging fees apply, with reservation or entrance.

Marsh Creek Lake is especially popular with sailboaters and windsurfers who take advantage of the prevailing wind to enjoy their sport. Nature lovers will enjoy a pleasant walk on hiking trails or the Larkins covered Bridge located in the northeast section of the park. Pool, Boat Rentals, Sledding, and Fishing.

Doylestown

MERCER MUSEUM

Doylestown - *84 South Pine Street (off SR202, rear SR313 and SR611) 18901. Phone: (215) 345-0210. www.mercermuseum.org. Hours: Monday-Saturday 10:00am-5:00pm, Sunday Noon-5:00pm. Admission: $8.00 adult, $7.00 senior (62+), $4.00 youth (5-17). Combo pricing if touring Fonthill also. Please note: The Mercer Museum is not heated or cooled; plan to dress appropriately for the seasons. Educators: their website has a treasure trove of downloadable activity sheets, scavenger hunts (highly recommended to print off your fav before you tour), vocabulary and bibliographies. Studying pre-Industrial Revolution history? These materials make it fun: http://mercermuseum.org/teacher_resources.htm.*

The receptionist promised us that the best part of the self-guided tour was the walk into the Center Court. It is amazing! Artifacts are hanging everywhere! While searching through junk in a barn, Henry Chapman Mercer found a jumble of objects made obsolete by the Industrial Revolution. His collection, housed in a "cement castle", represents more than

Cool old stuff housed in a big stone castle...

60 crafts and trades - pre 1850. Called "The Tools of the Nation Maker", play a game to try to find one tool from at least 50 trades (every year, they produce a different themed scavenger hunt worksheet - ask for one). Some are easy to see, but over 40,000 pieces of "junk" are in every nook and cranny. In the museum's Imagination Gallery, located nearby, young children can explore other hands-on activities related to the museum's collection, including puppet play, tile rubbings, puzzles, and storybooks. This is the most eccentric, yet curiously fun, museum you'll ever find! By the way, the cement and leaded glass windows truly give that medieval feeling inside and out.

MERCER MUSEUM FOLKFEST

Doylestown - Mercer Museum. www.buckscountyhistorical.org/folkfest/index.html. Traditional artisans make the skills and trades of early America come to life during this nationally acclaimed festival. Entertainment, militia encampment, and full picnic fare. Admission. (Mothers Day weekend - May)

MORAVIAN POTTERY AND TILE WORKS & FONTHILL

Doylestown - *130 Swamp Road/East Court Street (Court St. and Swamp Rd., off of Rte. 313, which runs north/south of Doylestown) 18901. Phone: (215) 345-6722. www.buckscounty.org/government/departments/Tileworks/index.aspx. Hours: Daily 10:00am-4:45pm, except closed select holidays. Admission: Averages $2.50-$4.50 per person for Tile Works or $4.00-$10.00 per person for Fonthill. Discount combo pricing with Mercer Museum. Tours: Self-guided - every 1/2 hour. Last tour at 4:00pm. Tower Tours for Families (explore basement to tower) the first Saturday morning of every month. Miscellaneous: Tile Shop.*

This facility, beginning in 1912, produced tiles and mosaics for floors, walls and ceilings. Mercer's artistic floor tiles adorn the rotunda and halls of the Pennsylvania State Capitol, depicting 400 scenes in the Commonwealth's history. Today, the facility makes reproductions of Mercer's original line of tiles. Mercer was a visionary architect who was one of the first designers to work with reinforced concrete as a building material.

Tours are offered every half-hour and consist of a 17-minute video and a self-guided walk through the facility. Watch the clay being prepared, then stamped with designs, then fired, glazed and fired again. Kids will appreciate FONTHILL (Mercer's mansion/castle that is next door) or the Mercer Museum a little more if they understand what made him rich and famous. His mosaics are probably the prettiest to look at. www.mercermuseum.org

44 rooms, 18 fireplaces and more than 200 windows...

SE Area

JULY 4TH CELEBRATION

Doylestown - *City Parks. Parades, music, food, fireworks & contests. Town ball game, Pony rides, contests. Admission.*

PUMPKIN FESTIVAL

Doylestown - *Moravian Pottery And Tile Works & Fonthill. Pumpkin painting and carving, pie-eating contests. Pumpkin patch (wagon rides out there). Refreshments. Admission. (last weekend in October)*

CHRISTMAS OPEN HOUSE

Doylestown - *Moravian Pottery And Tile Works & Fonthill. Tours of decorated, historical buildings. Refreshments and musical entertainment. Dolls, toys, crafts. Admission. (weekends in December)*

POLISH AMERICAN FESTIVAL

Doylestown - *National Shrine of Our Lady of Czestochowa. www.czestochowa.us. Polish folk song dance ensembles, polka bands, entertainment shows, Polish and American foods, and amusements. Admission. (1st two weekends of September)*

BYERS' CHOICE LTD

Doylestown (Chalfont) - 4335 County Line Road (Just north of Rt.309 & Rt. 202) 18914. Phone: (215) 822-0150. www.byerschoice.com. Hours: Monday-Saturday 10:00am-5:00pm, Sunday Noon-5:00pm (Closed major holidays) Admission: FREE.

The Byers Choice factory is the home of America's beloved, handcrafted Carolers® figurine collectibles. What started as a family Christmas gift 40 years ago has grown to a team of 180 artisans – all designing the caroler figures in a variety of settings with their heads raised in song. Family and friends (employees) hand sculpt precious Caroler figurines. By a walk-through observation deck, you can watch them mold delicate faces and then apply makeup (paint) to add dimension and features. See all the costumes and background landscapes available to make each singing doll unique. What you don't see in production that day, you can watch by pre-taped video. Want more? Stroll down a recreated London street scene and enter the Christmas Museum. You can peer into shop windows and residences filled with Christmas displays, view a short film about the history of the company in a theater reminiscent of Victorian England, and try on a top hat, scarf, muff or bonnet to have your picture taken.

RALPH STOVER STATE PARK

Doylestown (Pipersville) - *6011 State Park Road (State Park Road and Stump Road) 18947. Phone: (610) 982-5560.   www.dcnr.state.pa.us/stateparks/parks/ ralphstover.aspx.   Admission: to PA State Parks is FREE however swimming, marina and camping/lodging fees apply, with reservation or entrance.*

45 acres along the Tohickon Creek. Warm-water fish species found in Tohickon Creek include smallmouth bass, sunfish, carp and catfish. They stock trout, a cold-water fish. There is one mile of easy walking trails that pass through many habitats and near the millrace. The 'High Rocks' section of the park features an outstanding view of a horseshoe bend in Tohickon Creek and the surrounding forest.

Elverson

FRENCH CREEK STATE PARK

Elverson - *843 Park Road (off Route 345) 19520. Phone: (610) 582-9680. www. dcnr.state.pa.us/stateparks/parks/frenchcreek.aspx. Admission: To PA State Parks is FREE however swimming, marina and camping/lodging fees apply, with reservation or entrance.*

French Creek offers two lakes - Hopewell and Scotts Run, extensive forests and almost 40 miles of hiking trails. Adjacent to the park lies Hopewell Furnace. Pool, Boat Rentals, Horseback Riding, Mountain Biking, Campsites, Modern Cabins, Yurts, Fishing, and Cross-Country Skiing.

HOPEWELL FURNACE NATIONAL HISTORIC SITE

Elverson - *2 Mark Bird Lane (PA Rt. 724 East, turn right onto PA Rt. 345 South) 19520. Phone: (610) 582-8773.   www.nps.gov/archive/hofu/index.html.   Hours: Wednesday-Sunday 9:00am-5:00pm. Closed most holidays. Parking lots, restrooms and hiking trails are open every day except on those federal holidays when the park is closed. Admission: FREE. Tours: Self-guided tours enhanced by recorded voices of workers and their families. Miscellaneous: Younger children would prefer summers when living history actors are in costume throughout the village. Older kids really get into the stories told on the tour. Educators: http:// www.nps.gov/hofu/historyculture/index.htm In this section of their web site, you can learn more about the many stories Hopewell Furnace has to tell of the history of our nation, people and land.*

Hopewell spans two centuries; and presently stands as an example of America's development during the industrial revolution. Explore the museum which provides exhibits and audio-visual programs, including an 11 minute theater program giving a history of the Hopewell Furnace Community. Get the chance to experience living history programs and demonstrations that show the work and lifestyles of the residents of Hopewell.

The Visitor's Center features an audio visual program and exhibits of the original iron castings and tools used in Colonial cold blast charcoal furnaces. See a restored cast house, water wheel cooling shed, tenant houses and ironmaster's mansion (The Big House). Learn about "pig iron" (formed in troughs), and stoves and weapons produced here - recreated by actual blacksmiths shaping the hot slabs of iron alongside molders. This is mostly a living history village (summers and special events) and the "villagers" are well educated on iron casting. Call ahead to be sure you get to see live demonstrations during your visit.

During September and October the park's historic apple orchard is opened for picking by the public Wednesday through Sunday. The park's orchard includes many historic varieties not normally available in today's markets. Length of season and availability of varieties depends upon the success of the growing season. The apples are sold by the pound.

CHRISTMAS OPEN HOUSE

Elverson - Hopewell Furnace National Historic Site. Tours of decorated, historical buildings. Refreshments and musical entertainment. Admission. (first Saturday in December)

Fort Washington

FORT WASHINGTON STATE PARK

Fort Washington - *500 Bethlehem Pike (2 miles from PA Turnpike exit 26) 19034. Phone: (215) 646-2942. www.dcnr.state.pa.us/stateparks/parks/fortwashington.aspx. Admission: to PA State Parks is FREE however swimming, marina and camping/lodging fees apply, with reservation or entrance.*

This beautiful park interests historians of the American Revolution. The park takes its name from the fort built by George Washington's troops in the fall of 1777, before heading to Valley Forge. The park is popular with hikers and bikers. Birders enjoy the seasonal migration of raptors from the Observation Deck. Hawks, Washington Encampment, Fishing, Trails, Winter Sports. Disc Golf: The wooded, 9-hole course begins in Lot 2 in the Militia Hill Day Use Area at a kiosk with a map of the course.

Grantville

MEMORIAL LAKE STATE PARK

Grantville - RD 1, Box 7045 (I- 81 at exit 29 /Fort Indiantown Gap, take PA Route 934 North) 17028. Phone: (717) 865-6470. www.dcnr.state.pa.us/stateparks/parks/ memoriallake.aspx. Admission: to PA State Parks is FREE however swimming, marina and camping/lodging fees apply, with reservation or entrance.

This quaint park has a lake for canoeing, wind surfing and fishing, and hiking trails and lots of beautiful scenery. A short woodland trail winds along the northern shoreline. The open nature of the park allows the visitor to take casual walks through most of the park. Scenic views of the lake provide a tranquil setting, especially during the spring and autumn days. Boat Rentals, Fishing, Cross-Country Skiing.

Intercourse

INTERCOURSE PRETZEL FACTORY

Intercourse - 3614 Old Philadelphia Pike (at Cross Keys) (at the intersection of Route 340 and Route 772 East) 17534. www.intercoursepretzelfactory.com. Phone: (717) 768-3432. Admission: FREE. Tours: When weather permits factory production Monday - Saturday 9:00am-5:00pm (mid-February thru December). Miscellaneous: Snack Bar.

How do you like your pretzels? Soft, stuffed, or hard? Plan on visiting this factory for a lunch/ dessert treat. As you watch all the pretzels being made by hand and learn to twist your own pretzel…try to decide which flavors you're going to try now and which you'll take home. The FREE 10-15 minute tour explains pretzel making, twisting and baking. You are awarded with an official pretzel twister sticker for your work.

Their stuffed pretzels are wrapped around cheeses, meats, relishes, and jams. Soft and hard pretzels come in a variety of seasonings (doesn't brown butter topping sound warm and cozy?) and their chocolate covered varieties are smothered in Wilbur's (our favorite in Pennsylvania) chocolate. Do you see why we suggest to save "tummy room" for snacking?

SE Area

KITCHEN KETTLE VILLAGE

Intercourse - Route 340 17534. www.kitchenkettle.com. Hours: Monday-Saturday 9:00am-5:00pm. Closed Sundays.

Welcome to a village in the heart of Pennsylvania Dutch Country where there's always plenty of shopping, good foods, and a place for everyone to be a kid again. Visit the World Famous Canning Kitchen (samples) or stroll down Pepper Lane and eat as you go: hand-rolled fudge, homemade ice cream, hot pretzels, and freshly baked goodies. Walk that off browsing through almost 40 specialty shops.

EASTER EGG HUNT

Intercourse - *Kitchen Kettle Village. Easter crafts, entertainment, breakfast with Easter Bunny & Yummie. (Saturday before Easter Sunday)*

RHUBARB FESTIVAL

Intercourse - *Kitchen Kettle Village. Annual festival that teaches us that rhubarb (a red-stalked vegetable) is no longer just for pies. You won't believe the colorful menus of rhubarb-inspired foods, baked goods and beverages, and the Rhubarb Jams made special at festival time. Kids can play games (even build mini-racecars – The Rhubarb Race Car Derby). Food and games. FREE. (third Friday/Saturday in May)*

STRAWBERRY FESTIVAL

Intercourse - *Kitchen Kettle Village. Sample strawberry treats like fresh strawberry shortcakes and strawberry ice cream or sundaes. From great beverages and tempting sweets to colorful side dishes and barbecued meats grilled with berry sauces. Entertainment, demonstrations, contests and prizes. Kids' activities. (mid-June)*

7 SWEETS & SOURS TAILGATE

Intercourse - *Kitchen Kettle Village. Celebrate the fall and tailgating season with a celebration of food, music and sports fun. The Village comes alive with a sports themed scarecrow competition, tailgating food demos, pumpkin bowling, musical entertainment and more. Dress in your favorite "team" gear. (third Friday & Saturday in September)*

HOLLY DAYS

Intercourse - *Kitchen Kettle Village. Join in decking the hall, streets and shops with holiday décor. Caroling, brass bands, cookie baking, roaming musicians and oodles of specialty shopping, Experience Old Fashioned Christmas Friday Nights with Mrs. Claus & Yummie. "Hershey Chocolate S'more Area." Families can enjoy a holiday feast at The Kling House Restaurant (includes family style dining, storytelling with Mrs. Claus & Yummie and a special gift for children).*

Kempton

HAWK MOUNTAIN

Kempton - *1700 Hawk Mountain Road (I-78, exit 9B north to Route 895 east) 19529. Phone: (610) 756-6961. www.hawkmountain.org. Hours: Daily 9:00am-5:00pm (most of year), 8:00am-5:00pm (September-November). Admission: Trail Fees (to get to lookouts): $5.00-$7.00 adult, $4.00-$7.00 senior, $3.00 child (6-12).*

Located along the Appalachian Trail, scenic Hawk Mountain Sanctuary offers an outstanding nature experience with its mountaintop vistas, hiking trails, and thrilling autumnal raptor migration. With a total of 2,600 acres, anyone can enjoy these trails rated from easy to challenging. You can spend an entire day at the sanctuary or take an early morning hike and then onto your next stop. Between mid-August and mid-December an average 18,000 hawks, eagles, and falcons fly past this site. Bookstore. Wildlife viewing windows. Exhibits. Trails. FREE Live-raptor programs on weekends (April-November).

W.K. & S. STEAM RAILROAD

Kempton - *PO Box 24 (SR143 or SR737 into Kempton. - follow signs) 19529. Phone: (610) 756-6469. www.kemptontrain.com. Hours: Sundays (May thru mid-November, plus December), Saturdays also (July, August, October, November). Departures from 1:00pm-4:00pm leave every hour on the hour. Admission: $4.00-$8.00 (age 3+). Miscellaneous: The station facilities include a large free parking area, a gift shop with many railroad-related items, refreshment stand, waiting room, restrooms, and a large picnic area. Large grassy areas provide for the kids to run. On Sundays, the Schuykill & Lehigh Model Railroad Club's HO model train display is also open to the public.*

Known as the "Hawk Mountain Line", the WK&S has been open since 1963. Passengers enjoy a three-mile ride to Wanamaker through Pennsylvania's picturesque countryside, passing several historic sites and structures. Nice short ride (40 minutes) where you can get off at picnic groves throughout the countryside and get back on later. What could be better than a 45 minute train ride through beautiful scenic woods on a real locomotive? After your ride, you'll feel rested and ready to head south to your next destination. Gift shop. Snack bar.

EASTER BUNNY TRAIN RIDES

Kempton - *W. K. & S. Steam Railroad. Candy treats with the Easter Bunny riding along. Admission. (Easter Weekend)*

HARVEST MOON TRAIN

Kempton - *W. K. & S. Steam Railroad. Autumn moonlight train ride with musicians and light refreshments. Admission. (third weekend in October)*

SANTA CLAUS SPECIAL

Kempton - *W. K. & S. Steam Railroad. Join Frosty the Snowman, Santa & his Elves at the WK&S! Free gifts for the children as Santa walks through the train. Admission. (first weekend in December)*

Kennett Square

LONGWOOD GARDENS

Kennett Square - *US Route 1 (take SR 52 northwest to US 1. Left on US 1. Follow signs) 19348. Phone: (610) 388-1000. www.longwoodgardens.org. Hours: Daily 9:00am-5:00pm (open later during peak Spring / Summer & Holiday seasons) Admission: $16.00 adult, $14.00 senior (62+), $6.00 student (5-18). Miscellaneous: Stop by the Terrace Restaurant for Kids Value Meals (offered daily). Breakfasts with the Easter Bunny and Santa, and Family Fireworks BBQs are featured seasonally by reservation. Go online to find out more about how you make your visit to the Gardens more enjoyable and worth the admission.*

See exotic plants from around the world, examine insect-catching plants up close, enjoy dancing fountains that shoot water 130 feet in the air, and be dazzled by 40 colorful indoor and outdoor displays every day of the year. Daily activities feature fun and educational adventures and activities for kids and families. Special children's programs like Peter Rabbit and Friends, Christmas and Mazes.

LONGWOOD GARDENS (cont.)

Is Longwood Gardens a place for family fun? Yes, if you look for it. Explore three awesome tree houses, have your picture taken next to animal-shaped topiaries and be amused by colorful indoor and outdoor floral displays. The Indoor Children's Garden is an whimsical space of ramps, mazes, grottoes, and lots of running water (30 water features in all). A shooting jet that rings a bell, a spitting fish, a pond with rising steam, a cave with dripping walls, and a gigantic drooling dragon are just a few of the water wonders visitors will enjoy. Two mazes - one square accented by story tiles and shooting jets of water - and one Bamboo offering a jungle of tree-size bamboos for children to explore. Kids will enjoy frolicking in the Bee A-mazed garden designed especially for them. The Garden features three major areas: the Honeycomb Maze, Flower Fountain, and Buzz Trail. All the children's areas are accessible for kids of any age. We noticed lots of moms pushing strollers on the pathways. Within reason, kids can romp and squeal to their hearts content.

CHRISTMAS OPEN HOUSE

Kennett Square - *Longwood Gardens . Tours of decorated buildings. Refreshments and musical entertainment. Admission. (Thanksgiving thru early January)*

King of Prussia

SCOTTISH AND IRISH MUSIC FESTIVAL AND FAIR, GREATER PHILADELPHIA

King of Prussia - *Valley Forge Convention Center. www.eohebrides.com/events/ index.cfm. Scottish and Irish musical entertainment with Highland and step dancing, bands, singers, storytellers, exhibits, craft vendors Scottish and Irish foods and fraternal organizations. Admission. (mid-February weekend)*

SE Area

Kutztown

CRYSTAL CAVE

Kutztown - *963 Crystal Cave Road (Off US 22. Follow signs) 19530. Phone: (610) 683-6765. www.crystalcavepa.com. Hours: Daily 9:00am-5:00pm (March-November) Summer to 6:00 or 7:00pm. Holidays & Weekends to 6:00pm. Admission: $7.50-$11.50 (age 4+). Tours: 45 minutes includes video about cave formation. Miscellaneous: Food. Gift shop. Rock shop. Mini-golf. Gem Panning (extra fee). Museum and nature trails. Note: there are many steps to climb to get to the cave entrance and stairs to navigate inside the cave. Heavy or unhealthy persons may find this a challenge.*

The most visited cave site in Pennsylvania, Crystal Cave is known for its profuse and varied formations. The 45 minute tour begins with an eight minute video presentation in the theatre. Trained guides take you past milky white formations enhanced by indirect lighting. Look for the Giant's Tooth, Prairie dogs, Indian Head, Totem Pole, Natural Bridge and the Ear of Corn formations. Although the cave isn't spectacular, the added adventure of the guide momentarily turning off the lights is an interesting feature. We liked how the guides point out formations and tell some stories of why they named them. This site includes shops, fast food, trails, 125 acres and a museum.

RODALE INSTITUTE FARM

Kutztown - *611 Siegfriedale Road (off US222, just northeast of town) 19530. Phone: (610) 683-1400. www.rodaleinstitute.org. Hours: Monday-Saturday 9:00am-5:00pm, Sunday 10:00am-3:00pm (early May - mid-October). Admission: Average $3.00 per person (age 5+) Tours: Monday - Friday morning (By appointment). Miscellaneous: International Café features organic light fare and beverages. Gift shop - suggest you try homemade organic apple sauce or butter.*

Regenerative Organic Farming and Gardening - Do you know what that means? The Rodale Institute is located on a 333-acre organic certified farm in Kutztown, Pennsylvania, devoted to research, education and certified organic production.

If you've eaten one too many frozen or fast food meals this week - start feeling healthier here. Learn the connection between healthy soil, healthy food, and healthy people, all through demonstrations and children's gardens. A tour highlight for children is watching how earthworms help aerate and fertilize the soil. Initial shrieks turn to keen interest as the children handle the subterranean workers, feed them kitchen scraps and watch them burrow. They can then take a trip through a child-size "Earthworm Tunnel™" for a first-hand experience.

KUTZTOWN FOLK FESTIVAL

Kutztown - *Fairgrounds. www.kutztownfestival.com. An annual celebration of the Pennsylvania Dutch lifestyle with demonstrating craftsmen, entertainment, food, nature center, antique farm museum and much more. Delightful baby farm animals, puppets, make-and- take crafts, hay stacks and mazes, story time, singalongs, and hands on fun. Admission. (first full week in July)*

🏃

Lahaska

PEDDLER'S VILLAGE

Lahaska - *Routes 202 & 263. www.peddlersvillage.com. Phone: (215) 794-4000.*

Lightspace Play, an LED-lighted floor programmed to create games and activities, is the newest addition to Giggleberry Fair, a family-friendly attraction at Peddler's Village that includes an old-fashioned Grand Carousel, Giggleberry Mountain, Discovery Land, the Game Room and the Painted Pony Café.

STRAWBERRY FESTIVAL

Lahaska - *Peddler's Village. Sample strawberry treats like fresh strawberry shortcakes and strawberry ice cream or sundaes. From great beverages and tempting sweets to colorful side dishes and barbecued meats grilled with berry sauces. Entertainment, demonstrations, contests and prizes. Kids' activities. FREE. (first weekend in May)*

🏃

CELEBRATION OF FREEDOM

Lahaska - *Peddler's Village. Live entertainment, children's activities, and picnic-style favorites await you at this patriotic event. Fireworks display at 9:15pm. Free admission. Music accompanying fireworks. (July 3rd)*

🏃

SCARECROW COMPETITION & DISPLAY

Lahaska - *Peddler's Village. Unusual and delightful bird-chasing creations compete for over $1400 in prizes. Vote for your favorite traditional, contemporary, whirl-a-gig and amateur. Displayed throughout the village. Pumpkin painting, square dancing. Make one workshop. (Mid-September to Mid-October)*

🏃

APPLE FESTIVAL

Lahaska - *Peddler's Village. Live music, marionettes, pie-eating contests. Apples served up in fritters, pastries, butter, dipped in chocolate and caramel, or enjoyed plain. Take home a bushel fresh from the orchard. Juried Artisans sell their wares and demonstrate their skills at our Street Road Green Artisan Area. Live entertainment and apple pie-eating contests add to the festivities of this traditional autumn celebration. FREE. (first weekend in November)*

Lancaster

DUTCH APPLE DINNER THEATRE

Lancaster - *510 Centerville Road (off US 30west) 17601. Phone: (717) 898-1900. www.dutchapple.com.*

Children's matinee and Sunday twilight. Dine while watching children's musicals like Pinocchio, Adventures of Huck Finn, Willy Wonka or Cinderella. Regular show Tickets range $18.00-$33.00. Children's Theatre Schedule Ticket Price: For Kids of all ages $15.00 includes children's lunch and show.

HANDS-ON HOUSE CHILDREN'S MUSEUM

Lancaster - *721 Landis Valley Road (US 30 to Oregon Pike N exit) 17601. Phone: (717) 569-KIDS. www.handsonhouse.org. Hours: Tuesday-Friday 11:00am-4:00pm, Saturday 10:00am-5:00pm, Sunday Noon-5:00pm. Open Mondays and extended hours in the summer. Closed major winter holiday times. Admission: $7.00 general Miscellaneous: Recommended for ages 2-10. Everything is simply explained to allow parents and kids' imagination to explore possibilities.*

All of the exhibits at Hands-on House are custom-designed and unique. There exhibits include a variety of activities appropriate for children ages 2-10 years. Each exhibit has a theme with a variety of activities to do that relate to the theme. Favorite "spaces" include: a Lancaster Farming Area, Grocery Store and Art Smart Fun. In Marty's Machine Shop, you'll wear safety goggles to work on an assembly line or sort and deliver mail at a kid-friendly factory. The Space Voyage Checkpoint takes kids on a spaceship ride to learn about health and wellness as earthlings get a checkup before their journey into space. At Feelings, talk to a giant stuffed bear.

SE Area

LANDIS VALLEY MUSEUM

Lancaster - *2451 Kissel Hill Road (3 miles north on Oregon Pike - SR272) 17601. Phone: (717) 569-0401. www.landisvalleymuseum.org. Hours: Monday-Saturday 9:00am-5:00pm, Sunday Noon-5:00pm. Closed some major holidays. Admission: $12.00 adult, $10.00 senior (60+), $8.00 child (6-17). Miscellaneous: Weathervane gift shop.*

The largest Pennsylvania German museum in the U.S. (100 acres) includes 20 buildings including the craft shop, schoolhouse, country store, leather crafts, farmstead, blacksmith, transportation building, hotel, pottery shop plus others. Exhibits interpret rural life prior to 1900 through artisans and demonstrations of traditional skills. Children can discover a one-room school house, try their hands at woodworking and mingle with lambs in this recreated 19th- century Pennsylvania Dutch village. If they are conducting lessons in the schoolhouse, mind your ways as you might get sent in the corner with a dunce cap. Special performances, craft demonstrations and living history programs change monthly. The tavern, log home, family home and general store are the most informative presentations - besides the schoolhouse, when "school" is in session. Don't forget about the traditional walkways of dirt, pebble or brick. Lots of walking here. Besides the festivals listed below, they often have less formal events which are the ideal time to visit - events or festivals - as there are always more costumed guides leading the kids in hands-on activities.

HARVEST DAYS

Lancaster - *Landis Valley Museum. Tractor pulls, antique steam engines, parades, food (made with steam), threshing, baling, cider and apple butter making, hayrides, children's activities, petting zoo & fall crafts. Admission. (second weekend in October)*

PUMPKIN FESTIVAL

Lancaster - *Landis Valley Museum. Pumpkin painting and carving, pie-eating contests. Pumpkin patch (wagon rides out there). Refreshments. (last weekend in October)*

CHRISTMAS OPEN HOUSE

Lancaster - *Landis Valley Museum. Tours of decorated, historical buildings. Refreshments and musical entertainment. Lunch & Dinner tours. Admission. (first and second Wednesday-Saturday in December)*

AMISH FARM AND HOUSE

Lancaster - 2395 Route 30 East 17602. www.amishfarmandhouse.com. Phone: (717) 394-6185. Hours: Daily 8:30am-6:00pm (Summer). 9:00am-5:00pm (Spring & Fall), 10:00am-4:00pm (Winter). Admission: $8.25 adult, $7.50 senior (60+), $5.25 child (5-11). For an additional fee you can take a Countryside Bus Tour. Tours: 35 minutes Miscellaneous: Dutch Food Pavilion (April - October). Weekend craft demonstrations (branch carvings for example). Nighttime lamp tours (late September - late October). Buggy rides. They are pet friendly.

Guided tours of an Amish home (10 rooms) - learn the history, religious customs and a simple way of life. Self-guided tour of a working farm with local crops, barns, and farm animals. Most interesting is a unique Lancaster County device - a water wheel powered pump (smaller pump in meadow) operates a larger pump via wire. In the Spring House, a large water wheel powers a pump which forces cold spring water into a kitchen refrigerator. A limestone quarry on the property supplied stone to build this barn and house. New to the property is a tour of the Amish One Room Schoolhouse.

FALL FARM DAYS

Lancaster - *Amish Farm And House. Fall celebration of the harvest, especially the apple harvest. See cider being pressed, apple "schnitzing", taste historic apple varieties. Games for children. Corn maze, buggy rides and wood carving. Admission. (second weekend in October)*

BIBLICAL TABERNACLE REPRODUCTION / MENNONITE INFORMATION CENTER

Lancaster - *2209 Millstream Road - Off US30   17602. Phone: (717) 299-0954. www.mennoniteinfoctr.com.   Hours: Monday-Saturday 9:00am-4:00pm (April-October). 11:00am-3:00pm (November-March). Admission: FREE for info center. $7.00 adult, $6.00 senior (60+), $4.00 child (ages 7+). Tours: Guided group tours. 45 minutes. Every hour on the hour. Miscellaneous: Gift shop featuring crafts (reproduction) from biblical times & craft kits to recreate tabernacle.*

Film and displays explaining the faith and culture of Amish and Mennonites called "Postcards From a Heritage of Faith" or the 3-screen documentary from

Peoples' Place, "Who are the Amish?" Shown every hour. Included is a reproduction of a Hebrew Tabernacle with lecture tours given on the history, construction, function, and significance on the hour (every 2 hours in the Winter). Most kids leave with an understanding of the Arc of the Covenant and can answer as to why the 66 lumps in the candleholder were prophecy of the future. Even if you know little about Biblical history, this presentation is fascinating. But for those who know, this makes the story come to life.

DUTCH WONDERLAND FAMILY AMUSEMENT PARK

Lancaster - *2249 Route 30 East 17602. www.dutchwonderland.com. Phone: (717) 291-1888. Hours: Daily 10:00am-7:00pm (Memorial Day-Labor Day), Weekends only 10:00am-6:00pm (Spring & Fall). Admission: Range $27.00-$32.00 (ages 3+). Discount packages*

available adding nearby attractions. Preview Plan is FREE if you go the night before and pay for the next day. Miscellaneous: Also Wonderland Mini-Golf.

Monster Truck fun...

It's a Kingdom for Kids. Come and meet "Duke The Dragon" and the "Princess of Dutch Wonderland". It's cute...with many clean, safe rides for kids (probably best age range is 4-12, with their adults). Water splash and ride areas with new features every year. Cute little interactive shows and a wonderful "High Dive" show. It's hard to believe those guys really dive from 30 to 80 feet…until you see it! Rides include: Roller Coaster, Giant Slide, Double Splash Flume, Flying Trapeze, Lady Riverboat rides, Mini-Train rides, Sky ride, and Duke's Lagoon waterplay area.

WINTER WONDERLAND

Lancaster - *Dutch Wonderland. Selected rides and attractions open. Santa. Decorate cookies. Storytelling by the Princess of DW. FREE (rides & crafts, pay as you go). (late November-December)*

FULTON STEAMBOAT INN

Lancaster - *1 Hartman Bridge Road (US30 & SR896) 17602. Phone: (717) 299-9999 or (800) 922-2229. www.fultonsteamboatinn.com. From the first "Welcome Aboard" to the last splash in the Indoor Atrium pool – your kids will think it's cool to overnight in a steamboat. They have an indoor pool, jacuzzi, playground (really fun, outside) and an observation deck that looks onto the duck/koi pond and walking trail. This hotel is right in the middle of Dutch Country – easy to "pop" in and out of all day. Check out all of the ship's wheels and Victorian flare – esp. the lobby. The family-favorite Promenade Deck Queen w/Bunk rooms are located on the first level of the hotel and have one queen bed & a set of bunk beds. All rooms on board include, Flat Panel 32" HDTV's with remote, AM-FM clock radio, direct dial phone, refrigerator, microwave, hairdryer, iron/ironing board and in-room coffeemaker. Average daily rate runs about $80. After you spend the night sleeping on a steamboat, enjoy a meal in a room full of steamboat antiques. The outside of this Inn looks just like a steamboat complete with wheels and smoke stacks. As you hear occasional seagulls sounds, select from Steamboat or Mid-Ship Specialties for breakfast, lunch or dinner.*

LANCASTER SCIENCE FACTORY

Lancaster - *454 New Holland Avenue (and Plum St.) (near Industrial Area of downtown) 17602. Phone: (717) 509-6363. www.lancastersciencefactory.com. Hours: Tuesday-Saturday 10:00am-5:00pm, Sunday Noon-5:00pm (September-June). Opens Mondays also (June-August). Educators: Be sure to download the Scavenger Hunt for Young People before you go. Available on the Education icon, then Teacher Aids.*

Experience the interactive, hands-on learning environment of the Lancaster Science Factory. Through exhibits, work stations and mini-labs, children can experiment and create as they learn the principles of science and the application of science in engineering and technology. Can you make a long-lasting bubble? What about a building that withstands an earthquake? Next, run some electric or design and put a roller coaster in motion. And, our favorite - the maze that is a Kinetic Energy Machine. In this exciting learning environment, children of all ages will develop curiosity about how things work, will be challenged to think creatively and will build self-confidence as they discover that Science is Fun!

LANCASTER BARNSTORMERS BASEBALL

Lancaster - *Clipper Magazine Stadium, 650 North Prince Street (downtown) 17603. Phone: (717) 509-HITS. www.lancasterbarnstormers.com.*

Clipper Magazine Stadium in downtown Lancaster is the home of the Lancaster Barnstormers, the 2006 Atlantic League Champions. The Barnstormers are part of the Atlantic League of Professional Baseball and play from early May until October. The state-of-the-art stadium offers affordable and fun family entertainment. Fans enjoy the largest Kids' Play Area in minor league baseball, concession stands offering a "taste of Lancaster," unique promotions and giveaways and "up close" seats that will allow you to feel that you are part of the game. Single game tickets run $5.00-$12.00.

NORTH MUSEUM OF NATURAL HISTORY AND SCIENCE

Lancaster - *400 College Avenue (Franklin Marshall College) 17603. Phone: (717) 291-3941. www.northmuseum.org. Hours: Tuesday-Saturday 10:00am-5:00pm, Sunday Noon-5:00pm. Admission: $6.00-$7.00 (ages 3+). Small additional fee for planetarium.*

The North Museum has generated excitement and curiosity about natural history, science and technology for more than 50 years. Close to downtown Lancaster, the Museum features varied exhibits from outer space to local Native American peoples, from rocks and minerals to dinosaurs, from the Living Animal Room to the Discovery Room. While here, twist a 20-foot spiral wave machine, see how a tidal wave spreads across the Earth, play with a tornado, examine hundreds of birds, or explore the galaxy in the planetarium. The Technology Theater features the award winning ViewSpace system with downloads from the Space Telescope Science Institute. Linger to enjoy incredible images from the Hubble telescope and NASA missions. Planetarium shows weekend afternoons.

WHEATLAND

Lancaster - *1120 Marietta Avenue (PA 23 off US30west) 17603. Phone: (717) 392-8721. www.wheatland.org. Hours: Daily 10:00am-4:00pm, except Sunday (April-October) plus long weekends in November (Friday-Monday). Closed all major holidays. Admission: $8.00 adult, $7.00 senior, $6.00 student, $3.00 child (6-11). Tours: Costume guides for general or pre-arranged hands-on tours. Last tour begins at 3:00pm. Miscellaneous: Gift shop. Snack bar. Educators: click on Learn on the Wheatland homepage for biographies of Buchanan and others.*

The Federal Style mansion was home to the nation's 15th President (and the only President from Pennsylvania), James Buchanan. Tours begin in the

carriage house where you view a film about Mr. Buchanan and see the actual carriage his family used to travel around town. Also, see the library that served as a headquarters for his Presidential campaign. Kids are invited to dress in top hats or hoop skirts and may be asked questions like, "How often did people take baths in the mid-1800s?" Guess? (Answer - An average of 2 times per year!) His response to inquiries about "Wheatland" was…"I am now residing at this place, which is an agreeable country residence…I hope you may not fail to come this way…I should be delighted with a visit…"

CHRISTMAS OPEN HOUSE

Lancaster - *Wheatland. Tours of decorated, historical buildings. Refreshments and musical entertainment. Admission. (first and last week in December)*

AMERICAN MUSIC THEATRE

Lancaster - *2425 Lincoln Highway East (US 30) 17605. Phone: (717) 397-7700 or (800) 648-4102. www.amtshows.com.*

American Sights. American sounds. American Songs. American spirit. Musicals plus 30+ celebrity concerts year round. Morning, matinee and evening shows. Spring thru the Holidays. From concerts and Broadway Tours, to original musical revues that are fun for the whole family, there's something on stage for everyone at AMT. $10.00-$39.00 avg. Friday Family Night Rates (discounted early shows).

NATIONAL CHRISTMAS CENTER

Lancaster (Paradise) - *3427 US 30 (Lincoln Highway) 17562. Phone: (717) 442-7950. www.nationalchristmascenter.com. Hours: Daily 10:00am-6:00pm (May - first week of January). Open weekends in March & April. Admission: $11.00 adult, $5.00 child (3-12). Miscellaneous: Santa visits November 20th - December 23rd. Gift shop.*

As you enter, you're greeted by a cute 1950s Christmas morning scene as a little boy opens and tries on his new cowboy outfit. Another scene depicts "Yes Virginia, There is a Santa Claus". Can you find Santa patiently waiting for a

little girl to go to bed? This scene depicts a Christmas 100 years ago. Life cast artists create theme walk-thru displays with story lines. "Tudor Towne" is of Jolly Old England, a Once-Upon-A-Time World. "Return to Christmas Past" features antiques dating back to the early 1800s . The Electric Train display is wonderful.

"The First Christmas" probably has the most impact as you walk down a life-size recreation of the journey of Mary and Joseph to Bethlehem. It's very touching.

HANS HERR HOUSE

Lancaster (Willow Street) - *1849 Hans Herr Drive (between Pennsylvania route 741 / U.S. route 222 (Beaver Valley Pike) and Penn Grant Road) 17584. Phone: (717) 464-4438. www.hansherr.org. Hours: Monday-Saturday 9:00am-4:00pm (April-November). December special events. Admission: $5.00 adult, $2.00 child (7-12).*

The 1719 Hans Herr House, built in that year by Hans' son Christian, is the oldest surviving dwelling place of European settlers in what is now Lancaster County, Pennsylvania. It is the oldest still-standing Mennonite meeting house in the Western Hemisphere. The 1719 House, or "Hans Herr House" as it is known locally, was a home to several generations of Hans Herr's family until the 1860s, after which it was used as a barn and storage shed. It was restored to colonial-era appearance in the early 1970s. It is now part of a Museum complex which includes three Pennsylvania German farmhouses, several barns and other outbuildings, and an extensive collection of farm equipment spanning three centuries. Check their website for special events when re-enactors bring this place to life. Three regularly scheduled special events throughout the year include Heritage Day, a farm festival with many demonstrations and workshops; Snitz Fest, celebrating the apple in Lancaster County; and Christmas Candlelight Tours.

SIGHT & SOUND THEATRES

Lancaster / Strasburg - *Route 896 (off Rte. 30), 300 Hartman Bridge Rd (Millennium Theatre & Living Waters Theatre) 17579. Phone: (717) 687-7800. www.sight-sound.com.*

Sight & Sound continues the same mission to share the Word of God by turning stories you've always loved into shows you'll never forget. This special effects theatre is known for live Easter and Christmas performances. Shows the rest of the year focus on familiar bible characters like Ruth or Daniel. Through inspirational productions, they seek to encourage others to be dedicated and wise stewards of our God-given talents and resources. Epic stories unfold in front, beside and even above you! With innovative dream "cloud" sequences, lavish staging, colorful characters and vibrant music, this energy packed production is for all ages and is certain to stir your emotions with life-changing messages. Amazing side stage and live isle-way entrances/exits help bring Bible stories fantastically to life! Most major story scenes are mouth-droppers! Don't be afraid of the price, it's worth it. Tickets range from $16.00-$57.00. Seasonal shows each Christmas and Easter, too.

Langhorne

SESAME PLACE

Langhorne - *100 Sesame Road (I-95 to US 1 north to Oxford Valley exit. Next to Oxford Valley Mall) 19047. Phone: (215) 752-7070. www.sesameplace.com. Hours: Daily 10:00am-8:00pm (mid May - Labor Day Weekend), Weekends (early May, September & October) - Call for current schedule. Admission: ~$51.00 general admission. Parking $10.00. Discounts up to $10 are available at several online & retail partners and can be redeemed at front gate ticket windows. Miscellaneous: Late afternoon and family discounts. Bathing suits required for water attractions. We'd recommend staying all day to get your money's worth. Eateries, cafes and a bistro for sit down eating or set up a character meal.*

SESAME PLACE (cont.)

While your kids continue to peek over their shoulders for a glimpse of a Sesame Street character like Big Bird (great photograph opportunities), they'll be pulling your hand in every direction so they won't miss anything. Big Bird,

Elmo and the other stars of Sesame Street come out and play at Sesame Place, the only theme park in the nation featuring the popular TV show's most lovable characters. Catch a show like "Rock Around the Block", then jump on Ernie's Bed Bounce (that even sounds like fun to adults, doesn't it?) or scale "Cookie Mountain". Mechanical rides include: A roller coaster called "Vapor Trail", or, a 40-foot high balloon tower ride carries you up in one of eight balloon baskets - providing a bird's eye view of the park, and, also a character themed tea cup ride turns you "round and round" - as fast or as slow as you want to go. Everybody's favorite character hosts the new Elmo's World ride area. There's also 14 refreshing water attractions. As you float, zoom or chute through Big Bird, Ernie's and Slimey's Rides, you'll be splashed or trickled by a giant rubber ducky. Toddlers can be water trickled in Teany Tiny Tidal Waves. Bet your kids just can't wait to walk down a full-sized replica of Sesame Street and take pictures to show their friends back home!

TYLER STATE PARK

Langhorne (Newtown) - *101 Swamp Road (Follow I-95 north to the Newtown-Yardley exit 49) 18940. ww.dcnr.state.pa.us/stateparks/parks/tyler.aspx. Phone: (215) 968-2021. Admission: to PA State Parks is FREE however swimming, marina and camping/lodging fees apply, with reservation or entrance.*

The meandering waters of Neshaminy Creek flow through the park along with 10 miles of paved bicycling trails, a playhouse--Spring Garden Mill (www.langhorneplayers.org), and several children's play areas. Maze Picnic Area: This area is especially popular with families with young children because of the Children's miniature play barn and maze, Sand box, and Large play field. Gravel hiking trails to the east of Neshaminy Creek link each picnic area. Anglers may fish along the banks of Neshaminy Creek or from a canoe. A 27-hole Disc Golf course begins by the Upper Plantation Picnic Area. Neshaminy Creek offers calm, easy boating (electric motors only) upstream from the canoe rental. Horseback Riding, Trails, Winter Sports like Ice Skating, Ice fishing, Sledding & Tobogganing.

Lititz

STURGIS PRETZEL BAKERY

Lititz - *219 East Main Street (Route 772 - off Route 501) 17543. Phone: (717) 626-4354. www.juliussturgis.com. Hours: Monday-Saturday, 9:00am-5:00pm generally. Closed Sundays and winter Mondays. Admission: General $2.00-$3.00*

(A pretzel is given as your admission ticket. Be careful not to eat it all before the tour starts!) Tours: Every half hour. Weekdays 10:30am-3:30pm, Saturdays 9:30am-4:30pm. Miscellaneous: Gift shop with all sorts of fresh baked pretzels (flavorings, galore!) to purchase.

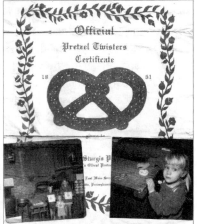

Boy, did the memories flow at this place! Over 20 years ago, my family (Michele's) took the same tour, in the same building and I still have my "Official Pretzel Twister" (see right) certificate. (By the way, they still do that - our daughter now has one too!). This is the first pretzel bakery in America (1861) and they still make their original soft pretzel by hand in the original 200

Michele & her brother & sister (left) and Jenny (right) earning their official <u>Pretzel Twister Certificate</u>...

year old ovens. Julius Sturgis started the pretzel industry with a recipe he learned from a hobo. Learn the history of the "pretiola" derived from monk's gifts to nearby children if they said their prayers. As you learn to fold your own pretzel, you'll learn how each step is related to prayer or marriage or the trinity. Definite "must see" while in Amish country.

WILBUR CHOCOLATE CO.

Lititz - *48 North Broad Street - (Route 501) 17543. www.wilburbuds.com. Phone: (717) 626-3249. Hours: Monday-Saturday 10:00am-5:00pm. Admission: FREE. Miscellaneous: Gift shop - suggest chocolate pretzels or Wilbur Buds (free sample).*

Wilbur Chocolate Company is known for its fine quality chocolate and currently produces more than 170 million pounds of chocolate products and other various food ingredients each year. The products are manufactured and shipped to confectioners, dairies, bakers, and candy makers across the nation.

Visitors to the modern candy kitchen can watch handmade chocolates created right before their eyes, including homemade marshmallow, almond bark, peanut butter meltaways, heavenly hash, mint drizzle, and almond butter crunch. They also make unique flavors of fudge in the Candy Shop. After the mouth-watering tour, check out the Wilbur Chocolate Co.'s Candy Americana© Museum - antique metal molds, tin boxes, and advertisements. View the Video – "The World Of Wilbur Chocolate" - see smooth chocolate made from the start...and learn a

Famous, yummy
Wilbur Buds

little cocoa bean history. Pick up a "lucky" cocoa bean as you walk in (don't eat it though!). Everyone walks out with a bag full of store bought variety chocolates and yes, they still offer FREE Wilbur Bud Samples to guests. P.S. - For a walk back in time, try their hot cocoa mix that you prepare over a stove - it's worth shoveling snow just to enjoy entering a warm house full of an aroma of the rich liquid chocolate.

WOLF SANCTUARY OF PA

Lititz - 465 Speedwell Forge Road (Follow Rt.501 North, at Rt.322 in Brickerville, turn left. Take the first left onto Long Lane, and follow to end, left onto Speedwell Forge Rd) 17543. Phone: (717) 626-4617. www.wolfsancpa.com.   Admission:

Weekend rates - $12.00 adults, $11.00 senior, Children under 12-$10.00, Cameras-$5.00. Weekday rates - $15.00 adults, $14.00 senior, Children under 12-$13.00 Tours: Weekend tours at 10:00am (summers) and noon (rest of year) only. Please arrive one half hour early to register. Weekday tours (Tuesday & Thursday) or by appointment only.

Located in the heart of Pennsylvania Dutch country on 22 acres of natural woodland, Wolf Sanctuary of Pennsylvania is the unlikely home of the Speedwell

Wolves. Kids enjoy meeting the wolves most of all. They enjoy hearing the wolves' stories and learning about their behaviors, personalities, and interactions with other wolves as well as volunteers. If they would like, they may bring dog treats to share with the wolves. Even though they love doggy treats, wolves make very bad pets. Find out why. Twice a year they have special events that include face painting, wolf identification, and other kid friendly activities. See website for updates. They also have numerous cats on the property that kids enjoy observing. Many girl scout and boy scout troops visit, as well as spend a few hours doing some volunteer work.

Manheim

CELTIC FLING & HIGHLAND GAMES

Manheim - *Mount Hope Estate & Winery (83 Mansion House Road, Route 72 & PA Turnpike Exit 20). www.parenfaire.com. Held on the festival grounds of the PA Renaissance Faire turns Amish Country into the Celtic Capital of the US! This Irish and Scottish heritage celebration covers the Faire's 35 acres in kilts, cabers and Celts with each day featuring musical sets, competitions and demonstrations. $10-$25 admission (age 5+). (third or last weekend in June)*

PENNSYLVANIA RENAISSANCE FAIRE

Manheim - *Mount Hope Estate. www.parenfaire.com. The Faire, with a cast of 100's of colorfully costumed merriemakers, is a rollicking recreation of a 16th Century country festival celebrating a visit by Her Majesty, Queen Elizabeth I, "God Save The Queen!" Hundreds of costumed merrymakers create a fantasy of bygone days and knights. Shows include jousting, cuttings from Shakespeare's immortal plays, Commedia Del Arte, puppet shows, sword swallowing, juggling, rope walking, and much more. Strolling minstrels and memorable street characters delight visitors hither and yon about the Shire. Admission. (weekends, mid-August thru mid-October)*

Media

LINVILLA ORCHARDS

Media - *137 W. Knowlton Road (Rte 352 north 3.5 miles. Left onto Knowlton Rd.) 19063. Phone: (610) 876-7116. www.linvilla.com. Hours: Regular hours are 9:00am-6:00pm daily with longer fall hours and shorter winter hours. Open every day of the year except December 25 and January 1.*

Once everyone has had their fill of Longwood Gardens, you'll be heading to Linvilla Orchards, one of the last working farms in the Delaware Valley.

With more than 300 acres, Linvilla hosts a variety of family-friendly events throughout the year. This is the oldest working farm in Delaware Valley where families can pick their own seasonal fruit, hop on a hayride and buy fresh-baked pies. Hayrides, tours, swimming and fruit and vegetable picking are offered in season. Try a Hayride to Bunnyland and Carolings Hayrides. Go out to look at the blossoms in spring and the autumn leaves each fall. After getting a nice lunch at the food stands, head out into the fields to pick some blue- or blackberries — they'll make a nice Philly-style souvenir for your ride back home!

- AUTUMN HAYRIDE AND TOUR – After a hayride, a tour guide will lead your group through a series of educational displays that teach about Johnny Appleseed, the Native Americans that lived on this site, the different varieties of apples and squash, and the process of making cider. The harvest is emphasized.

- SPRING / SUMMER HAYRIDE AND TOUR – After a hayride, a tour guide will lead your group through a discussion of planting and growing our food, how the Lenni Lenape planted in the spring, and show you some of the equipment we use today. The emphasis is on spring planting.

RIDLEY CREEK STATE PARK

Media (Newtown Square) - *Sycamore Mills Road or 351 Gradyville Road (entrances on PA3, PA 252 or PA352) 19073. Phone: (610) 892-3900. www.dcnr. state.pa.us/stateparks/parks/ridleycreek.aspx. Admission: FREE into park. Fee charged for Plantation tours.*

Shaded equestrian, hiking and bicycling trails lace the woodlands and old meadow. Within the park is the Colonial Pennsylvania Plantation (www. colonialplantation.org) that depicts a Delaware County Quaker farm prior to the American Revolution. On weekends from April to November, visitors can observe the farm family cooking over the open hearth, preserving foods, processing textiles, tending field crops and performing other chores necessary for survival in the 18th century world (small fee, 610-566-1725). There are hundreds of picnic tables in 14 picnic areas. Each area is equipped with restrooms and charcoal grills. Several of the areas have large fields suited to sports activities. Fishing and Winter Sports.

INDIAN POW WOW

Media (Newtown Square) - *Ridley Creek State Park. Native American singing and dancing. Arts and crafts. Native food storytelling and much more! Ridley Creek State Park. (610) 566-1725. Native Americans of the Delaware Valley present a Pow Wow at Colonial Pennsylvania Plantation. Admission. (second weekend in September)*

Morgantown

HAY CREEK APPLE FESTIVAL

Morgantown - *Historic Joanne Furnace. www.haycreek.org/festivals.htm. Homemade apple specialties. Scarecrows, pumpkin paintings, hay and pony rides. The Hay Creek Festival is known for its delicious homemade foods - Mabel's kettle soups, Schnitz Un Knepp (Apples & Ham), Ice Cream Floats, Apple Butter, Mint Tea, and Hamburgers & Hot Dogs. Entertainment. Historical activities for young children include rubber stamp and rubbing stations. Civil War Encampment. FREE. (mid-September long weekend, rain or shine)*

Morrisville

PENNSBURY MANOR

Morrisville - 400 Pennsbury Memorial Lane (Rte. 1 north, Morrisville to Rte 13 south. Exit onto Tyburn Road East. on the Delaware River) 19067. Phone: (215) 946-0400. www.pennsburymanor.org. Hours: Tuesday-Saturday 9:00am-5:00pm, Sunday Noon-5:00pm (open Summer holidays). Admission: $7.00 adult, $6.00 senior (65+), $4.00 child (3-11) Tours: 90 minutes long - a little difficult for pre-schoolers. Miscellaneous: Best for kids to visit (April - October) Sundays for living history days. Picnic areas.

A quaint, Quaker, simple homestead of William Penn, the founder of Pennsylvania. In 1682, William Penn sailed to Pennsylvania with one hundred other passengers on The Welcome. See a replica of the boat Penn used to "commute" to Philly. Horses, cattle, sheep and even a few peacocks roam the grounds as 17th century costumed interpreters demonstrate crafts and activities of the day. They may be baking bread (up to 30 loaves at one time!) in the bake house or check out the farm where sheep and geese roam. Inside the Visitor's Center try writing with the original "pen" - a quill pen. You can also learn about Colonial James writing style here.

CHRISTMAS OPEN HOUSE

CHRISTMAS OPEN HOUSE

Morrisville - *Pennsbury Manor. Tours of decorated, historical buildings. Refreshments and musical entertainment. Admission. (second weekend in December)*

New Hope

NEW HOPE AND IVYLAND RAILROAD

New Hope - *32 West Bridge Street (I-95 exit 51 west. Taylorsville Rd 5 miles. Rte. 32 north 5 miles. Depot at West Bridge and Stockton Street) 18938. Phone: (215) 862-2332. www.newhoperailroad.com. Hours: Daily (April-Holidays). Admission: Generally $11.50-$15.50 per ticket. Toddlers $3.00. Special trains more. Tours: Departure times vary, phone or visit website for schedule. 9 miles round trip-45 minutes.*

Climb aboard the New Hope & Ivyland passenger train and travel into a scene from the past. Relax and leave your cares behind as you journey into history, learning what rail travel was like for your parents, grand parents and great-grand parents. This ride is famous for the trestle called "Pauline" upon which actress Pearl White was bound to in the 1914 silent film "The Perils of Pauline". It might be the best way to expose young kids to the silent movies era (pictures available at the depot, too).

NORTH POLE EXPRESS

New Hope - *New Hope And Ivyland Railroad. Sing songs and eat treats as you ride the train with Santa aboard. Admission. (Thanksgiving - December weekends)*

NEW HOPE BOAT RIDES

New Hope - *18938.*

- **CORYELL'S FERRY HISTORIC BOAT RIDES**. 22 South Main Street at Gerenser's Ice Cream. (215) 862-2050. A Mississippi-style paddlewheel boat, the Coryell's Ferry offers trips on the Delaware River near New Hope. The boat departs daily at 11:00am from May to September. A Seniors special is offered on Tuesday, and Kids day is Wednesday. Buy your tickets at Gerenser's Exotic Ice Cream on Main Street. Learn about the history of the region and enjoy the scenery of the area. 1/2 hour tours on path once used to commute passengers by canoe (now they use paddleboats). Make sure to ask the driver about the area's importance as a colonial ferry crossing (Coryell's Ferry has been operating in the area since 1733), including the story about General George Washington's crossing.

- **WELLS FERRY** - Ferry Street and River Road. (215) 862-5965. Today, you can ride in comfort and savor the gentle river breezes on the 37-foot "Star of New Hope," a pontoon boat which departs New Hope at exactly the same spot as the original ferry, the end of Ferry Street. Guided tour on a 36 passenger boat highlighting history of river and canal plus famous homes and wildlife. Admission. Departs on the hour, from the end of May to mid-October, every day except Tuesday.

Norristown

ELMWOOD PARK ZOO

Norristown - *1661 Harding Blvd (I76 to Rte. 202 to Johnson Hwy.) 19401. Phone: (610) 277-BUCK. www.elmwoodparkzoo.org. Hours: Daily 10:00am-5:00pm. Closed major winter holidays. Admission: $8.50-$11.50 (ages 2+). Miscellaneous: Pony rides add $2.00 (seasonally). Snack shop. Gift shop. Picnic area. Easter Egg Hunts each spring. Butterflies in the summer. Educators: working on animal science reports? Glean some info from their Animal Profiles pages on the Animals/Education link online.*

This is not a big city zoo but it is a calm, friendly atmosphere where you have the opportunity to leisurely observe animals. Highlights of the zoo include: Petting Barn (goats & sheep), Duck Lake, Prairie Dog exhibits, Aviary Wetland (waterfowl, beaver, otters), and The Bayou (murky home to lovely alligators, turtles, and snakes - everything that hisses or snaps!). There's also your basic natural Grasslands (bison, elk, and new "bears" area). At certain places like the Elk and Prairie Dogs you can get very close to the animal as opposed to most zoos where you are kept at a significant distance. Animal shows on Summer weekends are entertaining as they play with and share stories about unique animals in the park. There's a cougar that doesn't feel ferocius and a monkey that only loves on you if you scratch him.

Nottingham

HERR'S SNACK FACTORY TOUR

Nottingham - *20 Herr Drive (US 1 and SR272 to Herr Drive) 19362. Phone: (800) 63-SNACK. www.herrs.com. Admission: FREE. Tours: Monday - Thursday 9:00am -11:00am and 1:00pm-3:00pm; Fridays 9:00am-11:00am (cannot guarantee production running on Friday). All tours take approximately one hour. When scheduling, please indicate the time of day (on the hour) you wish to take your tour. Miscellaneous: Gift shop. Chippers Café with crunch and munch lunchroom. Very reasonable snack bar prices.*

There's no fake machinery or actors - it's the REAL factory, the REAL workers, and the REAL process. "Watch a groovy-chip movie" starring "Chipper" your

tour guide and mascot. The whimsical (combination guide and TV monitor) tour takes you through the simple process of snack food production. Lots of hot oil and hot air drying, moisturizing and "spritzing" going on - a salon for snacks! Try samples warm off the "beltway" - those were a favorite point of the tour. Yes, you can have more than one! Also see other snacks made like cheesepuffs (corn meal dollops filled with air),

Jenny & Daniel and their good friend "Chipper"

tortilla chips, popcorn (huge poppers!) and pretzels (how do they make the outsides brown?). Your kids will be amused at the sideway mixers churning out 10 pound mounds of pretzel dough. The dough takes a long trip on a conveyor and then a "dough-bot" (robot) removes them to be shaped & baked. Like to try new things? Try Grilled Cheese Curls, sweet Chocolate Covered Pretzels or Kansas City Prime Steak Potato chips (yes, steak flavored!) An excellent, organized tour - voted our best pick of snack food tours.

Penns Creek

T & D 'S CATS OF THE WORLD WILD ANIMAL REFUGE

Penns Creek - *Mountain Road (off rte. 104) 17862. www.tdscats.com. Phone: (570) 837-3377. Hours: T & D's is a not for profit refuge and is opened May to September for visitors. Admission: $10.00 per person (ages 13+) and $5.00* *per child (3-12). Special Admission during June, July, and August (in addition to Saturdays and Sundays). Tours: Hour tours offered Mondays through Fridays at 10:00am and 2:00pm. Arrive early. Tours start on time. Admission - $10.00 per person. October through April-Groups by appointment.*

One family owns and operates an exotic wildlife refuge for unwanted, abused and confiscated animals. The tour through the woods takes approximately an hour and half to complete. Students will learn about the native habitat, diet, distribution, and adaptations of each species; as well as conservation activities, how the animals came to T&D's, and why these animals should not be kept as pets. Students will be able to get within four feet of the animals--close enough to count the whiskers on the lions and tigers! They will also have the opportunity to feed deer, goats, and ducks.

Philadelphia

PHILADELPHIA SPORTS

- **KIXX SOCCER** - MISL - Major Indoor Soccer League. May-September. Wachovia Complex. www.kixxonline.com. Look for their mascot, SocceRoo. PHILADELPHIA 76ers BASKETBALL - www.nba.com/sixers. Wachovia Complex. National Basketball Association. Family Pack Nights.

- **PHILADELPHIA EAGLES FOOTBALL** -www.philadelphiaeagles.com. Lincoln Field. NFL Professional football team (August-December). Meet and greet players at the annual Eagles Carnival in August.

- **PHILADELPHIA FLYERS HOCKEY** - www.philadelphiaflyers.com. Wachovia Complex. National Hockey League (October-March).

- **PHILADELPHIA PHILLIES BASEBALL** - http://philadelphia.phillies. mlb.com. Citizens Ballpark. Gameday: National League East MLB team. Take a romp in the Phanatic Phun Zone, the largest Softplay area for kids in Major League Baseball. Take a stroll through Ashburn Alley, an outdoor entertainment area. Features include the All-Star Walk, Citizens Bank Games of Baseball, Memory Lane, Rooftop Bleacher Seats, Wall of Fame, Alley Store, and more! Opens 2 1/2 hours prior to game time so fans can watch batting practice. Look out for the long lines waiting for an order of delicious crab fries at Chickie's and Pete's, the famous cheesesteaks at Campo's, sinfully amazing roast pork sandwiches at Tony Luke's, authentic Philadelphia hoagies at Planet Hoagies, and the creative cheesesteak variation from Chestnut Hill's McNally's that is the Schmitter.

PHILLY CHEESESTEAK

Philadelphia -

People usually come to Philadelphia for two things: the history and the cheesesteak. So what is an authentic cheesesteak and how do you order it? Here's the lowdown on this region's favorite sandwich:

A cheesesteak is a long, crusty roll filled with thinly sliced sautéed ribeye beef and melted cheese. Originally, the cheese of choice was Cheez Whiz, but American and provolone are common substitutions. Other toppings include fried onions, sautéed mushrooms, ketchup and hot or sweet peppers. The onions, cheese and beef are the most common. You'll find Cheesesteaks sold on every corner of historic and south Philly...mostly at small, family-owned pizza shops or delis. Some of the best we've had were from food carts stationed around the Liberty Bell. When ordering, there are two critical questions to answer: First, what kind of cheese do you want? (Whiz? Provolone? American?) Second, do you want onions? Be forewarned: Lines are often long at lunchtime and if you don't have your order and money ready to go, you might be asked to step back to the end of the line until you decide. This isn't your mall variety cheesesteak - these babies are dripping with juices (ask for extra napkins) and filled with meat!

Here's some of our favorites to try:

- More famous for its creative menu of hoagies, **CAMPO'S DELI** cooks up a respectable traditional cheesesteak. It's a small place but fun. Great for lunch. 214 Market Street. (215) 923-1000.

- **JIM'S STEAKS** has multiple locations, but the classic smell of fried onions wafting down South Street makes that location the most memorable. 400 South Street. (267) 519-9253 or www.jimssteaks.com.

PHILLY TRANSPORTATION & TOURS

Philadelphia - *(Downtown). Admission: Call for rates. Pay as you board.*

Parking can be difficult and pricey around downtown Philly. During their spring/summer and fall season they offer the Phlash, a Visitors' loop bus, as a great option for visitors. The rates are very reasonable. Many parking garages give significant discounts to guests who park in their garage (all day) and then transport to museums and sites via Phlash. Street parking is available for around $4.00 per two hours at kiosk meters but you must return every two

SE Area

hours to add time. For a full day downtown, budget $20.00 for parking and enjoy as many free attractions as you can!

- **SEPTA** (Southeastern Pennsylvania Public Transportation Authority) Part of Philadelphia's subway system. Visitors can purchase a One Day Independence Pass for unlimited rides on all of the subways and buses for a whole day. The pass is also accepted on the Phlash (in season). This year's prices were $25 for a family up to five. More details are available at www.SEPTA.org/fares or by calling (215) 580-7800. This pass can purchased at the Independence Visitor Center at 6th and Market Streets at all SEPTA Sales Office and Regional Rail Ticket Offices or online at www.shop.septa.org.

- **PHILADELPHIA TROLLEY WORKS** ('76 Carriage Company): www. phillytour.com. This longtime Philadelphia company offers several exciting options for touring town, including Victorian Trolley Tours, Horse Drawn Carriage Tours, LandShark Tours and Double Decker Bus Tours. Entertaining staff will treat you to a fun and informative trip around the city. Take advantage of free daytime shuttle service. www.phillytour.com.

- **PHILLY PHLASH** - (215) 4-PHLASH or www.phillyphlash.com. Look for Philadelphia Trolley Works Purple Phlash Trolleys for a quick, cheap and easy way to get around Center City Philadelphia. Phlash is the quick and easy connection between Penn's Landing and the Philadelphia Museum of Art, with stops at 21 key destinations covering most downtown hotels. $5 for an individual all-day pass, $10.00 family. Runs May thru end of October.

- **RIVERLINK FERRY** - (215) 925-LINK. Passenger ferry across the Delaware River between Penn's Landing and the Camden waterfront sites. Seasonal

- **BIG BUS TOURS** - www.bigbustours.com. Now you can experience the unique history and beauty of Philadelphia from an authentic London-style double-decker bus. An open-top tour of the city offers you spectacular views and make sure your ears are tuned in to the entertaining live commentaries from fully-trained and friendly guides.

PHILADELPHIA ORCHESTRA

Philadelphia - *260 South Broad Street, 16th Floor (most performances at Kimmel Center) 19102. Phone: (215) 893-1900. www.philorch.org.*

Sound All Around Series (ages 3-5), learn about the different families of instruments. Family Concert Series (ages 6-12) - music featuring puppets, magicians, storytellers, and young soloists. (Saturday mornings). Each summer The Philadelphia Orchestra performs free outdoor concerts in neighborhoods around the Philadelphia region.

ACADEMY OF NATURAL SCIENCES

Philadelphia - *1900 Benjamin Franklin Parkway (off I-676 and corner of 19th Street) 19103. Phone: (215) 299-1000.   www.acnatsci.org.   Hours: Monday-Friday 10:00am-4:30pm, Saturday, Sunday & Holidays 10:00am-5:00pm. Closed Thanksgiving, Christmas, and New Year's Day. Admission: $12.00 adult, $10.00 senior (65+), $10.00 child (3-12). Butterflies! Exhibit extra $2.00 per person. Part of CityPass discount card.   Miscellaneous: Ask for Scavenger Hunts sheets (age appropriate) when you enter. The kids stay focused this way. Films show daily. Ecology Café and gift shop.*

The oldest dinosaur and natural science exhibit in the world is here. Actually peer into, or walk under, dinosaurs. You're greeted by a roaring robotic dinosaur at one entrance. A giant dinosaur skeleton hangs over the information desk at the main entrance. Most families'

favorite area is the Dinosaur Hall. This is hands-on paleontology including a fossil dig (child equipped with goggles and tools), fossil prep lab, and Time Machine (get your picture image appearing with dinosaurs!). You'll also meet T-Rex, plus 11 friends, and even get to climb into a dinosaur skull. The North American Hall has some stuffed large animals that are almost 200 years old.

"Friendly" dinosaurs everywhere...

Butterflies!, a completely redesigned permanent exhibit, features a lush, tropical garden filled with colorful plants and a multitude of exotic butterflies from around the globe. Educational demos and computer interactives add to this Metamorphysis space ($2.00 extra admission). There are live animals shows and "Outside In"... hands-on, touching mice, snakes, frogs, and huge bugs. Touch a real meteorite, view a stream from underneath, crawl through a fallen log, look for fossil footprints, pan for shark teeth, watch a working beehive, build a sandcastle or read a book on Lucy's Back Porch. There's also a crystals and gems exhibit that features a 57 pound amethyst and "Living Downstream" - a showcase of life in a watershed or Egyptian Mummies.

SE Area

FRANKLIN INSTITUTE SCIENCE MUSEUM

Philadelphia - *222 North 20th Street (intersection of 20th Street and the Benjamin Franklin Parkway, downtown) 19103. Phone: (215) 448-1200. www.fi.edu. Hours: Daily 9:30am-5:00pm. Closed on November/December major holidays only. Admission: $14.75 adult, $12.00 child (4-11) and $13.95 senior (62+). Sci-Pass includes museum, science demos, and planetarium. IMAX and special exhibits extra.   Miscellaneous: Ben's Bistro - Lunch, Café, Museum Stores. Special exhibits change in the Mandell Center. IMAX Theatre (additional charge).*

If you've got older kids, you may want to check out the Franklin Institute instead of the children's museum. The Franklin is the area's premier science museum, housing a planetarium, IMAX movie theater, several permanent exhibits and rotating special exhibits (advanced tickets are typically required for the special exhibits). What began as a national memorial to Ben Franklin is now a hands-on exhibit and demonstration complex.

At the entrance are displays of some of Franklin's personal effects and a famous statue by James Earle Fraser. Some exhibits have been there forever. Walk through a "Human Heart" - hear a heart beating as "blood" races through the arteries. Also, see a full-size train or airplane cockpit! Learn how Sports and Physics mix or how Art & Physics collide. Highlights include The Sports

Challenge, which uses virtual-reality technology to illustrate the physics of sports; The Train Factory's climb-aboard steam engine; Space Command's simulated earth-orbit research station; a fully equipped weather station; and exhibits on electricity. Our favorite area is Space Command where you visit a research station right here on Earth!

Locate your house using a satellite home-tracking device. Travel through time to uncover what our ancestry thought about space. Embark on a mission to discover a lost, unmanned space probe. Check out equipment used by real astronauts to explore space.

Films like "Everest" and "The Lion King" assume grand proportions on the Tuttleman IMAX Theater's

Did You Know?

The Franklin Institute is Pennsylvania's most visited museum?

SE Area

79-foot domed screen; galaxies are formed and deep space explored in North America's second-oldest planetarium sporting the continent's most advanced technology. Don't miss the 3D Theater and the indoor SkyBike.

PHILADELPHIA ZOO

Philadelphia - *3400 West Girard Avenue (I-76, exit 36) 19104. Phone: (215) 243-1100. www.philadelphiazoo.org. Hours: Daily 9:30am-5:00pm (February-November). Daily 9:30am-4:00pm (December-January). Closed Thanksgiving, December 24, 25 and 31 plus New Years Day. Admission: $16.95 adult, $13.95 child (2-11) Zoo. $15.00 Zooballoon Ride. Parking $10.00. Seasonal Zoo Trolley transport from Independence Visitor Ctr. Is only $2.00. Educators: click on FOR SCHOOLS & SCOUTS, then Educational Lessons. Miscellaneous: Zoo shop. McDonald's restaurants. Victorian picnic groves. Stroller and wheelchair rentals. Camel, elephant and pony rides and "Treehouse" interactive areas have additional fees. Behind-the-Scenes tours available occasionally. Kids and grownups can climb inside one of the award-winning Dodge Wild Earth Durango adventure simulators for a thrilling 3-D ride through the plains of Africa.*

The first zoo in the country - now has 1800 animals on 42 acres of beautiful landscape. Favorites include the famous white lions, Jezebel and Vinkel, the first white lions ever to be exhibited in North America. Presently, there are no white lions in the wild. Big Cat Falls! - home to endangered big cats from around the world, including three new playful snow leopard cubs, three adorable new puma kittens and a beautiful new black jaguar cub. Carnivore Kingdom has the country's only giant otters. Bear Country allows you to interact (viewing, that is) with playful bears that love to show off. Check out the new primate habitat. The Children's Zoo has your typically petted animals plus cow-milking and other live demonstrations in the pavilion. The first passenger carrying balloon in the world to be located at a zoo is available for rides (Zooballoon). Zooballoon rises 400 feet above the treetops and overlooks giraffes, zebras and the Philadelphia skyline.

SANTA AT THE ZOO

Philadelphia - *Philadelphia Zoo. Food, arts & crafts, games, face painting, Santa & Mrs. Claus, sing-alongs, storytime and sweets. (weekend in December before Christmas)*

UNIVERSITY OF PENNSYLVANIA MUSEUM OF ARCHAEOLOGY & ANTHROPOLOGY

Philadelphia - 3260 South Street (I-76 to South Street exit to 33rd and Spruce Streets) 19104. Phone: (215) 898-4001. www.upenn.edu/museum. Hours: Tuesday-Saturday 10:00am-4:30pm, Sunday 1:00-5:00pm (Closed Mondays, Holidays, and summer Sundays from Memorial Day to Labor Day) Admission: $10.00 adult, $7.00 senior (62+) and $6.00 student (age 6+). "Pay-what-you-want" after 3:30pm Tuesday through Saturday, and after 4pm Sunday. Tours: Guided on Weekends at 1:30pm during the school year. Miscellaneous: Snack café. Pyramid Gift Shop. Most fun to come during a Family Fun Day Event (215) 898-4890.

Exhibits outstanding findings from Ancient Egypt, Asia, Central America, North America, Mesopotamia, Greece, and Africa, uncovered by University staff and student expeditions. See a giant Sphinx and real mummies. Gaze at an Apache tipi or a Navajo walk-in sky theater. On

Did You Know?

The Penn Museum is the only museum in the world to exhibit such a significant portion of an Egyptian royal palace.

one side of each gallery the exhibition focuses on the use of objects to display status and to transfer laws and traditions to upcoming generations, and on the ways in which some cultures have used objects to influence and communicate with the forces that control people's lives. The other side of the gallery displays objects of everyday life and invites you to compare the lifestyle of a group of hunter-gatherers with the lifestyle of subsistence farmers by looking at the objects each uses. The stories of the archeologists' thoughts and accompanying pictures of "digs" might inspire a budding career.

WORLD CAFÉ LIVE

Philadelphia - 3025 Walnut Street 19104. www.worldcafelive.com. Phone: (215) 222-1400. Peanut Butter & Jams at World Cafe Live is about creating fun and interactive live music experience for kids and parents. Perfect for a family outing, children's birthday parties, or just for a fun afternoon, the Peanut Butter & Jams series is a guaranteed crowd pleaser. Join them each Saturday morning for the show and follow it up with a family friendly lunch buffet (not included in ticket price). Doors generally open at 11:00 am with the show starting at 11:30am, but you should always check each performance listing for times or any changes. Show admission: $7.00-$10.00 per person. Add the all-you-can-eat Lunch buffet:$7.00-$10.00. Peanut Butter & Jams at World Cafe Live is about creating fun and interactive live music experience for kids and parents. Perfect for a family outing, children's birthday parties, or just for a fun afternoon, the Peanut Butter & Jams series is a guaranteed crowd pleaser. Join them each Saturday morning for *the show and follow it up with a family friendly lunch buffet (not included in ticket price). Doors generally open at 11:00 am with the show starting at 11:30am, but you should always check each performance listing for times or any changes. Show admission: $7.00-$10.00 per person. Add the all-you-can-eat Lunch buffet:$7.00-$10.00.*

ATWATER KENT, MUSEUM OF PHILADELPHIA

Philadelphia - *15 South 7th Street 19106. www.philadelphiahistory.org. Phone: (215) 922-3031. Hours: Wednesday-Sunday 1:00pm - 5:00pm. First Friday - 5:00 - 8:00pm, free and open to the public. Admission: $5.00 adult, $3.00 senior and youth (13-17). Admission structure may change after renovations.*

Whatever history you don't catch visiting buildings in the area, you'll get a touch of here. Included are: the wampum belt received by William Penn from the Lenni Lenape at Shakamaxon in 1682, the first German Bible in North America printed by Christopher Saur in 1743, personal items from Benjamin Franklin, and Phillies' Mike Schmidt's game-worn jersey. You'll also see Norman Rockwell's America showcasing all 322 magazine covers created by the country's most admired 20th-century illustrator for The Saturday Evening Post. Family Programs - toys of the past, hat making, children of the past.

BETSY ROSS HOUSE

Philadelphia - *239 Arch Street, Historic area (Between 2nd & 3rd Streets) 19106. Phone: (215) 686-1252. www.betsyrosshouse.org. Hours: Tuesday - Sunday & Monday Holidays 10:00am-5:00pm. Also open summer Mondays. Closed Thanksgiving, Christmas and New Years. Admission: Suggested donation: $2.00-$3.00 per person. Tours: Self-guided audio tours are $5.00 (includes admission). Self-guided tour lasts about 25 minutes. Miscellaneous: Hot dogs, drinks and snacks are offered in the courtyard from Thursday through Sunday in March and April and*

daily beginning May 1. FREEBIES: Ask for the "house hunt" sheet for kids.

The nation's most famous seamstress, credited with the creation of the first American flag, stitched her way into history in the small workroom on display at this house. In 1777, the first American flag made by Colonial Mrs. Ross was sewn here. Betsy, who made a living as a furniture upholsterer, rented the 1740 home, and the teeny-tiny rooms and tight little staircases give a good portrayal of a working class woman's life in colonial America. You can tour her modest, working class home. Did she design the flag? Each room has a description, in Betsy's words (in old English), of what led up to her sewing the flag. She and the fellas that made the Liberty Bell were just ordinary folks who had a skill needed to enhance the cause of Independence. What was considered a routine job lead to national recognition many years later! After you tour the house, make sure to meet Betsy Ross and plan to spend some time relaxing in the shady courtyard where you'll enjoy free family friendly programming, hear storytelling and see colonial crafters at work (seasonally).

CARPENTER'S HALL

Philadelphia - *320 Chestnut Street, Historic area (exit for Indep. Hall. Follow signs for 6th st to Chestnut, left on 2nd) 19106. www.ushistory.org/carpentershall/. Phone: (215) 925-0167. Hours: Tuesday-Sunday 10:00am-4:00pm (Closed January & February Tuesdays). Admission: FREE   Educators: Lesson Plans online by clicking TEACHERS icon. FREEBIES: icon marked FUN has interactive and downloadable quizzes, puzzles and coloring books.*

Displays of early carpenter's chairs and tools used by the First Continental Congress in 1774. A 10 minute video chronicles the history of the carpenter's company (they still own and operate the hall). Because the site is dedicated to the craft of carpenters and master builders, supplementing with lesson plans and puzzles is the best way to try and engage the kids. That, and the model of Carpenter's Hall which looks like a colonial "doll house" illustrating 18th century construction methods.

CHRIST CHURCH

Philadelphia - *20 North American Street 2nd Street (between Arch & Market Streets) 19106. Phone: (215) 922-1695. www.christchurchphila.org. Hours: Monday-Saturday 9:00am-5:00pm, Sunday 1:00-5:00pm (March-December). Wednesday-Sunday (Rest of year). Admission: Suggested Donation of $2.00-$3.00 to help maintain the church. Miscellaneous: Services (Episcopal) held on Sunday mornings and Wednesday at 12:00pm.*

Christ Church is bordered by a tree-lined brick path, small park and a cobblestone alley, which provide the perfect setting for this historic treasure. The tower and steeple made it the tallest building in America until 1856. Fifteen signers of the Declaration of Independence worshiped here including George Washington and Benjamin Franklin. A brass plaque marks each pew of famous Colonists including Betsy Ross. Families and groups can visit the church and burial ground to gain a deeper understanding of our early history and the importance of religious freedom. Tours given throughout the day. The church was built in 1727 and originally had dirt or wood floors. Ask a guide what those marble rectangles are in the floor. Careful - though they won't mind...you may be stepping on the memory of a notable patron of the church!

CITY TAVERN

Philadelphia - 138 South 2nd Street at Walnut St. (Columbus Blvd. Past 6 lights to left on Dock to right on Front St, left on Walnut) 19106. Phone: (215) 413-1443. www.citytavern.com. Hours: Lunch is served from 11:30am daily. Dinner is served from 4:00pm Monday-Saturday, from 3:00pm Sundays. This is an authentic Colonial tavern faithfully recreated to 18th century colonial America. Servers are dressed in colonial garb and the restaurant uses historic recipes like Turkey Pot Pie, Cornmeal Crusted Chicken, and Grilled Ham & Cheese (served on City Tavern's Sally Lunn bread, baked from the 18th century recipe, accompanied with pomme frites - potato fries). Honestly, the Turkey Pot Pie is the best ever! The City Tavern features an award-winning children's menu, high chairs and booster seats so even the little colonists can eat Olde-style in comfort. The children's menu ($8.00-$13.00 per entrée) are just smaller portions of the adult menu. Staying with the theme, they offer a fun drink called the Colonial Shrub - an 18th century beverage made from fruit juice, sugar, fizzed w/ ginger ale and soda (like a fancy Shirley Temple). A spiked version is available for adults. And parents, when was the last time you saw duck sausage, Roquefort salad dressing, pork schnitzel or beef pie on a menu (lunch avg. $14.00)? City Tavern bakes a variety of bread and pastries daily that may include such unique offerings as Sally Lunn, Anadama loaves or sweet potato and pecan biscuits - Thomas Jefferson's favorite.

¶◉¶ _____

DECLARATION (GRAFF) HOUSE

Philadelphia - 7th & Market Streets, Historic area 19106. Phone: (215) 597-8974. www.nps.gov/inde/declaration-house.html. Hours: Generally 9:00am-Noon. Vary by season. (Call ahead) Admission: FREE.

Catch the short video and then see the rooms that Continental Congress delegate, Thomas Jefferson rented in this building where he penned the actual Declaration of Independence. The bedroom and parlor that Jefferson occupied have been recreated and contain period furnishings. Also included are reproductions of Jefferson's swivel chair and the lap desk he used when he wrote the Declaration. Like the other buildings in this national park, our history studies come alive in these authentic places where great men once walked, worked, and lived.

SE Area

FEDERAL RESERVE BANK MONEY IN MOTION

Philadelphia - *100 N. 6th Street, ground floor of Federal Reserve (next to National Constitution Center) 19106.. www.philadelphiafed.org/education/money-in-motion/. Hours: Monday-Friday 9:30am-4:30pm. Admission: FREE. FREEBIES: Besides the souvenir pack of $$, ask the hostess for a Scavenger Hunt worksheet.*

This permanent exhibit explains the way our financial system works. The exhibit's 16 different stations offer artifacts ranging from wampum, the original colonial money, to a $100,000 bill, which was produced for one year (1934). Kids will gasp at the giant tube stuffed with $100 million in shredded cash and giggle at the "Match wits with Ben" game. At the end of the exhibit, visitors get a packet of shredded money worth $100.

FIREMAN'S HALL

Philadelphia - *147 North 2nd Street (Historic district near Elfreth's Alley) 19106. Phone: (215) 923-1438. www.firemanshallmuseum.org. Hours: Tuesday-Saturday 10:00am-4:00pm. Admission: FREE.*

Future firefighters get a head start at this restored 1902 firehouse that holds some of the nation's earliest blaze-fighting equipment and important historical artifacts. See memorabilia, films, and early equipment. Did your kids know Benjamin Franklin founded the first Philadelphia Fire Department in 1736? See old-fashioned leather buckets, fire wagons and an "around the world" display of firefighter helmets. Play pretend in the re-created living quarters or steer a fireboat. Taped firemen's stories recall high level exciting moments on the job. The Spider Hose Reel (1804) has a chariot look with brass bells and shiny mirrors. Also be on the lookout for the fire pole and injured firemen's hats (charred & broken).

FRANKLIN COURT

Philadelphia - *3rd, 4th, Chestnut & Market Streets (I-95 exit 22, Phila/Indep.Hall/ Callowhill to 6th & Race Sts) 19106. Phone: (215) 597-8974. www.nps.gov/inde. Hours: Usually daily 10:00am-5:00pm but can vary. Call for details. B.Free Franklin Post Office not open Sundays. Admission: FREE*

Today the site contains a steel "ghost structure" outlining the spot where Franklin's house stood and features an underground museum with a film and displays about his personal life. Check out Franklin's numerous inventions, then walk and talk in the Phone Room where dozens of phones can call famous friends of Franklin. Hear "voices" of historic men such as Thomas Jefferson and Mark Twain talk about Franklin and how they felt about his character. In the courtyard, peek in the pits below to see actual excavations of rooms of Franklin's home. "Bump into" Mr. Franklin as you roam his court and he'll invite you to gather around to hear stories of his life. What a wonderful way to study this amazing historic man!

Once owned by Ben Franklin who lived in Philadelphia from 1722-1790, the complex of buildings also includes:

- <u>NEWSPAPER OFFICE</u> - Working reproduction of 1785 printing press and bindery.

- <u>POST OFFICE</u> - In 1775, Ben Franklin was appointed as the first Postmaster General. The name "Free Franklin" was used as the hand cancellation signature because Mr. Franklin was referring to America's struggle for freedom. See actual hand-canceled letters, then, purchase a post card & send it from this working post office!

> **Did You Know?**
>
> Benjamin Franklin is accredited with being the first American to invent a musical instrument? He invented the glass armonica in 1761 after seeing wine glasses being used to make musical sounds.

FRANKLIN FOUNTAIN

Philadelphia - *116 Market Street (exit Indep. Hall and follow signs to Market St. Head east (left) on Market) 19106. Phone: (215) 627-1800. www.franklinfountain.com. Hours: Noon to Midnight every day. The Franklin Fountain, in Old City Philadelphia is an authentic early 20th century soda shop with tin walls and ceiling, original marble counters and mosaic floors. Servers dressed as old-fashioned soda jerks serve homemade hard ice cream, banana splits, thick shakes, egg creams, sundaes and flavored soda water creams. Ok, so because Franklin is in the name, you know the namesake has to follow in naming the sundaes... The Franklin Mint (mint chip ice cream, crème de menthe topping) or The Lightning Rod (dark chocolate brownie, espresso, choco espresso beans, coconut and pretzel rod), for example. Plain Janes will still love the basic Homemade Hot Fudge (PA made, Wilbur's dark chocolate creamed smooth into hot fudge). Adventuresome foodie - ever thought of ordering black Licorice or pink Teaberry Gum flavors? Wonderful on their own or in ice cream sodas. Most sundaes run $8.00-*

SE Area

$10.00 and are generally 3 scoops of ice cream (very sharable portions). With the menu's use of words like covered, glazed, suffocated, surmounted, bathed, finished, peppered, mountain, cascading, blanketed, doused, and ruffled...how can you go wrong?

FRANKLIN SQUARE

Philadelphia - *6th and Race Streets (close to the National Constitution Center) 19106. http://historicphiladelphia.org/day/franklin-square/. Hours: Daylight hours. Admission: Carousel tickets $2.00-$3.00 per person (age 3+). Philly Mini-Golf $6.00-$8.00 (age 3+).*

Franklin Square is one of Philadelphia's five original squares - and the only one dedicated just to fun. A day outside around Franklin Square could include a ride on an old-fashioned carousel, a game of mini-golf, a romp on a modern playground and a family picnic. A concession called SquareBurger sells burgers, hot dogs, fries, drinks and frozen treats. The 18-hole Philadelphia-themed course allows Guests to putt through favorite icons including Elfreth's Alley, Benjamin Franklin Bridge, Philadelphia Museum of Art, LOVE statue, Chinatown Friendship Gate, and on the 18th hole, putt through the crack in the Liberty Bell and land in front of Independence Hall. Plus, holes celebrating Philadelphia Sports teams and Philadelphia Music legends.

INDEPENDENCE HALL

Philadelphia - *520 Chestnut Street, Historic area (5th & 6th Streets on Chestnut - across from Liberty Bell) 19106. Phone: (215) 965-7676. www.independencehall.org. Hours: Daily 9:00am-5:00pm. Weekends 9:00am-6:00pm. Admission: FREE. Tours: Guided tours only throughout the day. Long lines move pretty fast. You must reserve a free timed ticket from the Visitor Center OR http://reservations. nps.gov ($1.50 handling fee per ticket if order in advance) to enter spring, summer and fall. Educators: Anything, we mean any angle of our country's founding is at this excellent website: www.independencehall.org. Miscellaneous: Congress Hall (where the first US Congress met and inaugurations of Presidents occurred) and Old City Hall (Supreme Court original house) are across the street. Hours vary but it is a must see for kids studying the setup of the United States Government.*

INDEPENDENCE HALL (cont.)

Hey…this is the place that we see in countless movies and pictures. You will get a patriotic chill as you enter the hall where the Declaration of Independence was adopted and the U.S. Constitution was written. They risked everything — "their lives, their fortune and their sacred honor." During the blistering summer of 1776, 56 courageous men gathered at the Pennsylvania State House and defied the King of England. George Washington's "rising sun" chair dominates the Assembly Room which is arranged as it was during the Constitutional Convention. The Assembly Room looks just as it did in 1776 (you'll feel like you're in a movie) and you can see the original inkwell the Declaration signers dipped quills in to sign the famous freedom document. If the story of Independence doesn't get them, the mini-jail in the courtroom where defendants literally "stood trial" will.

INDEPENDENCE SEAPORT MUSEUM

Philadelphia - 211 South Columbus Blvd, Penns Landing (I-95 exit 20) 19106. Phone: (215) 925-5439. www.phillyseaport.org. Hours: Daily 10:00am-5:00pm. Closed major winter holidays. Admission: $12.00 adult, $10.00 senior (65+), $7.00 child (5-12). Educators: an excellent Teacher's Activity Packet is downloadable to print by clicking on: EDUCATION, then TEACHER RESOURCES. Miscellaneous: The Museum Store. Ask about the Philadelphia Citypass - it's a great value if you're seeing more than just historic area. Family Saturdays at the Seaport is a programs where kids craft while pretending to be a pirate or ship captain.

With historic vessels to board, a ship's hull to rivet, and cargo to unload with miniature cranes, Philadelphia's maritime museum conveys what the Delaware and Schuylkill Rivers have meant to the city over the years. "Climb in, Pull this, Please"…are common signs here (hands on area). For example, ride a waterbed boat, blow a

"Everyone remain calm!" screams Capt. William…

fog horn, play the Crane Game or Climb aboard bunks on a ship. In clever dioramas, hear and see immigrant and crew stories. Take a few moments to watch and talk to boat builders as they build skiffs, then head outdoors to the walk-on battleship Olympia and submarine Becuna. This is what the kids really come for! The Olympia is the nation's oldest floating steel warship (1892) and most famous for being Admiral Dewey's flagship during his Spanish-

SE Area

American war victory in Manila Bay. The Becuna is a classic World War II submarine that fought battles in the South Pacific. Self-guided tour lets kids "feel" like sailors, captains, or pirates. The kids will move quickly following the self-guided arrows so try to keep up! Be prepared, they may want to tour again, and again. If parents don't want to tour the ships all afternoon, the Workshop on the Water working boat shop can be a nice diversion. Watch artisans building and restoring traditional wooden boats.

History lessons are woven between these additional exhibits:

* WHAT FLOATS YOUR BOAT? - Put weights in different places on a model boat to study its center of gravity, or pull different shapes through a ten-foot tank of water to examine how drag affects speed. Assemble a four-foot wooden boat puzzle. And further on, the curious can walk or crawl through a full size replica of a 22-foot 19th century Delaware River Shad Skiff.

* DIVERS OF THE DEEP - Diving gear and underwater archeology.

INDEPENDENCE VISITOR CENTER (FOR THE NATIONAL HISTORICAL PARK)

Philadelphia - *525 Market Street, Historic area (northeast corner of 6th & Market Sts - across from the Liberty Bell) 19106. www.nps.gov/inde. Phone: (215) 597-8974. Hours: Daily 8:30am-5:00pm. Extended summer hours. Admission: FREE. Parking garages in downtown Philadelphia are very steep ($4.00 per half hour up to $22.00). Cheaper alternatives: Philly Phlash buses, 2-3 hour parking meters (esp. open on Walnut & Chestnut sts). Tours: sign up for programs or walking tours (daily summers, weekends only rest of year). All ranger guided tours are free. Cell Phone Audio Tours are available using special code numbers attained at various stops or thru maps at the Center. Miscellaneous: This is where to park (below center) and purchase tickets or schedule times for tours. Plan to spend 5-8 hours in the Independence Historical Park. Secure areas (I. Hall & Liberty Bell) Do Not have restrooms so use them here. Educators: click on FOR TEACHERS link and download Lesson Plans. On that same page is a link to tour worksheets for students. Grab your pens and unleash your imagination for the Hedgehog Herald adventure! FREEBIES: you can download the Junior Ranger Activity booklet on the FOR KIDS link or pick one up at the Center. Search for the stamps found in the park, complete some activities and you'll earn a Ranger Badge. Coloring pages, too. This JR activity book is one of the best ever!*

INDEPENDENCE VISITOR CENTER (cont.)

Start here before you explore the well-known sites. See award winning historical and tourism films shown throughout the day. Ben Franklin, George Washington, John Adams and others come back to life to tell the Independence story. Older children will want to sign up for the walking tour here (little ones up to grades 1 or 2 will want to wander at their own pace and usually aren't interested enough to stay with the group). To keep attention spans high, we noticed they create a theme (seasonally) of historical significance. Actors called "Town Criers" present impromptu conversations and "street stage" presentations along with that theme. They admired our "carriage" (known to you and me as a wagon) and our "horse" that was pulling it (Daddy!) Most events are daily in the summer and weekends the rest of the year.

JULY 4TH CELEBRATION

Philadelphia - *Independence Visitor Center. www.americasbirthday.com. Welcome America Festival. Top name musical groups and dramatic readings by famous actors. FREE. Parades, music, food, fireworks & contests.*

JONES RESTAURANT

Philadelphia - *700 Chestnut Street at 7th Street (follow signs for Independence Hall, then go one block west) 19106. Phone: (215) 223-5663. www.jones-restaurant.com. Hours: Lunch Monday-Friday starting at 11:30am. Saturday/Sunday brunch starts at 10:00am. Dinner starts daily at 4:00pm until late. With a setting right out of the Brady Bunch, Jones restaurant puts a modern spin on comfort foods, such as macaroni and cheese and meatloaf. The talented kitchen staff created a menu of affordable comfort food, which is available seven days a week, from lunchtime through late night. Down-home dishes such as Baked Macaroni and Cheese (w/ crumb topping-be sure someone in your party orders this to sample!), Beef Brisket, Deviled Eggs, Meatloaf and Mashed Potatoes, and Thanksgiving Turkey Dinner with all the Trimmings are some of the all-American specialties on the list, with eclectic variations on more worldly treats such as Cheese Pierogies with Caramelized Onion. Jones' signature entree would be a hefty plate of Fried Chicken and Waffles, served with chicken gravy. For dessert, diners choose from Strawberry Jell-O Parfait, Coconut Cream Pie, and Duncan Hines Chocolate Layer Cake. For drinks, order something fun like Purple People Eater (grape juice, lemonade, sprite), Jungle Punch or Blackberry Soda. Appetizer portions (avg.$8.00) were just right sized for smaller appetites.*

SE Area

LIBERTY BELL

Philadelphia - *6th Street, between Market and Chestnut Streets (across from Independence Hall, entrance on Market Street) 19106. Phone: (215) 597-8974. www.nps.gov/inde. Hours: Daily 9:00am-6:00pm. Extended summer & many weekend hours. Admission: FREE Tours: Given by park rangers, relates the bell's history. Long lines (for security checks) - but they move fast. Miscellaneous: Glass encased bell is viewable 24 hours a day. Interpretive kiosk displays explain details of the Bell.*

Made a few blocks away by two crafters who only made pots and pans (usually), its famous "crack" has many folklore stories associated with it. It would be nice to believe that each crack was the result of zealous ringing; however, it just wasn't cast properly to withstand its large size and temperature variances. Initially, it was just a bell ordered to be placed in the tower of the meeting hall (now called Independence Hall). Later, abolitionists used it as a symbol of freedom for slaves

So close to history...

and proclaimed it the Liberty Bell (not until 1840 though!) - and the name stuck!

What does a cracked bell sound like?

Try clanging the sample cracked bells that show how a bell sounds before and after repairs.

X-rays give an insider's view, literally, of the Bell's crack and inner-workings. In quiet alcoves, a short History Channel film, available in English and eight other languages, traces how abolitionists, suffragists and other groups adopted the Bell as its symbol of freedom. It'll give you goosebumps to stand inches from it. Be sure to take advantage of the photo opportunity time provided by park rangers.

LIGHTS OF LIBERTY

Philadelphia - *Liberty Center, PECO Energy (Independence Hall exit. Left on N. 6th to the corner of Chestnut) 19106. Phone: (215) LIBERTY or (877) GO-2-1776. www.lightsofliberty.org. Hours: At Dark on Fridays & Saturdays (mid-April-early September). See website additional scheduled days during peak or seasonal events. Admission: $19.50 adult, $16.50 senior (65+) and student (w/*

ID), $13.00 child (6-12). Discount promotions on their website. Tours: 60 minute tours depart every 10 minutes. Miscellaneous: The Liberty Center is also home to Ben Franklin's Ghost -- a free exhibit where kids (and adults) can use a touch-screen computer "book" to query Ben with their own questions or choose from two hundred pre-formed questions, answered by Dr. Franklin, who appears as a dramatic, large screen image.

One evening during a visit, be sure you reserve a spot for the LIGHTS OF LIBERTY. The Lights of Liberty Show leads visitors on an evening journey to relive the American Revolution. Using headsets with 3D sound, visitors follow

the drama of the American Revolution as it happened, where it happened. The sound system and enormous five-story images projected on buildings immerse visitors into events leading up to the Colonists' fight for freedom from the British. Mom and dad can tune in to hear Walter Cronkite and Ossie Davis narrate the adult version of the tour while kids can listen to Whoopi Goldberg recite the children's version. Start in Franklin Court, end at Independence Hall where the battle rages with swirling smoke and flashes from imaginary musket blasts. Hear the hurried sound of horses' hoofs on cobblestone streets. You'll find yourself cheering for the Patriots and clapping on several occasions. The ending "God Bless America" is very moving. Our six year old really got engaged! Although anyone can see the giant projected images, only those wearing the high tech headsets hear the stories. Ask for the youth

show (a fictional family, the Warren children, serve as headset hosts). Recommended ages: 6+. So unique and what an adventure!

NATIONAL CONSTITUTION CENTER

Philadelphia - *525 Arch Street, Historic area (Independence National Park, between Arch & Race, 5th & 6th Streets) 19106. www.constitutioncenter.org. Phone: (215) 923-0004. Hours: Monday - Friday 9:30am-5:00pm, Saturday 9:30am-6:00pm, and Sundays Noon- 5:00pm (except Thanksgiving Day, Christmas Day, and New Years Day) Admission: $8.00 - $12.00 (age 4+). Active Military w/ID are FREE. Parking garage under the museum runs $8.00-$18.00. Educators: click online on RESOURCES page, then Bill of Rights game or civics lesson plans for all grades. FREEBIES - click on EDUCATION, then Students, then Studying the Constitution for resources, games and puzzles just for you.*

The first-ever national museum honoring and explaining the U.S. Constitution and the Constitution's relevance to our daily lives so that all of us -- "We the

People" -- will better understand and exercise our rights and our responsibilities. It's only four pages long, but the U.S. Constitution is among the most influential and important documents in the history of the world. Wandering a "street scene" in 1787 Philadelphia, you can eavesdrop on fellow citizens and discover the forces that inspired the creation of the document. You

then enter a theater-in-the-round, where you view The Founding Story, a dramatic multi-media production which orients you to the major themes of the Center and the basic historical context of the Constitution. "Signers Hall," is where visitors are invited to play the role of Signer amidst life-size statues of the Founding Fathers. Place notes or sign a modern Constitution book and then hang out taking pictures with famous folks present at the 1st signing. High-tech, interactive exhibitions let everyone-even those under 18-vote on legislative bills, weigh in on court cases and take the Presidential Oath of Office. Kids get to dress up in robes and push buttons and play games.

NATIONAL LIBERTY MUSEUM

Philadelphia - *321 Chestnut Street (Washington Ave. exit , left on Columbus. Follow signs to Market & Second St) 19106. www.libertymuseum.org. Phone: (215) 925-2800.   Hours: Daily 10:00am-5:00pm (Memorial Day - Labor Day). Closed Mondays the remainder of the year. Admission: $7.00 adult, $6.00 senior, $5.00 student, $2.00 child (5-17). "Family Admission" $15.00, includes two adult family members and all of their children. Educators: Lesson plans and activities/follow up questions are under EDUCATION, then PRE-VISIT MATERIALS.*

This museum is home to more than 100 works of glass art by Dale Chihuly. The exhibits celebrate heroes who fight for freedom around the world. From the stories of thousands of heroes of all walks of life... to awesome glass art... to lively discussions on youth-oriented topics, try to stop in and see some of the spaces that really engage questions because the art if so fun! Parents love the interactive themes including anti-bullying and non-violence, pride in oneself, civic responsibility, character education and more. The Jelly Bean People and Flame of Liberty are must sees!

RIDE THE DUCKS TOURS

Philadelphia - *6th & Chestnut Depot, Historic area (Exit at Callowhill St. Turn left onto 6th Street) 19106. Phone: (215) 227-3825. www.phillyducks.com.* **Tours: Daily, Daylight hours, mid-March thru December. Tickets for sale near depot or Independence Visitors Center. Admission: $26.00 adult, $16.00 child (3-12). AAA, senior & military discounts.**

This fun tour provides passengers with an 80 minute entertaining, historically accurate, land and water sightseeing adventure aboard amphibious WWII Duck vessels. Each tour features a scenic "bus" tour past Philly's historical and cultural sites, then splashes down into the Delaware River for a floating tour along

This tour vehicle is at "home" on land and water - QUACK!

Penn's Landing (the kids, and kids-at-heart, get to try driving the boat on the water, too). You'll find yourself quacking (with provided official quackers) at interesting people as the captain comments w/ theme music – party music – that really gets you in the mood! Learn about different ethnic eateries or some history "with a twist" – just little funny tidbits that never bore the kids (i.e.. What happened if you didn't have fire insurance? Who is famous for cake and ice cream?). Don't worry, the Duck Trucks look silly but you feel great as you travel this fun way…the new, hip way to see historic old Philadelphia!

SHANE'S CANDIES

Philadelphia - *110 Market Street (between 2nd & Front Sts.) (exit Indep. Hall/ Callowhill, bottom of ramp turn left onto 2nd St, then left onto Market) 19106. Phone: (215) 922-1048. www.shanecandies.com.*

America's oldest candy store still makes candy the old-fashioned way. Handmade, hand-dipped chocolates in traditional and novelty shapes have been tempting palates since 1876. It claims to be the oldest candy store in the country and the place hasn't changed in MANY years. Shane's Candies famous creamy buttercreams are slowly cooked the old-fashioned way in a copper kettle while being stirred with a wooden paddle. These irresistible delicacies are Shane's most popular piece because they possess an incredible creamy and rich taste. The ladies behind the counter try and stuff you with vanilla cream samples. They love kids!

THADDEUS KOSCIUSZKO NATIONAL MEMORIAL

Philadelphia - *301 Pine Street (I-95 Independence Hall exit/ Columbus Blvd. Follow signs to Society Hill) 19106. Phone: (215) 597-9618. www.nps.gov/thko. Hours: Wednesday-Sunday Noon-4:00pm. Admission: FREE.*

Visit the house where wounded Polish freedom fighter Thaddeus Kosciuszko lived and hear how this brilliant military engineer designed successful fortifications during the American Revolution. See the room where he received notable visitors such as Chief Little Turtle and Thomas Jefferson, who said he was "as pure a son of liberty, as I have ever known..." Exhibits & audiovisual displays (English & Polish language) describe the help Thaddeus gave to the American Revolution. Learn why he was loved and then kicked out of his native Poland, why he carried a crutch and how his skills helped Americans strategically beat the British. He was a genius engineer!

TODD HOUSE

Philadelphia - *4th & Walnut Streets, Historic area (just west of Carpenters Hall) 19106. Phone: (215) 597-8974. www.ushistory.org/tour/tour_todd.htm. Hours: Open house daily from 4:00pm-5:00pm. Admission: $2.00 adult.*

This was the home of Dolley Todd before her marriage to James Madison (Dolley Madison pastries will get the kids on the same page). While John Todd who dwelled in the house for two years would succumb to yellow fever in 1793, has become more or less a footnote on your Philadelphia tour, his wife Dolley remains a beloved historical figure and is the reason we are here. Dolley, by most accounts, was a fabulous and spirited hostess. Here fish, meat, fruit, and baked bread all purchased fresh daily from vendors at the High Street headhouse (now Market Street) would be prepared for the Todds, their two children, Dolley's younger brother and sister, and two law clerks who worked under Barrister Todd. Add to that a pet bird and a dog named Pointer and one has at the least a quite lively household. Representing a middle-class Quaker home, she became quite a First Lady when she moved from this house and married James Madison, fourth President of the United States.

U.S. MINT

Philadelphia - *5th & Arch Streets (Take I-95 to Exit 22 for "Central Phila/I-676".*
Follow signs for Phila/Independence Hall/Callowhill Streets) 19106. Phone: (215)
408-0112. www.usmint.gov/mint_tours/. Admission: FREE Tours: Weekdays
9:00am-3:00pm, except Federal holidays. If the Department of Homeland Security
level is elevated to CODE ORANGE, the United States Mint at Philadelphia will be
CLOSED to the public unless otherwise noted. All tours are free and self-guided;

no reservations are necessary. Note: The United
States Mint does not provide parking.

While in the historic district of Philadelphia, be sure
to take your family to the world's largest coinage
operation (seen through a glass enclosed gallery).
They make a million dollars worth of coins per
day! (29 million coins!). See them start with blanks
that are cleaned and then stamped, sorted, and

So many types of coins bagged. To see coins in large bins or spilling out
are minted here... of machines is mesmerizing! Even little kids eyes

sparkle. A "Stamp Your Own Medal" machine (press a big red button to
operate) is located in the Gift shop. Great souvenir idea!

DOUBLETREE HOTEL PHILADELPHIA

Philadelphia - *237 S. Broad Street (neighborhood: Convention Ctr / Chinatown/*
Market East-Broad St. exit south about 5 blocks) 19107. www.doubletree.com. Phone:
(215) 893-1600. Guests who want to stay in the middle of the action check in to the
Doubletree Hotel Philadelphia, located on the Avenue of the Arts. Families can spend
some time at the rooftop pool, sundeck and racquetball courts, and kids get a free
cookie at check-in. Especially nice if you want to stay in between the Science Museums
and the Historic Area. The views of the city are pretty cool, too. Some packages offer free
parking, which is a good value here as parking is $22.00 per day or more. You could walk
to everything (or take the Phlash) but that means a minimum of 10 blocks each way.

PHILADELPHIA CITY HALL OBSERVATION DECK

Philadelphia - *Broad & Market Streets (Broad St. exit south about 4 blocks)*
19107. Phone: (215) 686-2840. . Hours: Daily 9:30am-4:15pm. Admission: $4.00-
$5.00 per person (age 3+). Tours: Tower tours every 15 minutes from 9am to 2pm.
A full tour of City Hall, including the tower, starts at 12:30. Separate tower tours
resume at 3:00pm until 4:15pm.

Every city has one building that stands as one of the tallest in town and usually it has a lot of history behind it. Most noted is the courtroom (available to view on the tour only) where a motion picture film was made and the 548 foot tall tower that has a statue of William Penn on top. At the base of the statue is the observation deck. Its observation deck, which is open to the public, provides a panoramic view of the city. This building is so breathtakingly beautiful and stands in the center of downtown...believe us, you can't miss it!

Arguably the most popular sculpture in Philadelphia, LOVE, by artist Robert Indiana, debuted in John F. Kennedy Plaza during the 1976 Bicentennial celebration.

READING TERMINAL MARKET

Philadelphia *- 12th and Arch Streets (neighborhood: Convention Ctr/Chinatown/ Market East-Broad St. exit south, follow signs) 19107. www.readingterminalmarket.org. Phone: (215) 922-2317. Hours: Monday through Saturday: 8:00am-6:00pm. Note: Some of the Market's restaurants close after 4:00pm. Sunday: 9:00 am-5:00 pm. Wednesday - Saturday only hours for Pennsylvania Dutch vendors. Wednesday 8:00am-3:00pm, Thursday - Saturday 8:00am-5:00pm. Sunday 9:00am-4:00pm. Begin your historic adventure with an early lunch at the Reading Terminal Market, the nation's oldest continuously operating farmer market. Family-run vendors sell virtually every type of farm-fresh cuisine, as well as prepared food ready to eat there. The northwestern corner of the market is primarily devoted to Amish merchants from Lancaster County, who bring their farm-fresh products and distinctive prepared dishes to the Market four days a week. Watch as Amish bakers twist and bake soft pretzels right in front of your eyes - then try one while it is still warm from the oven. You can get a traditional Amish-style meal at the counter of the Dutch Eating Place (Famous blueberry pancakes, egg sandwiches, apple dumplings, fresh cut fries, deli sandwiches and scrapple) - or get an authentic Philadelphia cheesesteak at Ric? s Steaks. But those are just two options at this foodie paradise look around and see what you like!*

Did You Know?

The Reading Terminal is home to the best Macaroni and Cheese in the country? In 2003, Oprah Winfrey declared Delilah's Mac and Cheese (made from scratch with Gruyere and Asiago cheese) to be the best in America."

SE Area

EASTERN STATE PENITENTIARY

Philadelphia - *2124 Fairmount Avenue (I-95 exit 22, follow I-676 west. Get off at Art Museum/Benjamin Franklin Parkway Exit. Turn right and go five blocks past the Museum of Art) 19130. Phone: 215-236-3300. www.easternstate.org. Hours: Daily 10:00am-5:00pm. Closed Thanksgiving, Christmas Eve, Christmas Day and New Year's Day. Admission: $12.00 adult, $10.00 senior and $8.00 student, $8.00 child (7-12). Children under the age of 7 cannot be admitted to the site.*

Let's go to jail. This Penitentiary introduced Americans to a new- and a supposedly more humane-form of housing criminals: solitary confinement. Kids are fascinated by the massive cellblocks, dark cells, and stories of punishment and escape at Eastern State Penitentiary. There are special guided tours on the subjects of daily life, escapes, prison uprisings and artifacts available several times a day, every day April-November. These tours are hands-on, interactive experiences, designed for visitors age seven and up. Tours include: The central rotunda, restored cells, the solitary confinement yards, the baseball diamond, death row and Al Capone's Cell. A "Voices of Eastern State" audio tour is available during all hours. Although the subject matter is family friendly, it's recommended for kids 12 and up. Special Guided Tours with themes on Escape! Or Prison Life are highlighted versions of the audio tour. These tours are hands-on, interactive experiences, designed for visitors to engage in the spaces more.

PHILADELPHIA MUSEUM OF ART

Philadelphia - *26th Street and Ben Franklin Parkway (follow I-676 west. Get off at "Art Museum/Benjamin Franklin Parkway" Exit. Turn right) 19130. Phone: (215) 763-8100. www.philamuseum.org. Hours: Tuesday-Sunday, 10:00am-5:00pm. Friday evening until 8:45pm Admission: $16.00 adult, $14.00 senior (62+), $12.00 child & students (age 13+). First Sunday of each month: Pay what you wish all day. Miscellaneous: Museum restaurant.*

The 3rd largest museum in the country. 2000 years of fine and applied arts (crafts, interiors, architecture) with 200 galleries. Many rooms have themes that transport you back to when the works were created. Sundays are family days at the museum. The pay-what-you-wish admission is

The famous steps from famous movies...   budget friendly, and gallery games, musical performances and art projects entertain the whole family. Families can also take advantage of Self-Guided Family Tours and Children's Audio Tours to explore the collections on their own.

Outside, your kids (or parents!) will love running up the numerous steps to the top like Rocky (from the movie by the same name). Pretend you hear the crowd cheer as you step onto the brass glazed imprints of Rocky's shoes!

FAIRMOUNT PARK

Philadelphia - *Benjamin Franklin Parkway (info at Visitor's Center at Memorial Hall) 19131.   www.fairmountpark.org or www.smithplayhouse.org. Phone: (215) 685-0000.*

Along both sides of Schuylkill River, one of the world's largest city park's features include:

• **SMITH PLAYGROUND & PLAYHOUSE** - (215) 765-4325. Emphasis on playhouse (3 story) for preschoolers with trains, foam blocks and comfortable reading rooms. Pick up a Cozy Car and drive along the play roads with stop signs and traffic lights. This 100 year old playground has a Giant Wooden Slide that four generations have slid down.

• **ENVIRONMENTAL EDUCATION CENTERS**: Come check out Fairmount Park's two environmental education centers and its 112-acre working livestock farm. The Pennypack and Wissahickon Environmental Centers are open year-round. Experience their interpretive exhibits, wildlife viewing areas, picnic areas and miles of trails. Fox Chase Farm is an enjoyable place for children and adults to visit and explore. Open House the first Saturday of each month. Come experience Maple Sugar Day, Sheep Shearing or Apple Fest too.

• **FAIRMOUNT WATER WORKS INTERPRETIVE CENTER**: 640 Water Works Drive (215) 685-0723 or www.fairmountwaterworks.org. Who cares that you don't know the difference between a watershed and a woodshed? At the Fairmount Water Works Interpretive Center you and your family can learn about watersheds and have a ton of fun doing it. Fly a helicopter simulation from the Delaware Bay to the headwaters of the Schuylkill River. Or visit Pollutionopolis, America's most contaminated and disgusting town, to see how a city can really mess up its water supply. The Water Works is a pumping station from 1815 to 1909 where visitors can create rain, view historic photos and play with high-tech exhibits.

• **WISSAHICKON CREEK GORGE** - hiking trails.

MAPLE SUGARING FESTIVAL

Philadelphia - *Andorra Natural Area in Fairmount Park. (215) 685-9285. (Late February – Early March). Actual tapping of trees. Syrup making. Demonstrations of coopering and sugaring off in a realistic sugar camp. Pancakes and syrup served.*

PLEASE TOUCH MUSEUM

Philadelphia - **4231 Avenue of the Republic, Fairmount Park (Memorial Hall, GPS - Use 4231 North Concourse Drive for directions) 19131. Phone: (215) 581-3181. www.pleasetouchmuseum.org. Hours: Monday-Saturday 9:00am-5:00pm, Sunday 11:00am-5:00pm. Closed New Years, Thanksgiving and Christmas. Themed Shows presented several times each day. Admission: General $15.00 (over age 1). Parking fee $5.00. Miscellaneous: Please Taste Café. The Kids Store - take ideas from the museum home as souvenirs or projects. Nature's Pond and Fairy Tale Garden toddler areas for kids 3 and under.**

PLEASE TOUCH MUSEUM has moved and improved! The museum space is divided into six learning-through-play environments – based in the real world and fantasy themes. Here are some highlights: * Real Victorian era carousel & model of the Statue of Liberty's torch made of toys. * Kid-scaled city-scape * Road-side attractions section where kid "mechanics" can work on real Toyota Scion or "ride/drive" a real SEPTA bus. * Kid-scaled supermarket with shopping carts and food packages for kids to stock up. * Exploration of space where kids can pedal a propeller bike, play hopscotch on clouds or spin inside a giant hamster wheel. * Nature-inspired instruments that play music * Collection of 12,000 toys and games from 1945 to the present. OR *River Adventures. Race sailboats in water currents, play with bubbles, and rainbows.

This hands-on museum for kids 8 and under also kept our favorite:

ALICE IN WONDERLAND - The tale is explained in miniature (little doors to peek through) and then full size. Try on cover ups and pretend you're the Queen of Hearts ready for a tea party with Mad Hatter & rabbit (great photo op).

Although the setups are classic in here, the fresh aspects of creativity through role playing are really different. It's pricier than most kid's museums we've been to in our travels, but its uniqueness is often worth it. Frugal moms, If you have an ACM Reciprocal Program icon on your membership card from another children's museum, you will receive 4 free admissions to this museum. www.childrensmuseums.org/visit/reciprocal.htm#acmreciprocalprogramparticipants.

INSECTARIUM

Did You Know?
This is the largest insect museum in the nation.

Philadelphia - 8046 Frankford Avenue (1-95 Cottman Avenue exit 30 thru to right on Frankford for several blocks) 19136. Phone: (215) 338-3000. www.insectarium.com. Hours: Monday-Saturday 10:00am-4:00pm. Admission: $6.00 (ages 2+)

While in Philly, maybe add a creepy trip over to the INSECTARIUM, north of downtown. Philadelphia's only all-bug museum exhibits thousands of live and mounted insects from Africa, Tanzania and other exotic locations, as well as interactive displays and movie room. Did you know we eat bugs every day? They're ground up in plants as they are harvested. See a glow in the dark scorpion or bugs with noses. There's giant bugs and little bees (do you know what honey really is?). Pet live bugs like Martin the cockroach or Harry the millipede (yes, Mommy actually pet them!). Interact as you climb thru a spider web, eat fried worms, or push buttons. The highlight has to be the Cockroach Kitchen & Bathroom! How do they keep them inside the room? They live here and are welcome! Great photo ops and their gift shop has inexpensive craft kits and bug food and toys. You will learn so much here and the guides really add the "magic". Outside, there's a learning garden where you go on bug hunts.

George, "calmly" holding a scorpion... yikes!

SE Area

MUMMERS MUSEUM

Philadelphia - *1100 South 2nd Street & Washington Avenue (I-95 exit 20 west. Turn left on to Columbus Blvd. Take first left onto Washington Avenue. 2 lights up on the left) 19147. Phone: (215) 336-3050. www.mummersmuseum.com. Hours: Wednesday-Saturday 9:30am-4:30pm (October - April). Closed Sundays, Mondays, Tuesdays & all Holidays. Admission: $2.50-$3.50.*

What is a mummer? Opened in 1976, the museum is dedicated to the Philly celebration of the new year. Audio and interactive displays, musical instruments, costumes, and artifacts from the traditional New Year's Day parade. Some of the spectacular costumes date back to the turn of the 20th Century. See videos of past parades or watch how those colorful sparkly costumes are made.

PHILADELPHIA PHILLIES BASEBALL BALLPARK TOURS

Philadelphia - *Citizens Bank Park (south Philadelphia) (off exit 17 onto Broad St. & follow signs) 19148. http://philadelphia.phillies.mlb.com/phi/ballpark/index.jsp. Tour Pricing: Tickets are $9.00 for adults, and $6.00 for children (3-14 years) and senior citizens. Tour Times: Tours are offered year round, during the season, on non-game days.*

Come get an inside look at the Phillies home. Tour guests will be treated to a brief audio/visual presentation of Citizens Bank Park, followed by an up-close look at the ballpark. Tour stops include the Phillies dugout, Diamond Club (which features the glass-enclosed batting cages), Cooperstown Gallery (which features 32 original oil paintings by artist Dick Perez) and the unique Hall of Fame Club. Tours last approximately 90 minutes and start and end at the Majestic Clubhouse Store.

WACHOVIA CENTER TOURS

Philadelphia - *3601 South Broad Street (South Broad Street & Patterson Avenue) 19148. Phone: (215) 389-9543. www.wachoviacenter.com/tours.aspx. Tours: Groups of 15+ (may be added to another group if less than 15 in party). Weekdays (provided no events are scheduled). By reservation. $4.00-$5.00 per person.*

Guided tours of the home of the Philadelphia 76ers & Flyers. In your personal guided tour through the Wachovia Center, you will be given an exclusive chance to visit and explore the private luxury seating levels, the press box, Arena Vision studio control room, Comcast SportsNet, and the official NBA and NHL locker rooms. See playing floors and learn great inside scoops on the history of favorite players and teams.

FORT MIFFLIN

Philadelphia - *Fort Mifflin Road (I-95 to Island Avenue Exit 15 west - follow signs) 19153. Phone: (215) 685-4167. Web: www.fortmifflin.com. Hours: Wednesday-Sunday 10:00am-4:00pm. (March-December 1) Admission: $6.00 adult, $5.00 senior (65+) and $3.00 child (6-13) and veterans. Miscellaneous: Sundays suggested as there are military drills and craftspeople demonstrating their skills. Check out their educational Treasure Hunts for group tours.*

"What Really Happened at Fort Mifflin?"... you'll find out that a lot happened here. Starting in 1772, it was built by the British to protect the colonies. Ironically, in 1777, it was used by Americans trying to protect the Philadelphia and Delaware River from the British (7 long, grueling weeks of siege). It also protected the city of Philadelphia during the War of 1812 and was active as a Confederate and Union prison camp during the Civil War. Until 1954, it was still used to store ammunition for the United States military. A great place to check out and study several wars all in one spot.

HEINZ NATIONAL WILDLIFE REFUGE

Philadelphia - *Lindbergh Blvd. & 86th Street (I-95 exit 10west. left onto Bartram Ave, left onto 84th St, left onto Lindbergh Blvd) 19153. Phone: (215) 365-3118. http://heinz.fws.gov/.*

The refuge was established by an act of Congress in 1972 to protect the last 200 acres of freshwater tidal marsh in Pennsylvania. Hiking trails to explore butterflies, muskrats, frogs, flying geese, and loads of wildflowers is open dawn to dusk. Observation tower. The Cusano Environmental Education Center is open daily from 8:30am-4:00pm, free of charge.

PHILADELPHIA INTERNATIONAL CHILDREN'S FESTIVAL

Philadelphia - *University of Penn. Annenberg Center for the Performing Arts. (215) 898-3900. www.pennpresents.org. Performances throughout each day...you pick and choose from international acts like a circus from Finland, a dance company form the Ivory Coast, comedy from Denmark, fairy tales from England or folk singers from the USA. The Playworks area is where international artisans teach their art and help kids create versions of crafts such as African drums, Hmong tapestry, egg painting, dream catchers and Peruvian sundials. Stageworks is where emerging regional performers can share their talent. Admission/packages. (first week of May)*

BATTLE OF GERMANTOWN RE-ENACTMENT

Philadelphia - *Germantown Avenue on Market Square. www.cliveden.org. (215) 848-1777. This historic district is home to Cliveden (family homestead with original furnishings and bullet marks still visible) plus a museum with an overview of America's first German settlement. This land was the scene of a Revolutionary Battle of Germantown, the birthplace of writer Louisa May Alcott, and the site of the Underground Railroad. What some kids may feel are normally boring museums, become more interesting during a festival as history is relived. (first Saturday in October)*

MORRIS ARBORETUM

Philadelphia (Chestnut Hill) - *100 Northwestern Avenue (University of Pennsylvania) 19118. www.business-services.upenn.edu/arboretum/. Phone: (215) 247-5777. Hours: Daily 10:00am-4:00pm (year round). Open until 5pm on Saturday and Sunday (April - October) Admission: $14.00 adult, $12.00 senior (65+) and $7.00 student, military & child (3-17).*

Romantic 92 acre Victorian garden with many of Philly's rarest and largest trees, a sculpture garden, a rose garden and the Fernery. A canopy into the limbs of the Metasequoias is the latest addition to the Morris Arboretum experience. A stairway brings visitors front and center into one of the Arboretum's most spectacular groves of trees via an installation called meta Metasequoia. The model trains in the Garden Railway Display changes each season. Kids are sure to find several hidden side paths and little coves.

ADVENTURE AQUARIUM

Philadelphia area (Camden, NJ) - *1 Aquarium Drive (take Ben Franklin Bridge over to exit 5 or take RiverLink Ferry over from Penn's Landing) 08103. Phone:*

(866) 451-AQUA. www.adventureaquarium.com. Hours: Daily 9:30am-5:00pm. Avoid lines by buying and printing your tickets online. Best times to visit are posted online (beat crowds). Admission: $19.95 adult, $15.95 child (2-12). CityPass included in this attraction. 4D shows extra $5.00. Ferry extra. Waterfront Connections bus $2.00 roundtrip (summers only) Note: 4D Theater riders must be at least 36" tall. No babies in arms. Miscellaneous: Swim w/the Sharks - So, you think you've got guts? Well, why not go for a swim with their sharks. Sharks love guts. $165 per person w/ reservation. Other Adventures w/ Penguins.

The hippos were amazing to watch and this was <u>a first for us</u>...

Take a short trip on the ferry across the Delaware River to Camden, New Jersey's Riverfront. From here, it's just a quick walk to the Adventure Aquarium, home to more than 8,400 marine animals. From the moment you walk in you'll hear it: the unmistakable rumble of a massive rainforest waterfall or celestial music around the jellyfish. Some 500 species, including sharks, penguins, stingrays and hippos are there plus a 4D theater, dive shows, live animal talks, performances and a giant 760,000-gallon tank. Ask the trainers why penguins are such good swimmers or watch how smart and sassy seals are. Can you believe their hippos frolic and jump out of the water and press their snouts against

A VIRTUAL shark experience...well done!

the glass, going eye-to-eye with visitors? It's almost like they were trying to sneak a kiss! After you've made it through the shark tunnel, try your courage in Cage Match - a virtual Shark Cage experience. Movement and clanking noise allow you to feel vibrations of sharks approaching and pounding your cage. All pretend, of course. A little scary - but, you'll come out alive! The aquarium offers equal measures of entertainment and education with additional attractions including the Touch-a-Shark tank and the Caribbean beach, home to tropical fish and birds. Don't just look. Touch.

BATTLESHIP NEW JERSEY

Philadelphia area (Camden, NJ) - *62 Battleship Place (take Ben Franklin Bridge over to exit 5 or take RiverLink Ferry over from Penn's Landing) 08103. Phone: (856) 877-6262. www.battleshipnewjersey.org. Hours: Daily 9:30am-3:00pm. Extended hours May thru early September. Closed early January thru early February. The Battleship is closed Thanksgiving, Christmas Day and New Years Day Admission: 3 different tours offered: $18.50-$19.95 adult, $14.00-$15.00 seniors and child (6-11), FREE for Children < 6/Active Military/BB62 Vets. Combo Fish N Ship passes available for discount (combined w/Aquarium). FREEBIES: Print off your copies of the Battleship's Scavenger Hunt Enlisted Version on the EDUCATION icon online. Note: The tours of the Battleship New Jersey are interactive. You will be going up and down on ladders, stepping through passageways and sometimes maneuvering in tight spaces - just like the officers and the crew of the USS New Jersey did. We strongly recommend you wear comfortable flat shoes. If you do not feel comfortable with a complete tour, you can enjoy a main deck tour, which does not have any ladders. They also offer* *video tours of the Battleship in the Wardroom Lounge on the Main Deck. If you are bringing a toddler or baby, you cannot bring a stroller aboard the ship. We recommend that you wear a baby carry-on across your front to carry babies aboard.*

Wannabe sailors can tour the nation's most decorated battleship, the Battleship New Jersey. Be sure to ask for the Kids Audio Tour as a young crew member gives you funny details of the officers' and crew's mess halls, communications center and high-tech command center. Winding through tight, narrow companionways, visitors see even get to see the sleeping quarters, which range from small private rooms for senior officers to even smaller cots stacked atop each other for enlisted men. Not only do you see exhibits of artifacts

The "ferocious" main guns...

from the ship's past, but you are put into the exhibit as you go through the tour route. Sit in the chair from which Admiral Halsey commanded the fleet. Stretch out on the bunks where the sailors slept. Climb into the 16" gun turret and learn how the projectiles were loaded. Answer questions like: what is a coffin box bed and why can't enlisted men walk on blue tiles? Between climbing and sneaking peeks inside small spaces and trying to look for answers to the scavenger hunt - your kids will be totally occupied!

Not much room to "spread out" here...

CAMDEN CHILDREN'S GARDEN

Philadelphia Area (Camden, NJ) - *3 Riverside Drive (follow signs to exit 5 off I-676 east, adjacent to Aquarium) 08103. www.camdenchildrensgarden.org. Phone: (856) 365-TREE. Hours: Wednesday-Friday 10:00am-4:00pm, Weekends 10:00am-5:00pm. Admission: $5.00-$6.00 per person (age 3+). Admission per person at Aquarium/Garden Gate is $3.50 per person. Miscellaneous: 2 times/ month they hold a Family Festival with a different theme each time. Festival of Lights in December.*

A visit to Camden Children's Garden features a host of interactive habitats and exhibits — including the Dinosaur Garden, Storybook Garden, Tree House and Picnic Garden. Children can even take a train ride around the grounds or hop on the Garden's beautiful carousel. You might try one of the seasonal shows in the Piney Woods Amphitheatre, then hop on the Spring Butterfly ride. Or, when the weather's warm, you may just choose to splash around in the Violet Plaza Fountain. In addition to the Butterfly, Railroad, Dinosaur and Storybook gardens, the four-acre horticultural wonderland has added a new Fitness Garden where kids can crawl, climb and learn about healthy living. In the Burrowing Maze, act like a creature going through soil tunnels. By the way, why is Ben Franklin's Garden secret?

Jenny and Daniel become butterflies...

Quakertown

NOCKAMIXON STATE PARK

Quakertown - *1542 Mountain View Drive (PA Route 563, Northeast Extension of the PA Turnpike, Exit 32) 18951. Phone: (215) 529-7300 or -7308 (marina). www. dcnr.state.pa.us/stateparks/parks/nockamixon.aspx. Admission: to PA State Parks is FREE however swimming, marina and camping/lodging fees apply, with reservation or entrance.*

The name Nockamixon is synonymous with boating. Four public launching areas are provided on the lake and boats may be rented from a park concession. Visitors enjoy watching sailboats from a bench at the marina, and the equestrian, bicycle and hiking trails. Pool, Visitors Center, Horseback Riding, Modern Cabins, Fishing, and Winter Sports.

Quarryville

ROBERT FULTON BIRTHPLACE

Quarryville - *Box 33 (Rte. 30 west to Rte. 372 west to US222 South of Quarryville)*
*17566. Phone: (717) 548-2679.   www.padutchcountry.com/members/Robert_*
Fulton_Birthplace.asp. Hours: Saturday 11:00am-4:00pm, Sunday 1:00-5:00pm
(Summer). Admission: $1.00 adult, children FREE (12 and under).

Robert Fulton, the inventor, the artist, and the engineer was born here in 1765. On display are many of his drawings, miniature portraits, and models (located throughout the living room). Being most famous for his steamboat, "Claremont" (the first steamboat), you'll see a strong connection between his artistic ability and his engineering ideas. Because his drawings were so well done, supporters could easily visualize his inventive ideas.

Reading

MID ATLANTIC AIR MUSEUM

Reading - *11 Museum Drive - SR183 (Reading Regional Airport) 19605. Phone:*
(610) 372-7333.   www.maam.org.   Hours: Daily 9:30am-4:00pm. Closed major
holidays. Admission: $6.00 adult, $3.00 child (6-12).   Miscellaneous: Aviation gift
shop. Airplane rides weekends in summer for additional fee. The Mid Atlantic Air
Museum annually hosts a WWII Weekend on the first weekend in June.

Restored, ready to fly, classic civilian and military aircraft. This museum highlights the Mid Atlantic's contribution to flight as well as the general history of aviation, including military aviation. You'll find something for everyone at this museum. Take a tour and walk through the exhibit building, hangar and go out on to the museum ramp. Of special interest are the classic commercial airliners, and the first night fighter ever built, history of aircraft manufacturers, and aviation movies and toys.

READING PHILLIES BASEBALL

Reading - *1900 S. Centre Avenue (FirstEnergy Stadium) 19605. Phone: (610) 370-BALL or 375-8469. www.readingphillies.com.   Admission: $3.00-$7.00*

Minor League AA Class affiliate of the Philadelphia Phillies. The Mascot Band members are Quack the Rubber Ducky on lead vocals and guitar, Bucky the Beaver on bass, Change-Up the Turtle on the bongos, and Screwball bringing it all together on the drums – you really have to see it to believe it. While parking is always free and the concessions remain affordable, every game is a unique experience. Giveaways, fireworks and the five-member R-Phils Mascot Team keep things hopping throughout the season.

NOLDE FOREST ENVIRONMENTAL EDUCATION CENTER

Reading - *2910 New Holland Road 19608. Phone: (610) 775-1411. www.dcnr. state.pa.us/stateparks/parks/noldeforest.aspx.*

Year-Round Education & Interpretation Center. Nolde Forest encompasses more than 665 acres of deciduous woodlands and coniferous plantations. A network of trails makes the center's streams, ponds and diverse habitats accessible to both students and casual visitors. Teaching stations offer places for students to work and benches for those who wish to sit. There is a short, accessible trail by the mansion.

READING PUBLIC MUSEUM

Reading - *500 Museum Road (follow 222 South/422 East to West Reading/Penn Avenue exit) 19611. Phone: (610) 371-5850. www.readingpublicmuseum.org. Hours: Tuesday - Saturday 11:00am-5:00pm, Sunday Noon-5:00pm. Closed Christmas, New Years and Thanksgiving. Admission: $8.00 adult, $6.00 child (4-17). These costs apply to the Museum only. Star and Laser Shows at The Planetarium are separate costs, and listed on The Planetarium page online.*

Visit the Reading Public Museum and planetarium to take a ride back in time and then on to outer space. The Museum houses galleries and collections as well as events showcasing the discovery of art, science and civilizations.

While the art of many nations and people is represented in the permanent collection, special emphasis has been placed on painting. The fine art collection includes more than seven hundred oil paintings by American and foreign artists such as: Benjamin West, Milton Avery, John Singer Sargent, N.C. Wyeth, George Bellows, Raphaelle Peale, Henry Raeburn, Frederic Church, Joshua Reynolds, Julien Dupre, and Edgar Degas - names students are familiar with in art history class. In addition, the Reading Public Museum possesses over one hundred sculptures, thousands of graphics, and more than two hundred water colors. Learn about life in the Middle Ages, the code of chivalry, and how one became a knight in the Arms and Armor Gallery of Knights in shining armor. Mounted Specimens are prepared to resemble the organism as it would normally appear in the wild.

Visit the planetarium for a star or laser show. With specials on black holes, astronauts, and icy worlds plan on an informative trip. Public Star Shows on Sundays, Public Laser Shows on Saturdays (separate fee).

Ronks

AMAZING MAIZE MAZE

Ronks - *Cherry Crest Farm. www.cherrycrestfarm.com. Different design each year. (i.e. Noah's Ark). Petting zoo, refreshments, pumpkin patch, corn maze, pony or wagon rides. Also 4 smaller mazes and hay jump on property. Pedal carts. Sack slides. Admission. (weekends each fall, especially in October)*

Schaefferstown

CHERRY FAIR

Schaefferstown - *Alexander Schaeffer Farm Museum. Phone: (717) 949-2244. www.hsimuseum.org. There will be lots of great food and cherry goodies to eat, cherry pie eating and pitting contests, the Sit-&-Spit, cake walks, a family corner, a pig roast, garden and house tours, demonstrations and crafters, a raffle drawing, horse wagon rides, and saw mill demonstrations. Apprentices will be there and we will be baking, making candy and candles, and many more crafts. The Marini Family demonstrates their beautiful harps on the grounds and also performing a stage show along with the violin maker, and wheelwright shop, the spinners, and many others. Admission. (last Saturday in June)*

HARVEST FAIR

Schaefferstown - *Alexander Schaeffer Farm Museum. Phone: (717) 949-2244. www.hsimuseum.org. Tractor pulls, antique steam engines, parades, food (made with steam), threshing, baling, cider and apple butter making, hayrides, children's activities, petting zoo & fall crafts. Admission. (second weekend in September)*

Shartlesville

ROADSIDE AMERICA

Shartlesville - *Roadside Drive (I-78 / US22, exit 23) 19554. Phone: (610) 488-6241. www.roadsideamericainc.com. Hours: Weekdays 9:00am-6:30pm, Weekends until 7:00pm (July-Labor Day). Monday-Friday 10:00am-5:00pm, Saturday & Sunday 10:00am-6:00pm (September-June). Admission: $6.75 adult, $4.50 senior, $3.75 child (6-11).*

Roadside America is the Greatest Indoor Miniature Village in the heart of beautiful Pennsylvania Dutch Country. Its an unforgettable panorama of life in rural United States. The exhibit spans more than two hundred years in time and lets you see, in miniature, how people lived and worked in pioneer days... through the years since then...right up to the present. Our kids lost their breath as they entered the enormous and wonderful train village! It's the largest known indoor miniature train village!

As a young boy, Lawrence Gieringer saw buildings far away and felt they appeared tiny and toy-sized. As his carpentry skills grew, he began whittling blocks of wood into different scaled-

Something for every age here...all in miniature detail...wow!

down models of industries and buildings he saw all around him - all of them important to the development of the area. You'll see scenes of a coal breaker, a Pennsylvania Dutch farm, downtown small town USA, gristmills, and churches. Kids are enchanted by the moving trains (over bridges, through tunnels), trolleys, bubbling fountains, or aircraft swooping and diving through the air (there's even a hot air balloon). Parents relive childhood dreams playing with toy animals, people, machinery, etc. as they examine all the details. Kids' favorites are the 50+ pushbuttons that make trains or figures move - it gives them the chance to feel like they're helping to operate the huge display. Don't leave until you've seen the Night Pageant! Every half hour they turn day into night and back!

Spring Mount

SPRING MOUNTAIN ADVENTURES

Spring Mount - *757 Spring Mount Road (minutes from the Lansdale exit of the Pennsylvania Turnpike) 19478. www.springmountainadventures.com. Phone: (610) 287-7900.*

Spring Mountain has always been Pennsylvania's perfect place to learn to ski and snowboard, but now it's also the perfect place to experience the thrill of a canopy tour, rock climbing and geocaching. Skiers and Boarders participate in terrain park, half-pipe and eight trails. Plus, they have two tubing runs. The Ski and Snowboard School is renowned for the quality of instruction and instructors and multiple generations of families have learned here. Sunday night is Family Night.

* **TREE CANOPY TOURS** - Spring Mountain Adventures in Montgomery County is one of the only places in the country that offers treetop canopy tours - a series of zip line and rope challenges high up in the trees. Not for the faint-of-heart, the excursions keep visitors high off the ground, with nothing but their harness and a few cables used to land fighter jets on aircraft carriers! Honestly, though, outside of a fear of heights, we'd recommend canopy tours to families of all ages (ages 10+ probably the best). Those cables help you glide across the sky and, just like an aircraft carrier, try to prevent a "hot" landing. After a few glides, you may want to ask how to go faster…

Strasburg

ED'S BUGGY RIDES

Strasburg - *SR 896 (across from Sight & Sound Theatre) 17572. Phone: (717) 687-0360. www.edsbuggyrides.com. Admission: $9.00 adult, Children half-price.*

3 mile tour through Amish farmlands in an Amish buggy. Experience the beautiful Pennsylvania Dutch Country landscape, while watching the everyday routine of the Amish through hilly back roads in an authentic Amish buggy. Experience riding in an authentic Amish buggy. They have open and closed Amish family carriages and open Amish spring wagons. Daily, year-round.

AMISH VILLAGE

Strasburg - *Route 896 - PO Box 115 (1 mile south of US30 & 2 miles north of Strasburg) 17579. Phone: (717) 687-8511. www.800padutch.com/avillage.html. Hours: Daily 9:00am-5:00pm (Spring/Summer/Fall). Open at 10:00am on Sunday. Admission: $8.00 adult, $4.00 child (6-12). Online coupon. Tours: 20-25 minutes. Miscellaneous: Amish Village store.*

Take a step back into the 1800's. Tour an authentic 1840 Amish farmhouse, explore the farmland and animals, walk to school to the one-room school house built and furnished by the Amish. Visit the Smokehouse and taste the flavor of the 1800's. The highlight is an educational tour of an 1840 Old Order Amish home, authentically furnished. The site includes a blacksmith, one room schoolhouse, operating smokehouse, water wheel, farm animals, spring house and windmill.

CHOO CHOO BARN, TRAINTOWN USA

Strasburg - *Route 741 East, Box 130 17579. www.choochoobarn.com. Phone: (717) 687-7911. Hours: Daily 10:00am-5:00pm (April - December). Closed major winter holidays and Easter. Admission: $6.00 adult, $4.00 child (5-12)*

Gigantic model train display! A 1700 square foot mini display of Pennsylvania Dutch County with area landmarks, 20 operating trains plus over 150 animated and automated vehicles and figurines. The kids shriek with delight at everything there is to see - esp. when it changes from daylight to nighttime. Look for the skiers zooming down the slopes and the dump truck that really moves. The working fire display shows a house burning and then the fire truck comes to put it out, complete with a fireman who climbs the ladder and makes a hole in the roof to put out the fire. Most displays can be seen from "kids-eye" level with only occasional "lifts" to get the "big picture". You have to pass the well-stocked gift shop in and out of the exhibit so plan some extra time for shopping.

RAILROAD MUSEUM OF PENNSYLVANIA

Strasburg - *300 Gap Road - SR741 East 17579. Phone: (717) 687-8628. www.rrmuseumpa.org. Hours: Monday-Saturday 9:00am-5:00pm, Sunday Noon-5:00pm. Closed Monday & Winter Holidays (November-early April) Admission: $8.00 adult, $7.00 senior (60+), $6.00 child (6-17). Miscellaneous: Whistle Stop Shop. Outdoor yard restoration available in good weather. Hands-On-Center. Orientation video. 2nd floor observation deck. Strasburg Railroad is across the street.*

A nostalgic glimpse of railroading's glorious past awaits you at the Railroad Museum of Pennsylvania. Sit in an engineer's seat, explore a caboose, experience a turn-of-the-century passenger station and inspect a 62-ton locomotive from underneath! Pennsylvania's premier museum of railroading

Courtesy of Pennsylvania Historical & Museum Commission

The trains are bigger than life and each has a story...

exhibits a world-class collection of more than 100 historically significant locomotives and railcars, from mammoth steam engines to quaint Victorian coaches, and chronicles a society on the move.

This huge indoor/outdoor museum traces the development of railroads and rail transportation in Pennsylvania from restored locomotives to modern streamliners. Aside from viewing the

locomotives and rail cars from various vantage points, you can climb into a caboose or a steam locomotive. Docents are often on hand to explain special locomotives and show you how they worked, and other cars are opened during special events. Meet "Diesel", GG 1 Electric, Logging, Freight and Passenger (actually get to look in or walk in) trains! More access than most train museums. In the center of the museum is the railroad workshop where you can actually walk under a train! Great place to bring grandmas and grandpas to pass along stories to younger generations.

CHRISTMAS OPEN HOUSES

Strasburg - *Railroad Museum Of Pennsylvania. Tours of decorated, historical buildings. Refreshments and musical entertainment. Admission. (second Sunday in December)*

STRASBURG RAILROAD

Strasburg - *SR741 East - 17579. www.strasburgrailroad.com. Phone: (717) 687-7522. Hours: Daily 10:00am-7:00pm (July & August), 11:00am-3:00pm (April, June, September). Mostly long weekends (weather permitting) Noon-3:00pm (Rest of the year). Admission: Train Rides: $14.00-$16.00 adult, $7.00-$9.00 child (3-11), $2.00-$5.00 toddler. Activities: $1.00-$5.00 per activity (tokens). Tours: 45 minutes, departs on the hour. See schedule on website. Miscellaneous: Several gift shops with train souvenirs, books and loads of Thomas stuff! Restaurants with casual dining, picnic lunches and sweet treats on premises.*

Offering the most authentic train ride experience of the period, the Strasburg Railroad takes visitors back to a simpler time. This is the oldest short-line railroad. The restored Victorian open-air and coach cars offer wide views of the landscape (some cars even offer snacks and the "Lee Brenner" dining car offers meals). Visitors travel through farm fields still plowed by horses and mules. Amish buggies wait patiently at railroad crossings. Train travelers can even stop at an old-fashioned picnic grove and enjoy a snack while the trains rumble by. Each train has a narrator who tells the railroad's history spiced with a few tall tales.

All aboard !

Other activities on the premises: Hand-propelled cars, which date back to the 1930s, allow little ones to take control as they crank their way around a track; Cagney Train - built around 1920, this miniature steam train was originally used at an amusement park; President's Car Tour - Take a self-guided tour aboard the stationary "mansion on rails." This restored rail car was used for railroad tycoons and dignitaries. Also, tour the freight equipment display; Switch Tower Tour - Built in 1885, this is a classic example of Pennsylvania Railroad signal tower design. Get a bird's-eye view of the magnificent countryside and approaching trains; and Pump Cars - you provide the power when you operate vintage Pump Cars - with attendant - along a short track. Your young engineers are really going to enjoy the train ride and be sure to plan one or two extra activities because they'll be begging for more! Classy railroad.

A Day Out with Thomas ®!

Be sure to check on seasonal events that your "little engineers" will love like "A Day Out With Thomas the Train!" (One ride on a life-size Thomas plus storytelling, Sir Topham Hatt, Play Tables, Thomas Coloring and Videos, and Live Musical Entertainment for the wristband price of $18.00 per person/ages 2+ - June, mid-September, mid-November). This is the place where Thomas spends the most time visiting.

EASTER BUNNY TRAIN RIDES

Strasburg *- Strasburg Railroad. Candy treats with the Easter Bunny riding along. Admission. (Easter Weekend)*

TRAIN RIDES WITH SANTA

Strasburg - Strasburg Railroad. Sing songs and eat treats as you ride the train with Santa aboard. Admission. (two weekends before Christmas)

NATIONAL TOY TRAIN MUSEUM

Strasburg (Paradise) - *300 Paradise Lane (off SR 741 East & US 30) 17579. Phone: (717) 687-8976. www.nttmuseum.org. Hours: Friday thru Monday 10:00am-5:00pm (May-October), Weekends in April, November, and mid-December Admission: $6.00 adult, $5.00 senior (65+), 3.00 child (5-12), $12.00 family.*

Five operating push button layouts in panoramic viewing. Meet toy trains from the 1800s to the present in use as part of the layout. One of the displays features large-gauge trains used for outdoors. The Train Collectors Association operates it (they are often featured on national TV). A continuously running video show in the Museum's Theater area features cartoons and comedy films about toy trains.

Upper Black Eddy

DELAWARE CANAL STATE PARK

Upper Black Eddy - *11 Lodi Hill Road (Rte. 611 and Rte. 32 18972. Phone: (610) 982-5560. www.dcnr.state.pa.us/stateparks/parks/delawarecanal.aspx. Admission: to PA State Parks is FREE however swimming, marina and camping/ lodging fees apply, with reservation or entrance.*

A walk along the 60-mile towpath of the Delaware Canal is a stroll into American History. The Delaware Canal is the only remaining continuously intact canal of the great towpath canal building era of the early and mid-19th century. Mule drawn canal boat rides and the Lock Tender's House Visitor Center are at New Hope. Also, Horseback Riding, Mountain Biking, Fishing, Trails, Cross-Country Skiing.

The Delaware River Canal Boat Co. offers a unique, one hour journey aboard a replica canal boat drawn by a team of mules on the Delaware Canal through historic New Hope and into the scenic Bucks County countryside. Experience life along the Delaware Canal as it was in the 1800s and hear interesting tales of canal days related by an interpreter in period costume. Boats depart starting at noon on Saturdays and Sundays in April, (weather permitting), and daily May through October 31st.

RINGING ROCKS PARK

Upper Black Eddy - *(9 miles south of Easton) 18972. Phone: (215) 348-6114 or (215) 757-0571 Bucks Co. Parks n Rec. www.delawareandlehigh.org.*

Southbound, the site lies just off Route 32, two miles past its intersection with Route 611 at Kintnersville. From there, Narrows Hill Road runs past the General Store to Ringing Rocks Road which leads to the park.

This is literally a rock concert.

A quarter-mile trail meanders from a picnic area to the field of boulders. Take along your own hammer. Why? This vast field of boulders all ring like bells, with tones ranging from high ping to low bong. This is literally a rock concert. Whatever the score, "heavy metal" would lie at its heart, it is the iron content that makes them ring. No one knows where the boulders came from. No guards are needed to protect the singing stones at the field itself; they must weigh from half-a-ton up. Ringing Rocks Park, which also boasts a beautiful waterfall and lots of lovely flora and fauna, also is rich in the lore of magic and mystery. Compasses are said to spin madly in the vicinity of the boulder field. Can you solve the mystery?

Valley Forge

VALLEY FORGE NATIONAL HISTORICAL PARK

Valley Forge - *SR23 & N. Gulph Road - (I-76 to exit 24 - SR202 south to SR422 west to SR23 west) 19482. Phone: (610) 783-1077. www.nps.gov/vafo/index.htm. Hours: Daily 9:00am-5:00pm. Closed Thanksgiving, Christmas.   Admission: FREE. Tours: By trolley (summers) or self-guided driving with audio tape. Ranger led tours 2 times per day in the summer. Miscellaneous: Expanse of outdoor park areas available. Hiking and bike trails. Stop at the Visitor's Center first. Valley Forge Canteen open 10:00am-2:00 pm Saturday and Sunday. Educators: wow, an outstanding and thorough Valley Forge Curriculum Guide is here online: http:// www.nps.gov/vafo/forteachers/upload/CurriculumGuide.pdf.*

Explore the site of the Winter of 1777-78 encampment that was a difficult time for battling elements and disease. Some of the sites that you won't want to miss are:

- VISITOR'S CENTER - An eighteen-minute film, "Valley Forge: A Winter Encampment," is shown every 30 minutes on the hour and half-hour, starting at 9:30am, ending at 4:30pm. Be sure to take that in first and look over the dioramas. See a tent headquarters actually used by General Washington!

VALLEY FORGE NATIONAL HISTORICAL PARK (cont.)

- <u>ARTILLERY PARK</u> - long rows of cannons and forts. Get out a stretch and run areas.

- <u>WASHINGTON'S HEADQUARTERS</u> - Isaac Potts' House - looks exactly as it did when General George Washington and his wife, Martha were in residence. (Initially he shared the rough conditions with the soldiers in the field tents). Interpreters are excellent here (weekends and summers).

- <u>GRAND PARADE</u> - learn about the other hero (Von Steuben) who turned tattered, confused young men into soldiers.

- <u>WORLD OF SCOUTING MUSEUM</u> - A log cabin full of uniforms, handbooks, and badges. Daily, 11:00am - 4:00pm (Summer), Weekends (rest of the year).

Summer weekends are the best time to visit because the Muhlenberg Brigade is recreated in living history encampments - bringing the drudges of winter camp to life. Remember, these "huts" replaced tents but still only offered a little more warmth. Brave a visit Winter weekends to see scout troops living under similar conditions as the soldiers did or inside Washington's Headquarters. Battles may not have occurred here, but after 6 months of training in the worst conditions - those soldiers were a fighting force.

Warminster

BUCKS COUNTY ZOO & ANIMAL JUNCTION

Warminster - 1540-D Campus Drive 18974. Phone: (215) 394-5873. www. buckscountyzoo.com.   Hours: Tuesday-Friday 11:00am-4:00pm, Saturday 11:00am-3:00pm, Sundays 11:00am-4:00pm.(Memorial Day through Labor Day) Admission: $7.00-$9.00 (ages 2+).

This 5,000 square foot facility is an indoor zoological garden housing tropical plants and more than 60 animals, including giant pythons, alligators, mammals from around the world, amphibians, raptors and many more. All the animals represented are from wild corners of the world - hot jungles, wooded forests, dry deserts, grassy prairies, wet rainforests and other unusual habitats. Enjoy fun, safe, and friendly encounters with the unusual and the unexpected, presented by its staff of wildlife educators, which may include the infamous Jungle Joe.

Washington's Crossing

WASHINGTON CROSSING HISTORIC PARK

Washington's Crossing - SR32 and SR532 (off I-95, exit 31, head northwest on Rte. 532) 18977. Phone: (215) 493-4076. www.ushistory.org/washingtoncrossing. Hours: Tuesday-Saturday 9:00am-5:00pm, Sunday Noon-5:00pm. Closed some holidays. Admission: $4.00-$7.00 (age 3+) for walking tour. Park charges $1.00 per vehicle at entrance. Cash & check only. Tours: Guided tours of the McKonkey Ferry Inn section and the Thompson-Neely section occur everyday but Monday and select holidays/special events. Tours begin on the hour at 9:00, 10:00, 11:00, 1:00, 2:00, 3:00, and 4:00. During winter months, tours may conclude earlier in the day due to low light levels in the historic structures. A tour of the McKonkey Ferry Inn section is approximately one hour in length. Allow 30 minutes to tour the Thompson-Neely House. The Thompson-Neely grist mill is open seasonally for tours. Allow additional time to tour the grist mill. Miscellaneous: Events occur each month on the weekends, especially Sundays. Every Christmas (at 1:00pm) the park re-enacts Washington's crossing and special events also occur on his birthday. Also on grounds is the Bowman's Hill and Wildflower Preserve. FREEBIES: click on FOR KIDS icon to browse thru several games and FAQ. Be sure to print a copy of the Washington Crossing Scavenger Hunt to complete while you're on site.

It's December 25, 1776. Washington planned his attack on the British, first crossing the Delaware River by boat. In the Durham Boat House, you can see the boats that were actually used. A larger than life copy (20 ft. X 12 ft.) of the painting "Washington's Crossing" creates the best image of this historic Christmas Day for freedom. A total of 13

historic buildings are on site and your tour ticket includes Bowman's Hill Tower observation point, Thompson-Neely House (where Washington ate and slept), The Ferry Inn (where Washington dined before crossing the icy Delaware) and the Memorial Building where the giant painting stands. All of this, plus a short historical film is shown of the event. It'll give you goosebumps!

West Chester

AMERICAN HELICOPTER MUSEUM

West Chester - *1220 American Blvd. (Brandywine Airport - Next to QVC Studios) 19380. Phone: (610) 436-9600. www.helicoptermuseum.org. Hours: Wednesday-Saturday 10:00am-5:00pm, Sunday Noon-5:00pm. Admission: $6.00 adult, $5.00 senior (65+), $4.00 child (3-18) or student. Miscellaneous: Older kids will want more information about the engineering of the rotocraft. Films and mechanics are available to fill in all of the details. Helicopter Rides (every 4th Saturday for $40 per person) - ask for adventure here! Fly-bys…wow!*

This very kid-friendly museum exhibits the adventure and history of "rotary wing flight" at the country's only helicopter museum. Helicopters from the earliest to the most modern are here, inside and outside (Coast Guard, Navy, Army, M.A.S.H.), plus interactive exhibits. Climb aboard and play with the controls inside the giant helicopters being restored. Visitors come back here frequently because the kids can actually go on many units and work the rotors and play pretend. Plus a very exciting miniature wind tunnel blows air in the face of whatever child is standing behind it. It's lots of fun!

QVC STUDIO TOUR

West Chester - *Studio Park (I-76 or I-95, exit US202 to Boot Road - East to Wilson Drive) 19380. Phone: (800) 600-9900. www.qvctours.com. Admission: $7.50 adult, $5.00 child (age 6+). Tours: Daily between 10:00am - 4:00pm. Leaves every hour or hour-and-a-half. Groups of 10 or more must make prior reservations. Miscellaneous: Must be at least 6 years old. All adult tour guests are asked to bring identification.*

Imagine a shopping medium that reaches over 16 million homes instantly and can process more than 30 calls per second! Founded in 1986, this cable shopping service stands for "Quality, Value, Convenience" and has become the largest of its kind. Your tour begins as you are greeted by photographs of famous celebrities that have visited QVC to merchandise their products. You will see 34 sets and 8 studios (there is even an 8000 square foot 2-story house in the studio complete with a garage). All of the cameras are remotely controlled from one central source during taping and the complete facility uses over 1,000,000 watts of power (or enough to power 3000 average households!) You might even have a chance to see "Murphy the Dog" the QVC mascot - he is a golden retriever that is featured on the show and we are told he gets as much e-mail as any of the other hosts! See live broadcasts being done (without cue cards - everything is ad lib!). See the prop production and design facilities - the texture display is awesome! You can even be a part of a live studio audience with advance notice.

Wyomissing

BERK'S COUNTY HERITAGE CENTER

Wyomissing - Red Bridge Road (off Route 183) 19610. Phone: (610) 374-8839. www.berkshistory.org. Hours: Tuesday-Saturday, Holidays 9:00am-4:00pm (May - October). Admission: $2.00-$4.00 (age 7+) per museum. Discount combo prices.

The Berks County Heritage Center is a historical complex honoring important eras of our local transportation and manufacturing history. The Society's 20,000 artifacts tell many stories behind the development of the county. Three levels of museum exhibits interpret colorful history from the Conestoga Wagon to the 1902 Duryea to toys, crafts, fine arts, all related to our social history. This includes the Craft & Industry Room, Transportation Room, Firefighting & Toy displays and the Hands On History Room. Start learning about more Berks County heritage by taking a tour through landmarks of local history; including the Gruber Wagon Works and the C. Howard Hiester Canal Center.

GRUBER WAGON WORKS - Survives as one of the most complete examples of an integrated rural manufactory of its kind in the nation. Wagon wheels were constructed in the bench shop, and wooden parts of the wagon were made from patterns in the wood shop. Wheels were "tired" and wagons were "ironed" and assembled in the blacksmith shop. The distinctive striping and scrollwork were applied by hand in the paint shop.

C. HOWARD HIESTER CANAL CENTER: Canals saw their rise and fall in the 19th century. They offered means of bulk transportation and travel in the era prior to railroads when the only alternative to walking was the horse and wagon. Red Bridge (longest covered bridge in the state).

CIVIL WAR ENCAMPMENT

Wyomissing - Berk's County Heritage Center. The year is 1863, and Pennsylvania Federal Regiment try to enlist new recruits and demonstrate military life. Free. (second weekend in July)

Travel Journal & Notes:

SE Area

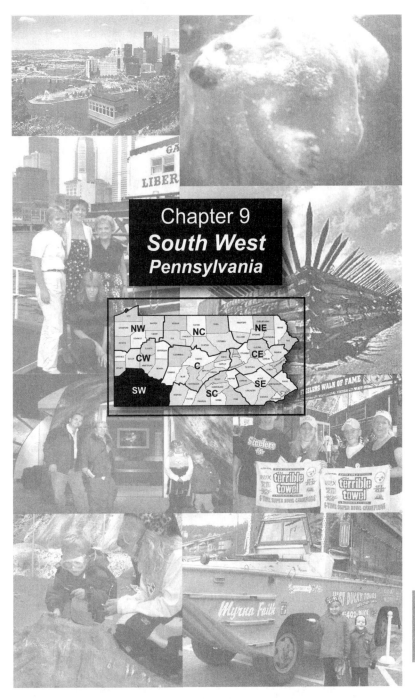

Chapter 9
South West
Pennsylvania

Brownsville
- Nemacolin Castle

Champion
- Seven Springs Mountain Resort

Clinton
- Hozak Farms Fall Festival

Donegal
- Living Treasures Animal Park

Elizabeth
- Round Hill Exhibit Farm

Farmington
- Fort Necessity Nat'l Battlefield
- Laurel Caverns
- Nemacolin Woodlands Resort
- Friendship Hill Nat'l Historic Site

Finleyville
- Strawberry Festival

Greensburg
- Westmoreland Museum Of American Art
- Overly's Country Christmas

Harrison City
- Bushy Run Battlefield

Hidden Valley
- Hidden Valley Ski

Latrobe
- DiSalvo's Station Restaurant
- Pittsburgh Steelers Summer Training Camp

Latrobe (Derry)
- Keystone State Park

Laughlintown
- Compass Inn Museum
- Forbes State Forest

Ligonier
- Fort Ligonier
- Idlewild Park & Soak Zone
- Ramada Inn Historic Ligonier

McMurray
- Simmons Farms Fall Playland

Meyersdale
- Pennsylvania Maple Festival

Mill Run
- Fallingwater

Monongahela
- Reilly's Summer Seat Farm

Monroeville (Trafford)
- Sherm Edwards Candies Tour

Mt. Pleasant
- L.E. Smith Glass Company
- Mt. Pleasant Glass & Ethnic Festival

North Huntington
- Big Mac Museum Restaurant

Ohiopyle
- Ohio Pyle State Park

Pittsburgh
- Pittsburgh Sports
- Primanti Brothers
- Sand Castle
- Pittsburgh Zoo & Aquarium
- The Frick Art & History Center
- Duquesne Incline
- Carnegie Science Center
- Children's Museum Of Pittsburgh
- Heinz Field Tours
- National Aviary
- Photo Antiquities
- Soldiers And Sailors Museum
- Allegheny Observatory
- Gateway Clipper Fleet
- Grand Concourse Restaurant
- Just Ducky Tours
- Monongahela Incline
- Ft Pitt Museum/Point State Park
- Heinz History Center
- Society For Contemporary Crafts
- Strip District Dining
- Beechwood Farm Nature Preserve
- International Children's Festival
- Pittsburgh Vintage Grand Prix
- Pittsburgh Light Up Nights
- Kids Holiday Crawl

SW Area

Pittsburgh (Avella)
- Meadowcroft Rockshelter/Village

Pittsburgh (Canonsburg)
- Little Lake Theatre Company

Pittsburgh (Carnegie)
- Pittsburgh's Motor Speedway

Pittsburgh (Gibsonia)
- Pittsburgh Holiday Train Show

Pittsburgh (Monroeville)
- Boyce Park Ski Area

Pittsburgh (Oakland)
- Carnegie Museum Of Art
- Carnegie Museum Of Natural History
- Phipps Conservatory
- Pittsburgh Playhouse Jr.
- Rodef Shalom Biblical Gardens
- Cathedral Of Learning Nationality Classrooms

Pittsburgh (West Mifflin)
- Kennywood Park

Rector
- Linn Run State Park

Rockwood
- Laurel Ridge State Park

Scenery Hill
- Westerwald Pottery

Scottdale
- West Overton Museums

Shanksville (Friedens)
- Flight 93 Memorial Chapel & Impact Site

Somerset
- Kooser State Park
- Laurel Hill State Park
- Somerset Historical Center

Tarentum
- Tour-Ed Mine And Museum

Uniontown
- Searight Toll House Museum

Washington
- Pennsylvania Trolley Museum
- Washington County Museum

Waynesburg
- Greene County Museum
- Battle Of The Bulge Re-Enactment

Wind Ridge
- Ryerson Station State Park

A Quick Tour of our Hand-Picked Favorites Around...

South West Pennsylvania

A Weekend in Pittsburgh and Its Countryside. Pittsburgh is so exciting! Pittsburgh is also so interactive! On any trip to the city by the Three Rivers, you'll find an overflowing handful of surprises.

Check out Mister Roger's Neighborhood exhibit, a hometown favorite at the **Children's Museum of Pittsburgh**, coupled with a very different approach to typical museums including "The River" water play space where you build bridges and water fountains to the sky.

Union Station and The Strip District have lots of dining and shopping options but it's also the depot for our favorite **Just Ducky Tour** of all. Venture aboard this funny land and water vehicles for a short, one-hour tour of Pittsburgh from a trolley boat. You'll quack, sing and laugh a ton.

On the outskirts of downtown are two other fabulous family sites. **The Pittsburgh Zoo** & PPG Aquarium is a double hit of animals in one place. You won't want to miss the polar bears and sea otters. What a treat to see these playful, curious water creatures from all angles. The setup actually allows you to look above, beside and below the water in a cute seaside town motif.

At **Meadowcroft** Rockshelter and Village re-live rugged rural life from 200 years ago as you walk the dirt and stone roads of this reconstructed village. By touring a settler log house, schoolhouse, country store, barn and blacksmith shop - you'll be introduced to inhabitants like the Native Americans, frontier settlers, farmers, lumbermen, coal miners, and conservationists who have worked the land. Get involved by taking a real school lesson. Shear sheep and then spin and weave wool. Then, dig some ancient rock at Rock Shelter.

Be sure to include a ride up the **Inclines** at least one evening during your visit. Wait until you see the view. And, if you get lost meandering

Pittsburgh streets around construction zones, just stop any native and they'll be glad to help you find your way. Some even wrote a map on napkins, others volunteered to drive ahead with us following.

The thriving metropolis of Pittsburgh, just one hour north of the Laurel Highlands, sits well amongst big cities. But every major town has countryside and the Laurel Highlands is such an area. Their natural area consists of 10 state parks and forests. Named for the Mountain Laurel, the hills and streams of these sleepy towns bloom with different colors from March through October. But quiet towns and beautiful blossoms don't wow the kids as much as The **Big Mac Museum**, a storybook forest, and a resort zoo or some French & Indian War forts!

Located in the scenic Laurel Highlands on 2800 acres, the 335-room **Nemacolin Resort** features an enormous variety of amazing activities. But did you know they have a Wildlife Academy? Just east of the main entrance, folks can schedule nursery tours or safari tours for a fee or just a pop in visit meandering near habitats of wolves in the wild, dozens of horses or maybe a panther. Or, scattered throughout the resort property, catch special Wildlife Habitats (black bears, zebras, elk, bison, and moose have habitats scattered around the golf course).

Forts – fun forts just for playing. **Fort Necessity** and **Fort Ligonier** commemorates the mid-1700s battles – George Washington battles – of the French and Indian War. The Visitor Center is the best place to begin your visit. After their movie introduces you to the park's story, sight and sound experiences engage the kids to listen closely as you enter exhibit spaces.

Now, I know we boast about few amusement parks but **Idlewild** and Storybook Forest are too fun to not shout about! Story Book Forest is a timeless walk through Nursery Rhymes but the park also has manageable rides, Mister Rogers Neighborhood and a Soak Zone waterpark.

Sites and attractions are listed in order by City, Zip Code, and Name. Symbols indicated represent:

 Festivals   Restaurants   Lodging

SW Area

Brownsville

NEMACOLIN CASTLE

Brownsville - *Front Street - US 40 east 15417. www.nemacolincastle.org. Phone: (724) 785-6882. Hours: Friday-Sunday Noon-5:00pm (Summer). Weekends only (Mid-March - May, September - Mid-October). Admission: $7.00 adult, $4.00 child (12 and under) Tours: 45 minutes.*

Previously known as Nemacolin Towers, the tudor style building dates back to the 1790s. The castle was built by Jacob Bowman who was appointed by George Washington as Brownsville's first postmaster. The Bowman family were businessmen and bank founders. It looks like a castle because of the turret towers and battlements. Tour 20 rooms of formal Victorian plus the oldest part that was the original trading post Bowman set up.

CHRISTMAS OPEN HOUSE

Brownsville - *Nemacolin Castle. Tours of decorated, historical buildings. Refreshments and musical entertainment. Candlelight tours. Admission. (Thanksgiving weekend and December weekends)*

Champion

SEVEN SPRINGS MOUNTAIN RESORT

Champion - *RR#1 Box 110 (I-76 exit 9 or 10, follow Rte. 31 or 711) 15622. Phone: (814) 352-7777, (800) 452-2223 (continental US). Snow Report: (800) 523-7777. www.7springs.com.*

Longest Run: 1.2 miles; 30 Slopes & Trails. Pennsylvania's largest ski and year-round resort. Be sure to get all of the latest details by calling or visiting their website. A perfect winter getaway resort, Seven Springs can accommodate more than 5,000 overnight guests in its 10-story high-rise hotel and nearly 1,000 condominium, town homes, cabins and chalets. The "resort cam" shows live pictures that are updated every 5 minutes. Tons of lodging & restaurants, indoor bowling, roller skating, swimming & mini-golf. Outdoor summer alpine slide, craft days, outdoor pool, horseback riding and tennis.

AUTUMNFEST

Champion - *Seven Springs Mountain Resort. Petting zoo, refreshments, pumpkin patch, corn maze, pony or wagon rides. Scenic chair lift rides, Alpine slide, open-spit cooked foods. (all October weekends)*

SW Area

Clinton

HOZAK FARMS FALL FESTIVAL

Clinton - Hozak Farms. www.hozakfarms.com. Petting zoo, refreshments, pumpkin patch, corn maze, pony or wagon rides. Admission. (October weekends)

Donegal

LIVING TREASURES ANIMAL PARK

Donegal - *SR 711 (south of Rte. 31) 15628. www.ltanimalpark.com. Phone: (724) 593-8300. Hours: Daily 10:00am-8:00pm (Summer). Daily 10:00am-6:00pm (April, May, September, October). Admission: $8.50 adult, $7.00 senior, $5.50 child (3-11).*

Watch kangaroos, tigers and wolves and ride the miniature horses. Kids love the petting area (babies, reindeer, camels) and feeding areas (bears, otters, monkeys, goats, sheep, & llamas). Cups of animal feed are available in the gift shop or at coin-operated food dispensers throughout the park. The Laurel Highlands location has several new additions each year including Black Leopards and Dingos. But the "biggest" addition is their Grizzly Bear family or baby camels!

Elizabeth

ROUND HILL EXHIBIT FARM

Elizabeth - *651 Round Hill Road (SR51 & SR48 to Round Hill Road) 15037. Phone: (412) 384-4701. www.alleghenycounty.us/parks/rhfac.aspx. Hours: Daily 8:00am-DUSK. Admission: FREE*

A small scale working farm dating back to the late 1700s. A brick farmhouse with barns and fields including dairy and beef cattle, pigs, chicken, sheep, horses, and a duck pond. Be ready to watch the cows being milked daily at 8:30am and 4:30pm. You can tour the grounds, play with the animals, plan a picnic, romp and play on the soccer fields, and walk the trails.

Farmington

FORT NECESSITY NATIONAL BATTLEFIELD

Farmington - *1 Washington Parkway - US40 15437. www.nps.gov/fone. Phone: (724) 329-5805. Hours: 8:00am-Sunset (park), Visitor's Center 9:00am-5:00pm, Closed many holidays. Admission: $5.00 adult, Children FREE (15 and under)*

Tours of the Mount Washington Tavern are available when staffing permits. The Tavern is a museum of life along the National Road and operated from 1828 to 1855. Miscellaneous: Picnic areas. Short 1/5th to 1/2 mile trail walks to fort and other museum sites along the National Road. Educators: Free lesson plans are at this link: (For Educators) ww.nps.gov/archive/fone/classroom/fiwar/adplans.htm.

Commemorating the 1754 battle - George Washington's first battle of the French and Indian War, this war was a clash of British, French and American Indian cultures. It ended with the removal of French power from North America. The stage was set for the American Revolution.

The Visitor Center is the best place to begin your visit. The twenty-minute movie "Road of Necessity" introduces the park story. Begin at Jumonville Glen - the site where the first skirmish occurred with the French. Washington feared they would return with backup forces, so, he had this fort built quickly, out of "necessity". It's a sight and sound experience as you enter spaces - ex. crossfire, characters talk at the roadside rest while you pull up a seat and listen in. Whose story of how the war started do you believe? Outside - soft play fort and Conestoga wagon with mini slides; pop in heads picture photo ops. Next, walk along the short marked trail to see the reconstructed fort - 53 feet in diameter, the gate is only 3.5 feet wide. Talks, tours, and historic weapons demonstrations are offered during the summer months.

LAUREL CAVERNS

Farmington - 200 Caverns Park Road (Chestnut Ridge in Laurel Highlands, off US 40) 15437. Phone: (800) 515-4150 or (724) 438-3003. www.laurelcaverns.com. Hours: Daily 9:00am-5:00pm (May-October). Weekends only (November, March, April). Admission: $8.00-$11.00 (age 6+). $5.00 extra per person for mini-golf course - recommended. Tours: 1 hour. Constant temperature, 52 degrees Fahrenheit. Miscellaneous: Visitors center, picnic areas.

> **DID YOU KNOW?**
>
> Kavernputt is the largest simulated cave in the world.

Pennsylvania's largest cave 2.3 miles. - well-lit tours of the "Grand Canyon" on the Family Tour. Laurel Caverns is a natural cave which follows the natural slope of the mountain. The family tour goes down approximately 1,700 feet. Kavernputt is so unique (additional activity fee required). A ten thousand square foot simulated cave is an eighteen hole golf course. The course is handicapped accessible with each hole conveying some unique aspect of caves.

SW Area

NEMACOLIN WOODLANDS RESORT

Farmington - *1001 LaFayette Drive 15437. www.nemacolin.com. Phone: (800) 422-2736.*

Located in the scenic Laurel Highlands on 2800 acres, the 335 room resort features a spa; golf course; the shooting academy; the off-road driving academy, a 3-stage instructional experience featuring hummer H1s and H2s; mystic mountain ski area; adventure course (ropes, Zipline, paintball, rock climbing wall, mountain bike rentals); miniature golf; every sport court imaginable; equestrian - trail rides, surrey rides, and sleigh rides; 6 swimming pools (2 indoor, one of which is just for children/families); and The Marina at Paige's Beach - canoes, kayaks, pedal boats and small sailboat rentals. Once you're settled in, your hardest decision is what to do first?

Lodging - as you step inside the Chateau foyer, modeled after the famed Ritz Paris, you may wonder if the place is a bit pretentious. That feeling leaves almost immediately as you quickly find families in every corner. Sightings of beach towels and the pit-pat of flip-flops makes you want to start exploring. But first, check into your Lodge room - original to the resort, the lodge is an English Tudor style hotel with room decor reminiscent of a comfortable English country inn. Very comfortable and kid-friendly. (This is upscale, yet comfortable elegance. Be prepared for overnight room rates starting at $300/night during non-peak times. Look for packages for the whole family so you get the most perks to make this fairy-tale place a special event).

Hungry? The Tavern has the world's largest free-standing cylindrical salt water aquarium with a wrap-around breakfast bar for dining. Look for the gold bar from the sunken Spanish galleon Santa Margarita. Try to see if you see the "Steelers" fish (black and gold). The menu is casual, American fare with offerings like homemade potato chips and root beer floats and pizza.

Retail stores - little 'streetside' shops and whimsical sculptures fill many corridors but the kids especially like the 50s soda shop, the arcade and the candy and toy shop (all conveniently located together in one large space). The kids activities and pool area is based from this same space so the kids can just settle into one area and feel comfortable

Property - Special wildlife habitats of black bears, zebras, elk, bison, and moose have habitats scattered around the golf course. You can take the shuttle around, walk the property (maybe walk off that huge banana split) or drive and park near the featured stops in the woodlands or around the links.

NEMACOLIN WOODLANDS RESORT (cont.)

• <u>NEMACOLIN'S WILDLIFE ACADEMY</u> - (nursery tours for a fee or safari tours) Just a pop in visit includes wolves in the wild, dozens of horses or maybe a panther.

• <u>MYSTIC MOUNTAIN SKI AREA</u>: Mystic Mountain is Western Pennsylvania's ideal learning environment for first-time skiers, with 25 acres of short lines, friendly trails and experienced instructors. Downhill skiing and snowboarding are available on 10 slopes at Mystic Mountain, with slope difficulty ranging from beginner to expert. Mystic Mountain has a 300-foot vertical drop, three lifts, and is 100 percent illuminated, making night snowsports great fun. Longest Run: .5 miles; 7 Slopes & Trails. A selection of resort lodging and activity packages are available year round with 5 swimming pools, mini-golf, trails and Equestrian Center, to name a few.

FRIENDSHIP HILL NATIONAL HISTORIC SITE

Farmington - *223 New Geneva Road (US 119 to PA 166) 15474. Phone: (724) 725-9190.   www.nps.gov/frhi/index.htm.   Hours: Daily 9:00am-5:00pm (spring thru early fall). Winter hours are Friday-Sunday only. Closed Christmas day only. Admission: FREE.*

Visit the home of Albert Gallatin (a famous local financier, scholar and diplomat of the early republic). "A country, like a household, should live within its means and avoid debt", says Albert Gallatin. Albert Gallatin is best remembered for his thirteen year tenure as Secretary of the Treasury during the Jefferson and Madison administrations. In that time he reduced the national debt, purchased the Louisiana Territory and funded the Lewis & Clark exploration. Gallatin's accomplishments and contributions are highlighted in his restored country estate, Friendship Hill. Ranger guided tours (summer) and self-guided Audio tours (rest of year).

Finleyville

STRAWBERRY FESTIVAL

Finleyville - Trax Farms. www.traxfarms.com. Sample strawberry treats like fresh strawberry shortcakes and strawberry ice cream or sundaes. From great beverages and tempting sweets to colorful side dishes and barbecued meats grilled with berry sauces. Entertainment, demonstrations, contests and prizes. Kids' activities. Watch them make strawberry jam. Pick your own. (second weekend of June)

SW Area

Greensburg

WESTMORELAND MUSEUM OF AMERICAN ART

Greensburg - 221 North Main Street (downtown) 15601. Phone: (724) 837-1500. www.wmuseumaa.org. Hours: Wednesday-Sunday 11:00am-5:00pm. Thursday 11:00am-9:00pm. Admission: Suggested donation $5.00 (age 12+).

"Arty-Facts" educational programs for children. Kidspace interactive area - Exhibitions include artwork from the permanent collection on display together with accompanying hands-on activities and a well-stocked reading corner. Regional industry, rural and cityscapes, toys of yesteryear, historical heroes.

OVERLY'S COUNTRY CHRISTMAS

Greensburg - *Westmoreland Fairgrounds. www.overlys.com. Glistening lights. Visit with Santa. Hot chocolate. Freshly baked cookies. Toy/gift shops. Mini-railroad display. Talking & dancing trees. Train ride. Weekend entertainment. Admission. (Evenings - mid-November thru early January)*

Harrison City

BUSHY RUN BATTLEFIELD

Harrison City - Bushy Run Road (off US22 to Bus66 to SR993) 15636. Phone: (724) 527-5584. www.bushyrunbattlefield.com/WelcomePage.html. Hours: Wednesday-Sunday 9:00am-5:00pm (April-October). Admission: $3.00-$5.00 (age 3+). Miscellaneous: Visitor Center

The battle that opened Western Pennsylvania to settlement - Pontiac's War in 1763. Native American forces lead by Chief Pontiac had occupied nearby forts. The British finally stopped advancements at Bushy Run - this reopened supply routes. Kids will either be scared or say "cool" when they see a life-size mannequin of an Indian Warrior dressed for battle with war paint from head to toe. In this same area, children can take turns dressing up like a British soldier (check out all the buttons!). Learn what "lock, stock, and barrel" means or discover all the different ways they used nature to provide basic needs (ex. Flour bags - fortification and wounds, or trees for gun stock, food, and dyes). View the electronic map of the battle - then walk outside to markers of the actual battlefield ground.

ANNIVERSARY OF THE BATTLE OF BUSHY RUN

Harrison City - *Bushy Run Battlefield. Live re-enactment of the Battle of Bushy Run, 1763. Period British and Native American campsites, and a variety of other programs. Admission. (first weekend in August)*

Hidden Valley

HIDDEN VALLEY SKI

Hidden Valley - *One Craighead Drive (PA Route 31) 15502. Phone: (814) 443-2600. Snow Report: (800) 443-7544. www.hiddenvalleyresort.com.*

Longest Run: 1 mile; 17 Slopes & Trails. Sleigh rides, Children's Snow Play area, Snowtubing and snowboarding. Year-round sports and recreation at Hidden Valley Resort from golf, outdoor swimming, indoor swimming, and mountain biking in the spring, summer and fall. Lodging in condos w/ kitchens.

Latrobe

DISALVO'S STATION RESTAURANT

Latrobe - *325 McKinley Avenue (Latrobe Train Station - downtown Amtrak station) 15650. Phone: (724) 539-0500.   http://disalvosrestaurant.com. An early 1900 train station that has been restored and decorated with railroad memorabilia. Ride from Pittsburgh on Amtrak to get here (adds to the railroad experience). When walking into the restaurant, you'll enter through a tunnel that trains pass over often. Feel and hear the rumble! Once through the tunnel, you may be seated in the atrium (formerly the train yard) with fountains, greenery and a full-size railroad dining car. Most families are seated in the original main concourse room with a continuously running model train above. A children's menu is offered. Hours: Tuesday-Sunday, Lunch and Dinner. Early Bird specials 4:00-6:30pm ($6.95). Reservations strongly suggested. Moderate to fine dining*

PITTSBURGH STEELERS SUMMER TRAINING CAMP

Latrobe - *US30 at Fraser Purchase Road (St. Vincent College) 15650. Phone: (724) 323-1200. www.steelers.com. Hours: Daily practice - get a schedule at the field. (Mid-July - August) Admission: FREE.*

Since 1967, this has been the site of the NFL - Pittsburgh Steelers pre-season training camp. Young fans can root for their favorite team member in a much

SW Area

smaller and more intimate setting. Children can also learn that the glamour and the glory of the NFL only comes from hard, focused work each day on the practice field. If you're lucky, you might have a chance to get some autographs. Be sure to bring a pen (a Sharpie? is best), paper, old program, or Steeler's memorabilia for the players to sign! A wonderful children's area offers face painting with Steeler's logos, photo boards and 3-D player props, plus kicking, passing, and running games. From our experience, it's tough to see the

Watching the PROS at work...

practice, and get autographs on the same visit. If you want autographs, stay up on the hill near the dorms by the entrance to the camp. The practices take place on the lower fields and the coaches usually enter from the dorm driveway farthest from the entrance. What fun!

KEYSTONE STATE PARK

Latrobe (Derry) - *RD 2, Box 101 (on SR 1018, the park is three miles from SR 981/SR 22) 15627. www.dcnr.state.pa.us/stateparks/parks/keystone.aspx. Phone: (724) 668-2939. Admission: to PA State Parks is FREE however swimming, marina and camping/lodging fees apply, with reservation or entrance.*

Camping, modern cabins, trails of all sorts, a lake, and a swimming beach provide an ideal setting for a summer outing. The park offers a variety of trails open year-round for hiking, cross-country skiing and snowshoeing. All trails have easy access with parking available at the trailheads. A sand beach is open from late-May to mid-September, 8:00am to sunset. A food concessionaire operates out of the Beach House Complex, which is across the road from the park office. The hours of operation during the summer months are 12:00pm to 7:00pm. Visitor Center, Year-round Education & Interpretation Center, Boat Rentals, Horseback Riding, Yurts and Camping, Sledding, Fishing.

SW Area

Laughlintown

COMPASS INN MUSEUM

Laughlintown - *PO Box 167 (US30 East, 3 miles east of Fort Ligonier) 15655. Phone: (724) 238-4983. www.compassinn.com. Hours: Tuesday-Saturday 11:00am-4:00pm, Sunday & Holidays 1:00-5:00pm. (May -October) Admission: $9.00 adult, $6.00 child (6-17). Tours: Costumed tour guides take you on a 1 1/2 hour tour. Note: ask the admission clerk for the paper scavenger hunt to use during the tour.*

A great chance to see a restored 1799 stagecoach stop that was a typical roadside inn - complete with cramped sleeping quarters. In the reconstructed cookhouse, you'll learn what terms like "uppercrust" (the bottom of the bread was sooty from the stove - so the upper crust was much better) mean. The bottom of the bread was "caked" with soot. "Let them eat cake" had a meaning of "Let them eat dirt". Also view the contents of The Barn & Blacksmith Shop. The tour utilizes many comparisons to modern-day things, so that students can relate the historical to the familiar while emphasizing the work children did and the important contribution this made to a family.

CHRISTMAS OPEN HOUSE

Laughlintown - *Compass Inn Museum. Tours of decorated, historical buildings. Refreshments and musical entertainment. Admission. (first Saturday in November thru second Saturday in December - weekends only)*

FORBES STATE FOREST

Laughlintown - *PO Box 519 (Del. Rt. 30E) 15655. Phone: (412) 238-9533. www. dcnr.state.pa.us/forestry/stateforests/forests/forbes/forbes.htm.*

Fishing, Camping, Trails, Winter Sports.

- BLUE HOLE DIVISION - a deep hole with water appearing blue, located on Blue Hole Creek and Cole Run Falls is located a few yards west of the Cole Run Road.

- BRADDOCK DIVISION - Pine Knob is an observation point overlooking Uniontown. Cabin Hollow Rocks is an interesting rock formation. Wharton Furnace was one of the last active iron furnaces in Fayette County. Old Water-Powered Grist Mill and Ponderfield Fire Tower.

SW Area

- LINN RUN DIVISION - Grove Run Spring is a walled, much used, spring. Adams Falls is a miniature water fall. Rock formations and Bluestone Quarry (stone from this quarry was used to pave the streets of Pittsburgh).

- KOOSER DIVISION - Beck Springs, Old Sawmill Site, & Kooser Fire Tower, Old Logging Railroad Grades & Bridges remain throughout the area.

- NEGRO MOUNTAIN DIVISION - many rock formations and Tarkiln is a kiln used to extract tar from the knots of pitch pine.

Ligonier

FORT LIGONIER

Ligonier - 200 South Market Street (US30 & SR 711) 15658. Phone: (724) 238-9701. www.fortligonier.org. Hours: Monday-Saturday 10:00am-4:30pm, Sunday Noon-4:30pm (mid-April thru mid-November). Admission: $7.00 adult, $5.50 senior, $4.00 child (6-14). Miscellaneous: Fort Ligonier Days in October - reenactments in summer. Quaint town shops within walking distance - some are toy stores!

Built by the British during the French and Indian War (1758), it was a vital link to the supply line to the West. You'll be able to view gun batteries, the very visibly and painful sharp wooden pickets of re-trenchment, the quarter master's store, a home, hospital (saws made from bone), and

We got the "point" here...

the commissary. Because you're free to roam in and out of buildings within the fort, it's ideal for antsy or playful children. The Museum displaying models and realistic dioramas, as well as a new audiovisual presentation about General Washington, serves as your gateway to the Fort complex.

FORT LIGONIER DAYS

Ligonier - Fort Ligonier. Commemorates the key battle of the French and Indian War. Hear the roar of the cannons and thunder of musketry at battle demonstrations at 2:00pm and 4:00pm on Saturday and Sunday. Visit the British and French military encampments, and journey back in time to an eighteenth century fort community. Experience the pageantry and color of Scottish Highlanders, American Provincial Troops and French Marines. Admission to fort. (second weekend of October)

SW Area

IDLEWILD PARK & SOAK ZONE

Ligonier - *Route 30 East, PO Box C (I-80 to I-76, exit 9, Donegal to 711, Left at Route 30) 15658. Phone: (724) 238-3666 or (800) 4 FUNDAY. www.idlewild.com.*

Hours: Opens at 10:00am (Memorial Day Weekend - Labor Day). Admission: $22.00-$30.00 GENERAL for Funday Pass (Children age 2 and under FREE). Miscellaneous: Goofy golf, rental boats and pony rides extra.

Now, I know we boast about few amusement parks but our recent visit back (after 30 years) to Idlewild and Storybook Forest was too fun! Story Book Forest is timeless. Idlewild Park lies between Pittsburgh and Johnstown and is considered to be one of the most

beautiful amusement parks in the country. Founded in 1878, Idlewild offers 16 unusual rides. Don't miss Raccoon Lagoon, one of the largest kiddie lands in the country; the Story Book Forest; Soak Zone water park; or the life-size tribute to Mr. Rogers' Neighborhood®, complete with the Neighborhood of Make Believe's famous residents. You can still meet Goldilocks, Snow White, the Old

Woman in the Shoe, and even get a lollypop from the Goodship Lollypop captain. Ride a real trolley into the Neighborhood of Make-Believe. Ask everyone on your trip to a Hug n' Song event at the castle. This village is like being zapped into a giant TV set!

Some other featured spots include:

- JUMPIN' JUNGLE - crawl, climb, swing, and bounce.

- SOAK ZONE - water slides, pool, Little Squirts Kiddie area.

- HOOTIN HOLLER - mining town with Cowboy shows, Old West games and food, Confusion Hill and Loyalhanna Railroad.

- OLDE IDLEWILD - roller coasters, merry-go-round, and Raccoon Lagoon kiddie rides (largest kiddie area in the US!)

School-aged kids can ride most every ride in the park and waterpark and families can bring in picnic baskets and grill. If you don't want all that fuss, they offer reasonable prices at Hootin' Holler' and the food is varied and good. Well before or after you eat, try a ride on the "Howler" replica tornado ride around a funnel cloud. There's entertainment from foot stompin', hand clappin' music and dancing to street actors.

Every part of the park is clean and easy to manage, even with younger kids. Look for discount days each month or get a membership. Still a great place for old-fashioned family amusement.

RAMADA INN HISTORIC LIGONIER

Ligonier - *216 West Loyalhanna Street (entrance off US 30) 15658. Phone: (724) 238-9545. www.ramadainnligonier.com. The closest family-friendly lodging to IDLEWILD (they almost always have seasonal Family Fun Packages to Idlewild-good value). Cozy doubles to spacious kings or suites at reasonable prices. Enjoy breakfast or dinner at the casual Bistro, see the sites, or relax by the outdoor heated pool. Kids Eat for only $0.99 in the restaurant. Great food in kid-friendly atmosphere featuring steaks, seafood and salads. Kids 10 and under eat for $.99 off the select children's menu. Walking distance to quaint shops and eateries or Fort Ligonier.*

Mc Murray

SIMMONS FARMS FALL PLAYLAND

McMurray - *Simmons Farms, 170 Simmons Road. www.simmonsfarm.com. Petting zoo, refreshments, pumpkin patch, corn maze, pony or wagon rides. Admission. (daily in October)*

Meyersdale

PENNSYLVANIA MAPLE FESTIVAL

Meyersdale - *US 219 Meyers Avenue Historic Buildings. www.pamaplefestival.com. Actual tapping of trees. Syrup making. Demonstrations of coopering and sugaring off in a realistic sugar camp. Pancakes and syrup served. War encampment, too. (last two weekends in March)*

Mill Run

FALLINGWATER

Mill Run - *1491 Mill Run Road, State Route 381 (I-76 exit 91, to SR31 East to Rte 381 south. 19 miles south of the Donegal exit) 15464. Phone: (724) 329-8501. www.fallingwater.org. Hours: Daily except Wednesdays 10:00am-4:00pm. (mid March thru Thanksgiving). December weekends only. Closed January and February Admission: $18.00 adult, $12.00 youth (ages 6-12). For safety reasons, children must be at least 6 years old to tour. Tours: 45 minutes - 1 hour. If you will be bringing very young children to Fallingwater, you may use their on-site Family Room. The Family Room is an unsupervised area where you or a member of your party must stay with your children while you wait for the rest of your party to complete their house tour. Note: No child care center anymore. Instead, try the Family Tour - a tour through the major rooms of the house, plus activities that explain how Fallingwater stands up. Appropriate for families with children ages 5-11. Children's tours for ages 5 and up are available by advance reservation. Falling Water restaurant. Want to see more, visit nearby Kentucky Knob, in Ohiopyle. FREEBIES: Click on the Learn icon, then Family Fun. You'll find architecture puzzles, bingo, word finds and coloring sheets.*

One of the most famous houses in America - and a memorable experience that is sure to delight all ages. The Edgar Kaufmann family used to vacation

the home is <u>ONE</u> with the <u>waterfall</u>...

on this exact spot in the woods during the summer months and loved to picnic by this waterfall. They loved it so much that they commissioned Frank Lloyd Wright (the famous architect) to build a home that would allow them to live on this spot, but not take away from its natural beauty. Wright commented, "I wanted you to live with the waterfall, not just look at it." The home is built from several cantilevers (stacked like Legos) that hang over the waterfall (actually - the stream goes right through the inside of the house!). Boulders were used as flooring and windows and walls on the first floor. Closer cave-like spaces were used as bedrooms. Children think Fallingwater is cool, with the waterfall, the natural landscape and all mysterious nooks and crannies throughout the house. As you tour, try to answer some questions: How many leaks in the stone? How many cantilevers in the building? This visit is sure to make a lasting impression!

SW Area

Monongahela

REILLY'S SUMMER SEAT FARM HARVEST FESTIVAL

Monongahela - *Triple B Farms, 823 Berry Lane. www.triplebfarms.com. Petting zoo, refreshments, pumpkin patch, corn maze, pony or wagon rides. Storybook Pumpkinland - with more than 200 pumpkin-headed, cartoon, storybook, and nursery-rhyme characters. Rope maze. Admission. (October Wednesday-Friday weeknights, all October weekends)*

Monroeville (Trafford)

SHERM EDWARDS CANDIES FACTORY TOUR

Monroeville (Trafford) - *509 Cavitt Avenue (near Rt. 130 & 993) 15085. Phone: (412) 372-4331. www.shermedwardscandies.com.*

Sherm Edwards Candies is the epitome of old fashioned candy making. In business for more than 60 years, Sherm Edwards is one of the very few Pennsylvania candy makers that still blends its own chocolate. Offering free factory tours, Sherm Edwards is known for its many creative confections, including Chocolate Covered Cordial Strawberries, Chocolate Covered Oreos, and even Chocolate Covered Pickles! Tours are given, by reservation. Hope they're making chocolate covered pickles when you visit - seeing is believing - and tasting...

Mt. Pleasant

L.E. SMITH GLASS COMPANY

Mt. Pleasant - *1900 Liberty Street (I-70 to SR 119 south, then off SR31 - follow signs) 15666. Phone: (800) 537-6484. www.lesmithglass.com. Admission: FREE. Tours: Monday - Friday 9:30am-3:00pm, Gift shop until 5:00pm. Ages 6+ only. Call ahead. Often it's just observation of crafters vs. tours.*

The oldest industry in America - making glassware by hand, started in the early 1600s. This company makes glass pictures, goblets, plates, figurines, and even exclusives patterns for famous people. Your guide starts the tour explaining the glass-making process from the beginning when glass powder (sand, cullet, color) are heated to 2000+ degrees F. in a furnace. Once melted, the molten glass is pulled on a stick and then molded or pressed, fire- glazed and then cooled in a Lehr which uniformly reduces the temperature to prevent shattering. They were making pedestal cake servers the day we were there.

They still use many old-time tools and techniques - for example, to frost glass, they dip it in acid. Their warehouse discount prices are great! Fascinating, almost unbelievable, work conditions create an interest for kids.

MT. PLEASANT GLASS & ETHNIC FESTIVAL

Mt. Pleasant - *Washington Street & Veterans Park. Over 100 arts, crafts and ethnic food booths. Two stages of national and regional entertainment. Parade, contests, rides and glass blowing demonstrations. www.mtpleasantglassandethnicfestival.com. FREE. (last weekend of September)*

North Huntington

BIG MAC MUSEUM RESTAURANT

North Huntington - *9051 Route 30 (Rte. 30 just off the PA turnpike at Exit 67) 15642.. www.bigmacmuseum.com. Hours: Lobby open 5am to midnight.*

Titled "the most tasteful museum in the world," the combo museum and restaurant features the world's largest Big Mac statue (measuring 14 feet high and 12 feet wide), and hundreds of historic artifacts and high-tech exhibits that celebrate the Big Mac, which was invented 40 years ago in Uniontown by Jim Delligatti. Say Cheese in front of the world's largest Big Mac replica and have a big bite of fun in the state-of-the-art jungle PlayPlace. While you're there, pull up a seat and enjoy a Big Mac with the inventor; race to sing the world famous tongue twisting recipe "jingle"; or just look at all the classic memorabilia on display.

Ohiopyle

OHIO PYLE STATE PARK

Ohiopyle - *PO Box 105 Rt. 381 North, Off Rt. 40 15470. Phone: (412) 329-8591. www.dcnr.state.pa.us/stateparks/parks/ohiopyle.aspx. Admission: to PA State Parks is FREE however swimming, marina and camping/lodging fees apply, with reservation or entrance. Miscellaneous: Suggested Whitewater Raft Companies in the area: Laurel Highlands River Tours, 800-4-RAFTIN. Mountain Streams and Trails Outfitters, 800-RAFT-NOW. Wilderness Voyageurs, 800-272-4141. White Water Adventurers, 800-WWA-RAFT.*

More than 14 miles of the Youghiogheny River Gorge churns through the heart of Ohiopyle. The famous Lower Yough, below the scenic Ohiopyle Falls, provides some of the best whitewater boating in the Eastern US. You can also hike or bike the 28-mile Youghiogheny River Trail. Ferncliff Peninsula Park -

SW Area

trails, flowers, trees, birds and wildlife abound. Sit in the creek bed and ride the water through two natural waterslides in Meadow Run. Parking is available adjacent to the SR 381 bridge. Visitor Center, Boat Rentals, Mountain Biking, Fishing, Trails, Winter Sports.

Pittsburgh

PITTSBURGH SPORTS

PITTSBURGH STEELERS FOOTBALL - www.steelers.com. (412) 323-1200. NFL Professional football team and 6-time Super Bowl Champs! Home games played at the new Heinz Field. Heinz Field's horseshoe shape allows for a

beautiful view of the city's unique skyline and the fountain at the Point while watching a University of Pitt (Saturday) or Steelers (Sunday/Monday) home game. Using the guidelines you can download from the Steelers.com website, we found parking for $5.00 at a garage at Sixth & Fort Duquesne Blvd., right across the street from the bridge to the North Shore. Once inside the park, we immediately noticed how modern, comfortable and clean the stadium

was. Better yet, the bright yellow-gold seats were super comfy. Something we'd recommend to any sports fan going to their first professional game is to get there at least two hours early. Pregames really set the tone & build excitement.

PITTSBURGH PIRATES BASEBALL - (412) 321-BUCS or (800) BUY-BUCS or www.pirateball.com. PNC Park. National League Professional Baseball (April-September). Watch the Pirates take on other League teams at PNC park. On game nights, the city closes the Roberto Clemente Bridge to vehicles

and street performers, vendors and pedestrians swarm the area - every other group walking towards the stadium might very well be a family - even babies dressed in their black and gold fan apparel. What a feeling to be part of on a nice summer's eve. The concessions at the park are upscale fair food and many are grilled upon ordering, not prepared ahead, so every sandwich is fresh.

- **PITTSBURGH PENGUINS HOCKEY** - Phone: (412) 642-PENS. http://penguins.nhl.com/. Mellon Arena. National Hockey League (October-early April). Official home of the Stanley Cup Champions. Look for Family Programs where kids get admission for around $10.00 with paid adult.

PRIMANTI BROTHERS

Pittsburgh - *www.primantibrothers.com. Locations are throughout Pittsburgh - even Heinz Field & PNC Park (gamedays and special events). Even the shortest visit to the*

Steel City will teach you that Pittsburgh pride runs deep—starting with the Steelers, and ending with the sandwich. The Primanti Bros. sandwich, that is. Every Primanti's sandwich begins with an inch-plus foundation of soft Italian bread. Moving from the ground up, it's piled with your meat and cheese of choice, layered with hot fries, slapped with peppered slaw, topped with tomato, and crowned with the second slice that somehow balances on top. It's all wrapped in waxed paper and given to you with a smile and offering to add Heinz 57 Sauce, if you like. We actually liked the Heinz 57 sauce and some Heinz mustard (it is Heinz headquarters, after all). The kids insisted all it needed was Heinz Ketchup. Fries ON your sandwich AND*

The original location is: 46 18th Street in the Strip District (open 24 hours, 7 days a week)!

crunchy coleslaw – crazy good. Some like the classic cheesesteak meat but others prefer pastrami. Start with the classic cheesesteak Pitts-burger and then see where that goes…

SAND CASTLE

Pittsburgh - *1000 Sandcastle Drive (I-376 exit 5, west Route 837) 15120. Phone: (412) 462-6666. www.sandcastlewaterpark.com. Hours: Daily (June-Labor Day); June 11:00am-6:00pm, July & August 11:00am-7:00pm. Admission: ~$30.00 general, Junior Whitewater Pass (46 inches and under) ~$20.00 and senior (65+). Parking $6.00. Tidal Wave Café buffet can be added for discount combo pricing.*

15 water slides including "Cliffhangers" pond slide and Two shotgun slides (patron rides on her/his back to a surprise ending - it drops in a free fall to the water below), giant Lazy River, Wet Willie's waterplay, Japanese tidal wave, kiddie and adult pools, Boardwalk and the world's largest hot tub. Riverplex Amphitheater.

SW Area

PITTSBURGH IRISH FESTIVAL

Pittsburgh - *Sand Castle. www.pghirishfest.org. Entertainment, food, marketplace, cultural and educational children's activities, bingo, Irish dogs, customs. Admission. (second weekend of September)*

PITTSBURGH ZOO & AQUARIUM

Pittsburgh - *One Wild Place (In Highland Park, SR 28 North to exit 6, follow signs) 15206. Phone: (412) 665-3640 or 1-800-4-PGH-ZOO. www.pittsburghzoo.com. Hours: Daily 9:30am-6:00pm (Summer), 9:00am-5:00pm (fall/spring). Reduced hours in winter. Zoo is open year-round except except Thanksgiving, Christmas, and New Year's Days. Closed for 3 weeks in January for maintenance. Admission: $11.00-$13.00 (age 2+). Parking Free. Reduced fees in the winter. Tours: The Zoo Tram provides a covered ride through the Zoo with stops at eight different locations. Simply purchase a Tram wristband and you can board or disembark as many times as you wish during the day. You can explore at your own pace, then proceed on the tram to your next adventure. The Tram stops at each well-marked location approximately every 20 minutes. The Tram is for your convenience in navigating the Zoo, and is not a guided tour. Miscellaneous: Food available. Fun "incline" escalator takes you up the hill to the zoo. FREEBIES: the Kids & Fun Stuff icon has links to online games, quizzes and printable downloads.*

Over 4000 creatures both great and small. Natural settings with themes like: Tropical Forest, Asian Forest (Amur Tigers), African Savanna (elephants), Water's Edge and PPG Aquarium - wonderful use of glass that allows you to feel you can almost "touch" the fish. Tunnels, too!

- WATER'S EDGE - Stories woven by Inuit natives who live side by side with these magnificent creatures provide the introduction to the bears and their environment. Paw prints lead to the polar bear den for a nose-to-snout encounter when the bears lounge in this temperature-controlled climate. Two large viewing windows intensify the excitement of seeing the young brother

Mr. Polar Bear having a little swim time...

bears as they splash in their freshwater waterfall and play in their dig yard. The paw prints continue to lead visitors down a nature trail to Pier Town, a replica of an Alaskan fishing village, complete with a cannery, a bait and tackle shop, and a sustainable seafood market. Wow!

PITTSBURGH ZOO & AQUARIUM (cont.)

- <u>KIDS KINGDOM</u> - Where kids can act like animals! This interactive facility is complete with playground equipment that replicates animal motions and behaviors so kids can play like the animals play. It's also full of hands-on animal experiences, like the walk-through Deer Yard, where kids can actually touch a white-tailed deer or the walk-through Kangaroo Yard where Australian gray kangaroos get so close, kids can reach out and touch them! There's also a friendly Goat Yard, the meerkat exhibit through a see-through tunnel, beaver and otter exhibits and a fabulous sea lion pool featuring several of these playful marine mammals. Swing-like spiders, Turtle Race, Penguin Slide, or climb through Mole Tunnel (big hits with the kiddies!).

You won't want to miss their newest exhibit of polar bears and sea otters. What a treat to see these playful, curious water creatures from all angles. The setup actually allows you to look above, beside and below the water in a cute seaside town motif. Another popular place to mark on your checklist of things to do: feeding time at the Bear habitat.

THE FRICK ART & HISTORICAL CENTER

Pittsburgh - 7227 Reynolds Street (I-376, Exit # 9) 15208. Phone: (412) 371-0600. www.frickart.org. Hours: Tuesday-Sunday 10:00am-5:00pm. Reservations suggested holiday weekends. Admission: FREE. Clayton is $12.00. Reduced for Family Days tours. $6.00 students. Tours:

Henry Clay Frick's (industrialist & art collector) mansion (Clayton) with original possessions, gardens, art museum and children's playhouse (now the Visitor's Center). Check out the floorboards that were once the bowling alley (playhouse). Kids will love the pretend food displayed in the dining rooms and Helen's bedroom. Family Days (ages 6-12) teaches about late 1800s life in Pittsburgh with a hands-on activity (dress up or craft) after the shortened tour with teen docents. The best theme tour for kids is: Growing Up at Clayton or something similar. Every room features a special "touchable" item, from a swatch of red velvet very like Mrs. Frick's chaise longue to stereoscopes and curious household tools. Got a question? Please ask! They want your children to be actively engaged as you learn about growing up in Pittsburgh over 100 years ago. Most appropriate for kids age 6 and up. Children 12 and under are FREE during this tour.

CHRISTMAS OPEN HOUSE

Pittsburgh - *The Frick Art & Historical Center. Tours of decorated, historical buildings. Refreshments and musical entertainment. Admission. Reservations suggested. (third Thursday in November - early January, Tuesday-Sunday)*

DUQUESNE INCLINE

Pittsburgh - *1220 Grandview Avenue (use either West Carson Street, or the Station Square access road which parallels the Monongahela and Ohio rivers) 15211. Phone: (412) 381-1665. http://trfn.clpgh.org/incline. Hours: Monday-Saturday 5:30am-12:45am. Sundays and Major Holidays 7:00am-12:45am. Admission: $1.00-$2.00 (age 6+) - Fares are each way. Seniors are FREE. Free parking at lower station.*

One of the few remaining cable cars still in use. Look for the red lights heading up the hill and the wood carved, paneled and trimmed cars. The cars climb and descend 400 ft at a 30 degree angle. The Upper Station, on Grandview Avenue, includes a new platform for the public to view the Incline's historic hoisting equipment, as well as displays

...the famous incline hard at work...

regarding the history of the Incline and the City of Pittsburgh, and pictures of other cable and rail cars from around the world. The observation platform outside has the best view of the city.

CARNEGIE SCIENCE CENTER

Pittsburgh - *One Allegheny Avenue (near Stadium - off I-279 or I-376) 15212. Phone: (412) 237-3400. www.carnegiesciencecenter.org/. Hours: Sunday-Friday 10:00am-5:00pm, Saturday 10:00am-7:00pm. Admission: $17.95 adult, $9.95 child (3-12). General admission includes exhibits, SportsWorks, Buhl Planetarium and USS Requin. Omnimax & Laser Fantasy Show extra. $5.00 parking. Miscellaneous: Discovery Store. Restaurant café. Educators: fun, downloadable Educator Guides are found here: www.wheresciencehappens.org/edu_resource.html.*

Bringing the world of science alive, the Carnegie Science Center is for visitors of all ages. This Science Center features more than 400 hands-on exhibits, three live demonstration theaters, a four-story IMAX Dome theater, an interactive planetarium, a 36,000 square foot science-of sport exhibition, a Cold War

SW Area

submarine moored on Pittsburgh's Ohio River, and a world-renowned model railroad display. Over 250 hands-on exhibits! Here's a menu of what you can expect at this fun-filled science center:

- <u>EXPLORATION STATION & JUNIOR STATION</u> - Habitats and live animals, structures & building, magnets and electric. Launching air rockets; Playing the laser harp and the PVC pipe organ; or Engineering dams, locks, channels and flood plains to control the flow of a river.

- <u>OMNIMAX THEATER</u> - Movies that literally make you a PART of the action.

- <u>INTERACTIVE PLANETARIUM</u> - Keeps you on "an edge". Also features laser light shows.

- <u>WW II SUBMARINE</u> - Climb aboard the authentic USS Reguin. See demonstrations on dives, power generators, even touch a real torpedo!

- <u>SCIQUEST LIVE SCIENCE DEMONSTRATIONS</u> or <u>KITCHEN CHEMISTRY</u> - Push a button to create a 4 ft. tornado or learn cooking chemistry (in a themed classroom setting). Lots of waves and air here!

- <u>SEASCAPE</u> - A large coral reef aquarium and water play table.

- <u>SPORTWORKS</u> - Best Virtual Sports Facility we've seen for kids! Experience virtual reality basketball and pitching cage. Cruise down Olympic bobsleds, hang glide the Grand Canyon or mini-golf Math. 60 + interactives - all included in admission price. This place is family-interactive and lets each family member "show off" their skills. Plan to spend half your time in here!

- <u>MINIATURE RAILROAD & VILLAGE</u> - 2300 square feet of a re-created village connecting the history and culture of southwestern PA between late 1800s and the 1930s.

CHILDREN'S MUSEUM OF PITTSBURGH

Pittsburgh - *10 Children's Way - Allegheny Square (off I-279, follow signs - just blocks from the stadium) 15212. Phone: (412) 322-5058. www.pittsburghkids. org. Hours: Monday-Saturday 10:00am-5:00pm, Sunday Noon-5:00pm. (Closed Monday during the school year). Admission: $10.00-$11.00 (ages 2+). Parking is $5.00. Miscellaneous: Pecaboo Café. Workshops on Saturdays and some Friday evenings. The Nursery Area for infants/toddlers. Changing Lower Level Gallery. Gift Shop.*

So, have all the dramatic changes to the museum worked? Yes, it's a success and this is what they found: Children learned more when their parents were interacting with them as opposed to standing back and watching. So, moms and dads, grandmas and grandpas, be prepared for not kid-centered exhibits, but family centered spaces. The expanded Museum offers exhibits based on the philosophy of "Play with Real Stuff." Children can tinker under the hood of a MINI Cooper and pound nails with a hammer in the Garage Workshop, build a boat and sail it down the rapids on a 53-foot waterway in Waterplay, stage their own performances with costumes and makeup in the Theater and much more. Many of the new exhibits are interactive art. Here are some favorites:

- GARAGE AND WORKSHOP - Roll up your sleeves and get busy, because the Garage/Workshop is a place where you can build things and take things apart, see how machinery and engines run, and learn how to fix them when they don't. You can also climb a rope net to go high into the planetarium dome on a platform where you can launch parachutes and use a pulley to bring them back up (funny, we saw more dads "supervising" this than kids). A giant slide brings you back to the ground floor. Tinkering is the rule.

- BACKYARD - The Backyard (outdoors) has clever interactive sculpture where you become part of the sculpture's movement and maybe even make music by your actions. Bubbling Mud has clay you "boil" to fit your mood - a babbling brook or an explosion.

- MISTER ROGERS' NEIGHBORHOOD - Loved Mr. Rogers Neighborhood? The Neighborhood features a video welcome from the beloved Fred Rogers, a closet of cardigans and sneakers to play pretend, a replica trolley and replica home. Music, folks playing with puppets in the castle; videos of shows; Mr. Roger's Sweater and Sneakers and "excerpts" from the set add to this open space.

- WATERPLAY - The River is so unique as its the only one we've seen with walk in water play spaces. RainCoats and Boots are required because you might build a water fountain to the sky and then want to jump around in it.

© Albert VecerkaEsto

Waterplay fun...

Make sure you interact with some art while you're here. You can have some psychedelic visual fun with Text Rain or Arc Tangent - playing with walls and floors is always fun!

HEINZ FIELD TOURS

Pittsburgh - *400 Stadium Circle (Heinz Field) 15212. Phone: Heinz Field Tour Hotline (412) 697-7150. http://news.steelers.com/heinzfield/. Admission: $6.50 adult, $4.00 senior (55+) or child (18 and under). Heinz Field Walk-Up Tours: Walk-up tours begin in June. Walk-up tours are offered to groups with less than 10 people. (If you have more than 10 in your group, please see "How to schedule a tour of Heinz Field" on the website or call the hotline). Saturday tours begin in April and run through August. The selected Saturday for tours will be posted*

monthly. Walk-up tours are offered Monday, Wednesday and Friday at 10:00am and Noon except in the months of September and October, only Mondays and Fridays at 10:00am. They are offered every Monday, Wednesday, and Friday at 10:00am ONLY. No reservation is needed. Just simply meet under the Coca-Cola Great Hall sign located on Art Rooney Avenue by 9:45 am. (Cash payment only). During the months of September and October, Walk-up tours are conducted on Mondays and Fridays at 10 am ONLY. Tours are not conducted on holidays, most weekends, or event days. Miscellaneous: McDonald's Steelers KidZONE Show - Show taping takes place at Heinz Field in the Coca-Cola Great Hall on select Tuesdays early Fall. Doors Open at 5:30pm, show taping begins at 6:30 p.m. Kids under age 12 are free, all others $5.00. Two shows are taped per night. Parking available in lot Gold 1A. The McDonald Steelers KidZONE Show airs Sunday mornings at 10:30am on CW Pittsburgh.

Heinz Field is not only the home of the Pittsburgh Steelers and the University of Pittsburgh Panthers football teams but a proud icon in downtown Pittsburgh. Tours of Heinz Field consist of the Coca-Cola Great Hall, club, suite and service levels, press box, warning track, south plaza and much more. The Great Hall is the biggest treat: From the Six, yes six! Championship trophies to the Immaculate Reception by Franco Harris in 1972 to the locker room personal artifacts in famous players lockers (ex. Bradshaw, Swann).

NATIONAL AVIARY

Pittsburgh - *Allegheny Commons West (off I-279 North Shore exit - follow signs)*
15212. Phone: (412) 323-7235.   www.aviary.org.   Hours: Monday-Saturday
10:00am-5:00pm, Sunday Noon-5:00pm (everyday but Christmastime and
Thanksgiving). Admission: $12.00 adult, $11.00 senior (60+), $9.50 child (2-12).

Miscellaneous: Get up-close-and-personal with African
Penguin "Stanley" or resident owls daily right before or
after lunchtime.

At the National Aviary on Pittsburgh's North Side,
visitors can meet African penguins, flamingos, and
many more colorful birds. See 220 species of birds
live in natural habitats like rainforests, deserts, and
marshes. The tropical areas have rare, exotic birds in
free-flight atriums. Favorites to look for are the live Toucan (so animated, it
appears mechanical!), a real cuckoo bird (that sings a loud, sweet sound), and

the funny billed marsh birds (boat and spoon shaped,
for example). The Tropical Rainstorm at 12:30pm
daily in the Wetlands of the Americas 200,000 cubic
foot walk-through exhibit is so-o-o cool! Don't you just
love the birds flying overhead…especially entertaining
during feeding times (early afternoons) and outdoor
shows.

PHOTO ANTIQUITIES

Pittsburgh - *531 East Ohio Street 15212. www.photoantiquities.org. Phone:*
(412) 231-7881.   Hours: Monday-Saturday 10:00am-4:00pm, except Tuesdays,
Sundays and holidays. Admission: $3.00-$8.00 (age 5+). Tours: guided tours are
given on every visit.

Photo Antiquities Museum of Photographic History offers a history lesson on
photography. The Museum, designed in the Victorian style with period music
playing in the background, lends to the feeling of being in the 19th century.
Photo and paper processes, antique cameras, vintage historical print exhibits.
Follow the history of photography with a guided tour, from the Daguerreotype
c. 1839 (the first commercially viable photographic image produced onto a
silver coated copper plate) to present day digital photography. Of particular
interest to American history students: period images of the Civil War era and
the difficulties of the photographers who risked their lives to make a visual
record of The Civil War.

SW Area

SOLDIERS AND SAILORS MEMORIAL MUSEUM

Pittsburgh - *4141 Fifth Avenue 15213. www.soldiersandsailorshall.org/index.html. Phone: (412) 621-4254. Hours: Monday-Saturday 10:00am-4:00pm. Admission: $5.00-$8.00. Military, Veterans and family of those deployed and their guests are invited to visit the museum at no cost.*

Soldiers & Sailors National Military Museum & Memorial is one of the country's largest museums dedicated to honoring & remembering our Veterans. The museum houses exhibits that span from the Civil War to present day conflicts that tell the stories of ordinary citizens called upon to do extraordinary duties for the United States of America. Also African-American and Revolutionary War films. Their goal is not to idealize war but to honor and educate about the sacrifices during it. Interesting perspective.

ALLEGHENY OBSERVATORY

Pittsburgh - *Riverview Park (US19 in Riverview Park off Perrysville Avenue) 15214. Phone: (412) 321-2400. www.pitt.edu/~aobsvtry/. Hours: Thursday-Friday (by appointment - evenings - April - October). Thursday night tours are held from May 1st through the third week of August and the Friday night tours are held from April 1st through November 1st. Admission: FREE. Tours: All tours begin at 8:00pm and last until approximately 10:00pm.*

One of the foremost observatories in the world. A short slide or film presentation is shown followed by a walking tour of the building finally ending up at the 13" Fitz-Clark refractor. If it's a clear night you would be shown whatever celestial objects are within range of the telescope that night. Dress for the temperature outside.

GATEWAY CLIPPER FLEET

Pittsburgh - *9 Station Square Dock - Downtown (I-376 exit Smithfield Street) 15219. Phone: (412) 355-7980. www.gatewayclipper.com. Admission: Average* *$14.00 adult, $9.50 child signtseeing. Add $8.00-$20.00 for lunch or dinner cruises. Tours: Sightseeing / Theme cruises usually depart between 11:00am-4:00pm (except Sunset at 7:00pm). Miscellaneous: On board gift shops and snacks available.*

A "Pittsburgh River Tradition" has sightseeing cruises sailing the three rivers. They are the largest and most successful sightseeing vessels in the America. There are several different boats in their fleet (all climate controlled) and many targeted toward ages 12 and under. These include Sunday Fun Cruises (w/ DJ Dance), Good Ship Lollipop Cruise (meet Lolli the Clown), Lock N Dam Adventure Cruises and 2 hour Sunset Cruises. Other mascots who frequent kids' cruises are Deckster Duck, and River Rover.

EASTER BUNNY BOAT RIDES

Pittsburgh - *Gateway Clipper Fleet. Candy treats with the Easter Bunny riding along. Easter crafts, DJ Dance Party. Admission. (Easter Weekend)*

SANTA FAMILY FUN CRUISES

Pittsburgh - *Gateway Clipper Fleet. 2 hours of DJ Dance Party with costumed mascots, visit from Santa with treat, and make your own ornaments. Admission. (weekends in December)*

GRAND CONCOURSE RESTAURANT

Pittsburgh - *100 West Station Square Drive 15219. Phone: (412) 261-1717. Kids Menu in the magnificent 1901 Victorian Train Station (kids like trying to find the most unique stained glass window themes) consists of items like pasta, chicken, fish, shrimp, burgers and grilled cheese ($6.99-$8.50). A great way to take in the "flavor" of old Pittsburgh at a real train station. Weekdays lunch. Dinners daily, Sunday brunch.*

JUST DUCKY TOURS

Pittsburgh - *Station Square - Downtown (I-376 exit Smithfield Street, next to Hard Rock Cafe) 15219. Phone: (412) 402-DUCK. www.justduckytours.com. Hours: Daily (mid-April - October). November weekends. Admission: $19.00 adult, $18.00 senior/student, $15.00 child (3-12), $5.00 child (2 and under). Tours: Departures 10:30 am, 12:00, 1:30pm, 3:00pm. Add 4:30pm (weekends) & 6:00pm (summer). Even more tour times in the summer. Approximately 1 hour.*

Venture aboard these funny, fully restored WW II Land and Water Vehicles! On land they use wheels and conventional steering. On water they use a propeller and a rudder.

...part bus...part boat...SPLASH!

By land - narrated tours include Pennsylvania and Lake Erie Railroad, Penn Station, South End and many historical downtown buildings. Learn Pittsburghese and about many movies made here. By water - see the Allegheny River and Golden Triangle or the Monongahela. Kids may get the chance to be captain of the boat for awhile (they get a sticker to prove it!). You'll quack, sing and laugh a ton. This is one of the best Ducky tours we've ever been on. It's so worth the price. Have fun!

MONONGAHELA INCLINE

Pittsburgh - *Carson Street at Station Square 15219. Phone: (412) 442-2000. www.portauthority.org/paac/customerinfo/inclines/tabid/119/default.aspx.*

Hours: Monday-Saturday 5:30am-12:45am, Sunday & Holidays 8:45am to midnight. Admission: Small fare each way.

The first US incline…boasting a 35 degree climbing angle and 358 foot elevation, this incline transports tourists and commuters daily from downtown to Mt. Washington. A special note to point out to the kids is that this engineering feat was designed in 1870 - before electric streetcars and the automobile! The trick is that one car climbs while the other descends - look for the green and yellow lights highlighting the track.

FORT PITT MUSEUM & POINT STATE PARK

Pittsburgh - *101 Commonwealth Place (off I-376, I-279, SR8, or SR51 on the forks of downtown, Ohio River) 15222. Phone: (412) 281-9284. www.dcnr.state.pa.us/ stateparks/parks/point.aspx. Hours: Daily 10:00am-5:00pm. Admission to Fort Museum: $5.00 adult, $4.00 senior (60+), $2.00 child (6-17). FREE admission to blockhouse and park. Miscellaneous: Blockhouse welcome center and gift shop (free to visit). Living history re-enactments (Summer-Sunday afternoons).*

This was the site of the largest British post in North America until they were forced to leave during the American Revolution. The fort played a pivotal role in the French and Indian War. Exhibits re-create the story of war, trade, and the founding of Pittsburgh. Listen to a taped explanation of the fort while viewing a scale model of Fort Pitt. A large diorama on the first floor contains a model of the fort. There's also an 18th century trading post.

Located at the tip of Pittsburgh's Golden Triangle, POINT STATE PARK has a fabulous water fountain, paved promenades along the riverfront & overlooks with dramatic views of the city, busy waterways, impressive hillside scenery. The traceries of both Fort Duquesne and Fort Pitt are lit by LED lights for a spectacular view from above at night. The original location of the rivers edge during the mid-1700s is depicted by a granite tracery within the Great Lawn area. Wayside exhibits and interpretive programs are planned for the park and are listed within the Point State Park Interpretive Plan.

JULY 4TH CELEBRATION

Pittsburgh - *Fort Pitt Museum & Point State Park. Parades, music, food, fireworks and contests.*

PITTSBURGH THREE RIVERS REGATTA

Pittsburgh - *Fort Pitt Museum & Point State Park. www.threeriversregatta.net . Downtown rivers and shores host the world's largest inland regatta. Air shows, powerboat races, hot air balloon races, fireworks and water-skiing demos. FREE. (first week in July including July 4th).*

HEINZ HISTORY CENTER

Pittsburgh - 1212 Smallman Street (in the Strip District, off I-376, Grant Street exit) 15222. Phone: (412) 454-6000. www.heinzhistorycenter.org. Hours: Daily 10:00am-5:00pm. Closed Easter, Thanksgiving, Christmas, New Years. Admission: $10.00 adult, $9.00 senior (62+), $5.00 student w/ id & child (4-17). Miscellaneous: Museum shop, café. Educators: click on the Education icon, then Materials & Resources, then Sports Museum Curriculum link or Social History or other assorted links to curriculum listed on the page.

An affiliate of the Smithsonian Institution, the History Center is the largest history museum in Pennsylvania.

The initiative of this museum is to preserve Western Pennsylvania history through intriguing exhibits such as:

- GREAT HALL - 1949 restored trolley with audio and a Conestoga wagon. ISALY's Dairy (Klondikes!) and a greeting from a robot that speaks fluent Pittsburghese.

SW Area

HEINZ HISTORY CENTER (cont.)

- <u>PITTSBURGH: A TRADITION OF INNOVATION</u>: Come face-to-face with a king of empire, Indians and inventors. Talk to George Washington, take a ride on America's First Superhighway or a sneak peak at innovations of the future.

- <u>SPECIAL COLLECTIONS</u> - Emphasis is placed on Steelworkers who were immigrants. Meet Mary, the mother of 5 children and married to a steelworker. Or, an African American journey to Freedom. Displays use ethnic costumes, toys, vehicles - even clothing - Mr. Roger's sweater and sneakers to be exact. A few years ago, the George Westinghouse Museum officially merged with the Senator John Heinz History Center & many of the early artifacts are found here. From the invention of the airbrake and automobile shock absorbers to the development of railroad signaling and the modern day weekend, the Westinghouse story is an integral part of Western Pennsylvania's 250 year history of innovation. MP3 audio players featuring local Pittsburgh personalities help to tell the stories behind many of the items so kids will engage in the items vs. passing by.

- <u>WESTERN PENNSYLVANIA SPORTS MUSEUM</u> - which includes exhibits dedicated to high school, collegiate, and professional sports in the Pittsburgh region (go Steelers!). A place where you can enjoy the great works of Maz and Mario. Art and Arnie. Roberto and Franco. Suzie and Swin. A place where you can relive the moments that made them great. The Immaculate Reception. The Home Run. Olympic gold. Super Bowls. Stanley Cups. The space promises to "get you in the game" with more than 70 hands-on interactive exhibits, a two-story video theatre and 20 audio-visual programs for visitors of all ages. The Interactive Football Exhibit, Make Your Own Medal, and Franco Harris' Immaculate Reception Shoes are the highlights for kids.

- <u>HEINZ 57 DISCOVERY AREA</u> – Three stations depict the lives of children who grew up in Western Pennsylvania, including a touch-screen, interactive trivia game called "Get to the Point" that challenges visitors to use their new found knowledge of Pittsburgh innovations. Kids can "go to work" as an apprentice in a beauty salon or climb through a steel mill. Children even as young as 12-14 were laborers – learn how some of them did their jobs (ex. packing pickles for Heinz or ironing clothes for pennies).

SW Area

- <u>KIDSBURGH</u> - Kidsburgh is an fun, interactive, two-tier playplace. Children will enjoy serving up Isaly's "ice cream" at their own play deli and milking a full-scale fiberglass "mooing" cow above Reymer's Old-Fashioned Deli. An interactive model of Pittsburgh allows kids to design their own city of Pittsburgh using models of buildings, boats, and sports stadiums. When they're done, kids can zoom down a 12-foot spiral slide, nicknamed the "Liberty Tube."

- <u>LEWIS AND CLARK</u> - Rediscovering Lewis & Clark: A Journey with the Rooney Family on the Corps of Discovery Trail. The Pittsburgh Steelers dynasty owners re-created that infamous trip along most of the same route.

Pittsburgh should be very proud and touched by this emotional history center!

SOCIETY FOR CONTEMPORARY CRAFTS

Pittsburgh - *2100 Smallman Street (Strip District) 15222. Phone: (412) 261-7003. www.contemporarycraft.org. Hours: MOnday-Saturday 9:00am-5:00pm. Admission: FREE.*

Visitors discover latest trends in the gallery, the store and the children's studio. Weekends for Families include demos, performances and workshops related to current exhibits. Because families are one of their primary audiences, they have developed the Drop In Studio, a free hands-on activity area for children and adults. The space, which is open during all public hours, allows visitors to participate in a hands-on art activity that has been developed by artists to tie-in to the special exhibitions.

STRIP DISTRICT DINING

Pittsburgh - *15222.*

The Strip District is several city blocks at the edge of downtown offering enticing food markets, coffee shops, restaurants and quirky shops (ex. a store that makes and sells handmade giant crayons that actually work).

Start your half-day trip with breakfast at <u>PAMELA'S</u> (60 21st Street, 412-281-6366). Serving Breakfast and Lunch everyday, most meals are around $5.00. Try the crepe hotcakes or french toast with chocolate and bananas.

After shopping and lunch, bring your crew into <u>KLAVON'S ORIGINAL ART DECO SODA FOUNTAIN</u> (Penn Avenue & 28th Street, www.klavonsicecream.com). They serve old-fashioned ice cream treats and "penny" candy.

For lunch, choose <u>PRIMANTI BROTHERS</u>. Ok, and this Pitts-burger sandwich.
. . .what's that about? We just love local flare on sandwiches and this one has
fries ON the sandwich NOT on the side! (check it out under separate listing:
PRIMANTI BROTHERS - www.primantibrothers.com).

And, if you get lost meandering Pittsburgh streets around construction zones,
just stop any native and they'll be glad to help you find your way. Some even
wrote a map on napkins, others volunteered to drive ahead with us following.

BEECHWOOD FARM NATURE PRESERVE

Pittsburgh - *614 Dorseyville Road (SR8 & SR28) 15238. Phone: (412) 963-6100.*
www.aswp.org/beechwood.html. Hours: Tuesday-Saturday, 9:00am-5:00pm.
Sunday, 1:00-5:00pm. Admission: FREE.

Headquarters of the Audubon Society of Western Pennsylvania. Acres of
fields, woodlands, ponds, and trails. Beechwood's 134 acres contain more
than five miles of walking trails, which are open to the public from dawn to
dusk everyday, year-round. The Bird observation room, Discovery Room &
Outdoor Discovery field programs are favorites for kids.

INTERNATIONAL CHILDREN'S FESTIVAL

Pittsburgh - *Allegheny Center, North Shore. www.pghkids.org/festival.htm. Indoor
main stage performances by world class professional theater companies along with
outdoor stages, strolling performers, workshops, and recreational, educational, and
cultural activities. Admission. (second week of May)*

PITTSBURGH VINTAGE GRAND PRIX

Pittsburgh - *Schenley Park. www.pittsburghvintagegrandprix.com. Racing and car
shows. Run by volunteers with proceeds benefiting mentally retarded and autistic
children and adults. (starts third weekend in July thru fourth weekend race)*

PITTSBURGH LIGHT UP NIGHTS

Pittsburgh - *Downtown. www.downtownpittsburgh.com. Celebrate the holiday season
in downtown Pittsburgh! Over 1,000 displays, performances, activities & events - many
free! Boat rides (www.gatewayclipper.com). Wintergarden Santa Display & outdoor Ice
Rink at PPG Center. Nativity Scene at US Steel. Holly Trolley; Polar Express and Mini*

SW Area

RR & village (Science Center). Includes Parade, fireworks and carriage rides. Go to the website for details! (every Saturday from third week November - first week of January)

KIDS HOLIDAY CRAWL

Pittsburgh - *Cultural District. www.pgharts.org/education/gallerycrawl.aspx. The Cultural District is crawling with fun activities for the whole family from cookie decorating and caroling to card-making and storytelling. Join friends at SPACE, the Pittsburgh Ballet Theatre, Pittsburgh Opera, Three Rivers Arts Festival and the African American Cultural Center as they celebrate the holiday season at over 10 venues throughout the Cultural District. Children can sit on Santa's lap, create crafts with the Pittsburgh Children's Museum and the Jewish Community Center of Greater Pittsburgh, meet the Radio City Rockettes and so much more. (first Saturday in December)*

MEADOWCROFT ROCKSHELTER AND VILLAGE

Pittsburgh (Avella) - *401 Meadowcroft Road (I-79 - Exit 11 Bridgeville to SR50 West) 15312. Phone: (724) 587-3412. www.heinzhistorycenter.org/meadowcroft.aspx. Hours: Wednesday-Saturday Noon-5:00pm, Sunday 1:00-5:00pm (Memorial Day-Labor Day). Weekends only (May, September, October). Open some weekends in November and December for special events. Admission: $10.00 adult, $5.00 (6-16) Rural Life Museum, Village and Rockshelter. Miscellaneous: Visitors Center and Café. Best during festivals for" hands on history" personalized sessions.*

Re-live rugged rural life from 200 years ago as you walk the dirt and stone roads of this reconstructed village. By touring a settler log house, schoolhouse,

country store, barn and blacksmith shop - you'll be introduced to inhabitants like the Native Americans, frontier settlers, farmers, lumbermen, coal miners, and conservationists who have worked the land. Get involved by taking a real school lesson (with slate and chalk) in a 1 room schoolhouse. Shear sheep and then spin and weave wool.

Meadowcroft Rockshelter has provided archaeologists with a rare glimpse into the lives of the first people to arrive in the New World. Visitors may go inside the open excavation and see evidence of tools and campfires made by these first Americans thousands of years ago. Discover how these ancient people survived - from what they ate to the weapons they relied on everyday - and, actually practice using a Native American "atlatl" (spear throwing). The grounds of this living history museum are on an archeological prehistoric dig site.

JULY 4TH CELEBRATIONS

Pittsburgh (Avella) - *Meadowcroft Rockshelter And Village. Parades, music, food, fireworks and contests. Historical patriotic activities. Admission.*

RURAL HERITAGE DAYS

Pittsburgh (Avella) - *Meadowcroft Rockshelter And Village. Tractor pulls, antique steam engines, parades, food (made with steam), threshing, baling, cider and apple butter making, hayrides, children's activities, petting zoo & fall crafts. Admission. (third weekend in October)*

TAFFY PARTIES

Pittsburgh (Avella) - *Meadowcroft Rockshelter And Village. Taffy pulling party in log house, holiday programs in one-room schoolhouse. Make an ornament. (mid-November and early December weekend)*

LITTLE LAKE THEATRE COMPANY

Pittsburgh (Canonsburg) - *500 Lakeside Drive, South 15317. Phone: (724) 745-6300. www.littlelaketheatre.org.*

Plays for the entire family for 50 years. Looking Glass Theatres, Fall Family Matinees. Youth plays run $8.00-$9.00 per person.

PITTSBURGH'S PENNSYLVANIA MOTOR SPEEDWAY

Pittsburgh (Carnegie) - *(US 22/30, Noblestown Exit) 15106. Phone: (724) 853-RACE. www.ppms.com.*

Auto Racing every Saturday Night, April through mid-September featuring the Super Late Models, Advance Auto Parts Crate Late Models, Pure Stocks, E-Mods, Amateur Stocks, Young Guns, and Demos on Dirt's Monster Half Mile. Visit their Sister Track Motordrome Speedway on Friday Evenings for exciting NASCAR Dodge Weekly Series Action. Tickets run $5.00-$13.00. Their slogan: "We'll sell you the whole seat, but you'll only need the edge!"

SW Area

PITTSBURGH HOLIDAY TRAIN SHOW

Pittsburgh (Gibsonia) - *5507 Lakeside Drive (I-79N exit Wexford to Rte. 910 east & Hardt Road). www.wpmrm.org. Holiday Miniature railroad displays the transportation systems in Pittsburgh during the 1950's. Accent on coal, steel, and steam production in use. Admission. (Friday evenings & weekends, mid-November - early January)*

BOYCE PARK SKI AREA

Pittsburgh (Monroeville) - *675 Old Frankstown Road (near U.S. 22 and right off of I-76) 15639. www.alleghenycounty.us/parks/bpfac.aspx. Phone: (724) 733-4656. Snow Report: (724) 733-4665.*

This ski area may be tiny and run by a county park, but lift tickets are inexpensive ($9.00 weekdays and $13.000 weekends). The park offers nine runs including moguls, halfpipe, Nastar timing runs with gates, jumps and night skiing. Lodge with a roaring fireplace, hot food and drinks. There's also a fitness center, roller skating, swimming, outdoor hot tubs, snow tubing, sleigh rides and even bowling.

CARNEGIE MUSEUM OF ART

Pittsburgh (Oakland) - *4400 Forbes Avenue (connected to Natural History Museum) 15213. Phone: (412) 622-3131. www.cmoa.org. Hours: Tuesday-Saturday 10:00am-5:00pm, Sunday Noon-5:00pm. Open until 8:00pm on Thursdays. Admission: $11.00-$15.00 (age 3+). Admission includes Carnegie Museum of Natural History. Miscellaneous: ARTventures: family art activities. Every Saturday 12:30-4:30 p.m., ongoing Ages 4 and up with an adult. Café open for lunch. FREEBIES: Ask at the admissions desk for the free kid's audio guide narrated by Art Cat.*

Check out whatever new exhibit is on display at the art museum - we saw packing tape philosophical art. Very funky and fun. With every kid visit, be sure to pick up a gallery search scavenger hunt card. Complete them and stop back for a prize at the end of your visit. Paintings, sculpture, film and video projections reflect values and ideas from cultures long ago and today. Hall of Sculpture. Hall of Architecture. Add this museum to your visit to the Museum of Natural History (included).

CARNEGIE MUSEUM OF NATURAL HISTORY

Pittsburgh (Oakland) - *4400 Forbes Avenue (I-579 to Oakland/Monroeville exit to Blvd. Of the Allies OR I-376E to Forbes Ave exit 2a) 15213. Phone: (412) 622-3131. www.carnegiemnh.org. Hours: Tuesday-Saturday 10:00am-5:00pm, Sunday Noon-5:00pm. Thursdays open until 8:00pm. Admission: $15.00 adult, $12.00 senior, $11.00 child (3-18). Admission includes same-day access to both Carnegie Museum of Natural History and Carnegie Museum of Art. Miscellaneous: Store, café. Earth Theater - 210 degree wrap around screen featuring tornadoes or meteors or dinos. Family Programs on weekends. Educators: Click on Programs/then Educator Resources/then choose a topic for research (student) or Teachers Guides specific to a time period presented in the museum. FREEBIES: (w/paid admission) Discovery Room & Family Museum Bags - Explore the Discovery Room with hands-on materials. Check out a Family Museum Bag for even deeper exploration of the exhibitions and collections. The BioTech Lab is often open for families to explore.*

...digging for clues...

See a world famous dinosaur collection with a T-Rex and 9 other species plus a PaleoLab and Bonehunters Quarry (Dino Hall fossil digs). You won't want to miss the Natural History's "revamp" of their dinosaur collection - "Dinosaurs in their Time". Take a few moments observing the Paleo Lab where actual dino doctors work on real pieces. The new exhibits showcase cast bones in natural settings with bright, contemporary lighting (not old dark hallways). Parts of the path allow guests to walk under the huge tails of several dinos.

In the Stratavator, a simulated elevator ride takes you 16,000 feet down into the Earth below the museum. Visitors enter the elevator cab, and meet their tour guide, a miner, seen through the cab's "window"—a video screen. The stratavator stops at the museum's

...all aboard, the "Stratavator"

basement storage rooms, a coal mine, a limestone cave, and other geological features. As the cab vibrates, rock strata whiz by between stops. (This is a "hot" one for the kids!) American Indians and the Natural World examine the belief systems, philosophies, and practical knowledge that guide Indian people. Polar World Dioramas illustrate the Arctic environment and the traditional Inuit way of life. Scenes depict kayak hunting, ice fishing, and a life-size recreation of an Inuit snowhouse. Additional sites include Egyptian mummies and a crawl-thru Egyptian tomb; a Discovery Room (hands-on); Hall of Botany; and the Hall of Minerals and Gems (fluorescent minerals, crystals). Watch, around every corner you may be greeted by a giant surprise!

PHIPPS CONSERVATORY

Pittsburgh (Oakland) - *One Schenley Park (I-376 East, take the Forbes Ave./ Oakland exit 2a). 15213. Phone: (412) 622-6914. www.phipps.conservatory.org. Hours: Daily 9:30am-5:00pm, Hours extended to 10:00pm on Friday. Admission: $9.00-$12.00 (age 2+). Tours: FREE docent-led tours occur daily right before or after lunchtime.*

A historic landmark 13 room Victorian glass house featuring tropical and desert motifs plus one of the nation's finest Bonsai collections. Feel the heat in the desert or smell the wafting fragrance in the Orchid Room. Explore the newer Amazon Rainforest or try to spy Chihuly glass (trust us, you'll know when you see it blended into many scapes). Discovery Garden - outdoor hands-on learning for children (boxwood maze, sensory garden). Visit a Discovery Table in the Conservatory for a hands-on, fun look at a specific subject. Summer-Butterfly Forest.

CHRISTMAS OPEN HOUSE

Pittsburgh (Oakland) - Phipps Conservatory. Tours of decorated, historical buildings. Refreshments and musical entertainment. Candlelight paths. Admission. (evenings mid-December thru the month)

PITTSBURGH PLAYHOUSE JR.

Pittsburgh (Oakland) - *222 Craft Avenue 15213. Phone: (412) 621-4445. www. pittsburghplayhouse.com/ThePlayhouse/Ourcompanies/PlayhouseJr.*

Over 50 years of children's classics and new works like Snow White or Winnie-the-Pooh (November - May). Playhouse Jr. brings children and young adults into the world of imagination through live theatre with fairy tales, modern and timeless stories adapted for young audiences and classics from children's literature. The productions are crafted to be family friendly for children of all ages. The second oldest continually running children's theatre in the nation, Playhouse Jr. is now performing for third generations of patron families.

RODEF SHALOM BIBLICAL BOTANICAL GARDENS

Pittsburgh (Oakland) - *4905 Fifth Ave. 15213. www.biblicalgardenpittsburgh.org. Phone: (412) 621-6566. Hours: Sunday-Thursday 10:00am-2:00pm. Also from 7:00-9:00pm on Wednesday and from Noon-1:00pm Saturday. (June - mid-September) Admission: FREE.*

The garden was established in 1987. It is the largest of its kind in North America (1/3 acre) and the only one with an ongoing program of research and publication. Visit the land of the Bible in a setting of a waterfall, a desert, a stream, the Jordan, which meanders through the garden from Lake Galilee to the Dead Sea. All plants are labeled with biblical verses accompanying them. See wheat, barley, millet and many herbs grown by the ancient Israelites along with olives, dates, pomegranates, figs, cedars. Biblical names given to local plants show the affection of each generation for the Bible. Free Admission.

CATHEDRAL OF LEARNING NATIONALITY CLASSROOMS

Pittsburgh (Oakland) - *1209 Cathedral of Learning (I-376 west to exit 7A, University of Pittsburgh) 15260. Phone: (412) 624-6000. www.pitt.edu/~natrooms/. Hours: Monday-Saturday 9:30am-3:00pm, Sunday 11:00am-3:00pm. Admission: $3.00 adult, $2.00 senior (60+), $1.00 child (8-18). Tours: 90 minute hour guided or tape recorded tours. Please request a tour that is adapted to younger audiences. Miscellaneous: While of campus, musically inclined may want to visit the Stephen Foster Memorial Museum (ex. Foster's piano, musical instruments and compositions. (412) 624-4100 or www.pitt.edu/~amerimus/museum.htm).*

"Tour the World in 90 Minutes!" - Visit 24 classrooms depicting heritages of different ethnic communities. In these rooms, themes are rendered in wood and glass, iron and stone, fabric, color, and words. Inspiration flows from such varied sources as Athens in the time of Pericles, a palace hall in Beijing's Forbidden City, an ancient monastic Indian university, flowers that grow in Czech and Slovak valleys, a 6th-century oratory from Ireland's Golden Age, an Asante temple courtyard in Ghana, London's House of Commons, and the intimate hearth-centered life of America's early New Englanders. See authentic examples of cultural architecture and décor from Africa, Asia, Middle East,

SW Area

and Eastern and Western Europe including: Ukrainian Room – wood carvings on beams and doors, hand painted pottery and tile. German - stained glass fairy tales. African - Sankofa birds. University classes meet in the classrooms from early morning to late at night, amidst surroundings designed to enhance learning and engage the senses. A steady stream of people -- often families of three generations -- come to see the world-famous rooms, which evoke pride in their own heritage and warm appreciation of other cultures. I don't think there's anything like it.

CHRISTMAS OPEN HOUSE

Pittsburgh (Oakland) - *Cathedral Of Learning. Tours of decorated, historical buildings. Refreshments and musical entertainment. Admission. (month-long in December)*

KENNYWOOD PARK

Pittsburgh (West Mifflin) - 4800 Kennywood Blvd. (I-376, Exit 9) 15122. Phone: (412) 461-0500. www.kennywood.com. Hours: Monday-Sunday 10:30am-after dark (Mid-May - Labor Day). Open some weekends in early May & early September. Admission: All day general passes available ~$36.00. $18.00-$23.00 general (Junior and senior passes). Children 2 and under are FREE. Parking is free. After 5:00pm reduced Night Rider $21.00. Miscellaneous: Shoes, shirts, pants or shorts are required in all parts of the park. If your family plans to ride the water rides, you may want to bring an extra set of clothes because the water rides WILL get you WET! Comfortable shoes and appropriate clothing to keep you warm/cool as temperatures change throughout the day are recommended. Lockers are available in the park for $1.00 per entrance.

Known as "America's Finest Traditional Amusement Park," Kennywood was established in 1898 in West Mifflin near Pittsburgh. Kennywood brings the old-fashioned amusement park feel into the 21st century with one of the highest rated roller coasters in the country. The park features thirty-one major rides, including three water rides, three classic wood coasters, the Phantom's Revenge steel coaster, and a one-of-a-kind indoor, dark coaster, the Exterminator. Kiddieland offers 14 "just for kids" rides. Home of the world's fastest coaster, live shows, arcades, mini-golf, paddle boats, and Lost Kennywood Lagoon area. In addition, Kennywood still maintains two of its original 1898 buildings, housing the carousel pavilion and restaurant. Want to take a break? Sit around the Dancing Waters for a while.

Rector

LINN RUN STATE PARK

Rector - *Linn Run Road (US 30east & PA Rte. 81south) 15677. Phone: (412) 238-6623. www.dcnr.state.pa.us/STATEPARKS/PARKS/linnrun.aspx. Admission: to PA State Parks is FREE however swimming, marina and camping/lodging fees apply, with reservation or entrance.*

The varied topography and mixed hardwood and evergreen forest make this park a scenic place for picnicking, hiking and cabin rentals. Grove and Rock runs join to make Linn Run, an excellent trout stream which has a waterfall, Adams Falls. Several trails are short - Adams Falls Trail is a 1-mile loop that features a mountain waterfall tucked in among rhododendron and hemlock. This very rocky trail passes by large boulders. Boat Rentals, Mountain Biking, Sledding, Campsites and Rustic Cabins.

Rockwood

LAUREL RIDGE STATE PARK

Rockwood - *1117 Jim Mountain Road 15557. Phone: (724) 455-3744. www. dcnr.state.pa.us/stateparks/parks/laurelridge.aspx. Admission: to PA State Parks is FREE however swimming, marina and camping/lodging fees apply, with reservation or entrance.*

Laurel Ridge State Park stretches along the Laurel Mountains from the Yougiogheny River at Ohiopyle to the Conemaugh Gorge near Johnstown. Most visitors come to hike the 70 miles of the Laurel Highland trails. The Laurel Highlands Hiking Trail is open year-round and is blazed approximately every 100 feet with 2-inch and 5-inch yellow blazes. Connector trails lead to and from parking and shelter areas and are marked with blue blazes. Mileage monuments are every mile. Pets are permitted. Snowmobiling and cross-country skiing on trails in winter.

Scenery Hill

WESTERWALD POTTERY

Scenery Hill - *40 Pottery Lane (US 40 - 7.5 miles east of I-79) 15360. Phone: (724) 945-6000. www.westerwaldpottery.com. Hours: Monday-Friday 8:30am-5:00pm. Saturday 10:00am-5:00pm, Sunday Noon-5:00pm. Admission: FREE. Tours: By appointment. Walk-ins, if you would like to watch craftsmen and women it is best to plan your visit for Tuesday thru Thursday, before 3:00pm. Miscellaneous: Gift shop. Discounted pieces outside.*

SW Area

Potters making their signature country-style decorative wares are simply amazing to watch! See a pre-measured lump of clay get hand thrown on a wheel and shaped before your eyes. They make pots, plates, mugs, and cute (and useful) apple bakers. The Westerwald signature is on every piece and they specialize in personalized giftware. You'll even get to see the drying (hardening kilns bricked up for 3 days) and the artists who glaze and paint each piece by hand. The blue and gray stoneware is a reproduction quality of those made in Germany's Westerwald region (thus the company name) as early as the 16th century. Look for a specialized name piece as a souvenir.

Scottdale

WEST OVERTON MUSEUMS

Scottdale - *Overholt Drive (West Overton Village - SR819) 15683. Phone: (724) 887-7910. http://westovertonvillage.org/visit.html. Hours: Friday-Saturday Noon-6:00pm, Sunday 1:00-5:00pm (mid-May - September). Admission: $4.00-$7.00 (age 7+).*

A 19th Century industrial village with a museum, barns, and a gristmill. Visitors to West Overton Museums may view the film, Pillars of Fire, which illustrates the process of turning coal into coke; visit the Overholt Homestead and Gift Shop; tour two floors of the Overholt Mill/Distillery, which contains a large collection of household, farm and industrial tools; visit the birthplace of Henry Clay Frick (millionaire by age 30 with steel coke business); and tour the wash house and smokehouse.

Shanksville (Friedens)

FLIGHT 93 MEMORIAL CHAPEL & IMPACT SITE

Shanksville (Friedens) - *Coleman Station Rd (Boulevard of Heroes) 15541. Phone: (814) 444-8339 or 444-1935. www.flt93memorialchapel.org. Hours: Friday-Monday 10:00am-3:00pm. Often open Tuesdays and Thursdays also. Miscellaneous: To continue journey to IMPACT SITE from FLIGHT 93 MEMORIAL CHAPEL - Continue 3 more miles to Stop sign in Shanksville. (Continuing Boulevard of Heroes). U.S. POST OFFICE, Shanksville, Immediately on right before Stop sign. LEFT one block, onto Lambertsville Road. (Continuing Boulevard of Heroes). 2.5 miles on Lambertsville Road to Lambertsville (Continuing Boulevard of Heroes). To Right onto Skyline Drive up and over the rise to IMPACT SITE.*

<u>**FLIGHT 93 MEMORIAL CHAPEL & IMPACT SITE**</u> (cont.)

Just three miles from the actual crash site, the non-denominational chapel is dedicated as a spiritual memorial and perpetual tribute in honor of the heroes of Flight 93 and all others who perished Sept. 11, 2001. The chapel is open to people of all faiths and is available for individual faith groups to worship together under the direction of their respective religious leaders. Everything about the design of the chapel is reminiscent of the story of Flight 93 and so the visual experience keeps bringing the visitor's thoughts back to that place and time.

Somerset

KOOSER STATE PARK

Somerset - *943 Glades Pike (PA Route 31) 15501. Phone: (814) 445-8673 or (888) PA-Parks. www.dcnr.state.pa.us/stateparks/parks/kooser.aspx. Admission: to PA State Parks is FREE however swimming, marina and camping/lodging fees apply, with reservation or entrance.*

Kooser State Park is bound by Forbes State Forest on two sides and is an ideal spot to start an overnight backpacking trip on the 70-mile Laurel Highlands Hiking Trail. The early settlers told of an American Indian battle that was fought nearby and a number of war arrows and spearheads have been found in the area. A 350-foot swimming beach is open from late-May to mid-September, 8:00am to sunset. Campsites, Rustic Cabins, Fishing.

LAUREL HILL STATE PARK

Somerset - *1454 Laurel Hill Park Road (Pennsylvania Turnpike Exit 110 (Somerset), drive west on PA Rte. 31) 15501. Phone: (814) 445-7725. www.dcnr. state.pa.us/stateparks/parks/laurelhill.aspx. Admission: to PA State Parks is FREE however swimming, marina and camping/lodging fees apply, with reservation or entrance.*

The 63-acre Laurel Hill Lake is a focal point of the park. A beautiful stand of old growth hemlocks lies along the Hemlock Trail. Remains of a logging railroad, like a wooden cross-tie or a rusty rail spike, can be seen along the Tramroad Trail. A 1,200-foot sandy beach is open from late-May to mid-September, 8:00am to sunset. Year-round Education & Interpretation Center, Boat Rentals, Campsites, Fishing, and Trails. Some feel this park is best in the winter with abundant snowfalls and winter sport recreation opportunities in abundance.

SOMERSET HISTORICAL CENTER

Somerset - *10649 Somerset Pike (SR601 and SR985) 15501. Phone: (814) 445-6077. www.somersetcounty.com/historicalcenter. Hours: Tuesday-Saturday 9:00am-5:00pm, Sunday Noon-5:00pm (May-October). Admission: $2.00-$4.00 (age 5+). Miscellaneous: 12 minute film about the history of the mountain barrier area.*

This center interprets daily rural life in southwestern Pennsylvania from 1750 - 1950. Isolated because of the Allegheny Mountains, they had to produce necessities from home - maple sugar, ginseng, and furs were traded - food was produced on the farm. With the Industrial Revolution came advances in farming (hand labor to machines and commercial crops). The site includes a log house, a smokehouse, a log barn, a covered bridge, a maple sugar camp, a general store, and various machines (corn husker & shredder, reaper, buggy). Pioneer and agricultural demonstrations daily.

Tarentum

TOUR-ED MINE AND MUSEUM

Tarentum - *748 Bull Creek Road (SR28 north, exit 14 - Allegheny Valley Expressway) 15084. Phone: (724) 224-4720. www.tour-edmine.com. Hours: Daily 10:00am - 4:00pm, except Tuesdays. (Memorial Day-Labor Day). Admission: $7.50-$9.00. Tours: Given by guides who are real miners - approximately 2 hours leaving every 30 minutes. Miscellaneous: Cool temperatures below - about 50 degrees F. - A jacket or sweater is suggested. Gift shop.*

Experience what it was like to be a coal miner in the 1850's and today. Your guides are experienced coal miners, who will treat you to an amazing, educational tour 160 feet below the Earth's surface. Wearing required hard hats and ducking down a little, you'll board a modernized mining car as you travel 1/2 mile underground into an actual coal mine. Original mines began in 1800 when labor was all done by hand. See demonstrations of this plus setting up a new mine area (installing the roof supports to prevent cave-ins), and the most modern mining - a continuous miner (robotic). Above ground, you can take a stroll to the past again as you view company stores, housing, strip mines, and a sawmill. Bring your camera. They have lots of photo ops above ground.

SW Area

Uniontown

SEARIGHT TOLL HOUSE MUSEUM

Uniontown - *US40 west 15401. Phone: (724) 439-4422. www.hmdb.org/marker. asp?marker=257. Hours: Tuesday-Saturday 10:00am-4:00pm, Sunday 2:00-6:00pm (Mid-May - Mid-October). Admission is $1.00 for adults and children are free.*

In 1806, the National Road began construction connecting the East and West. Searight Tollhouse received its name from its location near the village of Searight, named for its most prominent citizen, William Searight. Searight owned a prosperous tavern on the National Road, the ruins of which may still be seen today. The National Road tollhouse is kept as it once was, with a toll keeper's office, kitchen, and living room.

Washington

PENNSYLVANIA TROLLEY MUSEUM

Washington - *One Museum Road (I-79 to Meadowlands, exit 8) 15301. Phone: (877) PA-TROLLEY. www.pa-trolley.org. Hours: Daily 11:00am-4:00pm (Memorial Day-Labor Day), Long Weekends (Friday thru Monday) & Holidays only (April, May, September-December). Admission: $9.00 adult, $8.00 senior(65+), $5.00 child (3-15). Admission includes the orientation video, car barn tour and trolley rides. Once daily at 1:15pm is extra tour of the Trolley Display Building ($2.00-*

$4.00 more). Web coupon. Miscellaneous: Museum store. In cooler weather, heated trolleys are running. Trolley theatre videos. Air conditioned museum.

Because the kids will be heavy with anticipation once they see the rail yard full of trolleys - plan on taking a ride right away! The trolleys are run on four miles of Pennsylvania rail and each ride takes approximately 30 minutes. Along the rail, you'll learn the history of the vehicle that you are riding on and why it's so special. As you complete your guided or self-guided tour, you'll get to meet CAR #832 - "The Streetcar Named Desire" used in the stage play by Tennessee Williams. Be sure to peek in the car shop where volunteers are restoring cars for future use.

EASTER BUNNY TRAIN RIDES

Washington - *Pennsylvania Trolley Museum. Candy treats with the Easter Bunny riding along. Admission. (Easter Weekend & weekend before)*

PUMPKIN PATCH TROLLEY

Washington - *Pennsylvania Trolley Museum. Ride orange-colored trolleys and the kids get to pick a pumpkin, too! (second or third weekend in October)*

TRAIN RIDES WITH SANTA

Washington - *Pennsylvania Trolley Museum. Sing songs and eat treats as you ride the train with Santa aboard. Toy train lay-out. Admission. (Thanksgiving - December weekends)*

WASHINGTON COUNTY MUSEUM

Washington - 49 East Maiden Street (Route 40 - downtown) 15301. Phone: (412) 225-6740. www.wchspa.org/html/house.htm. Hours: Tuesday - Friday 11:00am-4:00pm and reserved group tours on Saturdays (March-December). Admission: $3.00-$4.00.

The stately stone house, located in downtown Washington, Pennsylvania, was built in 1812 by John Julius LeMoyne, the father of Francis Julius LeMoyne. Both father and son were practicing physicians, but it was the courageous Francis Julius LeMoyne who, despite the strict Fugitive Slave Law of 1850, risked his personal freedom and fortune to do what he knew was morally right — take a stand against the institution of slavery. This successful 19th Century doctor, reformer and builder of the first crematory in the western hemisphere, opened his home and properties as stops along the Underground Railroad. Dr. LeMoyne was also a leader in herbal health remedies. See the beds under which runaway slaves hid and the beehive in the herb garden on the roof.

CHRISTMAS OPEN HOUSE

Washington - *LeMoyne House. Tours of decorated, historical buildings. Refreshments and musical entertainment. Admission. (first & second weekend in December)*

Waynesburg

GREENE COUNTY MUSEUM

Waynesburg - *PO Box 127 (I-79, exit 3 to SR21) 15370. Phone: (724) 627-3204. www.greenecountyhistory.com/. Hours: Wednesday-Friday 10:00am-4:00pm, Saturday & Sunday Noon-4:00pm (May - August). Thursday-Sunday Noon-4:00pm (September, October). Admission: $3.00-$5.00. Miscellaneous: The Historical Society also maintains the Young Foundry and Machine Shop - Century old, belt driven machine shop and foundry with 25 fully operational machines.*

Colonial to Victorian... displays of local artifacts dating from the early native Monongahela culture to the early 20th Century. One of the rooms is devoted to an exhibit of early watches and clocks. The early watch and clockmaker was a talented craftsman, capable of very precise work. He was also the village jeweler. "Monongahela Culture" is the name for prehistoric Indians from the area. Look at the way they constructed their houses, the types of pottery they made and used, the stone materials they used for their tools, weapons, and cultivation of crops. Also on display are quilts, period clothing, early glassware & pottery, and an extraordinary birdhouse that stands over six feet tall and contains 104 rooms. The Early School and Early Children's Toys displays interest kids. A fun and informative worksheet is available for an interactive view of the exhibit. A fun project for families.

FALL HARVEST FESTIVAL

Waynesburg - *Greene County Museum. Tractor pulls, antique steam engines, parades, food (made with steam), threshing, baling, cider and apple butter making, hayrides, children's activities, petting zoo & fall crafts. Admission. (second weekend in October)*

CHRISTMAS OPEN HOUSE

Waynesburg - *Greene County Museum. Tours of decorated, historical buildings. Refreshments and musical entertainment. FREE. (December weekends)*

BATTLE OF THE BULGE RE-ENACTMENT

Waynesburg - *Fort Indiantown Gap. www.wwiifederation.org. World's largest WW II re-enactment with battle demos, equipment displays and many veteran reunions. (last weekend in January)*

Wind Ridge

RYERSON STATION STATE PARK

Wind Ridge - *361 Bristoria Road (both sides of Bristoria Road, just off of PA Route 21) 15380. www.dcnr.state.pa.us/stateparks/parks/ryersonstation.aspx. Phone: (724) 428-4254 or (888) PA-Parks. Admission: to PA State Parks is FREE however swimming, marina and camping/lodging fees apply, with reservation or entrance.*

Pool, Visitor Center, Boat Rentals, Sledding, Campsites, Fishing, and Winter Sports. The trails invite you to explore the park on foot during spring, summer, fall and on cross-country skis in winter. The trails traverse many habitats, like forests, wet valley bottoms, evergreen plantations and fields. There are several opportunities to observe the beauty of Duke Lake.

HISTORY (cont.)

HISTORY (cont.)

TOURS

TOURS (cont.)